D1165792

Child
Development
and
Social Policy

Child Development and Social Policy

KNOWLEDGE FOR ACTION

Edited by

J. Lawrence Aber, Sandra J. Bishop-Josef,
Stephanie M. Jones, Kathryn Taaffe McLearn,
and Deborah A. Phillips

DECADE
of BEHAVIOR

2000·2010

American Psychological Association • Washington, DC

Published by
American Psychological Association
750 First Street, NE
Washington, DC 20002
www.apa.org

To order
APA Order Department
P.O. Box 92984
Washington, DC 20090-2984
Tel: (800) 374-2721; Direct: (202) 336-5510
Fax: (202) 336-5502; TDD/TTY: (202) 336-6123
Online: www.apa.org/books/
E-mail: order@apa.org

In the U.K., Europe, Africa, and the Middle East, copies may be ordered from
American Psychological Association
3 Henrietta Street
Covent Garden, London
WC2E 8LU England

Typeset in Century Schoolbook by Stephen D. McDougal, Mechanicsville, MD

Printer: Data Reproductions, Auburn Hills, MI
Cover Designer: Naylor Design, Washington, DC
Technical/Production Editor: Devon Bourexis

The opinions and statements published are the responsibility of the authors, and such opinions and statements do not necessarily represent the policies of the American Psychological Association.

Library of Congress Cataloging-in-Publication Data

Child development and social policy : knowledge for action / edited by J. Lawrence Aber . . . [et al.].
    p. cm. — (Decade of behavior)
  Includes bibliographical references and index.
  ISBN-13: 978-1-59147-425-8
  ISBN-10: 1-59147-425-6
  1. Children—Government policy—United States. 2. Children—Services for—United States. 3. Children with social disabilities—Services for—United States. 4. Child development—United States. 5. Child development—Research—United States. 6. Child welfare—United States. 7. Zigler, Edward, 1930– I. Aber, J. Lawrence. II. Series.

  HV741.C484 2006
  362.7—dc22   2006001679

British Library Cataloguing-in-Publication Data
A CIP record is available from the British Library.

Printed in the United States of America
First Edition

APA Science Volumes

Attribution and Social Interaction: The Legacy of Edward E. Jones

Best Methods for the Analysis of Change: Recent Advances, Unanswered Questions, Future Directions

Cardiovascular Reactivity to Psychological Stress and Disease

The Challenge in Mathematics and Science Education: Psychology's Response

Changing Employment Relations: Behavioral and Social Perspectives

Children Exposed to Marital Violence: Theory, Research, and Applied Issues

Cognition: Conceptual and Methodological Issues

Cognitive Bases of Musical Communication

Cognitive Dissonance: Progress on a Pivotal Theory in Social Psychology

Conceptualization and Measurement of Organism–Environment Interaction

Converging Operations in the Study of Visual Selective Attention

Creative Thought: An Investigation of Conceptual Structures and Processes

Developmental Psychoacoustics

Diversity in Work Teams: Research Paradigms for a Changing Workplace

Emotion and Culture: Empirical Studies of Mutual Influence

Emotion, Disclosure, and Health

Evolving Explanations of Development: Ecological Approaches to Organism–Environment Systems

Examining Lives in Context: Perspectives on the Ecology of Human Development

Global Prospects for Education: Development, Culture, and Schooling

Hostility, Coping, and Health

Measuring Patient Changes in Mood, Anxiety, and Personality Disorders: Toward a Core Battery

Occasion Setting: Associative Learning and Cognition in Animals

Organ Donation and Transplantation: Psychological and Behavioral Factors

Origins and Development of Schizophrenia: Advances in Experimental Psychopathology

The Perception of Structure

Perspectives on Socially Shared Cognition

Psychological Testing of Hispanics

Psychology of Women's Health: Progress and Challenges in Research and Application

Researching Community Psychology: Issues of Theory and Methods

The Rising Curve: Long-Term Gains in IQ and Related Measures

Sexism and Stereotypes in Modern Society: The Gender Science of Janet Taylor Spence

Sleep and Cognition

Sleep Onset: Normal and Abnormal Processes

Stereotype Accuracy: Toward Appreciating Group Differences

Stereotyped Movements: Brain and Behavior Relationships

Studying Lives Through Time: Personality and Development

The Suggestibility of Children's Recollections: Implications for Eyewitness Testimony

APA Decade of Behavior Volumes

Note to Reader

The volume editors are listed alphabetically. All contributed equally to this volume.

Contents

Contributors

J. Lawrence Aber is a professor in the Department of Applied Psychology at the Steinhardt School of Education at New York University, New York, New York.

Joseph P. Allen is a professor in the Department of Psychology at the University of Virginia, Charlottesville.

LaRue Allen is the Raymond and Rosalee Weiss Professor of Applied Psychology at the Steinhardt School of Education at New York University, New York, New York.

Nancy H. Apfel is a research associate in the Department of Psychology at Yale University, New Haven, Connecticut.

Jennifer Astuto is an assistant research scientist in the Department of Applied Psychology at the Steinhardt School of Education at New York University, New York, New York.

W. Steven Barnett is a professor in the Graduate School of Education and director of the National Institute for Early Education Research at Rutgers, the State University of New Jersey, New Brunswick.

Sandra J. Bishop-Josef is the assistant director of the Edward Zigler Center in Child Development and Social Policy at Yale University, New Haven, Connecticut.

Kirsty C. Brown is the assistant director of the National Institute for Early Education Research at Rutgers, the State University of New Jersey, New Brunswick.

Alice S. Carter is a professor in the Department of Psychology at the University of Massachusetts, Boston.

Rachel Chazan-Cohen is a senior research analyst in the Office of Planning, Research, and Evaluation, in the Administration for Children and Families, U.S. Department of Health and Human Services, Washington, DC.

Dante Cicchetti is a professor at the Institute of Child Development at the University of Minnesota, Minneapolis.

Matia Finn-Stevenson is the associate director of the Edward Zigler Center in Child Development and Social Policy at Yale University, New Haven, Connecticut.

Olivia Golden is a senior fellow at the Urban Institute, Washington, DC.

Janice Gruendel is the senior advisor for early childhood to Connecticut Governor M. Jodi Rell and cofounder of Connecticut Voices for Children, New Haven.

Amanda E. Guyer is a postdoctoral fellow in the Mood and Anxiety Disorders Program at the National Institute for Mental Health, Bethesda, Maryland.

Kenji Hakuta is the dean of the School of Social Sciences, Humanities and Arts at the University of California, Merced.

Brenda Jones Harden is an associate professor at the Institute for Child Study at the University of Maryland, College Park.

Christopher Henrich is an assistant professor in the Department of Psychology at Georgia State University, Atlanta.

Stephanie M. Jones is an assistant professor in the Department of Psychology at Fordham University, Bronx, New York.

Sharon Lynn Kagan is the Virginia and Leonard Marx Professor of Early Childhood and Family Policy at Teachers College, Columbia University, New York, New York, and codirector of the National Center for Children and Families, New York, New York.

Jane Knitzer is the director of the National Center for Children in Poverty at the Mailman School of Public Health, Columbia University, New York, New York.

John M. Love is a senior fellow at Mathematica Policy Research, Inc., Ashland, Oregon.

Katherine W. Marsland is an assistant professor in the Department of Psychology at Southern Connecticut State University, New Haven.

Nancy F. Martland is a research assistant professor in the Eliot-Pearson Department of Child Development and executive director of the Child & Family WebGuide at Tufts University, Medford, Massachusetts.

Kathleen McCartney is the Gerald S. Lesser Professor in Early Childhood Development at the Harvard Graduate School of Education, Cambridge, Massachusetts.

Kathryn Taaffe McLearn is an adjunct professor of pediatrics at the Center for Children's Health Care Improvement at the University of North Carolina, Chapel Hill.

Susan Muenchow is a principal research scientist at the American Institutes for Research, Palo Alto, California.

Deborah A. Phillips is a professor of psychology and the codirector of the Center for Research on Children in the United States at Georgetown University, Washington, DC.

Ellen E. Pinderhughes is an associate professor in the Eliot-Pearson Department of Child Development at Tufts University, Medford, Massachusetts.

Helen Raikes is a professor of family and consumer sciences at the University of Nebraska, Lincoln.

C. Cybele Raver is an associate professor at the Irving B. Harris School of Public Policy at the University of Chicago, Chicago, Illinois.

Fred Rothbaum is a professor in the Eliot-Pearson Department of Child Development and president of the Child & Family WebGuide at Tufts University, Medford, Massachusetts.

Victoria Seitz is a research scientist in the Department of Psychology at Yale University, New Haven, Connecticut.

Anita Sethi is a research scientist at the Child and Family Policy Center at New York University, New York, New York.

Sheila Smith is the director of the Best Practices for Quality Childhood Programs at the Steinhardt School of Education at New York University, New York, New York.

Deborah Stipek is the dean of the School of Education at Stanford University, Stanford, California.

Sally J. Styfco is the associate director of the Head Start Section at the Edward Zigler Center in Child Development and Social Policy at Yale University, New Haven, Connecticut.

Heather B. Weiss is the director of the Harvard Family Research Project at the Harvard Graduate School of Education, Cambridge, Massachusetts.

Bernice Weissbourd is the president and founder of Family Focus, Chicago, Illinois.

Edward F. Zigler is a Sterling Professor of Psychology, *Emeritus*, and founder and director, *Emeritus*, of the Edward Zigler Center in Child Development and Social Policy at Yale University, New Haven, Connecticut.

Foreword

In early 1988, the American Psychological Association (APA) Science Director-ate began its sponsorship of what would become an exceptionally successful activity in support of psychological science—the APA Scientific Conferences program. This program has showcased some of the most important topics in psychological science and has provided a forum for collaboration among many leading figures in the field.

The program has inspired a series of books that have presented cutting-edge work in all areas of psychology. At the turn of the millennium, the series was renamed the Decade of Behavior Series to help advance the goals of this important initiative. The Decade of Behavior is a major interdisciplinary campaign designed to promote the contributions of the behavioral and social sciences to our most important societal challenges in the decade leading up to 2010. Although a key goal has been to inform the public about these scientific contributions, other activities have been designed to encourage and further collaboration among scientists. Hence, the series that was the "APA Science Series" has continued as the "Decade of Behavior Series." This represents one element in APA's efforts to promote the Decade of Behavior initiative as one of its endorsing organizations. For additional information about the Decade of Behavior, please visit http://www.decadeofbehavior.org.

Over the course of the past years, the Science Conference and Decade of Behavior Series has allowed psychological scientists to share and explore cutting-edge findings in psychology. The APA Science Directorate looks forward to continuing this successful program and to sponsoring other conferences and books in the years ahead. This series has been so successful that we have chosen to extend it to include books that, although they do not arise from conferences, report with the same high quality of scholarship on the latest research.

We are pleased that this important contribution to the literature was supported in part by the Decade of Behavior program. Congratulations to the editors and contributors of this volume on their sterling effort.

Steven J. Breckler, PhD
Executive Director for Science

Virginia E. Holt
Assistant Executive Director for Science

Acknowledgments

The festschrift in honor of Edward F. Zigler and this resulting volume were made possible by the support of the following organizations: the Smith Richardson Foundation, the William T. Grant Foundation, the American Psychological Association, the Harris Foundation, and the Society for Research in Child Development.

Child
Development
and
Social Policy

Introduction

J. Lawrence Aber and Deborah A. Phillips

Developmental psychology has been, from its origins, a hybrid science. At its best, this discipline addresses the twin goals of understanding children and applying this knowledge to efforts aimed at offering all children a rewarding childhood and a promising future. Edward F. Zigler's life and work have set the standard for bridging these two goals. His seminal experimental work on mental retardation and developmental psychopathology drew attention to capacities that reside in all children if given the right beginnings. The optimistic message of this work caught the eye of national leaders seeking to include children in the War on Poverty and they beckoned Zigler to Washington, DC. Head Start and other programs he envisioned remain the cornerstones of national policy for young children and their families. On returning to academic life, Zigler pledged himself to generating and deploying scientific insights about children and the factors that shape their lives toward the creation of more effective and humane policies on their behalf. In the process, he defined the now-burgeoning scientific field of child development and social policy, reaffirmed the practical importance of adhering to the highest standards of scientific rigor, and amply fulfilled his commitment to work tirelessly toward improved social policies for children and families. As such, he has redefined the responsibilities of developmental psychologists and inspired a new generation of scholars to blend the skill, rigor, and skepticism of scientific work with the passion, pragmatism, and devotion required to leave behind a better world for children.

This volume is the product of a festschrift in honor of Edward F. Zigler, Sterling Professor of Psychology, *Emeritus* at Yale University (see the Zigler festschrift Web site at http://www.yale.edu/zigler for more information). As the term *festschrift* implies, this volume is a celebration of a life of action, a life of contribution to the nation's children and families, and to the future for generations to come.[1] The main theme of this volume is reflected in its title, *Child Development and Social Policy: Knowledge for Action*. The chapters in this volume reflect two meanings of the title, both the influence of social policy on children's development and the unique perspective, insight, and skills that developmentalists bring to policy and its process. Zigler's career exemplifies

[1]We thank David L. Featherman, Director of the Center for Advancing Research and Solutions for Society at the University of Michigan, for his insights into the derivation of the term *festschrift*.

both meanings. He deeply believes in the critical role that positive policy can play in improving the well-being of children. There are dozens of examples from his work. We allude to just two now: the difference between the high-quality child care that children and families need and what he referred to as the "cosmic crapshoot" that most families face as they negotiate a child-care system that varies widely in quality. Zigler also believes that other social policies, including housing, transportation, defense, and economic policies, look radically different if viewed from the perspective of a developmentalist who evaluates policies in terms of their capacity to support human growth and change over the life course. The second example derives from Zigler's insistence that the child remain "whole" rather than partitioned into the pieces that compose the whole (language, cognitive, motor, social, emotional, motivational, and nutrition and health), in the context of interventions designed to improve the life prospects of the child. He designed Head Start with the whole child in mind and continues to criticize policies that attempt to address one aspect of development apart from the others.

It is our hope that the readers of this volume will come to know and appreciate Zigler as do the contributors to this volume and his hundreds of other colleagues, students, and friends. Zigler values rigorous and experimental scientific study, when achievable; logical and descriptive analysis at the least. And he disdains fuzzy thinking. Hard-won facts and clear thinking, empirical evidence, and the context of sound theory to guide interpretations of the evidence are what Zigler demands of students, expects of colleagues, and expects of federal- and foundation-funded sources. But Zigler also values action. Good science, rigorous research, and clear thinking are necessary, but not sufficient to benefit children. There are practical implications of knowledge—he reminds us day in and day out—practical implications for awareness of problems as well as for the design, implementation, and evaluation of solutions to those problems, whether they be programmatic or policy solutions. So, that is what the contributors of this volume address: *Child Development and Social Policy: Knowledge for Action.*

The volume's chapters offer an enormously rich menu from which the reader can sample. It simply is not possible to represent all of Ed's work at the intersection of child development and social policy, even in a large volume. It is inevitable that some aspects will be emphasized. Most, but not all, are covered in this volume. Some were lost. Here we cite just two examples of topics that, if you had a perfect representation of Zigler's interests and work, are not sufficiently addressed in this volume. The first is his seminal and long-standing work in mental retardation, institutionalization, and special education. The second is his extensive research on developmental psychopathology—for example, the effects of premorbid social competence on people's later development after a major psychotic break. Luckily, many of these issues have been addressed in an earlier festschrift on developmental psychopathology (Luthar, Burack, Cicchetti, & Weisz, 1997), but the policy implications were not fully developed.

Acknowledging from the start the enormous breadth and depth of Zigler's work in child development and social policy, it fell first to the planning committee of the festschrift (J. Lawrence Aber, Deborah A. Phillips, Stephanie M. Jones,

Sandra J. Bishop-Josef, Kathryn Taaffe McLearn [Executive Committee][2] LaRue Allen, Christopher Henrich, Katherine Marsland, Amanda Guyer, and Deborah Stipek) and then to the editors of this volume, to select the most essential areas of work and to bring to those areas some order and coherence. We chose four broad topics to organize the work of our mentor and colleague.

Part I of the volume, "Making History: Child Development and Social Policy," tells the story of the emergence of a new field of inquiry and action. It also makes explicit the leading, perhaps defining, role that Zigler played in both the creation of the field and its important early accomplishments. In chapter 1, Deborah A. Phillips and Sally J. Styfco place Zigler's work, and the entire volume, in historical context by detailing both the triumphs and setbacks in the field over its first 5 decades. In chapter 2, Olivia Golden, who held the same leading position in child and family policy in the Clinton administration as Zigler did 30 years earlier in the Nixon administration, draws on her years of public service in the federal government to describe helpful (and, by implication, unhelpful) research from the perspective of a decision maker. Following this discussion, in chapter 3, Janice Gruendel, cofounder of one of the most effective state-based child advocacy organizations in the country, and J. Lawrence Aber, who used to work in state government, challenge developmental researchers to be as bold and ambitious in the uses of research to influence government decisions as they are rigorous and scientific in the conduct of research. Chapter 4, by Kathleen McCartney and Heather B. Weiss, advances the theme of the volume by asking the question, "What does it mean to use data and research (child development knowledge) to influence policy (for action) in a democracy?" They answer this question by describing the recent history of the complex role of evaluation research in child and family policy decision making. Together, the four chapters in Part I place Zigler's work, and the rest of the volume, in very concrete historical and political context. The readers will be left with much to think about regarding the inherent tensions between values of fair, rigorous, impartial science and the committed, principled, and value-laden application of developmental science to collective solutions of social problems facing America's children and families.

Among the most important problems facing the nation's children and families is the enormous gap that exists between what we know children need in the first years of life and what they currently receive (Shonkoff & Phillips, 2000), despite the heroic efforts of individual parents, families, and communities. Zigler has spent a large part of his career analyzing and attempting to fill this gap, thereby striving to "ensure good beginnings for all children." This is the broad topic addressed in Part II of this volume.

In chapter 5, John M. Love, Rachel Chazan-Cohen, and Helen Raikes tell the story most commonly told by Zigler himself, the story of the creation of Head Start and the use of research both to critique and reform Head Start and to create adaptations suited for infants and toddlers. Susan Muenchow and Katherine W. Marsland in chapter 6 take on the task of describing how research and advocacy together have been used to promote the growth and devel-

---

[2]The Executive Committee also edited this volume.

opment of U.S. child-care policy. (Zigler might argue that the child-care system is such a crazy-quilt that the term *child-care policy* could be an oxymoron.) In chapter 7, W. Steven Barnett, Kirsty C. Brown, Matia Finn-Stevenson, and Christopher Henrich analyze the more recent movement toward universal prekindergarten education, where the best features of the child-care system (e.g., developmental appropriateness) and of the early elementary education system (universality, public funding) are being blended.

Decades of experience document that too many young children in the United States have been and will continue to be left behind by even the best universally available and high-quality child care and prekindergarten education. In chapter 8, Deborah Stipek and Kenji Hakuta discuss the challenges of and strategies for addressing the early needs of bilingual children. Throughout the chapters in Part II, readers will learn to struggle, as the field has, with the dueling perspectives of universal (child-care, pre-K) and targeted (bilingual, Head Start) strategies to ensure good beginnings for all the nation's youngest children.

Although Head Start is targeted to the nation's low-income children, Zigler always recognized that Head Start alone could not break the cycle of poverty and that poverty alleviation alone could not adequately "address the needs of the nation's most vulnerable children and families," especially maltreated children, foster children, and teen parents. Part III describes work in each of these areas, in all instances stimulated and supported by Zigler, if not always conducted by him. In chapter 9, J. Lawrence Aber, Stephanie M. Jones, and C. Cybele Raver follow in the Zigler tradition of striving to clearly define a social problem, both conceptually and operationally, and then working through the implications of problem definition for both scientific research and social problem solving. Researchers who examine the effects of poverty on child development and programs and policies meant to ameliorate the effects of poverty on development are strongly influenced by how poverty has been defined at different points in history and by different academic disciplines. The same can be said of the complex phenomenon of child maltreatment. In chapter 10, Dante Cicchetti first reviews the emergent highly interdisciplinary knowledge base on the neurobiological functioning of maltreated children and then goes on, in the spirit of Zigler, to identify the important implications of this new knowledge for both prevention and treatment programs and policies.

In chapter 11, Joseph P. Allen joins two of Zigler's closest colleagues from Yale, Victoria Seitz and Nancy H. Apfel, in describing one of the most dramatic instances of the influence of Zigler on a subfield, in this case, research on teen pregnancy and parenthood. Only recently have they recognized how profoundly their own work on viewing teen parents as "whole persons" has been influenced by Zigler's insistence on viewing a child with mental retardation as a whole person and not reducing the child's identity to a single deficit or characteristic.

Part III closes with chapter 12 by Ellen E. Pinderhughes, Brenda Jones Harden, and Amanda E. Guyer on children in foster care, perhaps among the nation's most vulnerable children because they have been deprived, by the actions of their families or the legal decisions of the state, of the protection of their own parents.

Of course, there are clear patterns of influence among these various vulnerable states: Teen parenthood is a major cause of child poverty, poverty causally increases the probability of child maltreatment, and child maltreatment is the most common reason for placement in foster care. Zigler's students have learned about these intricate and shifting interconnections from their mentor. Developmental science and child and family policy must not only view the child as a whole person but also view the family and policy as whole and interacting systems. One cannot make sufficient progress in understanding or addressing the complex influences on children's development if one tackles the major problems or their solutions one at a time.

Zigler, ever the Midwest pragmatist, found it practical, sensible, and enjoyable to learn from other giants in the field. His students remember the combination of awe and enthusiasm he felt for Urie Bronfenbrenner's advancement of an ecological perspective on human development. In addition, as a policy advisor to four generations of major politicians, he learned that to sell Americans on supporting the children's cause required a perspective that not only shored up their weaknesses but also promoted child and family strengths. These are some of the influences that led Zigler to a life-long focus on "strengthening children, families, and communities," the broad theme addressed in Part IV of this volume.

It goes without saying that parents are children's most important "ecology." But it is shocking how little the field of child development seemed to believe that (a) parents of vulnerable children had strengths that they could bring to child rearing and (b) parents could grow, develop, and become more educated and skilled at parenting. In chapter 13, LaRue Allen, Anita Sethi, Sheila Smith, and Jennifer Astuto describe the powerful influence that Zigler has had on the emergent field of parent education through his efforts on behalf of parents through the Head Start program.

In another echo of the whole-child perspective in chapter 14, Kathryn Taaffe McLearn, Jane Knitzer, and Alice S. Carter focus on the promotion of mental health in young children. Can young children whose major mental health needs go unmet, in part because they go unrecognized, arrive at the schoolhouse door ready for school? This rhetorical question leads to a cogent case for a whole-child approach to school readiness that lends children's social and emotional development as prominent a role as their cognitive and language development.

Again, echoing the theme of moving from the whole child to whole systems, parents cannot be educated and mental health cannot be promoted unless families qua families (not just the sum of their parts) are supported. In chapter 15, two leaders of the family support movement, Sharon Lynn Kagan and Bernice Weissbourd, analyze the recent history and strategies of this movement as a force for change in contemporary U.S. society.

Before the recent emphasis in social movements on media and communications strategies to advance causes, Zigler understood the critical role of media in moving the knowledge of child development into action. In chapter 16, Fred Rothbaum, Nancy F. Martland, and Sandra J. Bishop-Josef take up where Ed left off, by analyzing the potential of the World Wide Web to disseminate knowledge, especially to parents. Part I looks back toward the history of the emergence of the field of child development and social policy, and Part IV looks to the future, to new ways of strengthening children, families, and their communities.

There are two other features of this volume that both exemplify the influence of Zigler on the field of child development and social policy and that point toward its future. First, we call your attention to the new and multigenerational relationships that Zigler inspires. Ten of the 16 chapters involve brand new collaborations among Ed's former students, sometimes spanning periods of more than 30 years, who had never written together before. Like many ventures in life, developmental science and child and family policy can require skilled collaboration to yield fruit. Zigler has not only spawned the next several generations of top scholars and practitioners in the field of child development and social policy, he has also spawned a spirit of collaboration by his powerful example of inviting most of us to collaborate over the years.

Second, although the content of the chapters often focus on scientific challenges that have not yet been met and policy problems that have not yet been solved, there is a quiet and realistic sense of optimism in and across the chapters. Recognizing the complexity of human development and the extreme inadequacy of many policy initiatives on behalf of children and families has made Zigler sober and serious, but never pessimistic or defeated. This is captured eloquently in Zigler's epilogue to the volume, in which he traces his own journey from empirical scientist looking to the next experiment to the nation's leader in translating knowledge for action looking to a better future for our nation's children. Just as the enormity of the challenges fan Zigler's desire to conduct or support the next critical study, the next legislative effort, he calls on his students to continue contributing to the knowledge and the policies that will create this future. Zigler has infected his students with a sober and determined optimism that better science can lead to better policy. His love for America's children and families, his love for his own intellectual and professional children and families, and his desire to use knowledge of child development in the service of the well-being of all children and families are his legacies to his students, the field he helped create, and, in the end, the nation he loves.

References

Luthar, S. S., Burack, J. A., Cicchetti, D., & Weisz, J. R. (Eds.). (1997). *Developmental psychopathology: Perspectives on adjustment, risk, and disorder*. New York: Cambridge University Press.

Shonkoff, J. P., & Phillips, D. A. (Eds.). (2000). *From neurons to neighborhoods: The science of early childhood development*. Washington, DC: National Academy Press.

Part I

Making History: Child Development and Social Policy

1

Child Development Research and Public Policy: Triumphs and Setbacks on the Way to Maturity

Deborah A. Phillips and Sally J. Styfco

Over the last 3 or 4 decades, sentiments about the value of research at the intersection of child development and social policy have changed dramatically. Once viewed as a diversion from the true academic work of developmental scientists, such work has become an active and highly regarded subfield of scientific inquiry in its own right. Although histories of the role of social science in policy making have been written (e.g., Featherman & Vinofskis, 2001a, 2001b), none has specifically examined the role of developmental psychology. In addition to adopting this disciplinary lens, this brief history of the subdiscipline of child development and public policy is explicitly personal, embedded as it is in a volume honoring Edward F. Zigler. We offer an account of the ebbs and flows in the emergence and maturation of this subfield, highlighting some of the important influences on this history.

The boundaries of the intersection between research and policy on which this chapter focuses are necessarily indistinct. Its defining characteristic is the potential of the research to provide information on a problem situation that is external to the science itself. The research may be directed primarily at scientific questions about the problem, as is the case with researchers who study child care to explore the role of early experience in child development. Alternatively, the research may be motivated by an interest in addressing the problem directly, as is the case with evaluations of standardized testing of school populations. This spectrum of scientific inquiry, which deliberately includes what some may portray as basic or fundamental science (see also Zigler, 1980), is the focus of this account.

The authors thank John Hagan and Emily Cahan for their contributions to this chapter. Edward F. Zigler generously shared his own insights about this history through a series of conversations with Sally Styfco. Tom Cassel and Alexis Lester, graduate students in public policy at Georgetown University, did the painstaking work of reading and coding hundreds of articles in *Child Development*. Their careful efforts are deeply appreciated.

Ancestral Roots of the Subfield

Scholars who have traced the emergence of the social sciences (Bulmer, 2001), and specifically of developmental psychology (Cairns, 1989; Sears, 1975; Senn, 1975; White, 1992), often start at the turn of the 20th century. It was during this era (notably the 1890s to 1912) that basic questions about the origins and course of human development met up with highly educated and academically connected social reformers, such as Grace Abbott and Jane Adams. They carried social investigation about child development into the urban laboratories of the settlement houses for the explicit purpose of illuminating and building advocacy around social ills affecting children, especially poor and immigrant children (Davis, 1959; Lazerson, 1970; Takanishi, 1978). It is for this reason that Sears (1975) wrote, "the field grew out of relevance" (p. 4).

This early strand of developmental psychology gave rise to a virtual industry of applied research on children that allied the concerns of practitioners and decision makers with social science inquiry (Bremner, Barnard, Hareven, & Mennel, 1971; Takanishi, 1978). Amassed evidence on child labor, juvenile delinquency, and child and maternal health led to a panoply of local reforms, the establishment of child-specific social institutions (e.g., child guidance clinics and the juvenile courts), expansion of the legal doctrine of *parens patriae* that justifies public intervention in the lives of children, and compulsory school attendance. The first White House Conference on Children in 1909 confirmed the national significance of these developments. In 1912, the Children's Bureau was established to collect and apply systematic evidence about the conditions of children at the highest levels of the federal government (Ross, 1983; Zigler & Muenchow, 1985).

During this same period, practice-based investigators in the professions of pediatrics, education, and social work were increasing their interactions with psychologists aligned with the child study movement (Richmond, 1967; Siegel & White, 1982). White (1992) has written a marvelous account of G. Stanley Hall's seminal contributions to the child study movement, which linked empirical developmental psychology to educational practice and brought child development "research stations" into the fold of the university system. Companion developments, such as the social survey movement, the emergence of philanthropic support for the social sciences, and the establishment of research organizations such as the Social Science Research Council and the National Bureau of Economic Research, were mobilizing the broader research community to analyze social trends and conditions (Featherman & Vinofskis, 2001b). White and Phillips (2001) referred to this long-standing function of the social sciences as one of representation, in which the tools of research are used to translate complex social circumstances into symbols and ideas that can build public awareness and compel action. This explicit articulation of research with practical politics and practice did not, however, go unquestioned for long. The emergence of positivist social science in the 1920s recast research as an objective, apolitical enterprise to be judged primarily by its use of sound scientific methods rather than by its deployment for purposes of reform.

Thus, by the 1920s, three prominent strands of research representing different conceptualizations of the relationship between developmental science and its application to policy and practice had emerged. The leaders of the settlement house movement unabashedly deployed research as a tool of political advocacy on behalf of poor and immigrant children. The developmentalists who established the child study movement sought to inform practice and child rearing. The positivist strand lent a distinct voice to the mix, defining the value of science in terms of knowledge building for its own sake. This distinction between arms-length research and research as a tool of social reform remains an abiding dilemma facing the child development and public policy enterprise.

As the positivist approach to social science gained ascendancy, the social reform model for research receded (Haskell, 1977; Lyons, 1969). Developmental psychologists shifted their focus to empirical studies of child behavior and cognition. Scientific legitimacy became increasingly tied to quantitative statistics and experimental methods, rather than to the applications of the knowledge being generated. It would not be until the 1960s that applications of child development research would resurface as a salient activity within the field.

War, Science, and Child Development

World War II ushered in a new era of applied research. Just as President Lincoln established the National Academy of Sciences in 1863 to address technical problems arising during the Civil War and President Wilson turned to academic experts during World War I, scientists played very practical roles in World War II. Unlike the earlier wars, however, their continued involvement was sought by the federal government when the war ended. Although initially focused on defense-related issues, the social and behavioral sciences slowly gained prominence within the federal research infrastructure during the postwar period (Featherman & Vinofskis, 2001a; Smith, 1990).

A major catalyst was the Soviets' launching of Sputnik in 1957. Their triumph riveted national attention on the scientific and technological preparedness of the United States, including how well the nation was educating the next generation of scientists. As a result, educational and developmental research gained relevance as an instrument of the Cold War. Government support for research soon outpaced the contributions of private philanthropy, which had played such an instrumental role prior to World War II. Particularly significant for developmental psychology was the establishment in 1963 of the National Institute of Child Health and Human Development within the National Institutes of Health.

Another policy development enlisted research on children in yet another war, namely the War on Poverty. Reminiscent of the turn of the century, the 1960s launched a period when social science expertise was actively recruited into political decision making about how best to address the plight of those living in poverty. A handful of developmental psychologists, among many other social scientists, were brought into the inner circles of decision making to imagine, design, and implement the panoply of programs that defined the Great Society, including Head Start, the Elementary and Secondary Education Act (1965), and the Neighborhood Youth Corps. Those who were involved—Sheldon White, Urie Bronfenbrenner, Julius Richmond, Edmund Gordon, and Zigler—

were profoundly affected by the experience. Their own careers took new directions and they, in turn, sought to bring their experiences to bear on the future direction of developmental psychology.

The Reeducation of Edward F. Zigler

The 1960s witnessed a reawakening of social science's relevance to public policy (Featherman & Vinofskis, 2001a). Scores of political scientists, economists, sociologists, and psychologists served as consultants to federal agencies, testified before the U.S. Congress, and became involved in federal litigation on issues ranging from voting rights to school desegregation. They also engaged in large-scale social experiments such as the Negative Income Tax pilots. Modern schools of public policy began to be established, with economics and political science serving as the leading disciplinary orientations. Psychology in general, and developmental psychology in particular, were not part of the disciplinary mix that composed these programs and remain on their periphery to this day.

Zigler's journey from his research lab at Yale University to an office in Washington, DC, exemplifies both the newfound respect policymakers extended to experts and how unprepared most experts were to begin applying their science after having devoted their careers to basic laboratory research. Ed was immersed in studying the social and emotional aspects of mental retardation. Countering the deficit position dominant at the time, Ed argued that the performance of individuals with nonorganic mental retardation was affected by social deprivation, fear of failure, low self-esteem, and other factors known to affect those of normal intellect who experienced similar socialization histories.

Ed's pioneering work earned him invitations to speak at many forums, including one attended by the famous pediatrician Robert Cooke. Cooke was a friend of Sargent Shriver, who was President Johnson's chief strategist in the War on Poverty. Most of the war's efforts targeted poor adults, until Shriver decided that a good use of some of the funds—and a goal that would garner wider public support for these efforts—would be to prepare young children of the poor for school. Shriver asked Cooke to head a committee of experts to design a preschool program. Cooke remembered Zigler's thesis that many children with mental retardation perform below the level of their abilities because they have failed so often they no longer believe they can succeed. Cooke thought that children who live in poverty also encounter inordinate amounts of failure and, like the participants in Zigler's studies, could perform better in school if they experienced more success. He invited Ed to join the planning committee for what would become Project Head Start.

Ed was honored to accept the challenge, never imagining how far this foray into applied science would take him. The committee comprised people from a range of professional disciplines, including medicine, early childhood education, and social work. Ed, Urie Bronfenbrenner, and Mamie Clarke were the only developmental psychologists and the only basic researchers. At the time, there was only a small literature on early intervention for poor children, so members had to rely on their intuitions, personal experience, and best guesses. This was foreign to the scientist in Zigler, who demanded empirical proof and argued every point as if it were an untested hypothesis.

When the program guidelines were drawn and the committee's work presumably done, Ed insisted that the new program be rigorously evaluated to quantify its results and inform its future development. Most of the committee members did not see the point. After all, children would be getting medical care, nutritious meals, and social and academic experiences in a supportive, safe environment. What was there to measure? Julius Richmond, who became Head Start's first administrator, supported the idea of evaluation and ended the debate by telling Ed he could have his way if he would undertake the effort himself. Ed and some hastily recruited graduate students worked day and night to develop assessment measures in a few weeks' time. This hurried process did not return any useable information, but it did implant an evaluation component and research shop into Head Start that over four decades has created a vast knowledge base on early childhood intervention. Today, Head Start continues to be a national laboratory for early childhood research (see chap. 8, this volume).

Although Ed's efforts to bring science to an applied setting were not initially welcome there, neither was his entry into application appreciated by his academic peers. Indeed, a senior colleague told him, "You could become a first-rank developmentalist if only you would give up this policy nonsense." His response to such pressure was to take a leave of absence from academia and join the Nixon Administration as the first director of the Office of Child Development (now the Administration on Children, Youth and Families) and Chief of the U.S. Children's Bureau. As this anecdote suggests, at the beginning of the 1970s developmental psychology included a small subgroup of influential scholars who were deeply engaged in shaping federal policy affecting children and a majority group who had deep reservations about hands-on policy involvement and its presumed distorting effects on the course of basic empirical science.

Developmental Psychology: Challenges and Responses

These crosscurrents came to a head at the 1971 meeting of the Society for Research in Child Development (SRCD). The society's stated mission since its emergence in 1933 involved serving the dual goals of producing knowledge about child development and deploying this knowledge for the betterment of children. As portrayed earlier, however, practical research had gradually lost status among scientists. Regardless of whether SRCD rode or triggered this momentum, by the midpoint of the century it had drifted away from applied interests to concentrate on fundamental questions about developmental processes. Along with this came a loss of interest in, if not deliberate retrenchment from, efforts to mobilize knowledge for social purposes. Despite the intense federal activity around children that characterized the mid-1960s and early 1970s, many of the leaders within SRCD in 1971 had acquired their intellectual socialization during this earlier period. They remained strong believers in dispassionate and disinterested inquiry and were highly skeptical about forging a close alliance with policy concerns (Hagen, 2002).

The then-president of SRCD, Harold Stevenson, did not share this skepticism. He was a learning theorist whose work focused on understanding how children learn in order to help them learn better. He devoted his SRCD presidential session to a symposium titled, "Child Development and the National Scene." Invited participants were Senator Walter Mondale, Congressman Orval Hansen, and Zigler (by then director of the Office of Child Development), each of whom spoke about the value of an active exchange between research and policy on children.

The unique presidential session cracked open a door into the society's hard line scientific philosophy. Shortly thereafter, a number of socially conscious members were encouraged enough to seek SRCD's official endorsement of the Comprehensive Child Development Act of 1971. The bill would have created a universal system of child care in America, with fees calibrated to family income (see Cohen, 2001; Zigler & Phillips, 1987). The vision was to give all children of working parents access to high-quality, affordable care. With Ed behind the scenes, Bronfenbrenner made the formal proposal to a meeting of the SRCD business committee. The motion passed, marking the first time that this body officially supported national legislation. The fact that the Child Development Act, though passed by Congress with a wide bipartisan margin, was vetoed by President Nixon did not help encourage the society's future involvement.

The momentum to use the group's collective scientific knowledge to inform policy was slow to gather. For example, by the mid-1970s many young scholars were inspired by the more senior people we have been mentioning and were becoming interested in social policy issues and applied work. At a business meeting of SRCD, they asked the leadership to reserve some pages of the society's flagship journal, *Child Development*, for applied work. The journal was a hallmark of theory-driven, basic research, and the answer was an undebatable "no."

As recounted by John Hagen (1997, 2002), these fits and starts in SRCD's responses to policy-relevant requests endured for several years until, in 1977, the Governing Council of SRCD, on the recommendation of a four-person study group composed of T. Berry Brazelton, Harriet Rheingold, Alberta Siegel, and Harold Stevenson (Stevenson & Siegel, 1984), established the Social Policy Committee. The committee was charged with formulating recommendations and positions for the society about social policy issues affecting children. The council also created a liaison office for the society in Washington, DC, to track pending child policy issues and coordinate policy-relevant activities with other research groups to ensure timely responses from the scientific community.

James Gallagher served as first chair of the Social Policy Committee. He ascribed the resistance to explicit policy involvement within SRCD to misunderstanding of the role of research in policy deliberations. He received approval to include a preconference on child development and social policy at the biennial SRCD meetings in 1977 and to initiate a newsletter from the Washington liaison office, which continues to this day (*Social Policy Reports*). The newsletter was a delayed, diluted response to the earlier request for space in *Child Development*, but it was a response in the right direction. Somewhat ironically, in 1979 the American Psychological Association, which had always included the public interest as part of its mission, devoted an entire issue of the *American Psychologist* to "Psychology and Children: Current Research and Practice" (Scarr, 1979).

The policy preconferences at the SRCD meetings were rapidly absorbed into regular sessions during the biennial meeting. In 1978, SRCD joined the group of then 15 professional societies that sponsored Congressional Science Fellowships under the umbrella of the American Association for the Advancement of Science. The fellowship served two purposes: (a) to develop a cadre of developmental scientists who were conversant with policy issues and the policy process and who would pass on what they learned in Congress through teaching, writing, and research, and (b) to help establish a more effective liaison between child development research and public policy, thus lending the fellows an ambassadorial role on behalf of SRCD. The support provided for this new undertaking by the Foundation for Child Development and the W.T. Grant Foundation (and their subsequent support of the Washington liaison office) offered external validation of SRCD's growing acceptance, if not active reclaiming, of its role in mobilizing research to improve the lives and futures of children.

In 1983, the Social Policy Committee was renamed the Committee on Child Development and Social Policy, with Harold Stevenson as chair, and a number of important initiatives were undertaken to strengthen SRCD's link to policy.[1] This trajectory of increased engagement in policy came to a halt in 1985, when the Long Range Planning Committee concluded that the funding environment could not support the sustained presence of the Washington liaison office nor the continuation of the Congressional Fellows Program. The foundations had provided a decade of support and felt this was sufficient time for the society to assume full responsibility for these activities. Although the Planning Committee concluded, "We are mindful of the issues of social responsibility in our time" (Society for Research in Child Development Long Range Planning Committee, 1985, p. 5), they did not propose committing SRCD funds to the activities through which this responsibility had been formally manifested. The fellows program was discontinued, despite an attempt led by Zigler and Congressman George Miller to reconstitute it with federal funding. The Washington office stayed open until 1989 when John Hagen, then Executive Officer of the society, negotiated a liaison arrangement with the American Psychological Society to represent SRCD in Washington. This arrangement continued for a decade until a new Washington office for SRCD was established in 1999.

The 1970s and 1980s illustrate the tensions that have characterized the role of organized developmental psychology in public policy. The society's support of institutional expressions of this role came reluctantly and experienced a spurt that was tenuous and short-lived. Nevertheless, few within the society questioned the legitimacy of applied objectives of the field and, as we shall see, this rising and falling pattern of more explicit support for policy involvement rose again in the 1990s.

---

[1]SRCD's 1984 annual review volume, *Review of Child Development Research*, was titled *Child Development Research and Social Policy* (Stevenson & Siegel, 1984). A conference on Training and Research in Child Development and Social Policy was held in March 1983 at Vanderbilt University. Two summer institutes on child development and social policy were held at Cornell University in June 1984 and at the University of Texas in June 1985.

The Bush Centers in Child Development and Social Policy

While organized developmental psychology was struggling with its relationship to public policy, the small group of maverick members who had instigated the establishment of the Social Policy Committee turned their attention to the next generation of child development scholars. Future scholars were a neglected concern, addressed very partially by the Congressional Science Fellowship Program, which was limited to a handful of individuals, to postdoctoral training, and to the U.S. Congress as the site for learning about the issues and tactics of policy making. Policy schools, by and large, did not (and still do not) focus on child policy or include developmental psychologists. A vacuum thus existed for students interested in becoming "like Ed"—scholars who could cross-walk the worlds of developmental science and public policy. Ed and his colleagues, in turn, were eager to train the next generation of scientifically and politically sophisticated developmental psychologists who would become the leaders of the future, or, in Ed's words, "people who understand both how young children develop and how social policy is formed" (Cahan, 1992, p. 68). This led him— along with Bronfenbrenner, Richmond, and Sheldon White—to approach the Archibald Granville Bush Foundation to fund centers for training students to work in both research and social policy.

Four Bush Centers were established, headed by SRCD members Norma Feshbach (University of California at Los Angeles), Jim Gallagher (University of North Carolina), Harold Stevenson (University of Michigan), and Zigler (Yale University). Although each center had its unique program and emphasis, they all trained fellows in the combined fields of developmental psychology and social policy formation, conducted research into public policy issues relating to children and families, and made forays into public education (Cahan, 1992). Over the 10-year life of the program (1977–1987), approximately 254 fellows, including undergraduates, graduate and postdoctoral students, and midcareer professionals, were taught to use their knowledge in the solution of social problems.

Contributions of the Bush Centers to child and family policy are difficult to measure. One could argue that dissemination of policy-relevant child development scholarship blossomed because of the Bush Centers. Yet, as noted by Cahan (1992), the 1980s was a decade of retrenchment in federal support for child and family policy and thus not a particularly hospitable environment for the mission of the Centers. Policies are also overdetermined, making it extraordinarily difficult to tease apart the contributions of science in general, let alone the science that is emerging from discrete sources (Hayes, 1982; Takanishi & Melton, 1987; Weiss, 1987).

The actions of the host universities offer another insight into the acceptance of the Bush Centers. Although the centers were widely acclaimed and very popular, they were not given permanent status by any of their home universities once the seed money from the Foundation ended. The University of California at Los Angeles did provide some funds to keep its center open for a few more years. The North Carolina Bush Center was folded into its host, the Frank Porter Graham Child Development Center, and is still directed by Jim Gallagher. The Yale Center (now called the Edward Zigler Center in Child Development and Social Policy) has remained operative through private grants and a small amount of university support.

Impacts on the field of child development offer yet another yardstick for considering the contributions of the Bush Centers. As with impacts on social policy, this is a slippery outcome to capture. However, by the end of the decade-long support of the Bush Centers, the field of developmental psychology was once again showing signs of greater acceptance of precisely the kinds of activities they promoted. Like Cahan (1992), we conclude that there have been a number of changes in the character and definition of developmental psychology that are not coincidentally linked in time to the years of the Bush Centers. We turn to these developments in the next two sections, starting with a focused analysis of trends in the content of *Child Development*.

Trends in Child Development

We submit that the Bush Centers, through training a cohort of students who knew how to link their research to policy issues and to disseminate such research, contributed to renewed momentum within developmental psychology to embrace policy-relevant research. To lend tangible evidence to this assertion, we conducted an analysis of trends in the inclusion of policy-relevant articles in *Child Development* over 5 decades. Two graduate students in public policy at Georgetown University, under the supervision of Phillips, developed a coding system for assessing, first, whether a given article was policy relevant (addressed a topic that has direct relevance for social policy) and, second, whether the article included discussion of the policy implications of the research.

To ensure an inclusive process, a list of 125 policy topics (available from the first author) was generated through multiple methods. These methods specifically included (a) requesting that the Congressional Research Service provide a list of current legislative issues focused on children and families, (b) perusing six Web sites for liberal- and conservative-leaning think tanks, (c) asking policy advocates representing this spectrum of political persuasions to provide a list of topics related to child development that have been salient policy issues over the last 50 years, (d) scanning a complete set of the Packard Foundations' *The Future of Children* for policy topics, and (e) reviewing specific policy topics in four textbooks on child development and public policy (Stevenson & Siegel, 1984; Zigler & Hall, 2000; Zigler, Kagan, & Hall, 1996; Zigler, Kagan, & Klugman, 1983).

Once the list was developed, the students independently rated every article in the first issue of every decade of *Child Development* from 1950 to 2000 (i.e., all articles published in 1950, 1960, and so on). If the research presented in the article addressed a policy topic on the list, it received a one-star rating. These articles were considered to be policy relevant insofar as they had the potential to inform a policy debate about children and families. If the article went one step beyond policy relevance and explicitly linked the research to child and family policy, it received a two-star rating. Either the research in these articles was motivated by a stated interest in informing a specific policy debate, as portrayed in the introduction, or the findings were explicitly related to a

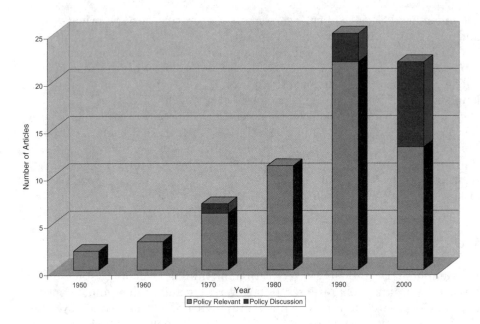

Figure 1.1. Number of policy articles in *Child Development*, 1950–2000.

policy issue. The independent ratings were then compared and disagreements were discussed among the students and Phillips until a consensus was reached.

The results of the consensus ratings are illustrated in Figure 1.1 (trends in the number of articles) and Figure 1.2 (trends in the proportion of articles). The trends are striking. In the 1950 and 1960 issues of *Child Development*, only 3 to 4 articles addressed policy-relevant topics. By 1970, this small number had doubled (although the share of total articles devoted to policy issues was still below 10%). By 1990, a more substantive number of the articles in the journal addressed policy issues (25 articles, or close to 16% of the total), but it was not until 2000 that a sizable share of these articles explicitly linked the research to a child and family policy issue.

The Broader Context of the Bush Centers

The Bush Centers were launched during a time of substantial turmoil for both child policy and social science research. The 1970s and 1980s marked a period of uncertainty with regard to the place of social science research, in general, in federal policy making. Those within SRCD who were uncomfortable with an explicit organizational endorsement of federal policy involvement were bolstered by the disappointing outcomes of several of the evaluations designed to assess the effectiveness of the Great Society programs. Developmental psychologists are most familiar with the controversy surrounding the Westinghouse Learning Corporation's evaluation of Head Start, but evaluations of Follow Through projects aimed to help low-income children transition successfully to elemen-

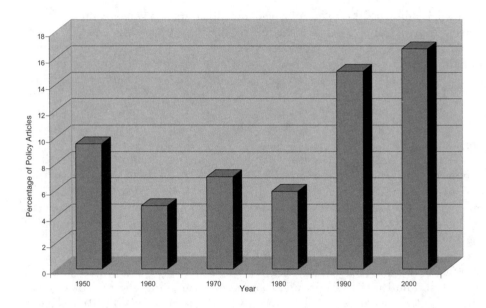

Figure 1.2. Percentage of articles in *Child Development* addressing public policy, 1950–2000.

tary school and of Title I compensatory education programs also revealed that the problems of the poor were more intractable than politically active social scientists had imagined. A period of public and scientific disenchantment with both the social policies of the 1960s and the contributions of social science to large-scale social reform efforts followed.

Disengagement from policy concerns, however, rapidly became a luxury. Dramatic cuts by the Reagan administration in federal research support, as well as in long-standing statistical series administered by federal agencies such as the Census Bureau, served as a wake-up call to the social scientific community. The Consortium of Social Science Associations and the Federation for Behavioral, Psychological and Cognitive Sciences both emerged during this period and helped to coordinate the responses of the separate social science disciplines to what was perceived as an explicit defunding of their basic enterprise. SRCD was a member of both organizations. Even scientists who were uncertain about political involvement could not help but recognize that the viability of their empirical work depended on political decision making. Moreover, the distinction between science policy and social policy became blurred as conservative national leaders justified cuts in research funding on the basis of poor practical returns on their investments. As a result, the social scientific research community necessarily became engaged in debates about their role in the construction of social policy (Bevan, 1980).

One highly influential forum within which these debates occurred was the Select Committee on Children, Youth, and Families, established in 1982 with the active involvement of the 1981–1982 cohort of SRCD Congressional Science

Fellows. Along with the Senate Caucus on Children, the select committee provided a central gathering place within the U.S. Congress for scientists, practitioners, and policymakers to consider questions of child and family policy, often in light of child development knowledge. Developmental psychologists served on the staffs (Republican and Democratic) of both the select committee and the caucus, and others were frequently called on to testify before these groups. The hearing records of the select committee provide a decade-long record of policy-relevant knowledge about child development that warrants its own historical analysis.

Other seminal reports issued by the Carnegie Council on Children (Keniston & Carnegie Council on Children, 1977), the Brookings Institution (Steiner, 1981), the National Research Council (1976), and the National Commission on Children (1991) juxtaposed worrisome demographic and social changes affecting children in the United States with proposals for reconsidering the federal role in child policy making. In 1980, the Committee on Child Development Research and Public Policy was established at the National Research Council to synthesize scientific evidence on child and family policy issues of national importance and recommend promising avenues of remedy. The committee issued reports on topics ranging from special education (Heller, Holtzman, & Messick, 1982) to teen pregnancy (Hayes, 1987) to child care (Hayes, Palmer, & Zaslow, 1990), as well as on the policy process itself as it plays out for children (Hayes, 1982). This committee was terminated in 1990, but it reemerged in 1993 as the Board on Children, Youth, and Families under the joint auspices of the National Research Council and the Institute of Medicine, with Sheldon White and Jack Shonkoff as its first two chairs.

Within the field of developmental psychology, the emergence of Bronfenbrenner's (1979) ecological theory provided a framework within which to consider the influences and interventions being proposed in this growing collection of policy reports. The ecological model directly highlights the role of the broad social context, including the political context, in shaping the trajectories of children. It is important to note that in a guest editorial for *Child Development*, Bronfenbrenner (1974) argued that science needs policy as much as policy needs science. The subsequent emergence of applied developmental science, which draws heavily on ecological theory as well as dynamic systems and life span theories, also contributed to the increasingly hospitable intellectual climate within which the Bush Centers operated (Fisher & Lerner, 1994; Lerner, Fisher, & Weinberg, 2000).

Cahan (1992), who traced this history and the contributions of the Bush Centers, concluded, "The Bush Centers helped to formalize and legitimate a process that had, in fact, been taking awkward forms for more than a century" (p. 4). We agree. By the end of the 1980s, scholarship on child development and social policy was assuming a prominent place in the major developmental journals, individuals trained to traverse this intersection in their research and professional roles were assuming leadership positions within the field, and offshoots of the Bush Centers were emerging in small and large versions at universities around the country. The fledgling subdiscipline of child development and public policy was poised to claim a place at the main table of the interdisciplinary developmental sciences.

Moving Toward Maturity: 1990 to 2003

Zigler (2000) wrote in his foreword to the second edition of the *Handbook of Early Childhood Intervention* that "each stage of development brings characteristic triumphs and challenges, with occasional setbacks and recurrences of the previous stage's struggles, not entirely abandoned as the young move forward into the new stages along their growth trajectory" (p. xi). The same is true of the young field of child development and social policy. From the early 1970s to the current day, this subfield has expanded greatly, become capable of more complex tasks and sophisticated understanding, and gradually (albeit haltingly) assumed an integral role within the institutional structures and operations of its parent field of developmental science.

We have traced the vicissitudes that characterized SRCD's involvement in matters of public policy during the Bush Center years. The Committee for Child Development, Public Policy and Public Information (now the Policy and Communications Committee) remained active during the 1990s, and in 1999 it persuaded the society to reestablish an office in Washington, DC. In 2000, a grant from the W. T. Grant Foundation allowed the congressional fellows program to be revived. The *Social Policy Reports* have become a regular publication, and substantial efforts have been made to enhance public dissemination of research presented at the society's biennial meeting. Further, the editor of *Child Development*, Lynn Liben, instituted a requirement for all accepted submissions that a brief, layperson's summary of the findings be prepared for publicity purposes and also initiated a new format, "From Another Perspective . . ." (FAP) in which commentary is sought on papers that warrant additional perspectives, including discussion of policy implications (see the Langlois & Liben, 2003, for the inaugural FAP). Policy activities are again thriving within SRCD, and unlike in the past, there is widespread belief in the value of these endeavors.

Perhaps the most obvious indicator of maturity concerns the successful development of the first generation of scholars trained in child development and social policy. The individuals in this fledgling cohort have established themselves in a wide array of leadership positions and developed a highly effective "issue network" of scientifically trained, policy-savvy experts on children and families. They are actively engaged in linking science to public policy at the federal, state, and community levels. This generation of "hybrid" scholars is involved in interdisciplinary teams evaluating the major societal reforms of the 1990s (e.g., welfare reform, education reform). They are situated not only in academic positions but also as foundation presidents, congressional and federal agency staff, and heads of nonprofit organizations. Others have become consultants, attorneys, physicians, and journalists. In each of these capacities, Bush Center graduates are shaping the direction of child and family policy and practice, as well as the research that will be available to inform these policies and practices in the future.

Many of the first-generation scholars are training a new cohort of students. A second generation of university-based child policy programs, composed of some of the long-standing centers as well as many new ones, has emerged. These programs are highly interdisciplinary; their university auspices include colleges of arts and sciences, policy schools, public health and medical schools, and law schools. They are engaged in an extremely wide range of activities focused on federal, state, and community-based issues and players.

Opportunities and Challenges for the Future

As the subfield of child development and public policy becomes a firm and valued fixture on the landscape of the developmental sciences, it faces many opportunities and challenges. In *Neurons to Neighborhoods* (Shonkoff & Phillips, 2000), the field was challenged to sustain attention to two complementary agendas: (a) How can our knowledge about child development advance the nation's human capital and ensure the ongoing viability of its democratic institutions? and (b) How can our knowledge contribute to nurturing, protecting, and ensuring the health and well-being of all young children as an important objective in its own right? Much earlier, Zigler (1970) also called for a dual commitment to policies that concern themselves with "their meaning for the child today and their meaning for the kind of person he will become in the future" (p. 166).

The first agenda speaks to society's economic, political, and social interests. As prevailing political agendas either embrace or retreat from leadership on children's issues and as the national economy goes through periods of growth and decline, policy-relevant research on children has the potential to sustain debates linking the care and protection of the young to the nation's future productivity. The second agenda speaks to society's moral and ethical values, focusing attention on the quality of life for all children.

As research at the intersection of child development and public policy addresses these agendas, it will confront both abiding and contemporary dilemmas. The abiding dilemmas concern the slippery slope between informing policy and becoming a political handmaiden, distinguishing informed recommendations based on established knowledge and reasonable hypotheses from policies guided by misuses of science (Shonkoff, 2000), and blending the values of scientific inquiry, which emphasize objectivity and empirical proof, with the incentives and pressures that characterize political decision making. As stated by White (1996), "We need to probe deeply into questions of how developmental psychology should properly deal with the ethical and political ramifications of its work" (p. 424).

Contemporary challenges also abound. They include the refractionating of the young child (see Zigler, 1984) seen in the current emphasis on cognitive and literacy development to the neglect of social–emotional development, continued pressure to further devolve responsibility for child policy to the states and localities with few safeguards, and the need to strike a balance between legitimate demands for accountability and the dual needs to ensure appropriate testing of young children and valid uses of test data.

Zigler has devoted his post-Washington years to addressing these dilemmas. He continues to train a cadre of scholars who are well-equipped to bridge the worlds of science and policy. Other chapters in this volume trace these specific contributions. This volume takes a step back to examine Ed's role in the broader development of the subdiscipline of child development and public policy. Absent Ed's abiding commitment not only to specific policy issues but to the development of this once fragile subdiscipline, we would likely still be struggling to lend legitimacy to the twin missions of our parent discipline to produce and deploy knowledge for the betterment of children.

References

Bevan, W. (1980). On getting in bed with a lion. *American Psychologist, 35*, 779–789.

Bremner, R. H., Barnard, J., Hareven, T. K., & Mennel, R. M. (Eds.). (1971). *Childhood and youth in America: A documentary history: Vol. 2. 1966–1973.* Cambridge, MA: Harvard University Press.

Bronfenbrenner, U. (1974). Developmental research, public policy, and the ecology of childhood. *Child Development, 45*, 1–5.

Bronfenbrenner, U. (1979). Contexts of child rearing: Problems and prospects. *American Psychologist, 34*, 844–850.

Bulmer, M. (2001). Knowledge for the public good: The emergence of social sciences and social reform in the late nineteenth and early-twentieth century America, 1880–1940. In D. L. Featherman & M. A. Viovskis (Eds.), *Social science and policy-making: A search for relevance in the twentieth century* (pp. 16–39). Ann Arbor: University of Michigan Press.

Cahan, E. (1992). *Research on child development and the formulation of social policy: Historical precedents and current perspectives.* Unpublished manuscript, Wheelock College, Boston.

Cairns, R. B. (1989). The making of developmental psychology. In W. Damon (Ed.), *The handbook of child psychology* (Vol. 1, 5th ed., pp. 25–105). New York: Wiley.

Cohen, S. S. (2001). *Championing child care.* New York: Columbia University Press.

Comprehensive Child Development Act of 1971, H.R. 6748, 92d Cong. (1971).

Davis, A. (1959). Spearheads for reform: The social settlements and the progressive movement, 1890–1914. Unpublished doctoral dissertation, University of Wisconsin, Madison.

Elementary and Secondary Education Act of 1965, H.R. 2362, 79 Stat. 27 (1965).

Featherman, D. L., & Vinofskis, M. A. (2001a). Growth and use of social and behavioral science in the federal government since World War II. In D. L. Featherman & M. A. Vinovskis (Eds.), *Social science and policy-making: A search for relevance in the twentieth century* (pp. 40–82). Ann Arbor: University of Michigan Press.

Featherman, D. L., & Vinofskis, M. A. (2001b). In search of relevance to social reform and policy-making. In D. L. Featherman & M. A. Vinovskis (Eds.), *Social science and policy-making: A search for relevance in the twentieth century* (pp. 1–15). Ann Arbor: University of Michigan Press.

Fisher, C. B., & Lerner, R. M. (Eds.). (1994). *Foundations of applied developmental psychology.* New York: McGraw-Hill.

Hagen, J. (1997). The Society for Research in Child Development: Early roots, history and current organization. *SRCD Newsletter, 40*(3), 3–5, 11.

Hagen, J. (2002). *The role of the Society for Research in Child Development in social policy: 1976–Present.* Unpublished manuscript, University of Michigan, Ann Arbor.

Haskell, T. L. (1977). *The emergence of professional social science: The American Social Science Association and the nineteenth-century crisis of authority.* Urbana: University of Illinois Press.

Hayes, C. D. (Ed.). (1982). *Making policies for children: A study of the federal process.* Washington, DC: National Academy Press.

Hayes, C. D. (Ed.). (1987). *Risking the future: Adolescent sexuality, pregnancy, and childbearing.* Washington, DC: National Academy Press.

Hayes, C. D., Palmer, J. L., & Zaslow, M. J. (Eds.). (1990). *Who cares for America's children? Child care policy for the 1990s.* Washington, DC: National Academy Press.

Heller, K. A., Holtzman, W. H., & Messick, S. (1982). *Placing children in special education: A strategy for equity.* Washington, DC: National Academy Press.

Keniston, K., & Carnegie Council on Children. (1977). *All our children: The American family under pressure.* New York: Harcourt Brace Jovanovich.

Langlois, J. H., & Liben, S. (2003). Child care research: An editorial perspective. *Child Development, 74,* 969–975.

Lazerson, M. (1970). Social reform and early childhood education: Some historical perspectives. *Urban Education, 5,* 83–102.

Lerner, R. M., Fisher, C. B., & Weinberg, R. A. (2000). Toward a science for and of the people: Promoting civil society through the application of developmental science. *Child Development, 71,* 11–20.

Lyons, G. M. (1969). *The uneasy partnership: Social science and the federal government in the twentieth century.* New York: Russell Sage Foundation.

National Commission on Children. (1991). *Beyond rhetoric: A new American agenda for children and families.* Washington, DC: U.S. Government Printing Office.

National Research Council. (1976). *Toward a national policy for children and families.* Advisory Committee on Child Development, Assembly of Behavioral and Social Sciences. Washington, DC: National Academy Press.

Richmond, J. (1967). Child development: A basic science for pediatrics. *Pediatrics, 39,* 649–658.

Ross, C. J. (1983). Advocacy movements in the century of the child. In E. Zigler, S. L. Kagan, & E. Klugman (Eds.), *Children, families, and government: Perspectives on American social policy* (pp. 165–176). New York: Cambridge University Press.

Scarr, S. (Ed.). (1979). Psychology and children: Current research and practice [Special issue]. *American Psychologist, 34*(10).

Sears, R. R. (1975). Your ancients revisited: A history of child development. In E. J. Hetherington (Ed.), *Review of child development research* (Vol. 5, pp. 1–73). Chicago: University of Chicago Press.

Senn, M. J. E. (1975). Insights on the child development movement in the United States. *Monographs of the Society for Research in Child Development, 40*(3/4, Serial No. 161).

Shonkoff, J. P. (2000). Science, policy, and practice: Three cultures in search of a shared mission. *Child Development, 71,* 181–187.

Shonkoff, J. P., & Phillips, D. (Eds.) (2000). *Neurons to neighborhoods: The science of early childhood development.* Washington, DC: National Academies Press.

Siegel, A. W., & White, S. H. (1982). The child study movement: Early growth and development of the symbolized child. *Advances in Child Behavior and Development, 17,* 233–285.

Smith, B. L. R. (1990). *American science policy since World War II.* Washington, DC: Brookings Institution Press.

Society for Research in Child Development Long Range Planning Committee. (1985, Spring). *SRCD Long Range Planning Committee report.* Unpublished report, University of Michigan, Ann Arbor.

Steiner, G. Y. (1981). *The futility of family policy.* Washington, DC: Brookings Institution Press.

Stevenson, H., & Siegel, A. (Eds.). (1984). *Child development research and social policy.* Chicago: University of Chicago Press.

Takanishi, R. (1978). Childhood as a social issue: Historical roots of contemporary child advocacy movements. *Journal of Social Issues, 34*(2), 8–28.

Takanishi, R., & Melton, G. B. (1987). Child development research and the legislative process. In B. G. Melton (Ed.), *Reforming the law: Impact of child development research* (pp. 86–101). New York: Guilford Press.

Weiss, C. (1987). Diffusion of child development research to legal audiences. In B. G. Melton (Ed.), *Reforming the law: Impact of child development research* (pp. 63–85). New York: Guilford Press.

White, S. H. (1992). G. Stanley Hall: From philosophy to developmental psychology. *Developmental Psychology, 28,* 25–34.

White, S. H. (1996). The relationship of developmental psychology to social policy. In E. Zigler, S. L. Kagan, & N. W. Hall (Eds.), *Children, families, and government: Preparing for the twenty-first century* (pp. 409–426). New York: Cambridge University Press.

White, S. H., & Phillips, D. (2001). Designing Head Start: Roles played by developmental psychologists. In D. L. Featherman & M. A. Vinokskis (Eds.), *Social science and policy-making: A search for relevance in the twentieth century* (pp. 83–118). Ann Arbor: University of Michigan Press.

Zigler, E. (1970). A national priority: Raising the quality of children's lives. *Children, 17*(5), 166–170.

Zigler, E. (1980). Welcoming a new journal. *Journal of Applied Developmental Psychology, 1,* 1–6.

Zigler, E. (1984). Issues in the construction of social policy for children and their families. *International Journal of Mental Health, 12*(4), 78–86.

Zigler, E. (2000). Foreword. In J. Shonkoff & S. Meisels (Eds.), *Handbook of early childhood intervention* (2nd ed., pp. xi–xv). New York: Cambridge University Press.

Zigler, E., & Hall, N. W. (2000). *Child development and social policy.* New York: McGraw-Hill.

Zigler, E., Kagan, S. L., & Hall, N. W. (Eds.). (1996). *Children, families, and government: Preparing for the twenty-first century.* New York: Cambridge University Press.

Zigler, E., Kagan, S. L., & Klugman, E. (Eds.). (1983). *Children, families, and government: Perspectives on American social policy.* NewYork: Cambridge University Press.

Zigler, E., & Muenchow, S. (1985). A room of their own: A proposal to renovate the Children's Bureau. *American Psychologist, 40,* 953–959.

Zigler, E., & Phillips, D. (1987). The checkered history of federal child care legislation. In. E. Z. Rothkopf (Ed.), *Review of research in education* (Vol. 14, pp. 3–41). Washington, DC: American Educational Research Association.

2

Policy Looking to Research

Olivia Golden

Shortly before I was asked to write this chapter, I had an experience that comes just a few times in a career. I learned, through the publication of the impact evaluation of Early Head Start, that a program that my colleagues and I had seen through from early dreams to full implementation had been shown by a rigorous research design to have made a significant, measurable, positive difference for vulnerable low-income babies and toddlers and their parents (Administration for Children and Families [ACF], 2002). For these very young children, attending Early Head Start meant that at 3 years old their burden of poverty and disadvantage was a little lighter than for other 3-year-olds from similarly vulnerable families, raising the hope that their chances for success in school and later life had been significantly improved. Among the improved outcomes for 3-year-olds who attended Early Head Start (compared with control group toddlers from comparably poor families) were higher average scores and a smaller percentage in the at-risk range on standardized tests of cognitive development, higher average scores and a smaller percentage at-risk in language development, better home environments and parenting practices, and better outcomes for parents.

Over the years of work on Early Head Start, an initiative to bring high-quality child development services to low-income children from birth to age 3 and their families, my colleagues and I focused with equal intensity on program design and implementation on the one hand and research design on the other. At the same time that we wanted to avoid failing children because of weak programs, we also wanted to avoid seeing good programs undercut by a research design not complex or rich enough to capture real effects. This focus on program and research in tandem paid off doubly for children: Early Head Start would not have been successful for young and vulnerable children had its design and implementation not relied powerfully on the lessons from early childhood development research, and it would not have yielded lessons about success to guide other programs had the research design not been sophisticated enough to capture knowledge about program implementation in the real world.

Yet despite the power of this two-way connection between early childhood research and policy, successful examples like Early Head Start are all too rare. Why? One reason, as I learned when I came to the federal government in a senior policy role, is that the different perspectives of researchers and policymakers can be a recipe for mutual frustration. Researchers' focus on knowledge in the abstract did not make sense to me in that role: there was no "in the abstract" in my life as assistant secretary. I was interested in how knowledge could improve children's lives, so I needed to figure out how to fit that knowledge into a complicated political, programmatic, and professional environment to change that environment for the better. At the same time, I had to worry about the possibility that knowledge misinterpreted or misused or insufficiently grounded could actually make things worse. Often when I talked about these issues to researchers, I would remember a conversation long ago with a talented journalist who pointed out to me that his job was to tell a true story, not to deal with the consequences of telling the story. My job as a policymaker, of course, was the opposite: to try to shape the consequences for children.

Exacerbating this disconnect, researchers and practitioners too often attribute the differences between them to bad motives on the other side. Researchers too often assume that policymakers are motivated primarily by the self-serving desire to defend existing programs; policymakers too often see researchers as motivated largely by their own cleverness and uninterested in how programs actually work. The end result is that researchers and policymakers too often talk past each other or buy into various common myths and excuses that obstruct the development of knowledge that is both true and usable.

The goal of this chapter is to draw on lessons from three successful experiences to help both researchers and practitioners bridge these gaps and engage each others' wisdom more successfully, to the ultimate benefit of children and families. All three examples are from my years at the U.S. Department of Health and Human Services [USDHHS] from 1993 to 2001, first as the Commissioner for Children, Youth, and Families and then as the Assistant Secretary for Children and Families. I came to USDHHS from a background in academia, state government, and the advocacy world, and thus brought to my federal role both a deep belief in the value of research, reflection, and the rigorous pursuit of knowledge *and* enough personal experience of research and researchers to question, challenge, and supplement researchers' underlying assumptions no matter how much certainty they displayed.

Three Examples of the Intersection Between Early Childhood Research and Policy

The three successful experiences span a full 8 years of policy making. The Advisory Committee on Head Start Quality and Expansion, convened in the first year of the Clinton administration, served as a base for much that came later, including the creation of Early Head Start. The multiyear effort to shape a policy-relevant agenda for child care research, along with the institutions to support it, was still evolving at the very end of the administration.

Advisory Committee on Head Start Quality and Expansion

The Advisory Committee on Head Start Quality and Expansion, announced by USDHHS Secretary Donna Shalala in June 1993 and chaired by Assistant Sec-

retary Mary Jo Bane, was convened at a time early in the Clinton administration when the administration's intention to invest substantially in Head Start
had run into opposition. A variety of stakeholders had expressed concerns that
quality in the program had eroded and that a condition of expansion should be
a look at quality and effectiveness. In response, the administration remained
committed to a major investment as a key step to improve the lives of poor
children and at the same time sought advice about the right approach from a
wide-ranging external committee. The consensus expressed in the unanimous
report of this committee of bipartisan experts and practitioners, issued promptly
in December 1993 (USDHHS, 1993), lasted through the 1994 and 1998 Head
Start reauthorizations and guided a whole series of improvements in regulations, policy, and practice aimed at enhancing the quality of programs and their
impact on children's development. Both the advisory committee's findings and
the bipartisan and research-based approach that made the committee so successful continue to have great relevance today, although as I write this chapter
the future looks very uncertain.

The advisory committee's membership included researchers, practitioners,
parents, and a bipartisan group of national policymakers, including the staffs of
the congressional committees that oversee Head Start and that would be involved in the next reauthorization. The committee's success in building a consensus from the extensive but disparate experience of its members owed a great
deal to the credibility of the researcher members and to their collective insistence on the core findings of the research. Although the researchers on the
committee disagreed on some specific findings of the research—for example,
how to interpret the findings about the long-run effects of Head Start on the
lives of poor children assessed many years later—they agreed on a set of critical
points that are laid out in the advisory committee's report and justify the key
elements of its approach (USDHHS, 1993):

- Head Start has accomplished important gains for children and families;
- quality of programs is key to outcomes for children;
- "most Head Start programs offer quality services" (compared, e.g.,
  with other child-care and preschool programs studied in the literature), yet "the quality of [Head Start] programs is uneven across
  the country" (p. 9); and
- research offers considerable guidance about the key elements of
  quality in early childhood programs, such as staff-to-child ratios,
  staff education, and the training and development opportunities
  available to staff.

Building on this consensus, the committee report proposes an approach
that blends expansion—because there are so many poor children still in need of
Head Start services who would benefit from the program's comprehensiveness
and high quality relative to other programs—with a set of very specific steps to
enhance quality and improve responsiveness to the changing needs of children
and families. The committee's researcher members played an important role in
explaining to other members the broad common ground that lies behind dis-

putes about whether Head Start works: In their view, we know from the research that Head Start provides important benefits to children, we know that high-quality early childhood programs work, and we know that Head Start comes closer to the lessons about what makes high-quality early childhood programs work than other large-scale programs available to low-income children. In addition, not only Head Start's practice but the principles that underlie Head Start—its "comprehensive approach, its commitment to parents, and its community focus" (USDHHS, 1993, p. 21)—are consistent with what we know about quality programs. Therefore, to the researchers as well as to the whole advisory committee, the next step was to build on these important successes to bring every single Head Start program up to the standards we know work for children.

The committee's work influenced statute, policy, and practice in Head Start and thereby improved poor children's lives in three major ways. First, it rebuilt a bipartisan consensus for expanding Head Start, which cleared the way for the major investments by the Clinton administration. Over the next several years, these investments allowed for expansion in the number of children served, important improvements in staffing, staff salaries, and overall program quality, and the creation of Early Head Start. Second, the committee's work contributed substantially to the 1994 Congressional Reauthorization of Head Start, which embodied the focus on both expansion and quality and also created Early Head Start. Third, it powerfully influenced practice through both the specific framework in the committee's report and the development of key relationships between committee members—particularly researchers—on the one hand and key implementers, both at USDHHS and in the Head Start community, on the other. Among the results of this partnership were new regulations governing quality in local Head Start programs (the Program Performance Standards) that more fully embodied the lessons of research and practice, a new focus on assessing developmental outcomes for children, revamped technical assistance for local programs, and a tougher approach to monitoring program quality.

Early Head Start

The idea of intensifying Head Start's focus on very young children, who had previously been served in Head Start primarily in programs for migrant farm workers' families and in parent–child centers, was raised by the advisory committee on Head Start Quality and Expansion as a not-quite-consensus recommendation:

> The overwhelming majority of Advisory Committee members recommend the development of a new initiative focused on serving families with children under age three. . . . The Advisory Committee did not reach consensus on the scope of the initiative or the exact amount of funds. . . . The Advisory Committee recommends that HHS convene a high level committee, like that which planned the original Head Start program, charged with developing program guidelines to allow Head Start to serve families with children under age three most effectively. (USDHHS, 1993, p. 52)

Through intense bipartisan negotiations, including particularly strong leadership from Senator Edward Kennedy, a provision setting aside an increasing percentage of Head Start funds for services to young children was included in the 1994 Head Start reauthorization, along with a provision authorizing an advisory committee of experts to design it. This group, the Advisory Committee on Services for Families With Infants and Toddlers, included as members primarily experts in early childhood programs, including both researchers and practitioners.

The committee, working on a very tight timetable, issued its statement on program design in September 1994 (USDHHS, 1994). The deliberations of the committee that led up to the statement were strongly shaped by the findings of child development research: the positive findings about features of programs that matter to success (staff training, intensity of services, development of nurturing relationships between adult caregiver and baby or toddler) and the negative findings that services do not work if they are insufficiently intense in terms of the hours of high-quality engagement directly with young children. In fact, the statement began with a careful overview of relevant research, focusing on quality and intensity of services and on four "cornerstones" of program design that emerged from the research: child development, family development, community building, and staff development. In turn, the statement, with its strong research base, undergirded the detailed program design of Early Head Start and provided guidance in the development of the Head Start Performance Standards for Infants and Toddlers, regulations that the agency had been unsuccessful in issuing in previous years but was able to promulgate successfully in the years following the Committee's work.

The Head Start reauthorization also called for a rigorous evaluation of Early Head Start, and the advisory committee spoke to that requirement in its report, recommending multiple purposes for the evaluation:

> determining the effectiveness of the initiative and . . . advancing our understanding about which services work best for different families under different circumstances . . . . The Secretary must approach evaluation . . . as a tool for individual programs so that they can continuously refine their practices based on feedback from their own program evaluation. (USDHHS, 1994, p. 23)

Chapter 5 of this book details the way that Early Head Start research was designed to approach—even if not fully achieve—all of these goals, for example, through national–local research partnerships. As indicated earlier, we now know that Early Head Start has benefited vulnerable babies and toddlers and their families in just the way it was intended to. In addition, the multilayered research design of Early Head Start has paid off in knowledge to help shape future policy and program decisions and increase the benefit to children. For example, the evaluation identifies characteristic strengths and weaknesses of different program designs (home based and center based) and offers insights about next steps for strengthening these different designs (ACF, 2002).

Child-Care Research

This third example is not a single, contained episode but rather encompasses the multiyear efforts of USDHHS policymakers, led by Joan Lombardi, Associate Commissioner of the Child Care Bureau and then Deputy Assistant Secretary, to create research and policy agendas that would inform and support national attention to quality child care for working families. Key steps included "launch[ing] a policy-relevant research agenda for the first time" (Joan Lombardi, personal communication, January 5, 2003), developing statutory and institutional support for this child-care research agenda, expanding the connections between policymakers and researchers so that research could become more immediately useful, drawing the attention of researchers in related fields to the importance of child care in understanding and explaining what they were finding about working families, and mining multiple data sources to build a picture of the role of child care in supporting the work efforts of low-income parents. Part of the challenge was to persuade researchers from different worlds to cross boundaries to build knowledge: Early childhood researchers had a deep interest in quality and much less interest in the changing work patterns of mothers or in welfare reform, whereas researchers working on welfare reform evaluations tended to see child care as an issue of work support only and to have limited interest in child-care policy or programs.

Our effort to create a policy-relevant research agenda on child care drew on an insight that was becoming obvious to individual practitioners but that had not yet surfaced as a consistent subject for researchers or a broad public issue, despite its enormous importance for individual families: The implications of the enormous increase in work effort among mothers, which by the mid-to-late1990s included not only married mothers but also single mothers, and not only mothers of school-age children but also mothers of the youngest children. As policymakers, we believed strongly that research could help surface the immensity of the change and guide us in understanding its policy implications; we were sure that any clear-eyed look at working families, particularly low-income families, would show how the availability and affordability of child care were intertwined with the ability of parents to combine working with nurturing their children. We also expected that research would continue to show the role of quality care in children's development, on the basis of everything that early childhood development research had already contributed. Finally, we believed that the time was right for this research to change public sector budgets and policies, because of the interest at both the federal and state level in investing in working families and because of the flexible resources available in state budgets as a result of welfare reform (Temporary Assistance for Needy Families) block grants.

Key early decisions included the creation for the first time of a unified policy home for child care within the ACF, the Child Care Bureau, thus providing an institutional home for research and policy. Another key early step was the creation of the Child Care Research Partnerships, which got the states involved as partners in research with academic institutions.

In addition to building institutions, we worked with researchers to make the most of the information already available. We mined all the state and national reports we could find for information on the relationship of child care to families' work, funded additional focused research, got questions about child care into the big national databases used to understand family income and demographics, and worked to connect researchers whose background was in employment, income, and welfare reform to the world of child development and child care. Because of ACF's key role in supporting welfare reform research, including an array of random assignment studies that were already following low-income working families who had earlier been on welfare, we were able to add child-care questions to the studies, assist the researchers in gaining a greater level of sophistication about child-care policies and the experiences of low-income families, and ensure that where they had policy-relevant findings about the role of state child-care policies in supporting family income or child well-being for former welfare families, those findings were made available to policymakers.

Throughout the multiyear effort to strengthen research and learn more about child care and family life, researchers sometimes lagged behind practitioners and parents in their focus on the dramatic nature of recent changes faced by families and, therefore, in their ability to find the most interesting research questions. When early on in the development of our national child-care work I decided to conduct focus groups with low-income working parents across the country, I expected that I would gain vivid stories that would illustrate points already looked at by the research. But I soon found that parents' experiences had been changing so rapidly that their experiences suggested many emerging questions.

To take just one example, parents spoke passionately about the instability of child-care arrangements and the ways in which the "system"—which often included the child-care subsidy system, the welfare system, the nature of low-wage employment, and the child-care market—contributed to that instability. For example, if a state's subsidy system requires that a child-care subsidy end when a job ends, then if a mother loses her job, she will probably have to pull her child out of his or her child-care setting, use one or more improvised informal care arrangements to search for a new job, and then—assuming she gets her subsidy back—move her child to what will most likely be a different setting that has a vacant place at the time she finds a new job. This means that the child experiences multiple changes in child-care arrangements each time a job ends, even if the mother finds a new job relatively quickly. On the basis of what we know about children's development, this scenario suggests that the number of child-care arrangements is an important topic for research into child-care quality, expanding the current research, which focuses only on quality in a single arrangement.

Over the years, these efforts achieved partial success. On the research side, we created several core institutions—the Child Care Bureau, the Child Care Research Partnerships, and a statutory set-aside for child-care research added by Congress—and increased the attention to child care as part of a broader research agenda about working families. On the policy side, we achieved greater attention to child care as an issue of critical importance to working families, as well as a substantial increase in federal and state investment in child care for low-income working families. Yet major gaps remain: Resources are still far from meeting the need for subsidized care, let alone for quality care, and among the broader public, child care has not yet benefited from the kind of focused attention to quality that is described in this section as an important contribution of researchers to the Head Start and Early Head Start debates.

Lessons

To me, the central lesson of these examples is that high-quality research in general, and child development research in particular, can make a major difference in the lives of children. This impact on children's lives is a powerful incentive for both researchers and practitioners to continue to struggle with the discomfort and challenges of partnership. Direct benefits for children from early childhood research include the following:

1. The Head Start advisory committee framed and distilled the research in a way that contributed to major budget investments in both expansion and quality; built a multiyear, bipartisan consensus on the direction of the program; directly influenced practice and therefore children's lives by shaping regulations (the "Performance Standards"), training, and monitoring of local programs; and built ongoing partnerships between researchers and federal and local program staff, which in turn led to more practice improvements.
2. The whole design of Early Head Start was closely based on research knowledge about quality services for very young children: The very existence of the program as well as its demonstrated improvements in the lives of infants, toddlers, and their families are consequences of the influence of research on practice. In particular, the research base for Early Head Start made it possible to insist on the high levels of investment in staff, including numbers of staff, training, and educational background, that appear to be critical to high-quality infant and toddler programs.
3. Evidence gathered from an array of studies and data sources about the role of child care in supporting families' work contributed to major increases at the federal and state levels in investments in child care for working families.

The second lesson, equally important, is that these positive results are not automatic or easy to achieve. No research finding, no matter how powerful, will affect children's lives automatically: It takes a strategy, in addition perhaps to some amount of luck, to influence the world. In these examples, four broad strategies for early childhood research that is most likely to affect practice seem to me to stand out.

Seize the moment when change is possible and research can make a difference. One key element of strategy is timing: seizing the moments of opportunity when research can influence policy. As illustrated in both the first and third examples, a time of change can create fluidity that gives research unusual influence. In the example of the Head Start advisory committee, political conflict created the moment of readiness for change. Times of intense political conflict are of course risky, because the intensity may drown out alternative voices or the conflict may be so deep-seated as to be unbridgeable by research knowledge. But with skillful partnership between policymakers and researchers—partnership directed, as in the case of the advisory committee, toward identifying and building on areas of consensus—political intensity can create a space for contributions from researchers much greater than could be made in routine, day-to-day operations.

In the child-care example, the moment of opportunity for research to influence policy came less from political turmoil than from economic and demographic change (the major increase in mothers' work) and policy change in the form of welfare reform—changes whose full implications had not yet been thought through. Again, a moment when the old approaches no longer seem to fit can create a space for change and a likely moment for research to influence practice.

Design effective research approaches by integrating research findings from many sources, placing individual findings into a broader context, and drawing on both research and policy partners to design individual studies. Not all individual studies and not all approaches to distilling common findings from a body of research knowledge are equally effective at influencing practice. Some research questions seem to practitioners relevant and up-to-date, whereas others seem off the point or too late to be useful; some evaluations are extremely helpful to practitioners, whereas others seem so narrowly focused in their effort to make the questions answerable that they fail to ask the right questions.

To have the best chance at being useful, all three of the examples highlight the value of lessons derived from a body of research, from the integration of individual findings sustained over time. Although researchers sometimes have incentives to draw attention to lessons from a single study even when inconsistent with much other knowledge—perhaps a sensible orientation in the research world, where counterintuitive findings create new research questions about the reason for the discrepancy—this practice deeply damages the possibility of effective partnerships with policymakers who "have enough trouble explaining intuitive findings."[1] This issue of placing findings into context is particularly sensitive for policymakers when an evaluation of a specific program shows no significant results, because they fear that if the evaluation is publicized and discussed as though it occurred in isolation from all other findings, then it may be overinterpreted to mean that all investment in the particular field is useless. However, if researchers and policymakers can join forces to ensure that individual evaluations will be seen in the context of evidence accumulated over time, then findings of no result can contribute to substantive progress without destroying partnerships.

For example, the statement of the Early Head Start advisory committee highlighted the importance of intensity of services to young children—the number of hours of direct interaction with young children required to achieve results. Among several sources of evidence that convinced me and other committee members of this principle were emerging findings from the evaluation of the Comprehensive Child Development Program (CCDP), which found individual sites with significant results for children but no overall results nationally. When the CCDP evaluation was issued, many policymakers were concerned that it would be overinterpreted to mean that all investment in young children was

---

[1]This is one of many wise points that Hale Champion, former Undersecretary of USDHHS, used to make to his students and colleagues at Harvard's Kennedy School of Government.

worthless and would derail the effort to enact Early Head Start. Instead, a wide range of legislative, advocacy, policy, and research leaders emphasized the ways that Early Head Start could learn from the CCDP evaluation to improve outcomes, for example, by increasing the intensity of in-home services and requiring that local sites ensure quality in all out-of-home child care received by program children.

The examples also illustrate lessons for designing individual studies that will be useful for policymakers. Perhaps most important, policymakers, practitioners, and advocates are the experts on what they need to know; therefore, if research is to be useful to them, it helps for them to have a strong voice in its design. For example, policymakers and advocates felt that past early childhood research designs were too often ill-suited to evaluate programs for very young children in important ways (in particular, that they included insufficient information on the quality and stage of implementation in individual sites and on the services received by control children), which led to a more complete research design for Early Head Start. More broadly, the USDHHS policy team spent a great deal of time on the Early Head Start research design, bringing to the discussion our knowledge as practitioners about what features of program implementation might affect results and our best guesses as policymakers and political appointees about what information we would want from the evaluation when faced with making the next set of decisions about the program. This detailed involvement has in fact paid off in findings that can shape the next round of program design and implementation.

In the child-care example, partnership with practitioners helped researchers identify policy-relevant questions and make necessary connections across academic boundaries to draw on related fields of knowledge. Child-care policymakers saw more quickly than researchers the dramatic changes in the policy environment that suddenly made a new set of questions exciting and relevant, for example, questions about how child care affects the retention and promotion opportunities of low-income workers. And policymakers found themselves forced earlier than researchers to consider the connections between different public programs that corresponded to different fields of research and study—in this case, between child development institutions and labor market institutions—as a result of the demands of the real situations they found in front of them. Thus, the experience of policymakers was able to help welfare researchers see connections to child care that they had initially missed, such as questions about how child-care subsidy regulations or the cost of child care affected job retention and advancement.

Build supportive institutions such as the "national laboratory" and university–state partnerships, and seek out and include people whose own experiences bridge the worlds of research and practice. As both the Head Start and Early Head Start examples illustrate, Head Start's vision of itself as a national laboratory presents a unique opportunity for research to influence practice—an opportunity that in both examples has substantially benefited children. In Head Start, the idea of a national laboratory contributed to the advisory committee's effectiveness and impact on practice because so many Head Start practitioners take pride in the national laboratory role and therefore in their obligation to learn from and act on research evidence. In Early Head Start, the national laboratory role helped to defuse what would otherwise have been an impossible dilemma: How do you implement a program at a level of expense per child that is necessary to achieve quality but very hard to imagine expanding to a universal level? The national laboratory concept offered an opportunity to start a program that was intensive enough to work for children, to start it at a substantial scale considerably larger than a pilot, and yet to hold off immediate pressure to reduce quality in order to expand. Future expansion strategies will of course have to address these issues, but at least they will benefit from the evaluation evidence showing meaningful improvements in outcomes for children.

The child-care example is at an earlier stage. At the beginning of the story, there was no history of supportive institutions, so part of the accomplishment was to create institutions to support partnerships, such as the Child Care Partnerships between universities and the states. Future strategies will need to build on what we have learned and take next steps to scale.

Beyond institutions that support partnership, it matters to find people who have lived it. In all three of these examples, the leading USDHHS policymakers included many with academic or related experience: the secretary of USDHHS (Donna Shalala), the two assistant secretaries for children and families (Mary Jo Bane and myself), and the leaders of the Child Care Bureau (Joan Lombardi) and the Head Start Bureau (Helen Taylor, the late associate commissioner of the Head Start Bureau, who had been involved in the national policy and research debate for years). The most influential researchers in the examples also had careers that reflected a link between research and practice, including the honoree of this collection, Edward F. Zigler. One consequence of these mixed backgrounds was that each of us saw ourselves as able to participate in both research and policy conversations, meaning that the policymakers were willing to press our views of what questions were important or what issues were left out in a research design, rather than being intimidated by a researcher's certainty, self-assurance, or insistence on specialized knowledge—and the researchers were willing to push us on our own underlying assumptions about politics and policy. A second key consequence was that knowing both languages and ways of thinking, as so many of us did, we could bring in others with more specialized knowledge and draw them into the full conversation because there were enough people conversant with both worlds to translate across the boundaries.

Choose areas of research that are not only deeply important to the individual partners but offer the greatest chance to make a difference. Although many different findings have the potential to influence practice, in my experience the single most influential set of lessons from the child development research is the consensus that quality matters to outcomes and the expanding set of findings about what quality is and how to know it and support it. These findings are especially powerful because they lead to practical next steps; because they are consistent with the intuitions of many practitioners, parents, and professionals yet provide rigor and clarity to those intuitions; because they command a broad consensus of support in the research community and draw on many different studies rather than relying on only one; because they demonstrably lead to results for children (as in the case of Early Head Start); and because they provide critical backing for high-cost strategies that would be difficult to invest in without the research but appear to be crucial to success.

Both the Head Start and Early Head Start examples illustrate the power of these paired lessons. In Head Start, the advisory committee built a consensus by starting from the research lessons about quality. In Early Head Start, the advisory committee went a step further in the specificity of its reliance on the research about "characteristics of effective programs that enhance both child and family development" (USDHHS, 1994, p. 6), that is, about what quality is. Drawing on research evidence about the importance of continuity in caregivers and the ability of caregivers to build relationships with children, the Early Head Start advisory committee chose to highlight staff development as one of the four cornerstones of the program. By doing so, the committee identified as central to program effectiveness such design features as high standards for staff, a commitment to staff training and professional skills, and staff salaries and opportunities for advancement sufficient to support continuity. This clarity in turn provided a mandate for Early Head Start to invest heavily in requiring strict staff-to-child ratios that would make possible one-to-one relationship building, in building a national network of training capacity for infant–toddler caregivers, and in other supports for and expectations from staff. Thus, one of the statement's most important contributions was the "cover" it provided for policymakers to spend money on what we know to be most important to young children: the quality of caregivers. The impact report has demonstrated once again the effectiveness of these investments, creating another opportunity for the research community to take the message back to other programs for very young children.

In child care, the same two themes—that quality programs lead to good outcomes for children and that we know quite a lot about what creates quality—ought to be just as substantively relevant to the policy discussion, but in fact they have not yet been influential at the national level. Understanding the reasons for this gap between knowledge and decision making and looking for research questions and designs that might bridge it are important next steps for both researchers and practitioners. One obstacle that researchers may be able to tackle is that it has been hard to make vivid what quality could look like in a child-care system as opposed to a single program; that is, to study not one terrific program but a community where parents have a lot of very different kinds of terrific choices.

In addition to the focus on quality, another area of research that seems especially relevant to policy and practice is the link among child-care systems and programs, patterns of low-wage employment, family outcomes including work success, and child outcomes. The child-care story suggests that this area of research has already been influential, yet there is much more to be accomplished. The child-care and related support programs for working families are relatively new and therefore flexible in design, offering opportunities for turning knowledge into practice, and it seems possible to me that researchers might be able to make major new discoveries: The research in each individual field offers considerable knowledge to build on and hypotheses to test, whereas research across the fields seems to an outside observer to be in its infancy and full of new opportunities. As new findings emerge, I would expect that the broad political consensus around work support as a strategy for low-income families could eventually provide openings for program creation and development.

Finally, researchers somehow need to build the expertise or the collaborations that would allow for joining these two threads to identify program strategies that consistently benefit both children's development and parents' employment and income across a range of working families (as several specific programs, including Early Head Start, have succeeded in doing for very-low-income families). Should we identify strategies that meet both goals, the consensus for attention and investment will be even stronger.

Conclusion

Throughout the months of writing and revising this essay—during which the nation went to war, debated major change in Head Start, and enacted tax cuts, among other events—I have often reflected on the relevance of these findings. Today, it seems impossible to predict when and how research into children's lives and experiences will again be able to affect the national debate. Yet at the same time, I believe that learning the lessons of success to achieve the greatest possible impact of research on policy and practice is more rather than less critical in difficult times. In a nation whose attention may be ever more focused on international crises and self-defense, society cannot count on past gains for children remaining secure, let alone on further progress, without the highest possible quality of thought and communication by both researchers and practitioners. And as the career of our honoree, Zigler, fully demonstrates, it is more, not less, important in difficult times to think over a period of years, not weeks or months. The contribution of research is not a short-run event, not the result of one moment or one study, but a long-term, lifetime process of bringing knowledge and wisdom to bear in ways that, in the end, make all the difference.

References

Administration for Children and Families. (2002). *Making a difference in the lives of infants and toddlers and their families: The impacts of Early Head Start*. Washington, DC: U.S. Department of Health and Human Services.

U.S. Department of Health and Human Services. (1993). *Creating a 21st century Head Start: Final report of the Advisory Committee on Head Start Quality and Expansion*. Washington, DC: Author.

U.S. Department of Health and Human Services. (1994). *The statement of the Advisory Committee on Services for Families With Infants and Toddlers*. Washington, DC: Author.

3

Bridging the Gap Between Research and Child Policy Change: The Role of Strategic Communications in Policy Advocacy

Janice Gruendel and J. Lawrence Aber

> You know, all of my life I've been waiting for a lobby. Why do the senior citizens get so much and kids get so little? Because they are organized and have a great lobby. One of the weakest things is that we have no lobby and have never had a lobby for children . . . there is just no force out there that fights for these things.
>
> —Edward F. Zigler (Coniff, 2002, p. 33)

In the 1970s, as graduate students in developmental psychology poking around in public policy under the tutelage of Edward F. Zigler, we once asked him how he managed the stresses and conflicts involved in public policy making and child advocacy. He wrinkled his eyes—and with a hint of a scowl and a hint of humor—he replied, "You need to have a great tolerance for ambiguity." He was right, of course.

More recently, in an interview published in the June 2002 issue of *The Progressive*, Ed's tolerance for ambiguity seemed to have reached an end.

> I study children . . . . They're my colleagues, really, all of these little kids. And I owe them. The fact that in this country we cannot move on child care, and after thirty years it's no better, in my estimation, than it was thirty years ago, that's a great deal of sadness . . . . Why are we doing that to children? (Coniff, 2002, p. 32)

Why indeed, in the face of ever-mounting data and the capacity to transmit it cheaply and easily, do we continue as a nation to make unquestionably poor public policy decisions about children's health and well-being? Why is there no "force" for children in America (and the world) powerful enough to alter the current course of public policy making and resource allocation?

The answer is both simple and complex. It is hard to get there from here because the road from empirical information to effective public policy in America is a messy one. It is fraught with ambiguity and littered with disagreements over values and battles over turf. In addition, the general public and the body politic suffer from an ever-shortening national attention span and, in the context of the needs of children and families, an ever-growing tolerance for incremental change. And as social scientists and students of child development, we are behind the curve in understanding the critical importance of strategic communication in the service of policy change.

Over the past several years, rigorous research has identified a series of policies and programs that actually reduce welfare dependence, increase family income, save money in future incarceration costs, enhance parental child rearing competence, *and* improve the likelihood that children will come to school each year healthy, eager to learn and ready for academic success . . . in other words, programs that provide a demonstrative return on investment. Yet, even before September 11, 2001 and America's resulting preoccupation with terrorism, before the war into Afghanistan and Iraq, before America's most recent recession and the nation's changing role in the global marketplace, information about these successful programs and policies did not serve as the basis for significant national resource reinvestment and public policy change.

This chapter is about building a broader context in which to think about the needs of children and families. It is also about adopting new frames in talking about these needs and becoming comfortable with a different set of principles and tools for public policy advocacy. And it is, at root, about the urgent need for members of the scientific community to move, competently, from fact to act.[1]

What will it take to turn research into policy action and to bring successful models to scale? Zigler's call for a new lobby for children certainly suggests one critical action component. Social scientists must, however, build a strategic communications and advocacy plan based on a clear set of policy goals, in partnership with other communities of interest, with messaging and persuasion directed at those in power, while keeping an intentional eye on the political salience of these strategies and conveying both urgency and a clear commitment to stay for the long haul.

Understanding Policy Change:
Building a Better Peanut Butter and Jelly Sandwich

In some intriguing ways, advocacy efforts in the service of public policy change have been not unlike a 3-year-old child making a peanut butter and jelly sandwich. First the requisite ingredients are assembled. But although we know, as adults, that you really do need two slices of bread, some peanut butter and some jelly, that knowledge base may not have been completely or reliably acquired by the young sandwich builder. So sometimes there is peanut butter only, sometimes jelly only, and sometimes there is only one piece of bread.

---

[1]It is of no small import that 100% of "act" is embodied in "fact." Alternatively, one might observe that you cannot have fact without act.

Then the tools are engaged. As adults, we generally use a knife—though grown-up fingers in the peanut butter jar are not unheard of—and we are quite adept at digging out and spreading the requisite substances, one on each of two pieces of bread. For a 3-year-old, however, a knife can be dangerous and a spoon is pretty inefficient. The peanut butter is sticky, the jelly is slippery, and the bread tears apart. Although in the end at least some level of nutrition usually reaches a hungry tummy, the process is downright messy from start to finish.

Effective public policy advocacy has some of the same messiness and also requires the coming together of two processes—research and policy advocacy—that are pretty much like the inside of peanut butter and jelly sandwich. Research provides the stickiness, the facts, and the data essential to building the sandwich of public policy change. Policy advocacy is the more slippery component because it means different things to different people and its use is based on varying comfort levels among us—as individuals, professionals in research and social science, and as citizens of our democracy. Try to put these two together without the bread, and you get pretty much the same thing as the 3-year-old: messy fingers and no sandwich.

In our view, the two slices of bread in this metaphor represent the two essential elements of effective advocacy—messaging (or informing) and mobilizing (or persuading)—without which you may have facts and you may have some ideas for new policy or programs, but you will not get policy change. Now you can have a peanut butter and jelly sandwich with only one slice of bread, but it is tricky to make, sloppy to eat, and if you drop it, it ends up face down on the floor or carpet—a loss of time, effort, and resources. Although business-based and political marketing has known for a long time that you need to inform and persuade to get a purchase or a vote, we in the nonprofit and academic communities are only recently beginning to get comfortable at this table of strategy and tactics.

Two other considerations are important in making a peanut butter and jelly sandwich or policy change: who is making it and whom it is for. For the child with the sandwich, they are probably both the same. For those of us seeking public policy change, however, they are not. Although we may be the messenger, we are most likely not the audience. Unless we are clear about our purpose and the audience—those who actually have the power to make public policy and those who influence policymakers—we are likely to make our sandwich with grape jelly and smooth peanut butter when strawberry jam and chunky peanut butter were really what was needed.

A Note on Purpose: Child (Case-Based) Advocacy or Policy (Class-Based) Advocacy

As social scientists and students of child development who may wish to move from research to advocacy, it is essential that we become clear in our purpose. Are we really looking for policy change that will address the developmental needs of children as a group, or is our personal and professional commitment that of making a difference one child at a time?

We are reminded of the well-loved "prevention" story about the children in the river and the towns' folks who gathered at the riverbed as children floated by, pulling them out one child at a time. The adults worked hard and with great passion, and they saved many children from the swirling water. But the children kept coming downstream. Finally, one person left the group of rescuers, angering them for they thought that he was giving up. But his purpose was different: to go to the head of the river and stop the people who were throwing the children in.[2] Both kinds of advocacy are critical to improving the lives of children—saving children one child at a time and working to save children as a group by going to the root of the problem—but they are very different in terms of desired outcome, audience, message, strategy—and perhaps most important, in terms of the ultimate return on our personal, social, and economic investment.

It is also important to note that policies affecting children's health, development, and well-being range from specific and traditional (i.e., education, health care, foster care, delinquency, and juvenile justice) to a rich range of specific but "historically new" concerns (e.g., infant and toddler care, child care and early education, linking health and early care). However, as students of developmental psychology, we are also learning that we need to focus, as well, on the more general and less traditional issues of children's well-being, including national economic security policy, the role of government, and the tax side of the budget as well as the expenditure side.

Although the more specific issues are most often considered the domain of child policy, we believe the more general policies are every bit as important to the well being of children and their families in the United States. Consequently, we have included opinion research focused on these domains to help tell our story about the role of informing and persuading in the mix of power, politics, and policy over children's issues.

Opinion Research: What Does the Public Think About the Issues?

As a key tool in making public policy change, Meg Bostrom of Public Knowledge asserted that there is

> no substitute for sponsoring your own opinion research tailored to the issues you care about, and conducted with the audiences that matter most to achieving your goals. However, we can learn quite a lot from the wealth of public opinion data that is available on the Internet for free or at a low cost. (Bostrom, n.d.b)

At one time in the not too distant past, opinion research was largely the domain of the business community and political campaigns. Marketers knew, of course,

---

[2]The new version of this story, on the basis of accumulating research on message and tactics as outlined in this chapter, would include some more information about what "policy influencing" credentials he brought to the head of the river, whether he found someone there who could actually stop the casting of the children into the water, and whether he had sufficient information to "make the case."

who was purchasing what and how to reach the buying public. And candidates, especially in major elections, always work hard to keep their fingers on the pulse of their constituency—the voting public. Today, the views of the American public are available to us all at little cost, on a 24–7 basis through Internet technology, and often segmented by population cohort.

In a recent FrameWorks Institute *Kids Count E-Zine*, Bostrom (n.d.b) lists 12 of "the best polling resources" on the Web. Public Agenda (2005b) presented a somewhat broader listing organized in terms of professional polling organizations, research firms, and media organizations that do polling. If you are not sure about how public opinion polling is conducted and how to understand some of the statistical measures used, see The Roper Center's Polling 101 online tutorial (The Roper Center for Public Opinion Research, 2004) or Public Agenda's section About Polling (Public Agenda, 2005a). Two particularly interesting articles on polling by Public Agenda are "20 Questions Journalists Should Ask About Poll Results" (Gawiser & Witt, 2005) and "The Seven Stages of Public Opinion" (Yankelovich, 2005).

What is the general public thinking about some of the key child policy issues facing this nation? Brief sketches of the results of recent public opinion research on personal and family economic security, the role of government, and tax and budget issues follow.

PERSONAL ECONOMIC SECURITY IN AMERICA. The dominant frame held by Americans with regard to work and family economic security is one of "personal responsibility." As reported by The Pew Research Center for the People and the Press (2003), "about two-thirds of Americans (67%–68%) disagree with the statement 'Hard work offers little guarantee of success' and also reject the view that 'success in life is pretty much determined by forces outside our control'." Six in 10 believe, however, that "many people think they can get ahead without working hard," and 7 in 10 worry that "poor people have become too dependent on government assistance." Nearly 9 in 10 admire "people who have gotten rich through hard work."

This focus on individual responsibility for one's own economic security and the economic well-being of one's family is borne out in other studies as well. In a National Public Radio (NPR), Kaiser Family Foundation, and Harvard Kennedy School of Government study (2001), between 52% and 70% of poll respondents identified a series of individual challenges as major causes of poverty: drug abuse (70%), medical bills (58%), decline in moral values (57%), too many single parents (54%), and poor people lacking motivation (52%). Fewer respondents ranked as major causes of poverty more systemic or policy-related challenges, such as a shortage of jobs (34%) and the public schools and the welfare system (47% and 46%, respectively); however, more than half of the respondents (54%) did identify having too many part-time or low-wage jobs as a major cause.

When asked in early 2002 about the role of government in helping low-income families, 82% of Americans polled said it is very important to require those receiving government-supported services to go to work and 79% indicated high importance for government to help recipients learn skills that will enable them to get good jobs (Action on the Poverty Front, 2002). Although these views posit acceptance of a role for government, they are clearly still based in the notion of personal responsibility and hard work. Similarly, 77% said a very important goal for government programs for poor people is to help noncustodial fathers become better parents, again a reflection of the dominant personal responsibility frame.

BELIEF IN GOVERNMENT AS A PROBLEM SOLVER. As the Pew (2003) study revealed, although Americans highly value work and responsibility, 66% agree that "it is the responsibility of the government to take care of people who can't take care of themselves," up from 54% in 1994 and 62% in 2001 (NPR, Kaiser, & Harvard, 2001). There has also been an increase in the proportion of Americans who believe "government should help more needy people even if it means going deeper into debt," up from 41% in 1994, to 49% in 1999, to 54% in 2003 (Pew, 2003).

Despite this belief in government assistance for needy people, nearly 50% of the respondents in the NPR, Kaiser, and Harvard study (2001) worried that government programs do not have much impact in making things better or worse, and 49% worry that poverty could not be eliminated even if "the government were willing to spend all that was necessary." Also, until immediately after the World Trade Center terrorist attacks, about 6 in 10 Americans lacked confidence in the federal government to solve a problem once it had identified a problem, a view that had held reasonably steady from 1991 through the summer of 2001. Immediately after the attacks, however, trust in the federal government shot up to 80% and the proportion of Americans who held a very favorable view of the government increased from 9% to 35% (Light & Labiner, 2001). Those holding a very favorable or somewhat favorable view increased from 50% to 88%. By January of 2002, however, that level of trust had both diminished and become differentiated (Langer, 2002). Although 68% of Americans said they trusted the federal government to do the right thing always or almost always regarding national security and the war on terrorism, only 38% did so regarding social issues including the economy, health care, Social Security, and education.

BUDGET AND TAXES. A recent *Kids Count E-Zine* (Bostrom, n.d.a) on budget and taxes summarizes opinion research on tax cuts passed in the first term of the current Bush administration. Nearly 7 in 10 Americans (68%) would prefer that the federal government spend more on domestic programs rather than cut taxes (29%), and more than 6 in 10 (64%) believe that there are better ways to stimulate the economy than cutting taxes. A January 2003 opinion poll conducted by Public Agenda (2003) found that 86% of respondents supported tax credits for families with children and 80% supported reducing taxes owed when both parents in a family work. Fewer respondents supported reducing dividend taxes (58%) or providing additional business taxes (65%). Note, however, that across nearly all of these tax-related budget choices, 6 in 10 Americans supported some form of tax relief.

Yet, though Americans were quite mixed on the likely outcomes of tax cuts to stimulate the economy and more than half (56%) believed the cuts would not help them personally, neither did they advocate tax hikes. An April 2003 *USA Today* survey conducted by Gallup Organization found that more than 8 out of

10 respondents wanted state governments to cut spending rather than raise taxes (Bostrom, n.d.a). Americans also perceive that government wastes nearly half (47%) of the tax dollars that it collects.

In sum, Americans have a deep and abiding belief in individual responsibility for economic success and they worry that too many people are not willing to work hard to achieve it. Although they do ascribe a role for government in aiding those who are "needy," they are not sure that government programs—even fully funded—can eliminate poverty. More generally, until immediately after the terrorist attacks of September 11, 2001, about 6 in 10 Americans did not trust in the government's capacity to solve problems (Light & Labiner, 2001). After the attacks, however, the proportion of Americans expressing a very or somewhat favorable opinion of government rose immediately and dramatically from 5 in 10 to 8 in 10. Still, a sizable proportion of the general public continues to believe that the federal government is wasteful in the use of its tax monies.

Opinion Research: People, Polls, the Press, and the Policy Process

A review of polling data available from The Roper Center for Public Opinion Research (n.d.) presented an important picture of how the general public views polling and other forms of information and influence in the policy decision process. Nine out of 10 poll respondents believe that nationally elected and governmental leaders should pay a great deal or a fair amount of attention to the views of members of the public who contact them on an issue; of these, 57% expect leaders to pay a great deal of attention. In contrast, more than half believe campaign contributors (56%) and lobbyists (54%) should receive little or no attention (56%).

Of respondents, 75% believe that policy leaders should pay a great deal or a fair amount of attention to public opinion polls, and only 20% believe that the public does not respond to polls honestly. About 6 in 10 respondents (61%) think that elected officials mainly consult polls because the officials believe that the public should have a say in what government does, although only 21% strongly believe that policy leaders believe this. More than 8 in 10 (84%) believe that the policy leaders mainly consult polls "because they want to stay popular and get re-elected" (The Roper Center for Public Opinion Research, n.d.).

Evans Witt (2001), president of Princeton Survey Research Associates, offered a cautionary tale for those who do polling in his summary of a 2001 Kaiser *Public Perspective* survey on polling and democracy. Just about 50% of respondents in the Kaiser survey agreed that sound scientific practice underlies polls, and 43% disagreed. Eight in 10 respondents said that poll questions do not allow them to say what they really believe about an issue, and nearly 6 in 10 (58%) believe that poll results "can be twisted to say whatever you want them to say." Only 1 in 3 believes that polls "accurately reflect what the public thinks at least most of the time" (p. 26).

In the same issue of *Public Perspective*, Thomas Edsall (2001) of the *Washington Post* unpacks data from the Kaiser survey concerning how the press views opinion research and how the public views the press. Slightly more than half of the media respondents (52%) believe that polling provides the best way for public officials to understand where the people stand on issues. Journalists also "tend more generally to be more confident of the accuracy of poll data than either policy leaders or the public at large" (p. 29).

Messaging Really Matters:
Strategic Frame Analysis and Making the Case

Although opinion research helps us to understand what the general public and other audiences believe about an issue, effective advocacy also requires the use of tools that enable us to make the case for policy action. Because people filter what they hear, read, and observe through their existing concepts of the world as a way of evaluating and integrating (or rejecting) new facts or data, strategic frame analysis has become an increasingly important tool in the new advocacy arsenal.

In a few different instances, the FrameWorks Institute (n.d.c, ¶ 2; 2001, p. 2 respectively) defined a frame as the following:

> A small set of internalized concepts and values that allow us to accord mean-
> ing to unfolding events and new information . . . . Over time, we develop
> habits of thought and expectation and configure incoming information to
> conform to this frame . . . When new facts are submitted that do not resonate
> with the frames we hold in our heads, it is the facts that are rejected, not the
> frames . . . . These frames can be triggered by various elements, such as
> language choices and different messengers or images. These communica-
> tions elements, therefore, have a profound influence on decision outcomes.

> Recognizing that there is more than one way to tell a story, strategic
> frame analysis taps into decades of research on how people think and com-
> municate. The result is an empirically-driven communications process that
> makes academic research understandable, interesting, and usable to help
> people solve social problems. This approach is strategic in that it not only
> deconstructs the dominant frames that drive reasoning on public issues, but
> it also identifies those models most likely to stimulate public reconsidera-
> tion and enumerates their elements (reframing). Strategic frame analysis
> offers policy advocates a way to work systematically through the challenges
> that are likely to confront the introduction of new legislation or social poli-
> cies, to anticipate attitudinal barriers to support, and to develop research-
> based strategies to overcome public misunderstanding.

In their work, FrameWorks Institute (n.d.c, ¶ 8) distinguishes between episodic and thematic frames:

> Episodic frames reduce life to a series of disconnected episodes, random events
> or case studies . . . . In contrast, thematic frames provide details about trends,
> not just individuals; they identify shortcomings at the community or sys-
> tems-level that have contributed to the problem . . . . The more episodically
> that children's issues are framed, the less likely it is that citizens will hold
> government accountable for solving the problem. The more thematic and
> contextual the message, the more likely it is that citizens will see the issue
> as one appropriate to government resolution.

Of great import is the recent study of more than 10,000 stories on foreign affairs on five television stations, which found that 97% of the coverage used episodic frames.

The authors of this particular *E-Zine* (FrameWorks Institute, n.d.c, ¶ 12) argued,

> The prudent choice of frames, and the ability to effectively contest the opposition's frames, lie at the heart of successful policy advocacy . . . . A frame isn't simply a slogan repeated over and over again; rather a frame is a conceptual construct capable of helping us organize our world . . . when new facts are submitted that do not resonate with the frames we hold in our heads, it is the facts that are rejected, not the frames.

Frames on Poverty

In a *Kids Count E-Zine* on child poverty, FrameWorks Institute (n.d.b, ¶ 5) provided a strategic frame analysis that matches up quite perfectly with the opinion research findings reported in this chapter.

> When adults think about poverty in general, they tend to think of it as the product of a deficit in character rather than as a product of social forces. They personalize poverty and, in this sense, they over-estimate free will and under-estimate social constraints . . . . "Individuals are solely responsible for their situation and their salvation . . . . Part of the American psyche is that any child can grow up to be President—there are not limitations on anyone. Ultimately, a message will not be successful if it collides with this core value."

A *KidsCount E-Zine* titled, "Anticipating the Opposition Using Framing Research" (FrameWorks Institute, n.d.a, § II) summarized five key values about poverty and low-wage workers that emerge from several years of opinion research. First, "charity and generosity toward the needy are appropriate responses." Second, "each individual is responsible for his or her own success and failure." Third, "with hard work comes reward." Fourth, "the goal is equal opportunity, not equal outcomes." Fifth, "anyone can achieve the American Dream."

In the child poverty *E-Zine*, FrameWorks Institute (n.d.b, Framing section) made a set of recommendations for framing the child poverty message. First, when it is possible to do so, use language other than *poverty* to describe the issue. Second, do not use case examples of the worthy poor, because they "simply underscore the personal nature of poverty." Third, when talking about child poverty "understand that the public will first want to know about the parents and why they are not taking responsibility for the child." Fourth, "stress values of nurturance, empathy, and adult responsibility (broadly construed) for children and for their healthy development" and use the "nation as family" metaphor to "put the responsibility squarely on government and community institutions to do a better job of preparing all children to take their part in our communities." Fifth, encourage "business leaders, mentors, seniors, volunteer leaders, athletic coaches, teachers and pediatricians" to speak to the importance of "social investments" and children's healthy development.

Frames on Budget and Taxes

Writing in *Kids Count E-Zine,* Bostrom (n.d.a) observed, "On every social issue we investigate—children's issues, poverty, child abuse, education, health care, environmental issues, foreign policy, etc.—the public's perceptions of taxes, government services and state budgets consistently emerge as barriers to supporting collective action." Bostrom made the following observations on framing these issues. First, because people assume that government wastes or mismanages substantial amounts of tax dollars, "abstract calls for increased funding will not gain public support." Second, "years of emphasizing crises has convinced the public that government cannot do anything right. Advocates need to talk about what works and what needs to be done, rather than just highlight what is broken." Third, "a lack of understanding about how state budgets work undermines support for taxes and government services." Fourth, "sometimes the issue is not really 'about' increased taxes; rather it is 'about' something else," for example, tax fairness. Fifth, on issues of taxation and budget, "political voices are of limited value; non-partisan voices need to be brought into the dialogue," especially those "without a vested interest, who have relevant experience and credibility." Next we provide three case examples of instances in which organizations used opinion research to develop and use frames that were the most effective at conveying their specific message.

Messaging and Framing: Three Case Examples

Our first example comes from work by the National Center of Children in Poverty and its three state partners—California, Connecticut, and Washington—to engage the public in policy advocacy through the marriage of research and strategic communications. The early name chosen for the initiative was The Children's Hour, and we all loved it for the message we thought it conveyed about changing policy through the commitment of small amounts of citizen time and action. However, what we learned by testing the name and some of our first message posters with focus groups in the three states sent us back to the drawing board.

   For most people in the focus groups, The Children's Hour conveyed a call to give an hour of personal time to children, through such activities as reading to younger children and mentoring older ones. Thus, it clearly called up the personal responsibility frame so dominant in the American psyche. It did not help the public to understand that some problems of children and families, such as poverty, have structural roots and can really only be solved at the policy level. We went back to the drawing board of message construction and, after a second period of focus group work and message testing, The Children's Hour became Let's Invest in Families Today (LIFT), with its clear messaging focus on frames that invoke ideas of investment, the importance of families, and the need for policy action today.

   Our second example is drawn from work by the national Early Care and Education (ECE) Collaborative over the past 3 years to create and implement "public education strategies for expanding the supply and quality of high-quality early care and education programs" in eight states—Colorado, Florida, New Jersey, Illinois, Pennsylvania, Connecticut, Missouri, and Kansas (see http://www.earlycare.org). Review of a rich base of opinion research revealed that the general public held several competing views of child care (ECE Collaborative, n.d.a). First, as a stand-alone issue, providing more support for child care is high and bipartisan; however, when matched against other issues demanding policy attention or additional national resources, only 2% to 3% of the general public rank it as a top issue. Second, 44% to 48% of the public views child care as a primary workforce support for parents, and they support child-care assistance for working families. Nearly as many (38% to 43%), however, believe that child care is a function best left to parents and that government has no role in providing child-care assistance. Third, although there is "no constituency for child care" (and, actually the very words *day care* or *child care* bring forth a "babysitting" frame for many people), there is a constituency for education, and when "child care is posed as a key element in school readiness . . . the issue gains additional support." Finally, the general public is more supportive of public involvement in early education for preschoolers than in child care for infants and toddlers.

Drawing on these findings, the ECE Collaborative described a set of messaging strategies to make the case for more resources (ECE Collaborative, n.d.b). Key elements in framing this issue included referencing the central role of parents and families, linking child-care issues explicitly to an early education and workforce development frame, and assuring that if policy recommendations focus on supports for low-income families, then they also convey that benefits must eventually accrue to middle-income families.

Our third case example is drawn from a research brief published by Child Trends in July 2003, titled, "How Children Are Doing: The Mismatch Between Public Perception and Statistical Reality" (Guzman, Lippman, Moore, & O'Hare, 2003). This analysis was drawn from three studies of public opinion between May 2002 and April 2003. Across a series of issues including child poverty, access to health insurance, children receiving welfare, children living in single-parent families, and the teen birth rate, researchers found that "most Americans think that children and youth are worse off than they actually are, and are either unaware of or are discounting progress made during the last decade" (p. 1). As examples, nearly 50% of those polled believe that 3 in 10 children live in poverty, about twice the actual rate. Nearly 75% believe the number of children on welfare has increased, yet the number has been reduced by about 50%, and about 75% believe that the number of children living in single-parent families has increased over the past half decade, but it has not.

The authors argued that the "public's overemphasis on the negative aspects of children's lives" (Guzman et al., 2003, p. 6) is a source of concern on several levels. First, the public does not seem to be aware of recent progress and successes in improving the circumstances of children's lives in America today. Guzman et al. postulated that this is a data delivery problem on the part of researchers, but the framing literature would also suggest that the academic and advocacy communities have been telling the stories of crisis in children's lives effectively enough and long enough that the public has actually accepted them. Second, the authors speculated that as long as "public perceptions dwell on the negative, policy and program development will tend to focus on addressing negative outcomes, rather than on investing in efforts that can boost positive outcomes" (p. 6). We concur.

Messaging and Framing: A Look at How Advocates Do It Now

Several years ago, Cultural Logic, an "applied cognitive and social science research group" (Aubrun & Grady, 2002, p. 24), was engaged by FrameWorks Institute and Public Knowledge to analyze the communications content and strategies used by a broad group of child advocacy organizations in the United States.

> The goal of the study was to identify the patterns in what advocates are currently trying, any important gaps (i.e., what they are not trying), and to compare these with what research—both from the larger FrameWorks Institute project and from major traditions in the cognitive and social sciences—suggests might work. (Aubrun & Grady, 2002, p. 1)

The authors found "an astonishing range of information and policy goals" expressed in the materials and worried that the public would miss the overarching issues and eventually "tune out" (Aubrun & Grady, 2002, p. 5). They also found advocates using "mixed messages that may leave consumers of the materials uncertain how to think about an important topic" (p. 5). In addition, they found that the emphasis on scientific research, particularly the use of new brain research with its emphasis on young children's cognitive development, may drive a wedge between "good parents" (usually with higher education and income) and "inadequate ones," and at the same time "make it harder for a picture of 'whole child development' to emerge into public consciousness" (p. 6). To correct these negative communication situations, the authors urged advocates to "move a set of simpler and more coherent frames into public discourse . . . that allow people to 'put the pieces together' in their own minds" (p. 5).

Lessons Learned From Communications Research

Reviewing this rapidly accumulating literature on communications research provides a series of helpful lessons as we, social scientists and students of child development, direct our personal, organizational, and professional attention to the journey from research to advocacy.

1. The media plays an enormous role in providing information to the general public and the frames within which to understand it. Because most of the media's stories are episodic in nature, they do not create or support the view that some problems must be solved in a public policy, rather than a personal responsibility, context. They do, however, present persuasive stories that come to constitute the dominant frame on many issues for the general public.

The media also places a high value on the polling process to determine where the general public stands on an issue. Presumably that information helps journalists to frame the way they select and present the issues. Taken together, however, this "press tells the people and people tell the press" cycle portends a self-fulfilling prophesy, with serious implications for the role of objective data and research findings in the marketplace of ideas and public policy.

2. Our field has a tendency to overintellectualize the presentation of issues, throwing all the facts we can at an issue to see what sticks. If, however, the facts do not match the frame brought to the engagement by the audience, then the facts will be ignored or rejected. Similarly, when messaging does not provide possible solutions or existing successes or does not suggest concrete actions, it can leave the audience with no place to go to resolve the angst that has been stirred up in their minds and perceptions.

3. Advocates, academics, and researchers tend to take great comfort in numbers, and we present them en masse and occasionally without interpretation. However, "unless numbers are married to a story, they are unlikely to mean anything to the public . . . . The better practice in fact sheets and brochures is to provide the meaning first and then use the numbers to support that meaning" (Bales, 2003).

4. We are, as a field, very tolerant of diversity in our messaging. We accept a broad range of messages on a subject and find it hard to hold to a common, repetitive message or frame, whether we are making key arguments or engaging in sound bites. We also underuse the findings of research on communications that the messenger is equally as important as the message.

5. A very common approach in our message framing is to use facts and data to declare and prove "a crisis" and then to exit the message without a solution. This teaches the audience that (a) the problem is too big to solve, (b) we have few or no successful models on which to build the solution, or (c) government is incapable of solving problems in which it is involved.

6. We pass up the opportunity to reframe an issue for the public or other audiences when we adopt issue-specific terms such as earned income tax credits *or* child-care turnover. "Strategic frame analysis adopts the position . . . that people reason out of deeply-held moral values, more than on the basis of self-interest or 'pocket-book' appeals." These values are "big ideas, like freedom, justice, community, success, prevention, responsibility." Higher level frames "map their values and reasoning" to lower-level frames (like the child-care or earned income tax credit) but not the reverse (FrameWorks Institute, n.d.c).

7. We need to become a lot smarter about the frames held by those who oppose our policy recommendations and disbelieve our research findings about successful program models. For some of us, *opposition research* may convey a political context that does not match our dominant frame as objective, nonpartisan conveyors of fact and knowledge. The framing literature suggests that it is time for us to "get over it" and learn (a) the dominant frames from which those who oppose us operate, (b) how to use bridging techniques to reframe exchanges that begin with an opposing frame, and (c) to stay on message regardless of twists and turns of our communications experiences.

8. Timing is everything, and using cross-media formats is essential. We live in a fast-paced, sound-bite world where increasingly the general public and others obtain their information from radio, television, and the Internet. We also live in a world where people are constantly bombarded with information, making the issue of salience of prime importance to us.

Conclusion

In this chapter, we have argued that strategic communications—especially the two elements of public opinion research and strategic frame analysis—are indispensable to effectively bridging the gap between research about and policy advocacy for children. It is time for researchers in child development and related fields to face the realization that although research can aspire to objectivity and fairness, the communication of research to important audiences—the public, opinion leaders, decision makers—cannot be neutral. These audiences already have opinions about the issues affecting America's children and families; any communication of research about children invokes frames within which they interpret and assimilate the "facts" of research. Thus, the issue becomes not whether frames are invoked by research reports, but rather which frames are invoked and how intentional and skilled researchers can be in invoking the frames that are consistent with their research findings and their policy recommendations.

As usual, nearly 3 decades ago, Zigler was ahead of the times on this issue. Because of Ed's experiences striving to communicate the importance of research findings to policymakers, he was among the first in our field to recognize the importance of strategic communications. So he hired a working journalist, Susan Muenchow, who was then a reporter for the *Christian Science Monitor*, to join the staff of the Bush Center in Child Development and Social Policy at Yale. Susan taught Ed how to frame the top line stories from research and how to craft op-ed pieces, and in turn Ed and Susan taught several generations of new workers in child development that the message matters. Is it any wonder that Ed was able to simultaneously accurately describe the research findings on the enormous variability in child-care quality and the dilemmas of parent choice in a world of variable quality by framing the phenomenon as "a Cosmic Crapshot"?

It is fortunate that just as the art of caring for children has evolved to integrate key findings from the advancing science of child development, so too has the art of communication about children's issues evolved to integrate the advancing science of communications studies. Today, it is possible (though not common) for researchers to communicate their research-based policy recommendations through evidence-based communications strategies.

Of course, research, strategic communications, and effective policy advocacy are necessary but not sufficient to improve policies for children and their families. Ed learned, and in turn taught us, that political strategies are the final common pathway in the policy change process. Over the last 3 decades, policy advocacy groups at the local (e.g., Citizens Committee for Children in New York City), state (affiliates of Voices for America's Children in every state in the union), and national (e.g., the Children's Defense Fund, Fight Crime/Invest in Kids) levels have endeavored to use research and strategic communications to inform policy advocacy. A balanced history of the child advocacy movement in the United States would include many successes and many failures and undoubtedly conclude that, in the absence of effective electoral advocacy, policy advocacy is essential but not sufficient.

In his 2002 interview with *The Progressive* (Conniff, 2002), Ed called for a new lobby for American's younger children, one as effective as the AARP is for America's older citizens. Indeed, a new organization, Vote Kids (http://www.votekids.org), has emerged in the last several years to (a) document the voting records of elected officials on key child policy issues and (b) use communications strategies to hold elected federal officials accountable for their votes on children's issues. It is highly likely that effective policy advocacy coupled with such electoral advocacy efforts as Vote Kids will finally provide the most effective bridge to a better future for all of America's children.

References

Action on the Poverty Front. (2002). *Addendum to action/discussion paper 1.* Retrieved March 18, 2005, from http://www.povertyaction.net/Documents/ActionPaper1addendum.doc

Aubrun, A., & Grady, J. (2002, May). *What kids need and what kids give back: A review of communications materials used by early childhood development advocates to promote school readiness and other issues.* Retrieved March 18, 2005, from http://www.frameworksinstitute.org/products/CL-PackMats8191.pdf

Bales, S. N. (2003, November). The storytelling power of numbers. *Kids Count E-Zine, 25.* Retrieved March 18, 2005, from http://www.frameworksinstitute.org/products/issue25framing.shtml

Bostrom, M. (n.d.a). Topic: Communicating on budgets and taxes. *Kids Count E-Zine, 24.* Retrieved March 18, 2005, from http://www.frameworksinstitute.org/products/issue24framing.shtml

Bostrom, M. (n.d.b). Topic: Finding and using polling data—for free! Case study: Taxes. *Kids Count E-Zine, 20.* Retrieved March 18, 2005, from http://www.frameworksinstitute.org/products/issue20polling.shtml

Conniff, R. (2002, June). Interview: Edward Zigler. *The Progressive, 66*(6), 30–35.

Early Care and Education Collaborative. (n.d.a). *Child-care polling analysis.* Retrieved March 18, 2005, from http://www.earlycare.org/ccpa.htm

Early Care and Education Collaborative. (n.d.b). *Sample message memo.* Retrieved March 18, 2005, from http://www.earlycare.org/messagememo2.htm

Edsall, T. B. (2001, July/August). The people and the press: Whose views shape the news? *Public Perspective, 12*(4), 29–31.

FrameWorks Institute. (2001). *Communicating global interdependence: A Frameworks message memo.* Retrieved March 18, 2005, from http://www.frameworksinstitute.org/products/messagememo.pdf

FrameWorks Institute. (n.d.a). Topic: Anticipating the opposition using framing research. *Kids Count E-Zine, 10.* Retrieved March 18, 2005, from http://www.frameworksinstitute.org/products/issue10framing.shtml

FrameWorks Institute. (n.d.b). Topic: Child poverty. *Kids Count E-Zine, 5.* Retrieved March 18, 2005, from http://www.frameworksinstitute.org/products/issue5poverty.shtml

FrameWorks Institute. (n.d.c). Topic: A five minute refresher course in framing. *Kids Count E-Zine, 8.* Retrieved March 18, 2005, from http://www.frameworksinstitute.org/products/issue8framing.shtml

Gawiser, S., & Witt, G. E. (2005). *20 questions journalists should ask about poll results.* Retrieved March 18, 2005, from http://www.publicagenda.org/polling/polling_20q.cfm

Guzman, L., Lippman, L., Moore, K. A., & O'Hare, W. (2003, July). How children are doing: The mismatch between public perception and statistical reality. *Child Trends Research Brief.* Retrieved March 18, 2005, from http://www.childtrends.org/Files/PublicPerceptionsRB.pdf

Langer, G. (2002, July/August). Trust in government . . . to do what? *Public Perspective, 13*(4), 7–10.

Light, P., & Labiner, J. (2001, October 18). *A vote of renewed confidence: How Americans view presidential appointments and government in the wake of the September 11th terrorist attacks.* Retrieved March 18, 2003, from http://www.appointee.brookings.org/events/oct19report.pdf

National Public Radio, Kaiser Family Foundation, & Harvard Kennedy School of Government. (2001, April). *National survey on poverty in America*. Retrieved March 18, 2005, from http://www.kff.org/kaiserpolls/loader.cfm?url=/commonspot/security/getfile.cfm&PageID=13807

Pew Research Center for the People and the Press. (2003, November 5). *The 2004 political landscape: Evenly divided and increasingly polarized*. Retrieved March 18, 2005, from http://people-press.org/reports/print.php3?PageID=753

Public Agenda. (2003). *The federal budget: Bills and proposals*. Retrieved March 18, 2003, from http://www.publicagenda.org/issues/major_proposals_detail2.cfm?issue_type=federal_budget&proposal_graphic=majpropbudgetproposals.jpg

Public Agenda. (2005a). *About polling*. Retrieved March 18, 2005, from http://www.publicagenda.org/polling/polling.cfm

Public Agenda. (2005b). *About polling: Sources and resources on public opinion research*. Retrieved March 18, 2005, from http://www.publicagenda.org/polling/polling_sources.cfm

Roper Center for Public Opinion Research. (2004). *Polling 101*. Retrieved March 18, 2005, from http://www.ropercenter.uconn.edu/pom/polling101.html

Roper Center for Public Opinion Research. (n.d.). *Role of polls in policymaking survey*. Retrieved March 18, 2005, from http://www.ropercenter.uconn.edu/sdaweb/pols015a/htmlcdbk/pol00006.htm

Witt, E. (2001, July/August). People who count: Polling in a new century. *Public Perspective, 12*(4), 25–28.

Yankelovich, D. (2005). *The seven stages of public opinion*. Retrieved March 18, 2005, from http://www.publicagenda.org/polling/polling_stages.cfm

4

Data for a Democracy: The Evolving Role of Evaluation in Policy and Program Development

Kathleen McCartney and Heather B. Weiss

Policies designed to improve the life chances of children and families often live or die on the basis of the findings from evaluation research. In the past 40 years, few have better understood the power of evaluation, nor done more to shape it, than Edward F. Zigler. From the beginning of modern evaluation efforts, a tension emerged that endures to this day, namely the role of the academy and its concern with scientific objectivity in the political decision-making process. Nowhere is this tension more evident than in child development research. The child study movement originated as an applied science, whereas psychology sought to establish itself as a laboratory science. As Zigler (1998) explained, research to improve education and child rearing was viewed by psychologists as incompatible with research on principles and theories of behavior; applied research "could compromise the purity of science" (p. 535). Leading developmentalists continue to note the false dialectic between basic and applied research. Nonetheless, the tension between the goal to maintain the integrity, discovery properties, and independence of science and the goal to contribute to the public good necessarily frames all discussions about the use of evaluation data.

In this 21st-century era of outcomes and accountability, there is renewed interest in the "right way" to do evaluation, its purposes and audiences, and how it should inform policy and practice. It is our intention to contribute to these discussions. Toward this end, we begin with a brief history of evaluation to highlight its relation with public policy decision making. This history traces how the purposes, uses, and users of evaluation research have grown since big investments in program evaluation began in the 1960s. We argue that past experience yields a number of important lessons about how to evaluate evaluation data. The national study of the 21st Century Community Learning Centers (CCLC) Program provides a significant case to which we apply our hard-won lessons learned. We conclude with thoughts about the meaning of data for a democracy.

A Brief History of the Use of Evaluation Data

The 1960s: Evaluation Comes of Age

Cronbach (1980) traced the roots of evaluation to the enlightenment, when science became "a powerful instrument for overturning natural beliefs" (p. 24). Evaluation did not come of age, however, until the 1960s, when President Lyndon B. Johnson's War on Poverty led to new initiatives to solve pressing social problems. President Johnson called for the active participation of leading social scientists not only in program development but also in the scientific evaluation of these programs. It was a time of great optimism, both scientifically and politically.

Politicians quickly realized that data could be used to advance their agendas, from managing existing social programs to winning support for new ones. Congress, seeing evaluation as a means to influence funding decisions, built data collection and evaluation efforts into the first big federal education legislation, the 1965 Elementary and Secondary Education Act. Robert F. Kennedy was particularly enthusiastic about the evaluation component, because he believed schools needed to be held accountable for their education of black students; thus, evaluation became a tool of the civil rights movement (Lagemann, 2000). Increasingly, major federal social and education legislation has an evaluation requirement and a funding "set aside."

From the beginning, Head Start served as the national evaluation laboratory. The first Head Start evaluation followed the early implementation of the Head Start program, which was mounted quickly as early childhood educators capitalized on a large policy initiative (Zigler & Muenchow, 1992). It was the black box era of evaluation in that its purpose was to determine whether an input produced a desired output. There was no real theory of change. In their enthusiasm to do good work, social scientists did not think through issues pertaining to program implementation, expected outcomes, and moderators of effects. Although early evaluation efforts led to advances in methodology, Head Start was continually placed at risk especially because expectations for program effects had been unrealistically high. Then and now, Zigler and others have warned the field not to embrace early evaluation results.

The 1970s: Broadening the Approach

As experience with evaluation grew, the limits of the black box experimental method became apparent. Cronbach (1980) and his colleagues on the Stanford Evaluation Consortium advocated for a broader approach to the uses of evaluation data. First, they argued that evaluation data provide only one source of information to shape policy. There are many others, including public will. Thus, decision making to fund or not to fund a program should not follow simple prescriptions from evaluation studies. Second, they expanded the methods in the evaluator's tool kit. There is no question that the random assignment experiment is a powerful tool if external validity is assured. Nevertheless, a rich qualitative study of a subgroup of participants can often reveal more about implementation issues than any other design. Finally, Cronbach and colleagues noted the need to expand the audiences of evaluation from policymakers alone to practitioners, advocates, and parents. The public can only be responsive to data when the data are available to them.

The 1980s: The Disconnect Between Federal and Local Problem Solving

Early evaluations of social programs typically used a top-down approach. Large scale studies, often conducted by the federal government, served as flagship evaluations. Following positive results, policymakers could argue for scale-up across a broad range of constituencies. This evaluation strategy is sometimes referred to as a *research and development* (R & D) *model*. In 20 years, the R & D model produced advances in methodology. For example, evaluators are now more likely to select outcomes that are both policy relevant and strategic, such as grade retention and special education placement; to include cost-effectiveness estimates to demonstrate savings for tax payers resulting from prevention efforts; and to engage in strategic communication efforts (H. B. Weiss, 2001). The R & D model also produced results in the form of significant experimental findings. These data provided influential national policymakers (Haskins, 1989) as well as scientists (Schorr, 1988) with the ammunition to call for the expansion of early childhood services.

Data do not always influence policy because there is a disconnect between research and practice. The bipartisan support of programs like Head Start has as much to do with values as with data (Zigler & Muenchow, 1992). Moreover, there are stunning case studies that demonstrate how data have been ignored in policy decisions. For example, a *New York Times* science reporter, Gina Kolata (1996), conducted an investigation of drug abuse prevention programs and discovered that 75% of the nation's schools use DARE, a program with mixed evaluation support. There is an alternative, more effective program that has been rigorously evaluated by a university-based researcher with a grant from the National Institute of Drug Abuse (NIDA). Unfortunately, neither NIDA nor the researcher had the skills or incentives to inform the public about this intervention, to develop training programs, or to execute a scale-up.

Then came the new federalism, which encouraged states and local communities to seek their own solutions to social problems. Typically states and communities adopt a bottom-up approach through which services are developed in response to a perceived need, resulting in a strategy that can best be described as opportunistic or entrepreneurial (H. B. Weiss, 1993; Zigler & Styfco, 2002). Community leaders often possess the leadership and political skills necessary to motivate state policymakers to build programs that reflect the community's prevailing social, ideological, and cultural values; however, they are hampered by the fact that policymakers want evaluation data but seldom provide funds to pay for studies. Sometimes, leaders are able to borrow R & D findings from similar programs, although these efforts are vulnerable to attacks about whether findings can be generalized. Other times, they scramble to obtain funding from foundations for evaluation efforts. Even when they are successful, leaders must then identify not only skilled evaluators but also cooperative program participants to conduct a study. As an adaptive strategy, leaders tend to use a defensive approach to evaluation—they are careful not to promise too much in the way of outcomes, or they say that their evaluations are "in progress."

The 1990s Into the New Millennium: Accountability and Scientifically Based Research

During the late 1980s, there were fierce debates about whether social interventions worked to help disadvantaged families. In addition, there was growing discontent with "big" government and its efforts to solve social problems. One result of this was the somewhat bipartisan effort to streamline and reinvent government to make it more efficient and effective (Osborne & Gaebler, 1992). To unfreeze bureaucracy and encourage effective innovation, the reinvention movement offered flexibility in return for an emphasis on outcomes and more transparent accountability. This culminated in the 1993 passage of the federal Government Performance and Results Act (GPRA), mandating that federal agencies set goals, develop performance indicators, and track and report their performance and results to Congress and the public. GPRA quickly had state and local counterparts. This push for accountability resulted in norms whereby nearly every public service did not just need to specify its intended outcomes but also report to funding agencies its progress toward achieving them. This is true of both old and new programs, regardless of funding source, be it public, nonprofit, or philanthropic.

Although the jury is still out about whether this will actually improve individual and community outcomes over the long run, accountability is transforming many organizations by forcing greater clarity about goals and outcomes, as well as strategies to achieve both (Bohan-Baker, Schilder, O'Reilly, Smith & Weiss, 1998; Schilder, 1998). Policymakers are now less willing to believe that experimental evidence on flagship programs can be generalized to their states or communities. Questions about who gets and uses data and information for what purposes—learning, accountability, rewards and sanctions, program termination, and continuous improvement—are at the center of debate.

The next wave of this reform movement is the new 21st-century emphasis on research-based policy and practice, first in education and increasingly across all service sectors. Slavin (2002) outlined three events that illustrate this burgeoning scientific revolution. First, in 1998 Congressmen David Obey and John Porter introduced legislation to provide schools with funds to adopt "proven, comprehensive reform models" (U.S. Department of Education, 1999). Second, in 2001 the Bush administration reauthorization of the Elementary and Secondary Education Act, referred to as *No Child Left Behind*, called for "scientifically based research" 110 times in the text. Third, in 2002 Grover Whitehurst, the director of the Office of Educational Research and Improvement (OERI), issued a request for proposals to evaluate early childhood programs using experimental designs only.

In an effort to clarify and specify the rules or norms behind scientific research in education, the National Research Council convened a study group and charged them to "review and synthesize recent literature on the science and practice of scientific educational research and consider how to support high quality science in a federal education research agency" (National Research Council, 2002, p. 1). This group responded with a monograph that outlined principles for scientific inquiry. The principles are now the subject of debate because they offer rules or standards for conducting research and evaluation, for judging their merit, and for determining when research and evaluation should be used to guide policy.

This movement could have a number of consequences—good and bad. It could generate knowledge that informs effective practices to improve outcomes for children and families, which would be good; it could create major disincentives for innovation, which would be bad; it could require practitioners to expend already scarce resources on endless cycles of research and evaluation, which would also be bad; and it could become the political lever to support an a priori decision to cut programs and expenditures on child and family services, which would be bad indeed. The outcome is more likely to be good if two conditions are met in the push for results, accountability and research-based policy and practice. First, social scientists and policymakers alike need to adhere to the rules of evidence. Second, social scientists and policymakers need to operate within a larger frame that emphasizes innovation and continuous improvement. These two conditions are consistent with Mark, Henry, and Julnes's (1999) view of the ultimate objective of evaluation as "social betterment that is the alleviation of social problems and the meeting of human needs" (p.17).

Lessons Learned: Rules of the Evaluation Game

We argue that at least five rules have emerged as hard-won lessons learned during these past 40 years as evaluation has come of age. Data will always be evaluated through a political lens. Moreover, in these postmodern times, many assert that data are merely constructed and therefore subject to as much bias as argument (Gergen, 1995). Although we accept that data are used to advance the goals of citizens—scientists, policymakers, and advocates—we believe that the use of rules will reduce the politicization of data, which is critical if data are to play any meaningful role in a democracy. In other words, it is crucial to maintain the integrity of science for findings to contribute to the public good.

Lesson 1: Use Mixed Methods Designs

In current debates, randomized field trials have emerged as the gold standard of evaluation methods in the minds of both policymakers and methodologists (Boruch, de Moya, & Snyder, 2002). The main argument in favor of this design is that it produces unbiased data compared with nonexperimental or correlational designs, where omitted variables bias may compromise interpretations of findings. This is a powerful argument. To date, randomized field trials have been relatively rare, largely for practical reasons (Cook & Payne, 2002). Nevertheless, the pressure to conduct them will continue to intensify because competition for limited program funds will increasingly rely on demonstrated effects. It is important that experimental work include both main effects research questions, which pertain to universal program outcomes, and moderating effects questions. It is possible, indeed likely, that effectiveness varies as a function of characteristics of children, for example their age, gender, or race; characteristics of families, for example, single-parent status or income level; characteristics of measures used as outcomes; and characteristics of the interventions themselves. Real advances in the field of program evaluation are likely to follow investigations of moderating influences.

Critics have voiced their concerns about adopting the experimental design as a gold standard. Gallagher (2002) worried that adopting a medical model for research in education will lead policymakers to expect breakthroughs that will be slow in coming. Gardner's (2002) objection is practical in that "Children cannot legitimately be assigned to or shuttled from one 'condition' to another the way that agricultural seeds are planted or transplanted in different soils" (p. 72). Twenty years ago, Cronbach taught us that educational experiments tended to sacrifice internal validity for external validity. For example, schooling experiments necessarily rely on a biased sample of schools willing to participate in a given study. Objections to randomized experiments abound, as do objections to the objections (Cook & Payne, 2002).

Many scholars are choosing a middle ground. Similarly, the National Research Council (2002) wrote that

> Particular research designs and methods are suited for specific kinds of investigations and questions, but can rarely illuminate all the questions and issues in a line of inquiry. Therefore, very different methodological approaches must often be used in various parts of a series of related studies. (p. 4)

In a recent article, Tom Brock (2001) of the Manpower Demonstration Research Corporation, a proponent of experimentation, described how interviews with participants of their New Hope Demonstration Project, a multifaceted welfare program, helped to elucidate the impact of findings by identifying the subgroups that benefited most and least from the intervention. Even Boruch and Mosteller (2002) advocated the use of mixed methods, although they view nonexperimental work as providing the groundwork for controlled studies of program effectiveness. For example, a survey might provide data on needs assistance, whereas a narrative study might provide data from children, parents, teachers, and policymakers on decision-making strategies.

The argument for mixed methods research is aided by an increasing number of excellent examples of such work. For example, Datta (2001) reflected on the evaluation of the Detroit Comer Schools and Families Initiative (Millsap et al., 2000) and showed how the extensive qualitative data revealed positive effects for participants where there was adequate implementation, effects that were not found in the quantitative analysis. As Datta noted, this mixed methods design prevented "death by control and comparison groups." She argued, and we agree, that no high-stakes random assignment study should proceed without a careful implementation study.

Lesson 2: Interpret Effect Size in a Research Context

Long ago, in a political climate far, far away, statistically significant findings were enough to justify a program's effectiveness. This is no longer the case, and for good reason. Statistical significance reveals whether there is an association between an independent and dependent variable in the case of randomized trials, or between a predictor and outcome in the case of nonexperimental studies. Statistical significance reveals nothing about the size of the effect, that is, whether an effect has practical importance. The computation of effect size estimates is straightforward and easy. From significance test statistics such as t or F, researchers can compute effect size estimates in standard units, such as r, the Pearson product–moment correlation, and d, which denotes the standardized difference between two means. Cohen (1977), a statistician, offered some conventions for effect sizes to help researchers conduct power analyses. With respect to d, he suggested that .20 was small, .50 was moderate, and .80 was large. Note, however, that social science research seldom yields effects as large as .80. If we, as researchers, apply Cohen's guidelines for power analyses blindly, we would end up dismissing most effects as small—even trivial. There is good reason to believe that this is not the case.

There is fundamentally no agreement on how to interpret effect size estimates, which are influenced by a number of factors, including measurement and design (McCartney & Rosenthal, 2000). This means that there are no easy conventions for determining the practical importance of effect sizes. Instead, researchers need to evaluate effect sizes in the context of the measures and designs used in the research. Measurement error biases effect sizes toward zero, and there is measurement error whenever anything is scaled. At least one psychometrician has warned that most psychological research can be thought of as construct validity research and that for this reason small effects should be expected (O'Grady, 1982). Experimental designs are likely to produce smaller effects than other designs, but for good reason, namely because they are less biased. And methodological choices that minimize error terms will increase effect sizes, for example the use of within-subject designs. These are the kinds of considerations that might enter debates about the practical importance of a program.

The National Evaluation of Family Support Programs (Layzer, Goodson, Creps, Werner, & Bernstein, 2001) offers a case to examine the inherent problems in evaluating effect size estimates (see McCartney & Dearing, 2002). Its authors identified 665 studies that represent 260 programs. Using meta-analytic techniques, they synthesized a large database to evaluate effect size estimates for child outcomes. The short-term average effect size across studies was .29 for child cognitive development. The use of Cohen's conventions would result in a dismissal of family support programs for producing small effects. Moving to moderating questions leads one to ask, Under what circumstances do programs work best? Programs were more effective when they included an early childhood education component (.48 vs. .25), when there were peer support opportunities for parents (.40 vs. .25), and when there were parent groups rather than home visits (.49 vs. .26). Even by Cohen's conservative standards, some programs had moderate effects. If there were data on method and assessment, we could extend the study of moderation to include research design characteristics. If there were data on cost-effectiveness, we could extend the debate about whether the results are worth public investment. We, as researchers, need to ground debates about effect size in these contexts before we dismiss significant findings.

Lesson 3: Synthesize All Research Findings

Cronbach argued many years ago that individual studies should not be used in and of themselves to direct policy. Nonetheless, there is often a desire among sponsors and stakeholders to bring the results of recent studies, especially large-scale ones, front and center on the policy stage. Yet a single study only provides an approximate estimate of intervention effects and may have little to say about the relation between the effect and features of the program. That is because effects can reflect methodological rather than procedural differences across studies (Lipsey, 1997). When there is a large literature on a given topic, then findings across studies can be brought to bear on a given question through synthetic work; more data mean more knowledge.

Synthetic work can be conducted qualitatively through critical review or quantitatively through meta-analysis. Good critical reviews are the more difficult of the two to conduct. They require a keen mind that can detect latent structures or patterns in the data. Good meta-analyses are easier to do, because the procedures for conducting them are clearly described and easy to follow. Using descriptive statistics, weighted effect sizes are computed from test statistics across studies, and using inferential statistics, moderators of effects are assessed. In fact, both methods are useful only insofar as reviewers sample the literature in an unbiased manner (i.e., through computer searches of library databases) and consider methodological differences across studies pertaining to characteristics of the sample, treatments, and outcomes. Neither method is preferable; rather, each has advantages and disadvantages.

Lesson 4: Adopt Fair and Reasonable Scientific Expectations

In a recent paper, McCartney (2003) discussed the meaning of statistical models generally, given that theory and conceptualization in developmental science far exceed method and measurement. She warned that "A significant association probably tells us little more than there might be something there, a kind of signal amidst the noise" (p. 34). In other words, the data can only take you so far given the state of the art. As a consequence, it is important to have fair and reasonable scientific expectations of the extent to which the data can inform a debate or direct a political decision.

This is clearly demonstrated by Lipsey (1997), who conducted an important analysis of the sources of between-study effect size variance, averaged over 300 meta-analyses. He found that program differences (e.g., treatment type, dosage, client type, and outcome) accounted for 25% of the variation in observed effects, whereas method (design, control type, measure, and study size) accounted for 21% of the variance; sampling error and residual variance accounted for 26% and 28%, respectively. From this analysis, it is clear that researchers need to distinguish program effects from methodological effects. Lipsey (1997) put it this way:

> To the extent that observed effects in evaluation studies reflect method-
> ological rather than substantive differences in the programs studied, we

> know we are looking at them through a distorting lens, a funhouse mirror
> that may make skinny effects look fat and robust effects appear anorexic.
> (p. 17)

A consideration of the methodological limitations in social science research
generally and evaluation research specifically may lead some to a nihilistic conclusion about the use of data in decision-making processes. On the contrary, we
believe that data advance argument, especially when they generate new knowledge. Nevertheless, one must not overstate what they can contribute to any
debate.

Lesson 5: Encourage Peer and Public Critique of the Data

Philosophers of science evaluate work in light of its heuristic value, that is, the
work's impact on the scientific community—the more impact, the more value.
In order for work to have impact, findings must be widely disseminated and
subjected to professional scrutiny by peers and the public. The National Research Council (2002) wrote that

> ongoing, collaborative, public critique is an indication of the health of a sci-
> entific enterprise. Indeed, the objectivity of science derives from publicly
> enforced norms of the professional community of scientists, rather than from
> the character traits of any individual person or design features of any study.
> (p. 5)

Scrutiny is especially important amidst political debates about the meaning of
data.

Similarly, it is important to encourage data sharing to promote multiple
independent analyses of evaluation data, especially where major policy issues
are at stake and especially when the data are generated by public funds. The
recent reanalysis of a school voucher study has sparked a productive debate
about data sharing (Viadero, 2003). Independent reanalysis of the data showed
different results than those from the original study. Although the original
team found learning gains for African American students who used tuition
vouchers to transfer to private schools, reanalyses by Winerip (2003) found
those gains to be statistically insignificant at one of the four study sites; unfortunately, data from the remaining three sites have not yet been made available
for secondary data analysis. Reanalysis and replication are hallmarks of the
scientific process.

A Framework for a Continuous Learning System

In addition to rules for interpreting data, we argue that a second condition
must be met for data to have a meaningful role in a democracy. Specifically,
data need to be directed toward innovation and continuous improvement. Zigler
noted this early in the development of Head Start, because he understood that

the best science is cumulative, where study builds on study (Zigler & Muenchow, 1992). The history of evaluation presented here suggests that the American approach to evaluation has been piecemeal, with relatively little emphasis on reflective learning. The new emphasis on accountability has the potential to ameliorate this, if researchers begin to think of evaluation as a key component in a larger, ongoing system of change. Such a system also has the potential to create a more engaged and informed citizenry.

Based on lessons learned, we lay out one possible learning framework as a heuristic device to stimulate creative thinking about the supports and investments necessary for the use of evaluation data in social problem solving. H. B. Weiss and Morrill (1998) outlined the rationale, structure, and operation of a continuous learning system to guide program innovation and evaluation as part of ongoing social betterment efforts. The framework for this system, presented in Figure 4.1, is designed to apply to programs and networks of service providers. Such a system will not work unless resources are realigned to support the learning, continuous improvement, and accountability efforts of individual programs and organizations. This means investing not only in building individual organizational capacity to gather and use data as part of performance management efforts but also in building necessary field level supports, such as easy access to syntheses of past and ongoing research.

It should be noted that this learning system also assumes the continuing need for the usual investments in R & D experiments to develop and test new approaches and models. Debate and discussion of experimental results is important for renewing, improving, and fostering innovation in existing services. Many program directors are willing to be part of the "experimenting society" that Donald Campbell (1969) outlined many years ago. But evaluations, outcome accountability efforts, synthesis and dissemination, and scale-up efforts are typically underfunded. Such systems will fail without the necessary resources for these activities. As Figure 4.1 indicates, there are five often overlapping stages in this learning system.

Stage 1

During Stage 1, the stakeholders design and initiate the learning system. They set the agenda and program goals, as well as the indicators of success. They also obtain resources and identify the research and evaluation questions and gaps. The program's agenda is keyed to an organization, agency, or field's long-term strategic plan and theory of change. Another key task at this stage is to determine how best to use evaluation resources to help understand how and why indicators change and which services affect them; in other words, to define mediators of effects. This ongoing discussion of the mechanisms of change enables more strategic targeting of evaluation to help improve performance. Because information penetrates policy and practice both incrementally and iteratively, information must be accessible and flow continuously in a learning system to promote course correctives and innovation. Given the importance of public support for social betterment policies and programs, understanding what the public values is essential. It is important at this stage that the stakeholders discuss the accountability consequences—the content and timing of their ex-

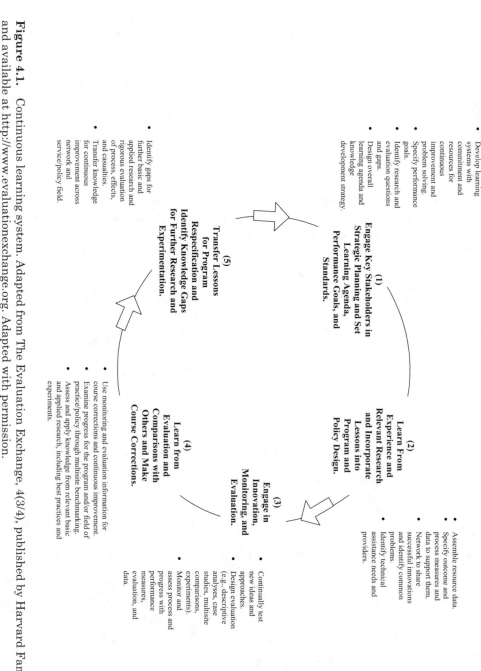

Figure 4.1. Continuous learning system. Adapted from The Evaluation Exchange, 4(3/4), published by Harvard Family Research Project and available at http://www.evaluationexchange.org. Adapted with permission.

pectations for progress in program indicators. Expectations should be reasonable and the learning system should factor in the private-sector experience of learning from failure. There should be opportunities and incentives for risk taking, innovation, and experimentation with new services and policies. This discussion must also include consideration of the point in a continuous learning system at which it is clear that a program or policy simply does not work well enough to warrant continued support.

Stage 2

In Stage 2, the stakeholders incorporate others' experience and relevant research into program and policy design. Activities include assembling resources, specifying outcome and process measures as well as the data necessary to support them, networking to share successful innovations and common problems, and identifying technical assistance needs and providers. In this stage the stakeholders must create the means to disseminate and synthesize relevant research and evaluation information. Dissemination strategies should attempt to initiate active discussion and consideration of the potential implications of the work for practice, organizational and policy change, as well as stakeholders' access to timely information about the latest research and evaluations.

Stage 3

In Stage 3, the stakeholders engage in program innovation, program monitoring, and program evaluation. Activities include continually testing new ideas and approaches, monitoring and assessing progress with descriptive performance measures, and designing the evaluation strategies to assess them. Data collection is at the heart of this stage of the learning system.

Stage 4

In Stage 4, the stakeholders look beyond their work again, as in Stage 2, to make course corrections based on evaluation data. Activities include benchmarking to compare one's progress against other programs or standards, as well as applying knowledge from relevant basic and applied research. The recent work of the National Academy of Sciences (NAS) on reading and literacy is a good example of the kinds of work required for a field in Stages 4 and 5 in a learning system (Snow, Burns, & Griffin, 1998). The consensus reached by the NAS panel helped resolve the disabling phonics-versus-whole-language debate and ultimately may help improve reading outcomes. It is in Stages 4 and 5 that programs and fields operate as learning organizations and systems.

Stage 5

Finally, in Stage 5, the stakeholders examine the lessons for program respecification, identify knowledge gaps for further research and experimentation, and look at the implications of the work for creation or respecification of performance standards and best practices. This is also the point where lessons should be debated and shared with key stakeholders, including the public, as part of the educative function of evaluation. For a learning system to work, stakeholders must buy in and commit to learning. Funders must commit as well, recognizing that "gotcha" accountability is not conducive to building effective programs or to encouraging innovation to solve social problems. All must recognize that it will take time, that clarity about the goals of the learning system is critical, and that there are important lessons from the past that must be considered.

Lessons Lost: The National Evaluation of the 21st Century Community Learning Centers Program

The most recent flagship evaluation is of the CCLC Program. We use this case to demonstrate how the two conditions we have outlined should be used to evaluate evaluation data. In 1998, the CCLC Program narrowed its mission to support school-based programs for children during out-of-school time. These programs support both academic and recreational activities during after-school hours, weekends, holidays, and summers. The increase in funding for these programs, from $40 million in 1998 to $1 billion in 2002, offered not only a means to provide preventive interventions for children in 7,500 communities but also an important support for their employed parents.

Sensibly, the U.S. Department of Education, in public–private partnership with the Charles Stewart Mott Foundation, decided to conduct an evaluation of this program and contracted with Mathematica Policy Research, Inc., to conduct the work (Dynarski et al., 2003). The methodology used by the Mathematica team was state of the art. For elementary school students, they were able to implement an experimental design involving seven programs. The middle school evaluation involved propensity score matching techniques, a powerful strategy for controlling for selection bias in nonexperimental designs. Nevertheless, it is important to note there were some important differences between the families of children who participated versus those who did not participate in programs on ethnicity, single-parent status, and income that call into question whether this strategy was up to the task. Participants were more likely than nonparticipants to be Black, to come from single-parent families, and to come from families with fewer economic resources (average income of $24,000 per year vs. $60,000 per year).

A report of the first-year findings was released by Mathematica and the Department of Education in February 2003 (Dynarksi et al., 2003). The descriptive data on implementation were disappointing because there were low levels of student participation. On average, students attended programs less than 2 days per week. Nonparticipants cited a number of factors influencing their decision not to attend programs, including their inability to obtain transportation home, a problem that could potentially be solved with program funds. Other issues for children included whether they had a choice concerning activities, whether their friends participated in the program, and whether they could work on their homework. In addition, staffing patterns may have affected program quality because most staff members only worked a few days each week, typically for short periods. Continuity in providers is a key index of program quality. This is just the kind of input that evaluators can offer program directors as part of an innovation cycle.

Despite limitations in participation and staffing, there were some significant outcomes. Participation in programs was associated with increased parent involvement; specifically, program parents of elementary school children were more likely to help their children with homework, whereas program parents of middle-school children were more likely to volunteer at school and to attend parent–teacher events. There was also some impact on academic achievement. Specifically, math grades were higher for CCLC Program participants than for nonparticipants. Effects were moderated by ethnicity. Grades for Black and Hispanic middle school participants were higher and their absenteeism was lower than for White students. By most standards the effects were small. There were null findings as well. For example, program participation was not associated with children's self-reports concerning feeling safe or being able to plan or set goals; nor were there lower rates of self-care for program participants.

Coinciding with the release of this report was a request by the President to cut funding for the 21st CCLC Program by 40%, from $1 billion to $600 million. The administration cited the "disappointing initial findings from a rigorous evaluation of the 21st CCLC program" as the reason for the proposed cuts (U.S. Department of Education, 2003). Is this recommendation reasonable?

To answer that question, we turn to our lessons learned. First, what would an evaluation of the methods reveal? As previously noted, the methods were state of the art. This is a flagship evaluation study, funded by the U. S. Department of Education and the Charles Stewart Mott Foundation at $15.8 million. That said, social scientists have noted some serious limitations (see Mahoney & Zigler, 2003).

Second, how were the effect size data interpreted? The Mathematica researchers highlight in their executive summary that these small effects were most likely due to the low attendance rates, the short follow-up period, and the lack of sustained, substantive academic support in most programs (Dynarski et al., 2003). Although it is easy to dismiss the effects as small, this conclusion is no doubt premature, especially in light of the fact that this is an ongoing evaluation.

Third, were the findings from the Mathematica Study synthesized with existing data on after school programs? The answer to this question is clearly no. Instead, they have been embraced as providing the only relevant information with which to inform funding considerations.

Fourth, did the administration have fair and reasonable scientific expectations? The country's leading scholars on after school research warned that one should not expect the 21st CCLC Program evaluation to yield short-term effects on tests scores (Rinehart, 2003), echoing Zigler's early warnings concerning Head Start (Zigler & Muenchow, 1992). It is sobering to think that preliminary findings from the implementation phase of this study might be used to undermine the program, despite the balanced report issued by Mathematica.

Fifth, were the findings subjected to professional scrutiny? Again, the answer to this question is clearly no, given that the administration's recommendations coincided with the release of the report. It is especially troubling to us, not only as citizens but also as researchers, that policy recommendations are preceding reactions from the scientific community.

Next, we ask whether the findings were used as part of an ongoing innovation cycle or learning system. In a brief issued by the Afterschool Alliance, a coalition of private and public organizations, Rinehart (2003) noted that the community of child advocates interested in after school care had hoped that this first report would be used to offer technical assistance to programs receiving funds from the 21st CCLC Program. In other words, she and others had hoped that this evaluation would be used as part of the innovation cycle of programs to promote continuous improvement. This does not appear to be a part of the administration's plan, given that the evaluation of the first-year data occurred during the implementation phase of the intervention.

We conclude with a final question: To what extent is a political lens guiding the administration's recommendation? You be the judge. If one plays by the rules of the game, we fail to see how the findings from the Mathematica Study, collected early in the implementation phase, lead to a recommendation to cut the 21st CCLC Program by 40%. This could be another sad example of death by evaluation (Datta, 2001). Or it could be an attempt by the administration to use the accountability movement as a political lever to cut programs and expenditures on child and family services.

Conclusion

Social scientists are often humbled, or should be, by the extent to which data are ignored in the political process (Gardner, 2002; Shonkoff, 2000). Researchers may privilege data, but policymakers do not. There is no guarantee that policymakers will listen to recommendations, even well-grounded ones that are derived from science. Instead, in a democracy like ours, data exist alongside compelling testimonies from ordinary citizens, newspaper exposes, and partisan politics. An often-used beltway adage, attributed to Daniel Patrick Moynihan, is that values trump data. Social programs for children and families are inherently "political creatures," in that they are not only proposed and funded through the political process, but also implemented and evaluated in a political climate (C. H. Weiss, 1987).

If this is the case, then what is the role of data for public policy? We have argued that research can generate usable knowledge that informs effective practices to improve outcomes for children and families. In other words, data can add to argument. For this to happen, two conditions must be met. The first is that social scientists and policymakers alike need to work within established rules of the evaluation game, rules that reflect 40 years of hard-won lessons. We, as researchers, do not have to privilege data, but we do have to use them in a way that minimizes their politicization. Otherwise, evaluation research has no added value to values. Probably the most important lesson learned is that evaluation studies need to be subjected to public scrutiny, both within and beyond the academy, before they can inform decision making. The second condition to be met is that evaluation data need to support innovation and continuous improvement. The heuristic value of meeting these two conditions would be great, because the resulting research would advance our theories of change as well as researchers' decision making.

In a perfect world, data from social science research would inform social policy completely. Basic research on developmental processes would provide data on theories of change, evaluation research would provide data on program effectiveness, and attitude research would provide data on the will of a people. In the real world, we must be vigilant in our efforts to evaluate evaluation data, so that data can have meaning for a democracy.

References

Bohan-Baker, M., Schilder, D., O'Reilly, F., Smith, J., & Weiss, H. B. (1998). *Learning from starting points*. Cambridge, MA: Harvard Family Research Project.

Boruch, R., de Moya, D., & Snyder, B. (2002). The importance of randomized field trials in education and related areas. In F. Mosteller & R. Boruch (Eds.), *Evidence matters* (pp. 50–79). Washington, DC: Brookings Institution Press.

Boruch, R., & Mosteller, F. (2002). Overview and new directions. In F. Mosteller & R. Boruch (Eds.), *Evidence matters* (pp. 1–14). Washington, DC: Brookings Institution Press.

Brock, T. (2001, January). *Viewing mixed methods through age implementation research lens: A response to the new hope and moving to opportunities evaluations*. Paper presented at the Conference on Mixed Methods in the Study of Childhood and Family Life, Ann Arbor, MI.

Campbell, D. T. (1969). Reforms as experiments. *American Psychologist, 24*, 409–429.

Cohen, J. (1977). *Statistical power analysis for the behavioral sciences*. New York: Academic Press.

Cook, T. D., & Payne, M. R. (2002). Objecting to the objections to using random assignment in educational research. In F. Mosteller & R. Boruch (Eds.), *Evidence matters* (pp. 150–178). Washington, DC: Brookings Institution Press.

Cronbach, L. J. (1980). *Toward reform of program evaluation*. San Francisco: Jossey-Bass.

Datta, L. (2001, January). *Avoiding death by evaluation in studying pathways through middle childhood: The evaluation of the comer approach*. Paper presented at the Conference on Mixed Methods in the Study of Childhood and Family Life, Ann Arbor, MI.

Dynarski, M., Moore, M., Mullens, J., Gleason, P., James-Burdumy, S., Rosenberg, L., et al. (2003). *When schools stay open late: The national evaluation of the 21st Century Community Learning Centers Program*. Washington, DC: U. S. Department of Education.

Elementary and Secondary Education Act of 1965. Pub. L. No. 89-10 (1965).

Gallagher, J. (2002). What next for OERI? *Education Week, 21*(28), 52.

Gardner, H. (2002). The quality and qualities of educational research. *Education Week, 22*(1), 72.

Gergen, M. M. (1995). Post-modern, post-cartesian positionings on the subject of psychology. *Theory and Psychology, 5*, 361–368.

Government Performance and Results Act of 1993. Pub. L. No. 103-62 (1993).

Haskins, R. (1989). Beyond metaphor: The efficacy of early childhood education. *American Psychologist, 44*, 274–283.

Kolata, G. (1996, September 18). Experts are at odds on how best to tackle rise in teenagers' drug use. *The New York Times*, p. A17.

Lagemann, E. C. (2000). *An elusive science: The troubling history of education research*. Chicago: University of Chicago Press.

Layzer, J., Goodson, B., Creps, C. Werner, A., & Bernstein, L. (2001). *National evaluation of family support program: Vol. B. Research studies: Final report*. Cambridge, MA: Abt Associates.

Lipsey, M. W. (1997). What can you build with thousands of bricks? Musings on the cumulation of knowledge in program evaluation. *New Directions for Evaluation, 76*, 7–23.

Mahoney, J. L. (2003, Spring). A critical commentary on the National Evaluation of the 21st Century Community Learning Centers. *21 Community News: A Newsletter for the Schools of the 21st Century.* Retrieved October 12, 2004, from http://www.yale.edu/21C/pdf/21CSpring2003.pdf

Mahoney, J. L., & Zigler, E. F. (2003). *A critical analysis of first-year findings from the National Evaluation of the 21st-Century Community Learning Centers.* Manuscript submitted for publication.

Mark, M. M., Henry, G. T., & Julnes, G. (1999). Toward an integrative framework for evaluation practice. *American Journal of Evaluation, 20*, 177–198.

McCartney, K. (2003). On the meaning of models: A signal amidst the noise. In A. Booth & A. C. Crouter (Eds.), *Children's influence of family dynamics: The neglected side of family relations* (pp. 27–36). Mahwah, NJ: Erlbaum.

McCartney, K., & Dearing, E. (2002, Spring). Evaluating effect sizes in the policy arena. *The Evaluation Exchange Newsletter, 8*, 4, 7.

McCartney, K., & Rosenthal, R. (2000). Effect size, practical importance, and social policy for children. *Child Development, 71*, 173–180.

Millsap, M. A., Chase, A., Obeidallah, D., Perez-Smith, A., Brisham, N., & Johnson, K. (2000). *Evaluation of Detroit's Comer schools and families initiative.* Cambridge, MA: Abt Associates.

National Research Council. (2002). *Scientific research in education.* Washington, DC: National Academy Press.

No Child Left Behind Act of 2001. Pub. L. No. 107-110 (2002).

O'Grady, K. E. (1982). Measures of explained variance: Cautions and limitations. *Psychological Bulletin, 97*, 766–777.

Osborne, D., & Gaebler, N. (1992). *Reinventing government: How the entrepreneurial spirit is transforming the public sector.* Reading, MA: Addison-Wesley.

Rinehart, J. (2003). *Policy brief on the National Evaluation of the 21st Century Community Learning Centers Program.* Washington, DC: Aftershool Alliance.

Schilder, D. (1998). *Aiming for accountability: Lessons learned from eight states.* Cambridge, MA: Harvard Family Research Project.

Schorr, L. B. (with Schorr, D.). (1988). *Within our reach: Breaking the cycle of disadvantage.* New York: Anchor Press/Doubleday.

Schorr, L. B. (2003, February). *Determining "what works" in social programs and social policies: Toward a more inclusive knowledge base.* Washington, DC: Brookings Institution Press.

Shonkoff, J. P. (2000). Science, policy, and practice: Three cultures in search of a shared mission. *Child Development, 71*, 181–187.

Slavin, R. E. (2002). Evidence-based education policies: Transforming educational practice and research. *Educational Researcher, 31*, 15–21.

Snow, C. E., Burns, M. S., & Griffin, P. (Eds.). (1998). *Preventing reading difficulties in young children.* Washington, DC: National Academy Press.

U.S. Department of Education. (1999). *Guidance on the comprehensive school reform program.* Washington, DC: Author.

U.S. Department of Education. (2003, February 3). *Fiscal year 2004 education budget summary and background information.* Retrieved June 14, 2005, from http://www.ed.gov/about/overview/budget/budget04/summary/edlite-section2a.html#clcs

Viadero, D. (2003, November 5). Researchers call for making data widely available. *Education Week on the Web.* Retrieved November 5, 2003, from http://www.edweek.org/ew/newstory.cfm?slug=10Access.h23

Weiss, C. H. (1987). Where politics and evaluation research meet. In D. J. Palumbo (Ed.), *The politics of program evaluation* (pp. 47–70). Newbury Park, CA: Sage.

Weiss, H. B. (1993). Building villages: Lessons from policy entrepreneurs. In M. A. Jensen & S. G. Goffin (Eds.), *Visions of entitlement: The care and education of America's children* (pp. 261–285). Albany: State University of New York Press.

Weiss, H. B. (2001). Program improvement. In D. Racine (Ed.), *Conference for funders on identifying, replicating, and improving successful early childhood programs* (pp. 90–103). New York: Replication & Program Strategies.

Weiss, H. B., & Morrill, W. A. (1998). Useful learning for public action. *The Evaluation Exchange: Emerging Strategies in Evaluating Child and Family Services, 4*(3/4), 2–4, 14.

Winerip, M. (2003, May 7). What a voucher study truly showed, and why. *The New York Times*, p. A27

Zigler, E. (1998). A place of value for applied and policy studies. *Child Development, 69*, 532–542.

Zigler, E., & Muenchow, S. (1992). *Head Start: The inside story of America's most successful educational experiment*. New York: Basic Books.

Zigler, E., & Styfco, S. J. (2002). A life lived at the crossroads of knowledge and children's policy. *New Directions for Child and Adolescent Development, 98*, 5–16.

Part II

Ensuring Good Beginnings for All Children

5

Forty Years of Research Knowledge and Use: From Head Start to Early Head Start and Beyond

John M. Love, Rachel Chazan-Cohen, and Helen Raikes

From the very start, under the leadership of Edward F. Zigler and others, a research agenda was set in motion within Head Start that eventually led to thousands of studies—from small-sample theses and dissertations to large-scale, multisite, national studies. The Head Start program became a national laboratory in which research and practice were linked to create new knowledge for program improvement. This chapter tells the story of these accomplishments. We trace the history of research within Head Start, with a special focus on federally sponsored national studies, describe the many ways the program has served as a national laboratory, and note the ways research has changed, with special attention to the innovations embodied in the Early Head Start research and evaluation study over the past 10 years. Key events and milestones in this history are depicted in Figure 5.1.

Although the goals of Head Start research have always been to inform policymakers, national program leaders, and local program leaders, in the drive toward continuous program improvement, the research questions have become more refined as the program and the research have developed. We review such themes as an increasing focus on two-generation outcomes of the program, an increasingly broad definition of child outcomes to embrace the whole child, increasingly sophisticated research designs, and greater emphasis on the question of "What works for whom?" with a focus on populations of special interest.

Head Start as a National Laboratory: The Evolution of Research Themes

Head Start began in 1965 not only with an ambitious social agenda but with a strong research and evaluation plan. From the very beginning, the program's planners recognized the importance that data could provide to the new program. The Office of Economic Opportunity (OEO) was created in 1964 to reduce

---

The content of this publication does not necessarily reflect the views or policies of the U.S. Department of Health and Human Services.

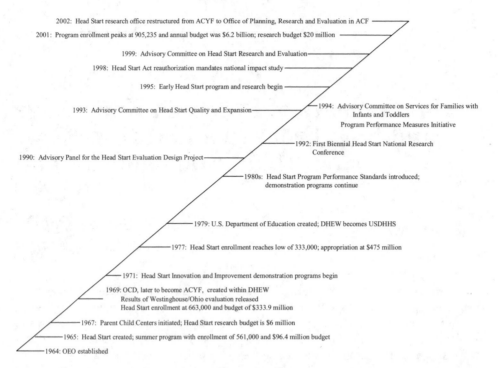

Figure 5.1. Key events in the history of Head Start research. ACF = Administration for Children and Families; ACYF = Administration on Children, Youth and Families; DHEW = Department of Health, Education and Welfare; OCD = Office of Child Development; OEO = Office of Economic Opportunity; USDHHS = U.S. Department of Health and Human Services.

poverty through such programs as Job Corps, Neighborhood Youth Corps, and Adult Literacy. A year later, under OEO director Sargent Shriver, pediatrician Robert Cooke headed a planning committee to recommend ways that the OEO goals might be advanced through projects for children, and Head Start was born. It is unlikely that researchers would have launched such a ground-breaking program on such a grand scale: The initial panel of experts recommended a comprehensive program for relatively few children—50,000—rather than the more-limited summer program created by politicians to enroll 561,000 children during its first summer.

Almost immediately, Congress and the Bureau of the Budget demanded accountability (Datta, 1976). The *planning, programming and budgeting systems* (PPBS) that Robert McNamara brought to the Pentagon influenced most federal agencies in the 1960s. As Alice Rivlin described it, the enactment of Head Start "coincided with another development: a new demand for 'accountability' for demonstrable 'outputs,' and measurable results of government spending" (Rivlin 1974, p. 10). Ironically, Head Start evaluations were already well underway, supported by a research and evaluation budget of about $6 million in fiscal year (FY) 1967 (about $26.3 million in 2002 dollars or 1.7% of the $349.2 million Head Start budget), when OEO established its Evaluation Division.[1]

---

[1]The Head Start research budget was $20 million in both FY 2002 and FY 2003.

Head Start's Early Research Agenda

Today, reading about the role of program evaluation 40 years ago, one sees—at least on the surface—strategies much like today's. Extensive studies were conducted in the very early years of the program, just as 30 years later a large-scale national study of Early Head Start was launched simultaneously with that new program. The questions were similar, with the intent of learning how well the program "worked," as well as efforts to understand and improve the program. One study, however, the Westinghouse/Ohio evaluation (Cicirelli, 1969), was designed to yield a quick report on the program's average effects on Head Start children's elementary school performance. It was rapidly implemented with a flawed design that would be unimaginable today. The study's flaws included its posttest-only design, lack of a true control group, questionable comparison group, inadequate measures of personal–social development, being conducted too early in the life of the new program (before the program design had been settled on), and lack of information on either the Head Start or post-Head Start curricular experiences of the children (Datta, 1976). Nevertheless, the study had important consequences for how Head Start research developed over the next 30 years. In Datta's thorough analysis, the consequences included (a) policies emphasizing experimentation before widely implementing new program strategies (reflected in the large number of subsequent demonstration programs), (b) methodologists questioning quasi-experimental designs, (c) researchers and policymakers alike striving to improve child assessment and observation measures, and (d) the Head Start office initiating a "new generation" of research that would include longitudinal studies and planned variation designs.[2]

Less well-known than the Westinghouse/Ohio evaluation, which began in 1968 and delivered its final report in spring 1969, are several other evaluation studies that were underway earlier. OEO's evaluation division took a broad approach to evaluation. It distinguished among summative, program improvement, and program monitoring studies. The Head Start Research Advisory Council, which Head Start director Julius Richmond had instituted, did not disagree with OEO's evaluation division about conducting summative evaluations, but it wanted a more balanced collection of studies. As Bronfenbrenner (1979) recalled, a research committee composed of Ed Zigler, Edmond Gordon, and Urie Bronfenbrenner was unsuccessful in arguing for an alternative to the proposed Westinghouse/Ohio evaluation because "it was the president's decision that all departments of the Office of Economic Opportunity were to undertake cost–benefit analyses . . . of all their programs. Head Start could not be an exception" (Bronfenbrenner, 1979, p. 88).

---

[2]Datta was Head Start's National Coordinator of Evaluation from 1968 to 1972. Her definitive analysis of the Westinghouse/Ohio evaluation and its aftermath is highlighted only briefly here. It is worth noting that, writing in 1976, Datta reported that

> the fragility of Head Start's situation in fall 1970 and the influence of the Westinghouse Report upon this situation is probably not too well known; Zigler's private discussions within DHEW and the strength of his presentations to Congress and to OMB are seen by those close to the situation as pivotal in encouraging [DHEW Secretary Elliot] Richardson to fight OMB for Head Start's survival. (p. 180)

Between 1965 and 1969, many evaluations were completed (Hubbell, 1983). In addition to the larger-scale studies sponsored by OEO, and subsequently by the Office of Child Development (OCD; the forerunner of the current Administration on Children, Youth and Families [ACYF]), academic researchers conducted many studies in an independent, uncoordinated fashion. Interested in a less-scattered approach, and hoping for a research effort that would be more sustained and better coordinated, in 1967 OCD created the Head Start Evaluation and Research (E&R) Centers. They combined research, evaluation, and technical assistance, through contracts with 14 university-based research scientists to conduct both investigator- and agency-initiated evaluations as well as to provide technical assistance to Head Start grantees in particular geographic areas. Institutions included Bank Street College; Boston University; University of California, Los Angeles; University of Chicago; Columbia University; University of Kansas; University of South Carolina; Southern University; Temple University; University of Texas; Tulane University; and others. Edmund Gordon (1979), Head Start's research director from 1966 to 1967, advocated for "some protection of self-initiated, even maverick work" (p. 403). This approach employed funding criteria that were more relaxed than customary for federal contracts during a time of increased federal accountability. The centers were soon eliminated.

The other major evaluation contemporaneous with the Westinghouse/Ohio study was the Educational Testing Service (ETS) Longitudinal Study, also begun in 1968. The OEO research committee believed the ETS study would be superior to the Westinghouse/Ohio study because of its longitudinal design, its intent to examine a broad range of developmental achievements, and its plan "to assess the extent to which individual program characteristics could account for differential impact across different program sites" (Bronfenbrenner, 1979, p. 88). ETS selected four sites and began following 1,650 3.5-year-olds through third grade. In the ensuing decade, a large number of reports fulfilled the original intentions, yet the findings lacked the coherence needed for clear conclusions about the national program's effectiveness.

Short-Term Studies and Enduring Legacies

Partly in response to disappointing findings from the Westinghouse/Ohio and other studies, in 1973 OCD contracted with the RAND Corporation to design a comprehensive evaluation of Head Start. At the outset, the RAND researchers noted that Head Start had "in fact, been exposed to more critical scrutiny than almost any other single federal program" (Raizen & Bobrow, 1974, p. 4). The authors went on to note that in the first 4 years of the program, OEO joined with the Bureau of the Census to do a descriptive study. The agencies surveyed a nationally representative sample of Head Start centers to measure compliance with program guidelines (overall compliance was high). Many small-scale evaluations were conducted, as previously noted, but they contained such diversity in their samples, measures, and evaluation designs that few clear conclusions could be drawn. However, one review team concluded that although children often showed gains on cognitive and affective measures during their

Head Start year, "virtually all the follow-up studies found that any differences . . . between the Head Start and control groups . . . were largely gone by the end of the first year of school" (Williams & Evans, 1972, p. 253). Thus, alarm about "fade-out" arose early.

During this period, in addition to the large-scale Westinghouse/Ohio study, the first meta-analysis of Head Start data was completed. This analysis of evaluations conducted by the E&R Centers in 1967–1968 and 1968–1969 was unfortunately hampered by highly selective samples (Research Triangle Institute, 1972; System Development Corporation, 1972). It is clear that Head Start research since this early period has made a number of strides toward increasing methodological rigor. One important legacy of this period, however, is the principle that evaluations should attempt to understand the kinds of programs that would produce the greatest gains—beginning to address the question of "What works for whom?"

An early consequence of this focus was a study of well-defined curriculum models known as the Head Start Planned Variation study (Klein, 1971). Beginning in 1969, eight curriculum developers implemented their models in multiple communities. These studies were plagued by inadequate measures (particularly in the social–emotional domain) and nonequivalent comparison groups; no clear conclusions emerged to guide program design. Thirty-five years later (2003–2005) the Administration for Children and Families (ACF) began an effort to design new planned variation studies to learn about the effectiveness of enhanced Head Start services.

But Head Start was (and is) more than classroom curricula. Two derivatives of the basic Head Start preschool model began in the late 1960s, focusing on opposite ends of the age spectrum: Parent and Child Centers (PCCs) and Follow Through. In 1967, 36 PCCs were funded to serve families and their children from birth to age 3. The PCCs continued as a small service-delivery model until 1995, when they were folded into the new Early Head Start program. Follow Through, also begun in 1967, was designed to apply the comprehensive services approach of Head Start in the kindergarten-to-third-grade years. The operation of Follow Through was assumed by the Office of Education in the Department of Health, Education and Welfare (DHEW) and continued in the U.S. Department of Education until 1999. Although not strictly speaking demonstration programs, these initiatives foreshadowed what was to become one of the most significant contributions of Head Start—an ongoing series of demonstration programs to test new programmatic strategies that began in the early 1970s and has continued to the present day.

The Demonstration Program Strategy

"I have always thought of Head Start not as a static program, but as an evolving concept," Zigler recalled in *Head Start: The Inside Story of America's Most Successful Educational Experiment.*

> So I tried to dazzle people with all types of new demonstration projects. . . .
> I wanted Congress and the public to associate both Head Start and OCD

with such a blur of useful activity that the administration would not dare close them down." (Zigler & Muenchow 1992, p. 150)

Datta (1976) suggested that the results of the Westinghouse/Ohio evaluation contributed to OCD's emphasizing experimentation with new programmatic ideas and strategies before adopting large-scale programs. Whether or not this was the reason, when Zigler became the first director of OCD, "He urged that Head Starts become centers of innovation, trying out new ways, and seeking many alternatives" (Datta 1976, p. 150). In the early 1970s, OCD launched a major strategy for learning about new initiatives before they became widespread. Dubbed the "Head Start I&I (improvement and innovation) effort," several demonstration programs were begun, evaluated, and where warranted, extended into national initiatives. These included Parent and Child Development Centers (PCDC; 1970–1975, 3 sites[3]); the first Health Start program (1971, 29 projects; with its "Healthy, That's Me" curriculum); the Home Start Demonstration (1972–1975, 16 grantees); the Child Development Associate credentialing program (1972, with 13 pilot projects established in 1973 and the first credentials awarded in July 1975); the Head Start Supplementary Training program to improve personnel preparation; mainstreaming handicapped children (10 pilot projects in 1972 followed by a congressional mandate that handicapped children shall make up at least 10% of Head Start enrollment, and 14 Resource Access Projects); Education for Parenthood (1972, eventually spreading to 3,000 schools); Child and Family Resource Program (1973–1983, 11 sites); Project Developmental Continuity (1974–1978, 15 grantees); and the Basic Educational Skills demonstration (1978, 18 programs).

Illustrative of these initiatives, OCD funded 16 Home Start demonstration sites and simultaneously began an evaluation with a randomized experimental design. OCD's purpose was to demonstrate "alternative ways of providing Head Start-type comprehensive services for young children in their homes" (Love, Nauta, Coelen, Hewett, & Ruopp, 1976, p. 1). Home Start director Ann O'Keefe was relentless in her mission to learn as much as possible from the evaluation to help shape the new program. For example, as soon as evaluators reported analyses showing that child impacts lessened as home visitor caseloads increased beyond 12 families, she issued a program memorandum with new guidelines limiting caseloads. Further, she promoted a Head Start "home-based option" so that home visiting strategies would be available to all Head Start programs when the evaluation demonstrated strong child and family impacts. By 1975, 283 grantees had been funded to operate the new home-based option, and OCD funded six Home Start Training Centers to train their home visitors. A decade later more than 500 grantees had adopted the new home-based option as a strategy for serving some or all of their families (Meleen, Love, & Nauta, 1988).

To respond to concerns that the many evaluation studies being funded often lacked measures of child outcomes that had sufficient reliability and validity in the Head Start context, in 1977 OCD began the groundbreaking *measures project*. Officially known as the Head Start Profiles of Program Effects on Chil-

---

[3]Three of the PCCs were selected to become research sites and renamed PCDCs; they operated for 5 years and then three replication sites were implemented.

dren project, this 5-year undertaking had the ambitious goal of revamping the way Head Start evaluations both conceptualized and measured the important program outcomes. The project, for a variety of reasons, never achieved its far-ranging goals (see Raver & Zigler, 1991). Nevertheless, it raised awareness of measurement issues and aided those who, responding to Zigler's notion of "social competence," sought support for focusing on the full spectrum of developmental outcomes (Mediax Associates, 1980).

By the end of the 1980s, Head Start had stimulated an astounding amount of research. Some observers even suggested that negative conclusions from the 1960s had been largely overcome. And a report to the President on the occasion of Head Start's 15th anniversary suggested that the program may have owed its survival to its evaluation component (U.S. Department of Health and Human Services [USDHHS], 1980).

Emergence of Social Competence as the Defining Goal of Head Start

It is not possible to leave the early days of Head Start without noting the substantial contribution to Head Start's approach to conceptualizing outcomes that resulted from Zigler's introduction of the concept of *social competence*. Head Start began with, and has consistently embraced, broad objectives for children's development as well as for family and community goals. One criticism of the Westinghouse/Ohio evaluation was that it concentrated on narrow cognitive outcomes. As director of OCD, Zigler had a very practical argument: Head Start's goal should be to enable children to function effectively in the environments where they need to succeed. His notion of social competence, frequently misinterpreted to mean only social behavior or social–emotional development, was codified in the first Head Start program standard in the 1973 *OCD–Head Start Policy Manual* to mean the following:

> Social competence means the child's everyday effectiveness in dealing with his environment and later responsibilities in school and life. Social competence takes into account the interrelatedness of cognitive and intellectual development, physical and mental health, nutritional needs, and other factors that enable a child to function optimally. (Raizen & Bobrow, 1974)

This conception of outcomes for children defined to span the major domains of growth and development has influenced Head Start research and evaluation studies ever since. For example, when RAND Corporation was awarded a contract to design a new national evaluation, it began with social competence as the critical outcome (Raizen & Bobrow, 1974). The Head Start measures project, already cited, adopted social competence as its starting point (Mediax Associates, 1980). The Family and Child Experiences Survey (FACES), the Early Head Start evaluation, and the national Head Start Impact Study (HSIS) are collecting data across these broad domains of development; the National Education Goals Panel specified five dimensions of early development and learning (Kagan, Moore, & Bredekamp, 1995); and many states concerned with assessing children's readiness for school acknowledge the importance of considering *readiness* as a broad developmental construct (Rhode Island KIDS COUNT, 2003).

The Growing Research Agenda

The 1990s ushered in a time of great expansion of the Head Start program as well as the research agenda. While continuing demonstration and field initiated efforts, the Head Start research agenda was expanded during the 1990s to include studies of nationally representative samples addressing issues of program quality, child and family outcomes, links between quality and outcomes, as well as impacts of the program. In 1992, under the leadership of Commissioner Wade Horn, ACYF began its series of biennial research conferences. These meetings provide a continuing forum for researchers, practitioners, and policymakers to share their latest findings and discuss associated policy issues.

The research agenda has been influenced by several factors, including expert advisory panels appointed at crucial times, congressional mandates, as well as issues of expansion and changing demographics within the Head Start program. We now review these external factors in more detail, note the continuation of demonstration projects, describe three major ongoing national studies, and present Head Start's vision of an integrated long-term research agenda.

The Role of Advisory Panels

In shaping the overall approach toward an expanded Head Start research agenda, ACYF relied on several expert advisory panels. Three pivotal panels were the Advisory Panel for the Head Start Evaluation Design Project (also known as the Blueprint Committee) in 1990; the Advisory Committee on Head Start Quality and Expansion in 1993 (USDHHS, 1993); and the 1994 National Academy of Sciences Roundtable on Head Start Research (Phillips & Cabrera, 1996). Taken together, these panels made broad recommendations for building a strong and enduring infrastructure for research that would ensure a leadership role for Head Start and that would place Head Start in the broader context of research on young children, families, and communities. Recommendations urged Head Start to focus on quality and other policy issues, conduct longitudinal studies of the gains for children and families, and establish researcher–practitioner partnerships for better communication and better use of data. Several recommendations noted the changing economic landscape as they sought to explore the challenges of increasing ethnic and linguistic diversity among the families served; to embed Head Start research within programs' community contexts, paying specific attention to violent environments; and consider the structure of income support policies for the poor and what it means to offer families a high-quality program. In sum, these advisory bodies advocated an expanded role for research in program planning, stressing the need for integration among programmatic questions, research, and program improvement activities. An enduring theme was to address questions about which Head Start practices maximize benefits for children and families with different characteristics under diverse circumstances.

Continuing the Tradition of Demonstration Programs

In the space available we cannot review all Head Start demonstration programs, but it is important to note that the impetus that started in the 1970s continued into the 1980s and beyond, although demonstrations became less frequent as the national studies described next took precedence. The Head Start Family Child Care Homes demonstration provides a recent example. ACYF had been funding family child-care projects within Head Start since 1984 through the Locally Designed Options (and in 1985 through Innovative Projects). Realizing the importance of full-day services for working mothers, Head Start considered providing this option more widely but wanted, first, to find out whether such services could meet the Program Performance Standards. Therefore, in fall 1992, ACYF funded eighteen 3-year family child-care demonstration projects, and contracted for an evaluation (ACYF, 2000a). As a consequence of generally positive outcomes, the Head Start Bureau created family child care as an official program option.

In 1988 Congress enacted the Comprehensive Child Development Centers Act to create an alternative approach to traditional human services delivery. Although technically not part of Head Start (being independently authorized by the 1988 Act), the Comprehensive Child Development Program built on earlier programs, both within Head Start and beyond, including the Parent Child Centers, the Child and Family Resource Program, and the Beethoven Project, a nonfederal, family-centered program in Chicago. It was administered by the Head Start Bureau within ACYF and implemented as a 24-site demonstration program in 1989 and 1990, with a second cohort of 10 projects funded in 1992 and 1993. They embodied the goals and approaches of family support programs (Hubbell et al. 1991).

In 1990, Congress authorized a new program designed to enhance the transitions of Head Start children and their families into public school. ACYF funded 31 Head Start/Public School Transition demonstration programs in fall 1991 to promote the use of developmentally appropriate practices and ensure continuity in children's educational experiences as they entered kindergarten following their Head Start experience. Educational activities were supported by parent involvement, family support services, and health and nutrition programs. The programs, which eventually involved more than 450 schools, operated until the 1997–1998 school year. The evaluation, consistent with other Head Start demonstration program studies, examined program implementation to learn about programs' challenges and successes and assessed children's progress from kindergarten through third grade (ACYF, 2000b). The tradition of demonstration program studies has continued into the 1990s, as will be seen in the final section of this chapter.

The Role of Congressional Mandates and Specific Studies: The 1994 Reauthorization

In the context of a vision of an expanding role for Head Start research, Congress mandated several specific studies. In the 1994 reauthorization, these included longitudinal studies designed to examine progress that children and families make during their time in the program and beyond. The law also mandated the development of program performance measures for Head Start (see Human Services Reauthorization Act of 1994). The act defines *program performance measures* as "methods and procedures for measuring, annually and over longer periods, the quality and effectiveness of programs operated by Head Start agencies" (§ 9836a, a(3)(b)) that will be used to identify strengths and weaknesses in the Head Start program—both nationally and by region—and to pinpoint areas requiring additional training and technical assistance.

As part of the performance measures initiative, and to provide information for Head Start in compliance with requirements of the Government Performance and Results Act of 1993, FACES was launched in the fall of 1997. FACES is a recurring longitudinal study of representative samples of Head Start children and families. The first cohort was identified in 1997, followed by others in 2000, 2003, and 2006. Children and families are followed during their Head Start experience (for 1 or 2 years) and through the child's kindergarten year with a broad array of child and family assessments. When possible, nationally normed assessments are used to allow comparisons of Head Start children with national averages. This descriptive study is answering many types of questions, permitting Head Start to learn about the characteristics of children and families served, what progress occurs during their Head Start experience, and how services (their quantity and quality) and community and family characteristics are associated with this progress. FACES research also documents the quality and quantity of Head Start services used by children and families and how characteristics of programs, children, and families (as well as children's progress in the program) vary across the waves of FACES. Do families served by Head Start change over time? Does quality or type of service (along with child outcomes) change with policy changes?

FACES was groundbreaking on many fronts. For the first time, it provided Head Start with the capacity to report on important aspects of outcomes, quality, and practices beyond the aggregated, administrative data the Head Start Bureau traditionally collected through its annual Program Information Report (PIR). Indeed, FACES enables Head Start to examine all facets of key outcomes and children's school readiness on an ongoing basis.

The 1994 amendment of the Head Start Act (Human Services Reauthorization Act of 1994) also instituted a new programmatic effort aimed at pregnant women and families with infants and toddlers, which later became known as Early Head Start. At the same time Congress authorized this new program, it also mandated the evaluation. So, unlike the preschool Head Start program— which went almost 40 years without a rigorous impact evaluation—the Early Head Start program began with such an effort (which we discuss later).

The Role of Congressional Mandates and Specific Studies: The 1998 Reauthorization

In 1998, the U.S. General Accounting Office released a report recommending that the USDHHS conduct "a study or studies that will definitively compare the outcomes achieved by Head Start children and their families with those achieved by similar non-Head Start children and families" (USGOA, 1998, p. 8). Following this recommendation, in the 1998 reauthorization of Head Start, Congress mandated a study, with an expert panel to recommend its design, to provide a "national analysis" of the impact of Head Start.

The HSIS is a rigorous prospective experimental impact evaluation of the Head Start program. Children and families were randomly assigned to the program or control group after they applied to the program. Five thousand children and families across 75 nationally representative grantee–delegate agency groups are participating in the study. To lessen the burden of random assignment on any one program, it was decided to include a large number of programs with a small number of children per site, and to have 60% assigned to the program group and 40% to the control group. The study is assessing children while they are in Head Start and following them into first grade. A broad range of child development and family functioning outcomes is being assessed, as is the quality of program and control children's Head Start and early care settings.

The HSIS has two primary goals. The first is to determine, with a nationally representative sample, the impact of Head Start on the school readiness of children and the well-being of families participating in the program compared with children not enrolled in Head Start. The second goal is to determine under which conditions Head Start works best and for which children.

Current and Future Research Activities

Today, the office overseeing Head Start research, the Office of Planning, Research and Evaluation, has an extensive array of ongoing studies, including the national studies reviewed in this chapter as well as studies of special populations (programs serving migrant and seasonal farm worker families and programs serving American Indian and Alaskan Native families) and grants to the research community and interagency agreements with other government agencies to supplement other national research with relevance for Head Start. (See http://www.acf.hhs.gov/programs/opre for more information.) Grants and cooperative agreements include field-initiated research (Head Start–university partnerships) as well as consortia aimed at specific topics, including the development of programmatic strategies (Child Outcomes Research and Support Consortium and the Early Promotion and Intervention Research Consortium) and planned variation random assignment studies (Quality Research Centers). To place Head Start research in the broader context of what is known about Head Start-eligible children and families, ACF also has supplemented national studies being conducted by other departments. These collaborations with the National Institute of Child Health and Human Development (NICHD; the NICHD Study of Early Child Care) and the Department of Education (Early Childhood Longitudinal Studies, Birth and Kindergarten cohort studies) have ensured a sharing of measures, methods, and knowledge. The most recent collaboration has been the Interagency Early Childhood Initiative, a joint effort of NICHD, ACF, the Office of the Assistant Secretary for Planning and Evaluation, and the National Institute of Mental Health in the USDHHS, and the Office of Special Education and Rehabilitative Services in the U.S. Department of Education. The initiative supports research on the effectiveness of interventions, programs, and curricula in promoting school readiness for children from birth through age 5. Together, these research components create an integrated research agenda.

The Role of Research in Program Development and Expansion: The Early Head Start Example

Early Head Start, the most recent addition to the Head Start family of programs, illustrates an approach to program development that has been coordinated with and informed by research. We offer it as an example in part because of our experience in conducting the Early Head Start research and evaluation project over the past 10 years and in part because it manifests a vision for a hand-in-hand linkage between research and program development promoted in an earlier era by expert advisors (among them, Ed Zigler).

As noted earlier, a major impetus to begin Early Head Start with research was the language in the 1994 legislation calling for evaluation of the new Head Start program for infants and toddlers, language that was strengthened by 1998 legislation requiring the impact study for Early Head Start and a plan to link the report to decisions about subsequent program expansion.

Although the evaluation was mandated, the vision for Early Head Start research (as well as for the program) was provided by the Advisory Committee on Services for Families With Infants and Toddlers, the committee of experts that provided principles, cornerstones, and the name for Early Head Start (USDHHS, 1994). Three decades of Head Start research and expert advisory committees were drawn together in the committee's recommendations for Early Head Start research. The committee members, including Ed Zigler, recommended ongoing research instituted systematically to address questions to inform program development. Whereas many on the committee argued that there already was sufficient evidence for effectiveness of this type of program, others suggested the burden of proof would be on Early Head Start to demonstrate effects. The committee recommended that the research quickly move to follow the recommendations of the earlier Blueprint Committee to study "for whom and under what circumstances" the program is effective, to build capacity in local communities through program–research partnerships to systematically use program data at the local level, and to use research to address specific areas in which the program needs improvement. Timely and focused research would support program excellence, creating an upward spiral of ever-increasing program excellence, both locally and nationally.

Following the guide of the advisory committee and prior committees, and with the legislative mandates in mind, ACYF launched a program of research for Early Head Start in conjunction with the roll out of the new program. The full program of research included designs to address eight questions of importance to the new Early Head Start program.

What do we know about the program descriptively? Today, more than 700 Early Head Start programs serve some 65,000 families. The Early Head Start research agenda builds from a descriptive base including in-depth information from the national study conducted in 17 sites selected to reflect the diversity and characteristics of all Early Head Start programs funded, more general descriptive information from the PIR collected from all Head Start and Early Head Start programs, and a survey of all Early Head Start programs conducted in 2005. The national study included an in-depth descriptive implementation study that provided some of the earliest information about the new program's development; suggested directions for early training and technical assistance; and, specifically, enabled a quick turn around for infusions related to child care, given changes in service needs due to welfare reform (ACF, 2002b; ACYF, 1999, 2000b, 2000c, and 2002d).

Does the program demonstrate overall impacts? ACYF implemented a rigorous random assignment design, involving 3,001 children and families in 17 communities, through a national contractor (Mathematica Policy Research and Columbia University) who, with 15 local research partners of the local programs, made up the Early Head Start Research Consortium. The final report from the national study (ACF, 2002a; Love et al., 2005) demonstrated that the program had modest significant impacts across a wide array of child development, parenting, and parent self-sufficiency outcomes. Impacts were notably larger in some subgroups.

Under what conditions is the program effective? The next level of question addressed variation in program models (whether home-based, center-based, or a mixture of home- and center-based services), and the extent to which new programs were implementing the program as designed. Given that programs must select models on the basis of community needs, participants in each program model must be compared with their own control groups. Doing so, the Early Head Start study demonstrated that all program models showed positive child and family impacts but that the pattern of impacts varied somewhat across the program models. By studying implementation within the impact study, the research could also address whether being "proud" affected outcomes. (Zigler often quoted Donald Campbell's dictum that programs should not be held accountable for outcomes until the programs were proud of their efforts.) Early and full implementation led to the broadest impacts. Furthermore, full implementation of the program model that combined center-based and home-visiting services (the *mixed approach* in the research nomenclature) led to the strongest pattern of impacts found in the study, offering impetus to a trend seen among programs to provide both center- and home-based services (ACF, 2002b; Love et al., 2005). The findings also underscored the importance of the Revised Head Start Program Performance Standards (USDHHS, 1996), the basis for ratings of implementation.

For whom is the program effective? Research advisory groups had long recommended disentangling Head Start effects by subgroups, noting that the extreme heterogeneity of the Head Start population made interpretation of effects difficult and that important effects (or their lack) for some subgroups were likely to be obscured. The Early Head Start study demonstrated that the program had impacts for most (23 of 27) population subgroups identified, and that child and family impacts were greater for several subgroups, including families enrolled during pregnancy, families at moderate levels of demographic risk, and African American families. These analyses also revealed that the program was not effective for families who experienced the highest levels of demographic risk. The findings were used by the program to enhance recruitment during pregnancy and to intensify the service package for families at highest levels of risk.

How does research suggest new practices in areas of ineffectiveness or to enhance impacts? The national study provided a working base for new hypotheses for program improvement. The Early Head Start program of research includes three vehicles for probing deeper to better understand mechanisms of intervention, deficiencies, strengths, and mediators and moderators of impacts. These include studies at each of the national study research sites, secondary analyses of the Early Head Start national study data, and systematic study in focused areas through new funding for Early Head Start–university partnerships. For example, a new consortium of five grantees, known as the Early Prevention and Intervention Research Consortium, explores critical mental health interventions found earlier to be an area in which Early Head Start services required intensification.

How can research aid program development on a continuing basis? The results from the national study have influenced many developments and training initiatives in the Early Head Start program, a few of which have been mentioned. Research findings have also influenced new initiatives in areas related to mental health, child care, father involvement, and child welfare. For example, the Early Head Start father studies added impetus for funding (in early 2001) 21 Early Head Start Fatherhood Demonstration grantees with local Offices of Child Support Enforcement. A descriptive evaluation study has documented challenges, successes, and best practices (Burwick, Bellotti, & Nagatoshi, 2004). Similarly, demonstration grants support 26 Early Head Start programs to form partnerships with child welfare agencies to strengthen supports for children whose early life situations bring them into the child welfare system (funded in fall 2002). In 2004, the Head Start Bureau funded 24 Early Head Start grantees to participate in the Enhanced Home Visiting Pilot Project, an initiative to develop and implement strategies for improving the quality of infant and toddler child care provided by relatives and other informal caregivers. Each of these demonstration programs has been accompanied by an evaluation. Furthermore, the results of the national study have informed the development of Program Performance Measures for Head Start programs serving infants and toddlers (Early Head Start and Migrant Head Start), by highlighting the areas of expected outcomes for children and families (see http://www.acf.hhs.gov/programs/opre).

However much the national program may be making timely improvements, based in part on research findings, the Advisory Committee on Services for Families with Infants and Toddlers recommended more—for research to be employed at each local program so that programs engage in annual, data-driven, continuous-improvement feedback loops. Early on, the application for Early Head Start funds called for local research–program partnerships to fulfill this purpose, and the national study included local research partners in each site. The new work in performance measures and program-friendly assessments will provide programs with much-needed frameworks and tools to complete their own continuous improvement efforts.

What are the long-term effects of the program? The study of developmental trajectories of children under various intervention scenarios provides vital understanding for policy and science. The Early Head Start longitudinal study complements the program of research and is studying the developmental status and environmental supports of children immediately before kindergarten entry. Initial results from this study are expected to inform children's transitions from Early Head Start to preschool early childhood programs.

How can Early Head Start continue the progress toward program excellence? The vision that has accumulated from Head Start advisory committees over 2 decades suggests that a program of research offers the optimal way to conduct research with the aim of enhancing programmatic development. Such a program of research completes a cycle from descriptive understanding of the program, to understanding overall impacts, to understanding under what conditions and for whom the program has impacts, to learning more about populations and conditions under which the program is not (or is less) effective—and cycles all the information in a timely fashion back into the programs locally and nationally so that adjustments can be made. Such a model suggests that research findings have the potential to contribute to the agency's efforts to achieve program excellence. Such has been the model in the development of the Early Head Start program.

Closing Thoughts

Since 1965, Head Start has sponsored, stimulated, promoted, and inspired thousands of studies by thousands of researchers with highly varied research interests. We have not attempted to describe all the studies conducted without federal funding, as important as they may be, but have focused on the history of the federal research initiative. Throughout this period, Head Start research has been characterized by a variety of approaches to learning whether programs were operating as they were intended and achieving their desired effects, with both purposes often combined in the same research study. More important, however, has been the emergence of a program of research. Since the early 1990s, Head Start research has continued to include demonstration studies but now integrates them into a cycle of research that includes descriptive studies, impact evaluations, and feedback to programs for continuous improvement. Today, the impact studies may be more effective than those of earlier years, as ACF has added several national, large-scale studies based either on nationally representative samples or samples sufficiently reflective of the national population of programs and families that meaningful policy conclusions can be drawn. Although the founders of Head Start expressed interest in learning not just whether programs worked but how and for whom they worked best, detailed investigations of these questions have grown and become more central since the mid-1990s. As we see in the case of Early Head Start, the findings have become even more directly linked to program features, their changes over time, and continuous improvement. When Head Start was just 13 years old, Zigler and Valentine (1979) described the program as a legacy of the War on Poverty. Today, it is clear that 40 years of research funded and stimulated by Head Start has created its own legacy.

References

Administration for Children and Families. (2002a). *Making a difference in the lives of infants and toddlers and their families: The impacts of Early Head Start.* Washington, DC: U.S. Department of Health and Human Services.

Administration for Children and Families. (2002b). *Pathways to quality and full implementation in Early Head Start programs.* Washington, DC: U.S. Department of Health and Human Services.

Administration on Children, Youth and Families. (1999). *Leading the way: Characteristics and early experiences of selected Early Head Start programs: Vol. I. Cross-site perspectives.* Washington, DC: U.S. Department of Health and Human Services.

Administration on Children, Youth and Families. (2000a). *Evaluation of Head Start Family Child Care Demonstration: Final report.* Washington, DC: U.S. Department of Health and Human Services.

Administration on Children, Youth and Families. (2000b). *Head Start children's entry into public school: A report on the national Head Start/Public Early Childhood Transition Demonstration study.* Washington, DC: U.S. Department of Health and Human Services.

Administration on Children, Youth and Families. (2000c). *Leading the way: Characteristics and early experiences of selected Early Head Start programs. Executive summary.* Washington, DC: U.S. Department of Health and Human Services.

Administration on Children, Youth and Families. (2000d). *Leading the way: Characteristics and early experiences of selected Early Head Start programs: Vol. III. Program implementation.* Washington, DC: U.S. Department of Health and Human Services.

Bronfenbrenner, U. (1979). Head Start, a retrospective view: The founders. In E. Zigler & J. Valentine (Eds.), *Project Head Start: A legacy of the War on Poverty* (pp. 77–88). New York: Free Press.

Burwick, A., Bellotti, J., & Nagatoshi, C. (2004, October). *Paths to father involvement: The Early Head Start fatherhood demonstration in its third year.* Princeton, NJ: Mathematica Policy Research.

Cicirelli, V. G. (1969). *The impact of Head Start: An evaluation of the effects of Head Start on children's cognitive and affective development* (Vols. 1–2). Washington, DC: National Bureau of Standards, Institute for Applied Technology.

Comprehensive Child Development Centers Act of 1988, Pub. L. No. 100-297 (1988).

Datta, L. E. (1976). The impact of the Westinghouse/Ohio evaluation on the development of Project Head Start: An examination of the immediate and longer-term effects and how they came about. In C. C. Abt (Ed.), *The evaluation of social programs* (pp. 129–181). Beverly Hills, CA: Sage.

Gordon, E. W. (1979). Evaluation during the early years of Head Start. In E. Zigler & J. Valentine (Eds.), *Project Head Start: A legacy of the War on Poverty* (pp. 399–404). New York: Free Press.

Government Performance and Results Act of 1993. Pub. L. No. 103-63 (1993).

Hubbell, R. (1983). *A review of Head Start research since 1970 and an annotated bibliography of the Head Start research since 1965.* Washington, DC: CSR.

Hubbell, R., Cohen, E., Halpern, P., DeSantis, J., Chaboudy, P., Titus, D., et al. (1991). *Comprehensive Child Development Program—a national family support demonstration.* Washington, DC: CSR.

Human Services Reauthorization Act of 1994. Pub. L. No. 103-252 (1994).

Kagan, S. L., Moore, E., & Bredekamp, S. (Eds.). (1995). *Reconsidering children's early development and learning: Toward common views and vocabulary.* Washington, DC: National Education Goals Panel, Goal One Technical Planning Group.

Klein, J. W. (1971). Planned variation in Head Start programs. *Children, 18*(1), 8–12.

Love, J. M., Kisker, E. E., Ross, C., Raikes, H., Constantine, J., Boller, K., et al. (2005). The effectiveness of Early Head Start for 3-year-old children and their parents: Lessons for policy and programs. *Developmental Psychology, 41*, 885–901.

Love, J. M., Nauta, M. J., Coelen, C. G., Hewett, K., & Ruopp. R. R. (1976). *National Home Start evaluation: Final report.* Ypsilanti, MI: High/Scope Educational Research Foundation and Abt Associates.

Mediax Associates. (1980). *Accept my profile! Perspectives for Head Start profiles of program effects on children: Vol. I. Technical report* (Rev. ed.). Westport, CT: Author.

Meleen, P. J., Love, J. M., & Nauta, M. J. (1988). *Study of the home-based option in Head Start: Final report* (Vol. I). Hampton, NH: RMC Research.

Phillips, D. A., & Cabrera, N. J. (Eds.). (1996). *Beyond the blueprint: Directions for research on Head Start's families.* Washington, DC: Roundtable on Head Start Research/Board on Children, Youths, and Families, National Research Council, and Institute of Medicine.

Raizen, S., & Bobrow, S. B. (1974). *Design for a national evaluation of social competence in Head Start children.* Santa Monica, CA: RAND.

Raver, C., & Zigler, E. (1991). Three steps forward, two steps back: Head Start and the measurement of social competence. *Young Children, 46*(4), 3–8.

Research Triangle Institute. (1972). *A report on two national samples of Head Start classes: Some aspects of child development of participants in full-year 1967–68 and 1968–69 programs.* Durham, NC: Author.

Rhode Island KIDS COUNT. (2003). *2003 Rhode Island KIDS COUNT factbook.* Providence, RI: Author.

Rivlin, A. (1974). *Social policy: Alternate strategies for the federal government.* Washington, DC: Brookings Institution Press.

System Development Corporation. (1972). *Effects of different Head Start program approaches on children of different characteristics: Report on analysis of data from 1968–1969 national evaluation: Technical memorandum.* Santa Monica, CA: Author.

U.S. Department of Health and Human Services, Fifteenth Anniversary Head Start Committee. (1980). *Head Start in the 1980s. Review and recommendations: A report requested by the President of the United States.* Washington, DC: Author.

U.S. Department of Health and Human Services. (1993). *Report of the advisory committee on Head Start quality and expansion.* Washington, DC: Author.

U.S. Department of Health and Human Services. (1994). *The statement of the advisory committee on services for families with infants and toddlers.* Washington, DC: Author.

U.S. Department of Health and Human Services, Administration for Children and Families (1996, November 15). Head Start program: Final rule. *Federal Register, 61*, 215.

U.S. General Accounting Office. (1998). *Head Start: Research insufficient to assess program impact* (GAO Rep. No. GAO/T-HEHS-98-126). Washington, DC: Author.

Williams, W., & Evans, J. (1972). The politics of evaluation: The case of Head Start. In P. H. Rossi & W. Williams (Eds.), *Evaluating social programs* (pp. 247–264). New York: Seminar Press.

Zigler, E., & Muenchow, S. (1992). *Head Start: The inside story of America's most successful educational experiment.* New York: Basic Books.

Zigler, E., & Valentine, J. (1979). *Project Head Start: A legacy of the War on Poverty.* New York: Free Press.

6

Beyond Baby Steps: Promoting the Growth and Development of U.S. Child-Care Policy

Susan Muenchow and Katherine W. Marsland

It is time to simplify and to organize a real child care system in America.

—Edward F. Zigler and Elizabeth Gilman (1993, p. 176)

In 1970, the White House Conference on Children named quality day care as the number one need of American families and children (White House Conference on Children, 1970). Despite much work in the ensuing 3 decades to improve the availability, quality, and affordability of child care in the United States, the central question raised more than a decade ago by Edward Zigler and Mary Lang (1991) remains as pertinent as ever: "How can we make the mixed system of child care in the United States an effective institution that supports families in their responsibilities?" (p. 26).

In this chapter we begin with an update on the status of child care and the baby steps that have been made in improving its quality, availability, and affordability in the United States. We then turn to a discussion of what would constitute giant steps toward creating a coherent high-quality early care and education system and the changes necessary to build the public support needed to achieve them. Finally, we offer a research agenda to inform such action.

Throughout the chapter the focus will be on *early care and education*, a term which in and of itself suggests some of the changes that have occurred in the American understanding of child care (i.e., that early care cannot be separated from early education, and that the two must be addressed together). Early care and education will be defined broadly here to include child-care centers, family child care, relative and informal care, Head Start, nursery schools, and school-based preschool programs for children from birth to 5 years. Although some of the programs began strictly to promote school readiness, the reality is that many families also rely on them as part of the package of child supervision that allows them to work. Similarly, even though infant and toddler care may once have been dismissed as babysitting, neurological research now confirms that a lot of education is going on in these settings; the only question is what quality of education. Although care for school-age children is no less important, the challenges specific to school-age child care are substantially different from those affecting early care and education; hence, they merit full discussion elsewhere.

Baby Steps: Progress in Improving Availability, Quality, and Affordability

Availability

The availability of child care has certainly increased, but access is uneven. As of 2002, there were more than 113,000 licensed centers and 300,000 regulated family child-care homes across the nation (Children's Foundation, 2002; Lombardi, 2003), reflecting roughly a 500% increase in licensed child-care centers and a 200% increase in regulated family child-care homes since 1979. However, pockets of unavailability of licensed care exist, particularly for infants and toddlers, children with special needs, school-age children, and children whose families work nontraditional hours (Lombardi, 2003). There are wide disparities in the availability of formal early care and education, and facilities are sometimes more lacking in low-to-middle income working areas than in the poorest neighborhoods, where a majority of the families qualify for publicly subsidized programs (Fuller, Kagan, Caspary, & Gauthier, 2002). Moreover, informal care may be less prevalent than previously thought, with nearly two thirds of welfare families having no friend or relative who could provide child care, and their access to formal arrangements limited by cost and transportation (Lombardi, 2003; Phillips, 1995)

Quality

Research over the last 3 decades has significantly advanced the definition and understanding of what constitutes quality child care and the importance of child care as a context for children's development (for comprehensive reviews of this literature, see Love, Schochet, & Mechstroth, 1996; Vandell & Wolfe, 2000). Today researchers know that good quality child care meets children's social, cognitive, physical, and emotional needs. Studies have shown that children's experiences are influenced by both process (e.g., positive caregiver's interactions with children) and structural (e.g., caregiver-to-child ratios and caregiver training) features. Further, quality of care is also related to caregiver compensation and turnover.

Edward Zigler recognized the importance of quality early care and in 1972 developed proposed revisions in the 1968 Federal Interagency Day Care Requirements (FIDCRs) that would have set standards for staff-to-child ratios based on the developmental needs of children at different ages; unfortunately, the revisions were never enacted and the FIDCRs were never enforced. In the absence of federal quality standards, the responsibility for establishing and enforcing quality requirements has rested at the state level.

There have been concerted efforts over the past 3 decades to improve structural features of child care, the only indicators of quality that can be regulated; and although safety and quality are still unreliable, some progress has been made. In 1979, the National Day Care Study (Ruopp, Travers, Glantz, & Coelen, 1979) reported that 15 states permitted 10 or more toddlers to be cared for by one caregiver, group size requirements varied widely, and training requirements were virtually nonexistent. Today, every state requires the licensure of center-based child care and most also license large family day-care homes. States have established monitoring programs for the enforcement of health and fire codes, as well as, in some cases, supplemental standards to address children's development (Phillips & Zigler, 1987). Staff-to-child ratio requirements for infant classrooms in centers have improved substantially: No state currently permits one adult to care for more than six infants, and the highest ratio for toddlers is 1:9 (Children's Foundation, 2002). Similarly, requirements governing group sizes have improved, with most states limiting group sizes for infants, toddlers, and preschoolers. Ongoing professional development and training requirements for caregivers and directors have also increased. For example, more states now require that caregivers participate in annual training, with the amount of training ranging from 3 to 25 hours (Azer, LeMoine, Morgan, Clifford, & Crawford, 2002). To strengthen the link between professional development and compensation, 22 states operate TEACH (Teacher Education and Compensation Helps) programs that provide scholarships to encourage further education and salary increases on completion of the education. More than 30 states have enacted some form of tiered licensing system to link increased funding for programs to the achievement of higher standards, such as national accreditation (National Child Care Information Center, 2002).

Despite these concerted efforts at quality improvements, field studies continue to paint an unflattering portrait of the safety—not to mention the quality—of both center and family child care. For example, the Cost, Quality and Outcomes Study found that the quality of most child-care centers is at best mediocre, with only 14% of the centers providing services of sufficient quality to promote healthy development and nearly 13% actually posing a threat to children's health and safety (Helburn & the Cost, Quality and Child Outcomes Team, 1995). Furthermore, 40% of the infant–toddler rooms in this study were found actually to pose risks to children's safety. Conditions in family child care— the preferred setting for infants and toddlers—are even more disturbing, with 35% found to pose harm and only 9% rated as promoting healthy development (Galinsky, Howes, Kontos, & Shinn, 1994). Thirty-nine states still do not require teachers in private settings to undergo any preservice training, and only half of the states that offer state-financed pre-K programs require teachers to have bachelor's degrees (Ackerman, 2003). Preschool teachers earn less than half of the salary of kindergarten teachers, and the gap between their salaries and those of other staff members with similar qualifications actually widens as their level of education increases (Barnett, 2003). Although the incentive structure represented by accreditation and tiered licensure and reimbursement clearly shows promise, even in the pioneering state of North Carolina only 3.5% of centers and 2.8% of family child-care homes are licensed at the five-star level (North Carolina Division of Child Development, personal communication, January 7, 2003).

Affordability

Public expenditures for early care and education have increased dramatically—quadrupling over the last decade alone—but quality child care is still not affordable for most families. Efforts to make early care and education more affordable have used different financing mechanisms for different income brackets, with subsidies as the mechanism for families near the poverty level and tax credits directed to more affluent families. Under the Child Care Development Fund (CCDF), states are allowed to establish income eligibility limits up to 85% of the state median income. All states have at least one child-care subsidy or assistance program designed to help low-income parents with the cost of care, with the primary goal of these programs to help parents become or stay employed and to prevent welfare dependency (Children's Defense Fund, 2000). The child and dependent care tax credit, commonly referred to as the *dependent care credit*, was enacted in 1976 and is the second largest source of federal child-care assistance (Donahue & Campbell, 2002).

Despite these important efforts, the average annual cost of child care for a 4-year-old in an urban area child-care center is higher than the average annual cost of public college tuition in all but one state, and the cost of infant care is even greater (Schulman, 2000). Meanwhile, no state has provided sufficient funding to support quality child care for all low-income families who need and request assistance. All but nine states set their income cut-offs for child-care assistance below the level allowed by the federal government (Administration on Children, Youth and Families, 2001). In addition, states have long waiting lists, low provider reimbursement rates, and parent copayment policies that directly or indirectly compromise affordability. As for the Dependent Care Tax Credit, three factors hinder its effectiveness: The credit is not refundable, leaving families who do not owe any tax ineligible for the credit; the maximum credit ($2,100 in tax year 2003) is paltry in the face of the child-care expenses incurred by most working families; and it is not indexed for inflation.

Giant Steps Toward Developing a System: Reframing Child Care

Many of these efforts to improve the quality, availability, and affordability of child care have met with success, at least within a limited locale. Some have been implemented in most every state, some in just a few, and some only in urban areas. If progress were being systematically tracked, one could view such varied child-care policy development as a natural experiment, enabling researchers to compare the costs and benefits of 51 or more different approaches to piecing together affordable access to good quality early care and education. However, in the absence of any systemic comparison data and analysis, the result is a "dizzying" (Phillips & McCartney, 2002) array of initiatives, some of which complement each other and many of which function at best in isolation and at worst in conflict.

What has been missing is the development of an early care and education system. As Gallagher and Clifford (2000) noted, there has been a striking "absence of a comprehensive infrastructure or support system to stand behind the delivery of services" (p. 1). By the term *system*, they mean a professionally trained and compensated workforce, boards to certify personnel, upgraded facilities to house programs, and the stable revenue sources to finance the services.

In *Not By Chance: Creating an Early Care and Education System for America's Children*, Kagan and Cohen (1997) defined an early care and education system as a combination of the programs that touch children and families and the infrastructure that acts behind the scenes to support programs—parent information and engagement, professional development and licensing, a stable funding source to help make child care affordable, and governance to ensure accountability.

Part of the problem has involved determining which level and which part of the government—federal or state, human services or education—should have the responsibility for child care. The closest this nation has come to the creation of a federal or national child-care system occurred more than 30 years ago. In 1971, when Edward Zigler was director of the Office of Child Development, Congress passed the Comprehensive Child Development Act (1971), which contained federal quality standards (the FIDCRs), money to train child care providers, and the allocation of funds to purchase child-care facilities (Zigler & Muenchow, 1992). Perhaps most revolutionary, the bill even stated that its purpose was to lay the groundwork for universal access to child care on a sliding fee scale. Unfortunately, Congress could not agree on whether the funds should flow directly from the federal government to local programs or pass through the states. President Nixon ultimately vetoed the legislation, which set back the prospects of any federal role in administering a child-care system for years to come. Subsequently, there have been numerous efforts to increase the federal funding for subsidized child care and to improve the quality, but the only real federal system of early education and care that has emerged is the Department of Defense's Child Development Program, which provides care to dependent children on a sliding fee scale and requires that providers meet minimum quality standards, based in part on the FIDCRs.

The primary focus on creating an early care and education system has moved to the state level, and to a model that might merge elements of child care as a human service and as an educational program. Beginning with the enactment of Smart Start in North Carolina in 1993, at least nine states have developed state- and county-based initiatives to develop a comprehensive system of early childhood services for children from birth to age 5. All but one is led by a state council or board comprising members from a variety of agencies and perspectives, and each one has provisions for local commissions or councils to oversee the administration of programs. Each of these state initiatives is in some way beginning to address how to create an early care and education system, but they differ greatly in their authority to control the allocation of resources and in their access to funds to invest in such a system.

Policy research has increasingly focused on how to create an early care and education system, especially one that builds on the considerable investment already made in the patchwork of fragmented efforts. A growing body of work is beginning to identify the characteristics of an early care and education system that is genuinely responsive to the needs of children and families and to estimate the time and resources needed to get there. On the basis of this body of work, as well as the lessons learned from the efforts to improve child care over the last 3 decades, we suggest that the major barrier to establishing a quality, affordable early care and education system is not a lack of knowledge concerning the components of quality or even a lack of funds to finance such a level of quality. Rather the major barrier is the lack of public will to do so. Reflecting on the efforts of the last 3 decades, it seems that progress beyond baby steps toward the development of a true early care and education system will require reframing the issue on the basis of three core principles.

Redefine the Constituency: Access for All

The early care and education system should be designed to provide access to all children whose families wish to enroll them. One of the main reasons the United States does not have an affordable, quality child-care system is that efforts to create a system have focused almost exclusively on the disadvantaged— children defined as being at risk and low-income working adults. Publicly supported child care has been touted as a means to help economically disadvantaged children get ready for school, to protect abused and neglected children from further harm, to help children with disabilities reach their full potential, to help teenage parents complete school, and, most of all, to help low-income adults avoid welfare and go to work. In short, child care has been presented as a compensatory program to help children and families with problems, rather than as a normal part of the lives of most young children and their families. Limiting programs to the disadvantaged has undermined the public will even to serve all of the targeted children, as is evident in the failure of the federal and state government to provide funds necessary to help families with incomes up to 85% of the state median income, as allowed under CCDF.

Edward Zigler correctly foresaw the downside of such a targeted approach as early as 1965 when he recommended a socioeconomic mix in Head Start. In part, Zigler's thinking was based on research indicating that task persistence, verbal skills, and self-concept of disadvantaged children improved more in Head Start classrooms that included children from more affluent homes (Boger, 1969). But his views were also based on the concern that it would prove difficult to define disadvantage and that focusing exclusively on the low-income families would generate resentment among many nonpoor families.

Three decades later, with 50% of infants and toddlers and three out of four preschool children in some form of nonparental care, many researchers and advocates are revisiting the role and responsibility of government with respect to child care. The question is no longer whether most young children will experience some form of nonparental care but rather what quality of care they will experience. Moreover, although there is evidence that disadvantaged children do benefit the most from early care and education, at one time or another, a growing number of children at some point in their lives may meet someone's definition of disadvantage. Children with one or more of the following risk factors—living in poverty, or in a single parent household, or with a mother who has less than a high school education, or in a family of English language learners—are two to three times more likely not to have kindergarten readiness skills according to an analysis of a study of 22,000 children entering kindergarten (Zil & West, 2000). Furthermore, two thirds of the children entering school in urban areas with populations of more than 250,000 have at least one of these risk factors (West, Denton, & Germino-Hausken, 2000).

The call for a universal approach to child care has expanded rapidly over recent years, primarily focusing on preschool for 4-year-old children, which is discussed in more detail in chapter 7 (this volume) on universal prekindergarten. Although only one state, Georgia, currently operates a truly universal preschool program open to all 4-year-old children, Florida has just enacted legislation requiring implementation of universal prekindergarten, and many other states, including California, Illinois, Massachusetts, New York, New Jersey, South Carolina, and Texas, have made or are planning substantial steps in this direction.

In 2002, the publication *Preschool for All: Investing in a Just and Productive Society,* by the Research and Policy Committee of the Committee for Economic Development, a group of more than 200 top business and education leaders, called on the United States to invest in universal access to preschool for all 3- and 4-year-old children: "It is time for the United States to acknowledge society's stake in and responsibility for early education, as it long has for older children, by making publicly-funded prekindergarten available to all preschool children whose parents want them to enroll" (p. viii).

Providing universal access to preschool and other forms of early care and education will not, of course, guarantee that the programs will be of high quality or even affordable. But the basic principle here is that providing access to all is a prerequisite for developing the public demand for quality, affordable services. Without the element of universality, it is unlikely that quality will ever be achieved.

Change the Paradigm: Early Learning and Education

The foundation of the early care and education system must be early learning. Another major reason why the United States does not have a quality early care and education system is that there has been reluctance to frame the issue as education. Child advocates have feared that an early education focus would lead to formal schooling for 4-year-old children—watered down kindergarten. Critics of linking child development programs with education have also pointed out that school hours do not match parents' work hours, and that any child-care system constructed on a school model would give family work needs short shrift. Thus, more than 25 years ago, when American Federation of Teachers president Albert Shanker said that child care was a job for the public schools, the early childhood community responded with a resounding no.

Unfortunately, the reluctance to emphasize the education in early care and education contributed to a custodial approach, a sense that child care involves little more than babysitting. The term *education* simply resonates more positively with the public than does the term *child care* (Farkas, Duffet, & Johnson,

2000). As Brauner, Gordic, and Zigler (2004) pointed out, Americans tend to see education as something for children and therefore worthy of public investment; in contrast, they view child care as a private and individual responsibility (Lakoff & Grady, 1998). Because the major policy goal of providing financial assistance for child care has been viewed as helping adults work, there has been little recognition of the tremendous amount of learning going on from birth, or of the fact that education is going on in all child care settings—the only question is what quality of education. As a result, neither the federal nor the state governments has invested the funds necessary to build the facilities, the organizational infrastructure, or, most important, the workforce that would be considered necessary to provide a quality education program.

Mindful of the missed opportunity, for more than a decade early childhood leaders have been encouraging a greater focus on child care as education. One of the first to make this shift was Bettye Caldwell, who coined the phrase *educare* and who recommended that the field abandon entirely the term *child care* (Caldwell, 1989). In 1989, Edward Zigler and Matia-Finn Stevenson proposed a system to link child care with education: the School of the 21st Century (for a more in-depth description of the model and its current status, see chap. 7, this volume). The program calls for implementing a child-care system within the existing educational system and—where possible—using available school buildings, already subsidized by taxpayers, as the hub for the coordination of high-quality programs for families and children from birth to age 12 (Zigler & Lang, 1991). Included in the model are two on-site components—all-day, year-round child care for preschoolers from age 3 to kindergarten entry, and before- and after-school care for school-age children. In this model, the School of the 21st Century also coordinates a network of family child-care homes to serve younger children, includes a resource and referral system to provide area families with information about other child-care facilities in the area, and a home-based family support and parent education program based on the Parents as Teachers program in Missouri. As Sheila Kamerman, a national and internationally known expert on child care, has noted, the main asset of the School of the 21st Century model is its connection with "an institution that's well-established, well accepted, known to parents and lends itself to universal access" (Reardon, 1989, p. B12).

More recently, the school readiness movement has further helped to reframe child care as education. Several studies in the late 1990s helped to link the quality of early care and education to school readiness. Children who attended higher quality child programs were found to do better in math and language in elementary school (National Institute of Child Health and Human Development [NICHD], 1999). Findings, according to the National Research Council report *Eager to Learn* (Bowman, Donovan, & Burns, 2000), indicated that children, especially those whose mothers have a low level of education, have better language ability, fewer behavior problems, and higher cognitive performance if they attend well-planned, quality early childhood programs. A study by the Smart Start Evaluation Team indicated that children participating in high-quality child-care programs score significantly better on language, book awareness, math, and counting skills than do children from low-quality centers (Bryant et al., 2003). Moreover, the child-care quality had an equally great impact on children from nonpoor and poor families, underscoring the importance of quality programs for all income groups.

As an outgrowth of the education accountability movement, states have begun to develop child outcome measures for early care and education programs that are based generally on the six developmental domains recognized by the National Educational Goals Panel for what children should know and be able to do upon kindergarten entry. The Child Development Division of California's Department of Education (2000), for example, has developed *Prekindergarten Learning and Development Guidelines* for center-based programs, and is now developing similar guidelines for infant and toddler programs and family child-care settings. In addition, the state requires every publicly funded child-development program, including contracted child-care centers as well as state preschool programs and school-age child-care programs, to be assessed annually on the basis of a system called Desired Results. Desired Results consists of a developmental profile that a teacher uses to observe each child's social and emotional, language, cognitive, and physical progress. At the same time that the department instituted Desired Results to measure children's progress, it also began to require the use of the Early Childhood Environment Rating Scale to track program performance in publicly funded child-development programs, including contracted child care-centers and state preschools. Similarly, Florida, as part of its 1999 school readiness legislation, established a readiness assessment system designed to measure children's status in approaches to learning, and language, cognitive, social–emotional, and physical development on entry into kindergarten. The legislation also requires pre- and postassessments of children in all publicly funded early care and education programs, whether operated by Head Start, schools, or private providers.

Another approach to reframing child care as education is modeled after the higher education system. Under this model, as described by Teresa Vast (2001), early care and education could continue in a variety of settings and operate under numerous auspices, but there would be a central financial aid system similar to that for higher education. Families would complete one standard application form, regardless of whether parents were applying for school- or community-based child care. There would be one central hub agency in the community, such as a resource and referral agency, which would provide information to families on the types of early care and education available, and at the same time process applications for aid. To participate in the financial aid system, programs would have to meet quality and accountability standards (e.g., accreditation). In addition to providing direct aid to families, such a model could also include grants to providers to cover part of the cost of care and loans or tax credits to help middle- and upper-income families pay the cost (Brandon, Kagan, & Joesch, 2000).

In summary, there are a variety of approaches to reframing child care as education that may or may not actually include formal linkage to the kindergarten–grade 12 public education system. Ultimately, a quality early childhood system must include both care and education. As Joan Lombardi (2003) wrote in *Time to Care*, settings for young children must have both the comfort of home and experiences to promote education across all developmental domains. Even though reframing child care as early education will not guarantee a quality early childhood system, it is the key to garnering the public support necessary to finance a well-trained and compensated workforce, an infrastructure necessary to support a quality system, and the financing to make services available to all children and families who wish to use them.

Redefine Early Education: Leave No Infant or Toddler Behind

Care for infants and toddlers—in its various permutations—should be integral to a systemic solution. The principles of universality and ties to education—in the broad sense of the term—apply to the child-care needs of infants and toddlers as much as they do to the older preschool period. Yet, especially in the early years, it is important that a child-care system be policy neutral as to whether families use out-of-home early care and education or in-home parent education. A coherent system needs to afford parents both the choice to stay home or work and the ability to pay for good quality early care.

According to the National Research Council and Institute of Medicine Report *From Neurons to Neighborhoods: The Science of Early Childhood Development* (Shonkoff & Phillips, 2000), early experience clearly affects brain development.

> During infancy, there is a pressing need to strike a better balance between options that support parents to care for their infants at home and those that provide affordable, quality child care that enables them to work or go to school. (p. 392)

The report called for expanding coverage of the Family and Medical Leave Act of 1993 to all working parents, pursuing the complex issue of income protection, lengthening the exemption period before states require parents of infants to work as part of welfare reform, and enhancing parents' opportunities to choose from among a range of child-care settings that offer the stable, sensitive, and linguistically rich caregiving that fosters positive early childhood development.

In 1991, Zigler and Lang proposed a universal child allowance that would allow parents either to stay home or to purchase quality care for their infants and toddlers. The allowance would be in the form of a cash benefit and would not be restricted by income eligibility. It would constitute a form of "social security for children" (Zigler & Lang, 1991, p. 215). Just as the Social Security Act of 1935 was based on the rationale of relieving the economic burden of supporting elderly and handicapped family members who could no longer support themselves, so too the child allowance would be designed to ease the financial burden of caring for young children. Similarly, Helburn and Bergmann (2002) have proposed a funding system that would require parental copayments of no more than 20% of the difference between a family's income and the federal poverty level. Together with refundable tax credits, such funding mechanisms would do much to enable parents to purchase quality early care for their infants and toddlers or opt to care for their children at home—particularly if these initiatives included financial incentives for selecting high-quality programs.

Recognizing the shortage of quality infant and toddler care, Lombardi (2003) proposed expanding Early Head Start and giving regular Head Start grantees the flexibility to serve children ages birth to 5 years, depending on the avail-ability of other services in the community. In this way, Head Start can play a much-needed leadership role in developing quality services for the age group that is currently most lacking.

Another promising approach to improving the quality of infant and toddler care is the family child-care provider network component of the School of the 21st Century model, and a similar approach is integral to the Department of Defense's child-care system. In both models, small, community-based providers are linked to professional training and development opportunities, resources, peer mentorship, and assistance in seeking national accreditation. In addition, as Lombardi (2003) pointed out, existing child-care research and referral sys-tems could be enhanced to improve outreach to and support of these providers.

The Next Wave of Child-Care Research: An Action Agenda

As Phillips and McCartney (2002) discussed, child-care research has progressed from questions concerning "main effects" of child care on children's develop-ment, to questions regarding the effects of quality of care, to analysis of the interactive effects of family and child characteristics in child care settings of various type and quality. This third wave of research is enormously promising in that it is characterized by large-scale, multisite studies involving multidisci-plinary collaborations including developmental psychologists, political scien-tists, economists, and sociologists.

Indeed, the literature of policy-relevant findings from these studies is grow-ing rapidly. For example, data from both the Cost, Quality, and Child Outcome and the NICHD studies have been submitted to economic models to examine the relative benefits of various indicators of caregiver training for both process measure of the caregiving environment and child outcomes (Blau, 2001).

To inform the movement toward universal access to quality early care and education, additional research is needed in the following areas.

Estimation of System Use, Costs, and Best Combination of Approaches to Achieve a System

If access to quality nonparental child care were truly available and affordable to all children from birth to school entry, how much and what type of child care would families use? If the affordable access to care for children birth to age 5 were accompanied by an alternative of the same amount of funds for a children's allowance, at least for infants and toddlers, which option would families choose? This question is pertinent because of the experience where access is available to all. In Georgia, where there is universal access to preschool for 4-year-olds, 70% of the eligible children are enrolled. In France, where there is voluntary, free preschool available for all children, virtually all 3- and 4-year old children are enrolled (Neuman & Peer, 2002). At the same time, perhaps because of the availability of benefits to help parents care for their children at home, only 35% of 2-year-old children are enrolled in preschool. In their project Financing Universal Early Care and Education for America's Children, Richard Brandon and Sharon L. Kagan have developed a demand module to predict use of care separately for each type of care (center, family child care, relative, parent) and each age group (infant, toddler, and preschool; Brandon et al., 2000).

How much would it cost to finance universal access to early care and education, at least for 3- and 4-year-old children, based on various levels of staff qualification and compensation and investments in infrastructure? And, to what extent would the return on investments in increased tax revenues from working parents help offset these costs? Again, Brandon and Kagan are developing a computer model to help states estimate the per-child cost of universal birth to age 5 care and education. The project entails a protocol that guides state-level stakeholders through the process of defining minimally acceptable and high-quality care by establishing goals for ratios, group sizes, caregiver training, education, compensation, and so forth. Now in its fourth year, the project has been piloted in Ohio; is underway in South Carolina, Illinois, and Mississippi; and is set to begin in four more states (Sharon L. Kagan, personal communication, January 20, 2003).

What is the cost of targeting early care and education to the disadvantaged? What percentage of the public funds for early care and education in the United States are spent on various levels of bureaucracy to determine eligibility based on the various state and federal rules for different programs? If preschool were available at no cost to all 3- and 4-year-old children, then how much of the cost of the early care and education would be offset by the decrease in the need for eligibility determination? Even if families continued to pay fees but financial aid was modeled after the higher education system as previously described, how much money currently spent on eligibility determination could be redirected toward direct services for children?

Given the basic problem of economics—scarcity and hence the necessity of choices—what is the best way to phase in universal access to quality early care and education? California's First 5 Children and Families Commission is committed to the principle of universal access to quality early care and education. But the cost of a full system, even for 3- and 4-year-olds, had been estimated at $5 billion, and the commission had only $200 million to invest in a School Readiness Initiative. The commission determined that it would begin by making the school readiness funds available to be spent on any child, regardless of family income, living in a priority school district, meaning a school with low scores on the Academic Performance Index. Will this approach be less stigmatizing and evolve more quickly into true universal system than a system that begins by targeting programs to individual children with certain risk characteristics?

Effective Strategies to Reframe Child Care as a System That Provides Nurture and Promotes School Readiness

How can policymakers build on the interest in financing part-day universal preschool to address both the school readiness of children and the work needs of their parents? As documented by a report by the Packard Foundation's Center for the Future of Children, many children of working families have been unable to access enriched preschool programs because the schools operated only part of the day (Gomby, Larner, Stevenson, Lewit, & Behrman, 1995). To what extent are states that have already significantly expanded access to preschool incorporating extended hours to meet the needs of working parents? What percentage of the children enrolled receive full-day services, how much are families paying for the extra hours, and how is the quality of the full-day program perceived?

Identifying Strategies to Improve the Quality and Availability of Infant and Toddler Care

What is the best way to obtain one of the major advantages of association with the formal education system—teachers with qualifications set at a level comparable to that of kindergarten teachers, with training in early childhood education, and better salaries and working conditions to contribute to a stable workforce? In *Not By Chance*, Kagan and Cohen (1997) recommended the licensing of all staff responsible for children in centers and family child care. To obtain licenses, teachers of 3- and 4-year-old children in public schools would have the option of obtaining public school teacher certification or the Early Childhood Educator license. The latter would require an associate or bachelor degree in early childhood education or child development.

If teachers in early care and education had bachelor's degrees and compensation equivalent to that of kindergarten teachers, then would it be possible to reduce staff-to-child ratios for the older end of the spectrum—4-year-olds—to 1:15 and achieve equally or more favorable outcomes for children than with a 1:8 or 1:10 staffing pattern with less well-trained personnel? How would these various program trade-offs affect cost? Given the deplorable staff-to-child ratios still allowed by many states for infant and toddler care, and the poor educational qualifications for most child-care programs serving preschool children, child advocates have been reluctant to raise this issue. But this may be, ironically, one of the keys to breaking the deadlock on quality.

Without question, the biggest challenge regarding the care of infants and toddlers is the affordability of good quality care. Indeed, purchasing good care for children, who need constant, individualized, nurturing and stimulating care, is so exorbitantly expensive that such care is truly beyond the means of many working parents. And yet, as has been noted repeatedly, the stimulation afforded by quality early care environments is essential to early brain development. Therefore, much research is needed to inform decision making regarding the relative costs and benefits of various quality enhancement strategies. In addition, policy research is needed to determine how quality infant and toddler care can be made more affordable for working parents. As noted, one possibility would be a child allowance that would partially subsidize the costs of nonparental care and that would provide a financial incentive for the selection of high-quality settings. Were such a system available, would parents actually choose better quality care?

Conclusion

It took nearly 100 years for the full flowering of the kindergarten movement in the United States—from the initiation of the first kindergarten in Wisconsin in the 1850s until kindergarten became something basic for all children after World War II. Seen from this perspective, perhaps the halting steps that have characterized the movement for quality early care and education is not so far off track. Thus, Edward Zigler's advice to his students seems more sage than ever: Be prepared to devote the better part of your professional life to this struggle, or you might as well not begin. Zigler has been involved in virtually every step of progress in early care and education in this nation for nearly 4 decades. Ultimately, the achievement of a quality system accessible to all would be the most fitting tribute to his work.

References

Ackerman, D. (2003). *States' efforts in improving the qualifications of early care and education teachers.* New Brunswick, NJ: NIEER.

Administration on Children, Youth and Families. (2001). *Child care and development fund: Report of state plans for the period 10/01/99 to 9/30/01.* Washington, DC: U.S. Department of Health and Human Services.

Azer, S., LeMoine, S., Morgan, G., Clifford, R. M., & Crawford, G. M. (2002, Winter). Regulation of child care. *Early Childhood Research Policy and Briefs, 2*(1).

Barnett, W. S. (2003). Low wages = low quality. Solving the real preschool teacher crisis. *Preschool Quality Matters, 3.* Retrieved April 10, 2003, from http://nieer.org/resources/policybriefs/3.pdf

Blau, D. M. (2001) *The child care problem: An economic analysis.* New York: Russell Sage Foundation.

Boger, R. (1969). *Heterogeneous versus homogeneous social class groupings of preschool children in Head Start classrooms.* Washington, DC: Office of Economic Opportunity.

Bowman, B., Donovan, M., & Burns, M. (2000). *Eager to learn: Educating our preschoolers.* Washington, DC: National Academy Press.

Brandon, R., Kagan, S. L., & Joesch, J. M. (2000). *Design choices: Universal financing for early care and education.* Seattle, WA: Human Services Policy Center.

Brauner, J., Gordic, B., & Zigler, E. (2004). Putting the child back into child care: Combining car and education for children ages 3–5. *Social Policy Report, 18*(3), 3–16.

Bryant, D., Maxwell, K., Taylor, K., Poe, M., Peisner-Feinberg, E., & Bernier, K. (2003). *Smart start and preschool child care quality in North Carolina: Change over time and relation to children's readiness.* Chapel Hill, NC: Frank Porter Graham Child Development Institute.

Caldwell, B. (1989). A comprehensive model for integrating child care and early childhood education. *The Teachers College Record, 90,* 404–415.

California Department of Education, Child Development Division. (2000). *Prekindergarten learning and development guidelines.* Sacramento, CA: Author.

Children's Defense Fund. (2000). *Child care subsidy policy: A primer.* Washington, DC: Author.

Children's Foundation. (2002). *The 2000 child care center licensing study.* Washington, DC: Author.

Committee for Economic Development, Research and Policy Committee. (2002). *Preschool for all: Investing in a productive and just society.* Washington, DC: Author.

Comprehensive Child Development Act of 1971, H.R. 6748, 92d Cong. (1971).

Donahue, E. H., & Campbell, N. G. (2002). *Making care less taxing: Improving state child and dependent care tax provisions.* Washington, DC: National Women's Law Center.

Family and Medical Leave Act of 1993, 29 U.S.C. § 2601 (1993).

Farkas, S., Duffet, A., & Johnson, J. (2000). *Necessary compromises: How parents, employers and children's advocates view child care today.* Washington, DC: Public Agenda.

Fuller, B., Kagan, S. L., Caspary, G. L., & Gauthier, C. A. (2002). Children and welfare reform. *The Future of Children, 12*(1), 97–119.

Galinsky, E., Howes, C., Kontos, S., & Shinn, M. (1994). *The study of children in family child care and relative care.* New York: Families and Work Institute.

Gallagher, J., & Clifford, R. (2000). The missing support infrastructure in early childhood. *Early Childhood Research and Practice, 2*(1), 1–24.

Gomby, D., Larner, M., Stevenson, C., Lewit, E., & Behrman, R. (1995). Long-term outcomes: Analysis and recommendations. *The Future of Children: Long-Term Outcomes of Early Childhood Programs, 5*(3), 6–24.

Helburn, S., & Bergmann, B. (2002). *America's childcare problem: The way out.* New York: Palgrave for St. Martin's Press.

Helburn, S., & The Cost, Quality and Child Outcomes Study Team. (1995). *Cost, quality and child outcomes in child care centers* (Public Report, 2nd ed.). Denver: University of Colorado Economics Department.

Kagan, S. L., & Cohen, N. E. (1997). *Not by chance: Creating an early care and education system for America's children.* New Haven, CT: Bush Center in Child Development and Social Policy.

Lakoff, G., & Grady, J. (1998). Why early education benefits us all. In S. Bales (Ed.), *Effective language for discussing early childhood education and policy* (pp. 7–19). Washington, DC: Benton Foundation.

Lombardi, J. (2003). *Time to care: Redesigning child care.* Philadelphia: Temple University Press.

Love, J. M., Schochet, P. Z., & Mechstroth, A. L. (1996). *Are they in real danger? What research does-and-doesn't tell us about child care quality and children's well-being.* Princeton, NJ: Mathematica Policy Research.

National Child Care Information Center. (2002, November). *Tiered strategies: Quality rating, reimbursement, licensing.* Retrieved January 25, 2003, from http://www.nccic.org/faqs/tieredstrategies.pdf

National Institute of Child Health and Human Development Early Child Care Research Network. (1999). Child outcomes when child care centers meet recommended standards for quality. *American Journal of Public Health, 89,* 1072–1077.

Neuman, M., & Peer, S. (2002). *Equal from the start: Promoting educational opportunity for all preschool children—learning from the French experience.* New York: The French-American Foundation.

Phillips, D. (1995). *Child care for low-income families: Summary of two workshops.* Washington, DC: National Academy of Sciences.

Phillips, D., & McCartney, K. (2002, June). *Lessons learned from the disconnect between research and policy on child care.* Paper presented as part of the conference in honor of Sheldon H. White, Developmental Psychology and the Social Changes of Our Time, Wellesley College, MA.

Phillips, D., & Zigler, E. (1987). The checkered history of federal child care regulation. In E. Z. Rothkopf (Ed.), *Review of research in education* (Vol. 14, pp. 3–41). Washington, DC: American Educational Research Association.

Reardon, P. (1989, December 17). No recess for child care needs. *Chicago Tribune,* pp. B1, B12.

Ruopp, R., Travers, J., Glantz, F., & Coelen, C. (1979). *Children at the center: Final report of the national day care study.* Cambridge, MA: Abt Books.

Schulman, K. (2000). *The high cost of child care puts quality child care out of reach for many families.* Washington, DC: Children's Defense Fund.

Shonkoff, J., & Phillips, D. (2000) *From neurons to neighborhoods: The science of early childhood development.* Washington, DC: National Academy Press.

Social Security Act of 1935, 42 U.S.C. § 301–§ 1397jj (1935).

Vandell, D., & Wolfe, B. (2000). *Child care quality: Does it matter and does it need to be improved?* Retrieved August 20, 2002, from http://www.aspe.hhs.gov/hsp/ccquality00/ccqual.htm

Vast, T. (2001). *Learning between systems: Adapting higher education financing methods to early care and education.* Indianapolis, IN: Lumina Foundation for Education.

West, J., Denton, K., & Germino-Hausken, E. (2000). *America's kindergartners. Findings from the Early Childhood Longitudinal Study, Kindergarten Class of 1998-99* (NCES No. 2000-070). Washington, DC: U.S. Department of Education.

White House Conference on Children. (1970). *Report to the President.* Washington, DC: U.S. Government Printing Office.

Zigler, E., & Gilman, E. (1993). Day care in America: What is needed? *Pediatrics, 91*(Suppl.), 175–178.

Zigler, E., & Lang, M. (1991). *Child care choices.* New York: Free Press.

Zigler, E., & Muenchow, S. (1992). *Head Start: The inside story of America's most successful educational experiment.* New York: Basic Books.

Zil, N., & West, J. (2000). *Entering kindergarten: A portrait of American children entering kindergarten. Condition of Education 2000* (NCES No. 2000-062). Washington, DC: U.S. Department of Education.

7

From Visions to Systems of Universal Prekindergarten

W. Steven Barnett, Kirsty C. Brown, Matia Finn-Stevenson, and Christopher Henrich

Over the last 4 decades, the United States has gradually moved from a focus on preschool programs for the most needy, low-income children toward preschool education for all children. Whereas it was rare in 1960 for children under 5 years of age to be educated outside the home, today 60% of 3- and 4-year-olds attend some kind of preschool program, with the percentage of 4-year-old children in the Northeast reaching 80%. The preschool programs that children attend are a diverse mix that are unsatisfactory in many ways, including problems of coherence and conflict that increasingly demand a response. Universal prekindergarten (UPK) is one prominent response, but there are many possible visions of UPK. These visions owe much to major past preschool programs, most influenced directly or indirectly by Edward F. Zigler.

The need for new systems of early childhood education has become painfully evident as society has outgrown the visions and programs of the past. Those visions, unfortunately, did not turn into a seamless, effective system that provides early childhood educational programs to all children. Rather, a fragmented, hodgepodge of programs has been implemented that target children who qualify by virtue of disability or risk status, family income, parental employment, or other child and family characteristics. As momentum grows in this country for universal access to high-quality preschool programs, a critical examination of past visions and experiences—what worked, what did not work, and why—is essential to creating the systems of the future.

In this chapter we illuminate key issues in formulating UPK policy by focusing on commonalities and differences in the visions and experiences of four important types of programs: Head Start, federal child care initiatives, state prekindergarten programs, and the 21st Century (21C) School. We examine the ways in which these programs evolved to inform and illustrate the various policy challenges facing the development of a UPK system. Finally, we offer recommendations for ways in which these programs and aspects of their visions might be transformed into a new system.

Examination of the four types of programs, as will become evident, causes a number of interrelated themes to recur that can be posed as questions.

- Who should be served? Should programs be targeted or universal, and, if the latter, how should they deal with diverse needs? Is the program for children or families?
- What services should be provided? Is it education or child care? What qualifications do teachers need? Should education focus on academics or the whole child? To what extent should nutrition, health, and social services be provided?
- Who should set standards and determine accountability? Should that be left to private enterprises or should federal, state, or local governments be responsible?
- Should the funding streams be made up of federal, state, or local dollars, or a combination of public and private monies? Should government provide UPK even for wealthy families or should there be some sort of sliding scale arrangement?
- What role should (and can) research play in policy and program development?

Where Are We Now?

Before reviewing the programs individually, it is useful to have some general background on the preschool program mix that exists today and how it evolved. Figure 7.1 graphically illustrates the steady upward trend in preschool attendance. As can be seen, the long-term pattern of increased attendance has been nearly identical for children with stay-at-home moms and for children whose mothers work outside the home. Thus, the trend toward increased preschool program participation is not primarily driven by increased labor force participation of women and their need for child care. Rather this trend evinces a desire to invest in nonparental early education that contributes to children's learning and development broadly defined.

Of course, the programs children attend vary greatly. Hours of operation range from 2 to 3 hours a day offered only 2 or 3 days a week during the school year, up to 12 hours per day, 5 days a week, 50 weeks a year. Content and quality vary as widely as quantity. Programs are operated by Head Start, public schools, private for-profits, private nonprofits, and faith-based organizations. Cost varies greatly, and parents pay a far greater portion of costs than for K–12 education. Public funding is overwhelmingly federal, in stark contrast to K–12 education, though state and local funding have grown. Despite the relatively high overall level, participation remains quite variable, with major differences by region and state, and by such family background characteristics as parental education and income (Barnett & Yarosz, 2004).

How Did We Get Here? Past Programs and Visions

When planning a better future, it is valuable to understand the existing array of preschool programs and how it developed. What are the major programs and funding streams? What are their goals? How and why were they developed?

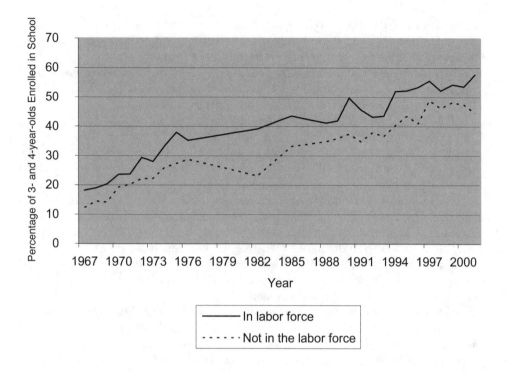

Figure 7.1. Preschool participation by maternal employment from 1967 to 2002. (From *Current Population Survey 1967–2002*; data for the following years have been interpolated: 1977–1981, 1983, 1984, and 1986.) Reprinted with permission from W. Steven Barnett and Donald J. Yarosz, "Who Goes to Preschool and Why Does It Matter?," NIEER Policy Brief (Issue 8, August 2004), NIEER: New Brunswick, NJ.

These questions are addressed in the following sections on Head Start, child care, local school initiatives as illustrated by 21C schools, and state prekindergarten.

Head Start

An in-depth examination of Head Start is presented in chapter 5 of this volume. However, any review of the visions of the past must take into account the starting point—Head Start. At least in part, Head Start was created on the basis of research indicating that the environments of children in poverty impaired their development and, thereby, damaged their chances for success in school and life more generally. Over subsequent decades, research would validate the view that high-quality preschool programs can improve the life course of children in poverty: increasing their achievement, school progress, and educational attainment while decreasing crime and delinquency (Barnett, 1993; Barnett & Hustedt, 2003).

Initially developed as part of the War on Poverty, Head Start was hastily launched in 1965 as a relatively large 8-week summer program serving 561,000

3- and 4-year-old children. With equal haste, the first evaluation was launched, conducted in 1969 by the Westinghouse Learning Corporation (Cicirelli, 1969). As a retrospective follow-up study, it found that summer Head Start programs had little or no effect on children, that full-year Head Start programs benefited children's school achievement, but that such effects were subject to rapid "fade out" and disappeared by the third grade (Cicirelli, 1969).

These evaluation findings (later found to be flawed) placed the fledgling Head Start program under fire. The Nixon administration and others sought to dismantle Head Start on the basis of this evidence. However, in 1970 Zigler became director of the newly formed Office of Child Development (OCD), to which Head Start had just been moved. Zigler and his OCD staff showcased Head Start as a national laboratory for innovative programs serving low-income children and families (Henrich, 2004). They emphasized the superior performance of school-year programs over summer programs in the evaluation and argued for program improvement rather than dismantlement (Zigler & Muenchow, 1992).

Zigler and Muenchow (1992) also argued that insufficient attention had been given to impacts on children beyond relatively narrow measures of cognitive abilities. He stressed the significance of producing well-adjusted individuals across a wide spectrum of intellectual ability (Zigler & Muenchow, 1992, p. 410) and pointed out the need for much broader criteria that included school performance as well as important aspects of health, nutrition, and attitudes toward self and society (Zigler & Muenchow, 1992, p.83). Subsequent research would confirm their arguments for Head Start's attention to social and emotional development (Barnett & Hustedt, 2003; Bowman, Donovan, & Burns, 2001).

The OCD piloted a series of innovative new programs that experimented with different ways in which the government could serve low-income families. Home Start, Parent and Child Centers, Family and Child Resource Centers, and Project Developmental Continuity resulted. Zigler saved Head Start and began a tradition of using the OCD (now the Administration for Children and Families) to experiment with new federal programs to serve children and families. The tradition has continued with the Comprehensive Child Development Program and Early Head Start (Henrich, 2004; St. Pierre, Layzer, & Barnes, 1998). Much has been learned from these programs about what works and what does not. Many of the lessons remain incomplete or at least incompletely understood. One of the lessons is that research rarely produces definitive and fully satisfactory results.

Although its budget was saved in 1970 and steadily increased thereafter, Head Start enrollment declined until 1978, when it began to rise again. As the budget rose, quality enhancements were made. In 1998, Congress required that half of Head Start's teachers have at least a 2-year college degree by 2003. By 2002, the Head Start budget had grown to more than $6.5 billion, and the program enrolled nearly 1 million children (still considerably short of serving all eligible children, a commitment Congress made in the 1998 reauthorization). However, in 2003, Head Start once again came under attack for failing to produce stronger gains in children's cognitive development (U.S. Department of Health and Human Services, 2003). The research base for this attack is again flawed (Barnett & Hustedt, 2003). Yet, Head Start's budget growth was stalled and the program was targeted for a radical overhaul while the first randomized trial to evaluate its impact was just getting started. Research over the past several decades does suggest that Head Start could improve its efforts to enhance children's language and cognitive abilities development. Caution must be exercised to ensure that this is not at the expense of other domains of development. Neither can it be achieved by means of a quick and inexpensive fix.

In 2003, the White House proposed changes to Head Start designed to alter how it is administered, delivered, and held accountable. Most notably, it sought to give states "a more prominent role in coordinating and providing a high-quality preschool experience before children enter preschool" (U.S. Department of Education, 2003, ¶ 2). The School Readiness Act of 2003, H.R. 2210, sought to implement this approach by offering at least some states the option of applying to use Head Start funds. Other features of the proposed Head Start reform are greater emphasis and more federal direction on teaching for early literacy, and testing for school readiness across Head Start programs.

Comprehensive Child Development Act of 1971

While director of OCD, Zigler also played a key role in the Comprehensive Child Development Act of 1971, which brought this country to the brink of federally subsidized early care and education for all families and the establishment of a national child-care system. The Comprehensive Child Development Act proposed a radical shift in federal policy. Initially supported by the Nixon administration, the legislation declared that the availability of quality child care was a right for all American families (Cohen, 1996). Quality child care would be provided to all families: free to all low-income families and at a reduced rate, based on a sliding scale, for higher income families (Cohen, 1996). Even though a large and powerful coalition of advocates led by Marian Wright Edelman supported the child-care bill, it was eventually vetoed (Zigler & Muenchow, 1992).

Child Care: Federal and State Policy After 1971

The defeat of the Comprehensive Child Development Act (1971) marked a turning point in national policy. Yet, the legacy of the act remains pertinent today as many states take over where the federal government left off more than 30 years ago. Moreover, several aspects implemented in the intervening years have contributed to the effective delivery of high-quality early care and education. Results of the defeated Comprehensive Child Development Act in 1971 include the following:

1. Head Start was recognized for its effective delivery of a broad set of services to children and families.
2. A systematic definition of what constituted quality care was developed, which became the precursor to voluntary accreditation standards that set a benchmark for assessing the quality of early care and education (Heinrich, 2004).

3.   The Child Development Associate (CDA) credential, which could
be earned by workers with specialized training in early childhood
development, became a critically important credential in the push
for quality early care and education.

Since the veto of the Comprehensive Child Development Act (1971), the
federal government has not made any subsequent attempts to oversee high-
quality preschool programs for nonpoor families. However, federal funding for
child care regained some momentum in 1988 with the passage of the Family
Support Act, which provided child-care subsidies to low-income families receiving Aid to Families with Dependent Children. This legislation was followed by
the 1990 Child Care and Development Block Grant, which provided child-care
subsidies through the states for low-income working parents. These pieces of
legislation, though, include virtually no standards for the quality of care. In
fact, government has done little to set high quality standards for the many
government child-care programs developed in response to Welfare-to-Work programs and welfare reform or for private child-care programs that have experienced a steady increase in enrollment of middle-class children over the past 30
years. The National Council of Jewish Women concluded in 1999 that there had
been little, if any, improvement in the state of child care since its 1972 *Windows*
report that emphasized the acute shortage of quality programs and the high
costs that made them unaffordable for most families (National Council of Jewish Women, 1999).

The only current federal guidelines pertaining to the quality of early care
and education are the Head Start Performance Standards. States have guidelines governing the operation of child care, but these vary in quality and many
fail to adequately address the health, safety, and (especially) developmental
needs of children (Young, Marsland, & Zigler, 1997). Most states have minimum qualifications for child-care staff, with only one state requiring child-care
teachers to have a 4-year college degree (Barnett & Hustedt, 2003). Because of
a lack of government oversight, many early care and education programs have
turned to the voluntary National Association for the Education of Young Children accreditation standard and the CDA certificate as benchmarks of quality.
Especially as the Temporary Aid to Needy Families (TANF) caseload declined
rapidly in the first years of welfare reform, states greatly increased child-care
assistance for low-income working families. In 2002, states allocated more than
$5 billion in TANF and state maintenance of effort funds to child care (Greenberg
& Rahmanou, 2003). However, the increased spending has not been accompanied by widespread improvements in state standards.

The School of the 21st Century

Zigler's work on Head Start and other early intervention programs, together
with his concerns for the quality and availability of child care, led to his
conceptualization in 1987 of 21C, or the School of the 21st Century (Zigler,
1987). In announcing 21C, Zigler promoted the idea that good quality child care

should be available to all preschool children, just as public education is now available to all.

21C represents a departure in design and concept from Head Start and other programs in its (a) use of public schools to provide services and (b) provision of universal access, ensuring that child care and other services are available to all children and their families. The 21C core components provide continuity of care and support from birth to age 12 and include home visitation for families with children from birth to age 3; all-day (6 a.m.–6 p.m.), year-round child care for children ages 3, 4, and 5; before- and after-school and vacation care for children in elementary school; outreach to, and collaborations with, community-based and family child-care providers; and health, nutrition, and various other support services as may be needed in the community. 21C's pragmatic approach leverages the nation's investment in school buildings and the infrastructure of public education. Further, it includes parental fees with a sliding scale calibrated to family income. The realities of increasingly limited public funds led Zigler to develop 21C as a child-care system that blended federal and state programs and funding streams.

21C meets children's educational and developmental needs and addresses working parents' need for child care. Implementation studies show that effective 21C programs occur when they become an integral part of the public school system, ensuring that services for young children and families are considered in space allocation, and that funding and other decisions by school districts are based on K–12 teachers interacting and collaborating with early childhood teachers and other 21C staff members. The commitment of educational administrators, especially principals, also was found to be necessary for success.

More than 1,300 schools have implemented 21C programs; many are more than a decade old. 21C has been implemented by individual school districts with three exceptions. In 1988, the Connecticut legislature appropriated funds for Family Resource Centers (FRCs) on the basis of the 21C concept, including all 21C components and guiding principles. In 1990 the Kentucky Education Reform Act (KERA) included Connecticut's FRC legislative language, phasing in FRCs in Kentucky schools over a 5-year period. These state provisions target low-income communities, but the schools include fee-paying children as well. In 2001, a $3 million investment by the Winthrop Rockefeller Foundation established 21C statewide in Arkansas, phasing in program implementation over a 5-year period, under the direction of the Yale 21C National Center. Although this effort is still in its early stages, it is illustrative on establishing partnerships between states and the philanthropic sector.

Studies of 21C show the start-up phase followed by a growth and program enhancement phase to be especially important (and a consideration for other UPK programs). In its start-up phase, 21C focused on program design and exploration of the use of schools to deliver services. 21C's design includes comprehensive services, parent involvement, and locally driven implementation. Because 21Cs are located in public schools, they add little or nothing to overhead expenditures for maintenance and insurance, and they more easily participate in many school-administered grant programs that provide substantial financial support.

21Cs facilitate universal access by charging parents fees on a sliding scale (calibrated to family income) for some 21C components (child care for preschoolers and school-age children). Grants and some program surplus cover other 21C components, and public child-care funds cover low-income children. Additional grants are needed to cover start-up expenses for a period of about 1 year. Some school districts have paid start-up expenses as a loan that is repaid once each school begins to realize a surplus in operating revenues. This approach has been more feasible in districts with fewer low-income families. In Kentucky, state support for low-income children made programs more financially viable. Some 21C schools incorporate special needs preschoolers to generate revenue and address mandates for mainstreaming. In other 21C schools, Head Start and fee-paying children in the same classrooms with Head Start families needing all-day child care pay only for the wrap-around care (Zigler & Finn-Stevenson, 1996).

The growth and program enhancement phase focuses on staffing needs. In 21C the need for early childhood educators and program administrators must still be addressed. As a result, in this phase 21C sites explore linkages to local teacher training institutions to participate in scale-up efforts on two fronts: providing pre- and in-service training to 21C educators and working with the school to achieve and maintain good quality care.

State Prekindergarten Programs

Until very recently, federal and state governments paid little attention to the education component of early care and education outside of Head Start. Rhetorically, this changed with the 1994 Educate America Act and Goals 2000. The first goal stated that all children would have access to high-quality preschool and start school ready to learn. With the development of Goals 2000 and its concomitant emphasis on school readiness, the focus of government attention is swinging back toward education. The Goals 2000 legislation provided states with an impetus to emphasize early education, but it did not provide additional financial assistance (Gilliam & Zigler, 2001). State preschool initiatives responding to the goals have had to cobble together state and local funds with targeted federal funds (from Head Start, the Family Support Act [1988], the Child Care and Development Block Grant, the Individuals With Disabilities Education Improvement Act [2004], and other programs). State spending on prekindergarten programs rose by roughly a factor of 10 over the last decade or so, in constant dollars, from a few hundred million to over $2.8 billion by 2005 (Barnett, Hustedt, Robin, & Schulman, 2005). Local spending adds an unknown but not insignificant amount (Barnett & Masse, 2003). As these programs have expanded, states have developed program standards specifying teacher qualifications, class size, ratios, and other program characteristics.

More than 40 states now have preschool programs, and some are moving toward UPK. As they do so, they illustrate both possible pathways and potential roadblocks. Serious issues to be considered when drawing a road map to UPK include blended funding streams, uniform program standards including teacher qualifications (and, implicitly, compensation), and common governance for diverse programs. Programs in Oklahoma, Georgia, Kentucky, New York, and New Jersey illustrate some of the diversity in approaches.

Oklahoma, in 1998, became the second state to seek to offer voluntary pre-K to all 4-year-olds, and the first to actually reach more than 90% of the entire population (combined with Head Start). Local districts collaborate with private providers and Head Start programs in some cases, but most children are served through public schools. Districts are reimbursed for offering half- or full-day programs through the regular public school funding formula, just as for kindergarten. All teachers have bachelor's degrees and certification in early childhood education and are paid at public school salary levels.

Georgia implemented a UPK program in 1995 for all 4-year-olds, paid for through lottery funds. The state program and Head Start (which has not merged with the state program) currently serve about 70% of Georgia's 4-year-old children. The minimum requirement for a teacher is a 2-year degree, though the state has initiated an incentives program for early childhood teachers, linking salary increases to increased educational attainment. They also have developed a tiered reimbursement system to enhance quality (Jacobson, 2002). Budget problems have led to suggestions that this program be targeted to low-income children, as the state attempts to cover college tuition and preschool costs from the same lottery fund.

Kentucky created a preschool program as part of the 1990 KERA. Their preschool programs are part of Family Resource Centers, based on the 21C model. The state funds 4-year-old children in families below 130% of poverty level and 3- and 4-year-olds with developmental delays, regardless of income. However, the Kentucky FRCs also serve children from higher income families that pay for services. Programs are required to meet minimum standards. The program has moved from joint administration by the Cabinet of Human Services and the Department of Education to the Department of Education alone. A team of educators provides state-level assistance to local districts.

New York's UPK program originally sought to serve all 4-year-old children by 2002–2003, but it has faced funding shortages and was implemented first in targeted districts with high concentrations of poverty. Services are delivered by a mix of public school and private programs that meet state standards. Districts blend funds from other sources with state dollars to cover program costs. In recent years, proponents had to fight the governor's efforts to eliminate the budget for this program altogether. Although they have succeeded in maintaining the initial funding that launched the UPK in some communities, proponents have been unable to expand funding to move toward universal coverage.

New Jersey's preschool program is administered by the state department of education and supported by a state supreme court mandate to provide high-quality preschool to all 3- and 4-year-old children in New Jersey's 31 poorest school districts (called *Abbott* districts, after the court case). Legislation provides funding for preschool to more than 130 school districts with relatively high concentrations of low-income children. However, only children in the Abbott districts (about 25% of New Jersey's 3- and 4-year-olds) are guaranteed full state funding for a full-day preschool program. The maximum class size is 15, and all teachers must have a state preschool teacher certification. Programs can be provided by public schools, Head Start, or private preschools, and most of the children attend private programs. Head Start receives state funding supplements to enable them to meet state requirements for teacher qualifications and class size. By 2005–2006, the program had scaled up to serve 80% of the children in the Abbott districts. Thus, New Jersey's Abbott program is one of the closest approximations to a system of universal prekindergarten to date, albeit in selected cities. Ongoing research to document the effectiveness of the Abbott programs should prove helpful in providing guidance to other states.

Support for UPK is growing. Most recently, Florida has made the commitment to provide UPK to 4-year-old children. In 2002, Florida voters approved a constitutional amendment requiring the state to offer all 4-year-olds a free, high-quality pre-K education by 2005. In 2005–2006, Florida may add as many as 100,000 children to the 800,000 plus served in other states' prekindergarten programs across the nation. California has a universal prekindergarten initiative on the ballot for voter approval in 2006. Other states have steadily expanded coverage without officially committing to serve all children. Thus, a substantial number of states already face issues raised by emerging systems of federal, state, and privately funded preschools that, together, may approach universal coverage of 4-year-old children.

Despite their differences, all these states will encounter some similar challenges. They will all have to address the questions set out at the beginning of this chapter as they consider how best to ensure adequate access and quality for all children. States leading the way toward universal coverage will provide examples to answer key questions and produce the needed capacity, but each state will have to adopt policies that address their unique political, economic, and social contexts. At the same time, the nation must determine what role the federal government should play in UPK.

Where Do We Go From Here? Systems for the Future

As public preschool programs continue to expand, new visions will be required to guide key decisions in creating state preschool programs, including UPK: Who will be served, what services are provided, who governs, and who provides the services? Inextricably linked to these decisions are issues of funding, standards, quality, infrastructure, and incorporation or coordination of existing preschool programs in the new system. Some of the ways in which new visions might emerge from existing programs are suggested briefly before focusing on each specific decision.

Head Start provides a vision of a free program provided by community organizations with nationally uniform standards and funding for a targeted population. The 21C vision is one of many services provided by public schools to all children with local standards and pooled funds from many sources, including parents. State programs vary greatly, with this variation itself suggesting one vision of the federal role—increasing uniformity across states in standards and access to high-quality programs. Georgia's program is free and universal to the entire state but leaves Head Start as a separate program. Georgia's low state-funding level raises questions about the extent to which local schools, parents, and others may (unofficially) pay to raise quality for some children. Within

30 cities with high concentrations of poverty, New Jersey's Abbott program is free and universal with high uniform standards and adequate state funding. In Georgia and New Jersey, private providers as well as public schools deliver services. In Texas, only the public schools participate.

Targeted Programs or Universal Access?

Whether to offer programs only to targeted groups or to all children stacks up as probably the most significant policy decision. Many criteria can be used to target by income, children's abilities and needs, and parental employment. The strongest argument for targeting is that limited state resources can be focused on children with the greatest needs and for whom the benefits of preschool education are most clearly established. Head Start remains the premiere example of targeting. Local programs are expected to meet the specific needs of their communities, but detailed program standards and funding are national. After 40 years, Head Start's success with targeting must be judged as mixed. Head Start funding per child is higher than that for many state programs. Head Start provides the most comprehensive services in the nation to families and children. Standards are uniform, and funding does not depend on local or state economies. However, even after 40 years Head Start is insufficiently funded to serve all eligible children. Quality is neither high nor uniform. For example, the percentage of Head Start teachers with 4-year college degrees (not a requirement) ranges from 64% in New York to 14% in Mississippi and 12% in Alaska and Alabama. New Jersey's (targeted) Abbott program provides another example, and though it has a short history, it does provide the highest per-child funding in the nation.

The argument for universal preschool education begins with the view that any dividing line used in targeting is to some extent arbitrary and excludes children who could significantly benefit. The poverty line is a fairly arbitrary cut off that results in many near-poor children having no access to similar services even though they differ little from children in poverty in their educational needs. Also, children in middle-income families are not immune to problems that interfere with later school success. More than 1 in 10 middle-class children fail a grade or drop out of high school. Moreover, research on the effects of child-care quality frequently finds that quality benefits the development of all children, not just those in poverty or with other problems. Who then should be excluded from the benefits of public preschool programs?

Practical limitations of targeted programs provide arguments for universal programs. It is costly and difficult to ensure that all ineligible children are excluded and that all eligible children are identified and enrolled. In practice, targeting is quite imperfect, with ineligible children served and many eligible children not even identified. Without a universal program, it is unclear how effective child find can be—how can programs determine whether a child who does not come to the program qualifies? Targeted programs also are potentially stigmatizing and segregate children by economic status, abilities, parental work status, or other characteristics when they might educationally benefit from greater integration (Zigler & Muenchow, 1992). Finally, a universal program can ensure that all children begin kindergarten with a shared background of common educational experiences.

As noted earlier, the evidence about whether support for quality is stronger or weaker in a universal program is mixed. Experience with Head Start and child care fuels concerns that without a universal program, there is no public commitment to quality (Finn-Stevenson & Zigler, 1999; Lewis 2001; Skocpol & Greenstein, 1991). Yet, so far universal state programs are not of obviously higher quality. However, they are better than Head Start in coverage—Head Start still reaches only half the eligible population. Thus, the best system might be universal and targeted. In such a system, the federal government could ensure (a) that children with greater needs receive additional support (with Head Start enhancing and adding services within state programs) and (b) that there is greater uniformity across states (offering matching funds to states that meet certain standards). Similarly, states can provide greater funding and set higher or broader standards to serve children with greater needs within a statewide program.

What Services?

In addition to education, preschool programs provide child care and more comprehensive services (health, nutrition, and social services) to children and their families. Programs vary in the service mix they provide partly because children and families differ in their needs for these services to be delivered together with education. Not every parent works outside the home. Some children benefit from spending much of their time in settings other than preschool. Many families have adequate resources of their own to provide for their children's nutrition, health, and other needs. Yet, even some of these families may be prevented from participating in a preschool program that does not accommodate their needs for child care directly or through the addition of wrap-around services. Of course, programs also vary in their ability to provide broader, higher quality services because of limited public and private funds. A system that provides targeting for these other services, within the framework of a universal education program, can be envisioned from the 21C model and the possibilities from merged visions of Head Start, public school, and private programs. Both suggest blending federal and state funding streams, perhaps even including parent fees, to develop UPK programs. Flexible rules will be required if such an approach is to be effective.

Who Governs?

The question of who will be responsible for setting policy and ensuring it is implemented (e.g., by directing funding, by setting and monitoring standards and regulations) seems likely to be another area where new visions move beyond old debates over either–or to both–and, with shared federal, state, and local governance as well as a role for parents. For example, it seems unlikely that the federal government would continue its level of funding for Head Start while relinquishing its governance role. Although it is possible that Head Start standards might be abandoned if Head Start funds were shifted to the states, both Congress and the President have moved to increase rather than decrease federal governance of education policy. States have a dominant role in education, but in most states there is strong support for local control as well. Private organizations are reluctant to relinquish their autonomy and might be expected to push for vouchers or similar arrangements that would minimize regulation and government oversight. Any new structure will have to provide some role for parents in governance.

Joint governance raises at least two concerns: (a) conflict leading to problems including confusion, unfunded mandates, and an inability to innovate; and (b) accountability declining as each governing body sees opportunities for others to bear more of the cost and responsibility for effective programs. Such shared governance may make it easier to escape blame for funding cuts or poor services. The 21C school offers one vision for joint governance, following the public school model. Yet, even this seems stretched to accommodate faith-based organizations, for-profit and not-for-profit organizations, and Head Start. Religious organizations need not be democratic in their decision making. For-profit organizations are responsive to owners as well as customers. Head Start has its own policy councils. How do these other governing arrangements interact with school boards? Contracts offer an approach by which states or districts could contract to specify services to be delivered by mutual agreement.

Who Provides Services?

Public funding need not imply public provision, as many state programs demonstrate. And, as the 21C school demonstrates, private funding need not imply private provision. Many visions of future systems seem possible, from purely private to purely public, at least within states. In fact, it is difficult to imagine one vision that would apply to all states at this point, unless it is a mixed public and private system. Even Head Start is delivered by a mix of private agencies and public schools. In most circumstances, proposals for UPK programs that do not use the full range of existing programs to provide services should expect excluded programs to be sources of political opposition rather than support.

Head Start and the Future

As a federal program with more funding than all of the state prekindergarten programs together, Head Start's role in any future system requires special attention. There are a number of ways in which Head Start might adapt to the changing state situation. Head Start could shift its focus to children ages 3 and younger from low-income families, though it is unclear that state programs could make up the lost funds. Where states implement free UPK, Head Start might have the greatest impact by serving children in poverty before they enter prekindergarten. This change could be accomplished within existing federal legislation as current law permits Head Start to children at any age from birth to kindergarten entry.

Another alternative is for Head Start to merge with state UPK programs. This would permit states to incorporate Head Start funding, expertise, staff, and facilities into UPK, thereby reducing costs to the state and making maximum use of existing resources in the field. For example, local or state education agencies could contract with Head Start either to raise standards for children already served or to serve children not covered by the federal grant. Such contracts might provide partial payment for each Head Start eligible child who is federally funded and full payment for each child who is not Head Start eligible.

Although some states contract with Head Start as part of their state pre-K programs, others, such as Georgia, do not. Some modification or waiver of federal Head Start regulations may be needed to enable Head Start to effectively operate under contracts with state programs. For example, Head Start policy councils and local boards of education constitute potentially incompatible governance structures. Alternatively, the federal government could raise the educational standards of Head Start and provide funds so that Head Start could meet or surpass state pre-K standards. This could be done uniformly or on a state-by-state basis. It would allow Head Start to effectively "merge" without accepting state or local funds and governance.

Other ways to merge Head Start with state UPK could provide even more flexibility. One way would be to allow Head Start dollars to follow the child to any program participating in UPK (public or private) chosen by the parents. Another would be for Head Start to shift its focus to providing supplemental services to Head Start eligible children and families attending UPK programs while withdrawing from the provision of direct classroom services. These children would then receive the advantages associated with participating in both Head Start and UPK. Both of these broader approaches, as well as contracting with Head Start to serve the general population, could reduce the isolation of children in poverty from their more economically advantaged peers. These options also would require changes in federal legislation.

Unfortunately, any major changes in Head Start must take into account that it still acts as an educational safety net for 4-year-old children. Too many states still treat preschool education as an extra that can be cut back when budgets tighten (Barnett et al., 2005). Eleven states still offer no state prekindergarten program, and many others still serve only a small fraction of even those children in poverty. This situation will change, but it has not changed yet, and some states will continue to lag for a long time.

Conclusion

Public recognition of the value of preschool is found in steadily growing attendance rates and state movements toward UPK, including the overwhelming support that passed Florida's UPK ballot initiative in 2002. Yet, preschool will fulfill its promise only if educators take on the hard work of creating new approaches to move from the current uneven patchwork of private and public programs to uniform and highly effective UPK systems. Much can be learned from the past to help generate new visions for such systems. Rigorous research can play a critical role in providing information about the effectiveness of these visions as the federal, state, and local governments move toward new systems. It also will require the reprisal of what Zigler called the real miracle of Head Start, "a diverse people uniting through the political process to achieve a common goal" (Zigler & Muenchow, 1992, p. 54).

References

Barnett, W. S. (1993). Benefit–cost analysis of preschool education: Findings from a 25-year follow-up. *American Journal of Orthopsychiatry*, *63*, 500–508.

Barnett, W. S., & Hustedt, J. T. (2003). Preschool: The most important grade. *Educational Leadership*, *60*(7), 54–57.

Barnett, W. S., Hustedt, J. T., Robin, K. B., & Schulman, K. L. (2005). *The state of preschool: 2005 state preschool yearbook*. New Brunswick, NJ: National Institute for Early Education Research.

Barnett, W. S., & Masse, L. (2003). Funding issues for early childhood education and care programs. In D. Cryer & R. M. Clifford (Eds.), *Early childhood education & care in the USA* (pp. 137–165). Baltimore: U.S. Department of Education.

Barnett, W. S., & Yarosz, D. (2004). *Who goes to preschool and why does it matter?* NIEER Policy Brief. New Brunswick, NJ: National Institute for Early Education Research.

Bowman, B., Donovan, S., & Burns, S. (Eds.). (2001). *Eager to learn: Educating our preschoolers*. Washington, DC: National Academy Press.

Cicirelli, V. G. (1969). *The impact of Head Start: An evaluation of the effects of Head Start on children's cognitive and affective development*. Athens, OH, and New York: Ohio University and Westinghouse Learning Corporation.

Cohen, A. J. (1996). A brief history of federal financing for child care in the United States. *The Future of Children*, *6*, 26–40.

Comprehensive Child Development Act of 1971, H.R. 6748, 92d Cong. (1971).

Family Support Act of 1988, Pub. L. No. 100-485 (1988).

Finn-Stevenson, M., & Zigler, E. (1999). *Schools of the 21st Century: Linking child care and education*. Boulder, CO: Westview.

Gilliam, W. S., & Zigler, E. (2001). A critical meta-analysis of all evaluations of state-funded preschool from 1977 to 1998: Implications for policy, service delivery, and program evaluation. *Early Childhood Research Quarterly*, *15*, 441–473.

Goals 2000: Educate America Act, H.R. 1804, 103d Cong. (1994).

Greenberg, M., & Rahmanou, H. (2003.) *TANF participation in 2001*. Washington, DC: Center for Law and Social Policy.

Henrich, C. C. (2004). Head Start as a national laboratory. In E. Zigler & S. Styfco (Eds.), *The Head Start debates* (pp. 517–532). Towson, MD: Brookes Publishing.

Individuals With Disabilities Education Improvement Act of 2004, H.R. 1350, 108th Cong. (2004).

Jacobson, L. (2002). Quality Counts 2002. *Education Week*, *21*, 108–109.

Kentucky Education Reform Act of 1990. Kentucky General Assembly. Regular Session, House Bill 940, § 104 (1990).

Lewis, A. C. (2001, October). Time to talk of early childhood. *Washington Commentary*, *83*, 103–104.

National Council of Jewish Women. (1999). *Opening a new window on child care: A report on the status of child care in the nation today*. New York: Author.

School Readiness Act of 2003, H.R. 2210, 108th Cong. (2003).

Skocpol, T., & Greenstein, R. (1991). Universal appeal: Politically viable policies to combat poverty; relieving poverty: An alternative view. *The Brookings Review*, *9*, 28–36.

St. Pierre, R. G., Layzer, J. I., & Barnes, H. V. (1998). Regenerating two-generation programs. In W. S. Barnett & S. S. Boocock (Eds.), *Early care and education for children in poverty: Promises, programs and long-term results* (pp. 99–121). Albany: State University of New York Press.

U.S. Department of Education. (2003, February 3). *President Bush's plan to prepare children for kindergarten*. Retrieved March 15, 2006, from http://www.ed.gov/news/pressreleases/2003/02/index.html

U.S. Department of Health and Human Services. (2003). *Strengthening Head Start: What the evidence shows.* Retrieved March 15, 2006, from http://aspe.hhs.gov/hsp/StrengthenHeadStart03/report.pdf

Young, K., Marsland, K., & Zigler, E. (1997). The regulatory status of center based infant and toddler care. *American Journal of Orthopsychiatry, 67,* 535–544.

Zigler, E. (1987, September 23). *A solution to the nation's child care problem: The school of the 21st century.* Paper presented at the Bush Center Policy Luncheon, New Haven, CT.

Zigler, E., & Finn-Stevenson, M. (1996). Funding child care and public education. *The Future of Children, 6*(2), 104–121.

Zigler, E., & Muenchow, S. (1992). *Head Start: The inside story of America's most successful educational experiment.* New York: Basic Books.

8

Strategies to Ensure That No Child Starts From Behind

Deborah Stipek and Kenji Hakuta

Children who live in poverty and children of color typically begin school with significant disadvantages. On average, they are already substantially behind their middle-class and Anglo peers in their cognitive skills, and those who enter school without proficiency in English face additional challenges. Children who are relatively less prepared for school are not doomed to a life of failure. But early experiences do set children on a pathway that can have long-term implications for their success in school and in life.

It would be ideal if schools served a leveling function, reducing the effects of ethnicity, poverty, or other family circumstances on children's academic success. Instead, the evidence suggests that schools reinforce the effects of family variables by providing differential resources and opportunities. Rather than receiving the extra support children need to catch up early in their academic careers, their disadvantages prior to school entry appear to be compounded by relatively low-quality education in school. This chapter is about economically disadvantaged children's double jeopardy and what needs to be done to improve their chances of success.

Starting From Behind

During the 1960s, Edward F. Zigler and a few colleagues called the nation's attention to the gap in cognitive and social skills between children living in poverty and children from middle-class and affluent families. Moving beyond scholarship to social action, he helped fashion the first national early education program designed to stop the cycle of poverty. Nearly 4 decades later, the Head Start program has grown to serve a large number of children living in poverty. The gap, however, persists. Head Start and other preschool programs have chipped away at the achievement gap and offered important services to many children who would not otherwise have had them, but children growing up in poverty continue to start school from behind. Today Zigler admits the naive expectations of child experts and advocates during the days of the War on Poverty. Older and wiser, with unmitigated energy and dogged persistence, he plugs away, enlisting the assistance of his students, their students, and others he has inspired. We have our work cut out for us.

Study after study shows that, on average, children from economically disadvantaged homes, including those who have had the benefits of early intervention programs, begin school with significantly poorer academic skills than do middle-class children. In a study of 262 children, Stipek and Ryan (1997) found a year's gap between low-income and middle-class children on a diverse array of cognitive and academic achievement tests; on many of the tests middle-class preschool children scored significantly higher, on average, than did the economically disadvantaged kindergarten children. Similar gaps were found in the nationally representative sample of 19,000 children in the Early Childhood Longitudinal Study (ECLS; National Center for Education Statistics [NCES], 2001b). In kindergarten children with one risk factor (e.g., having a mother with less than a high school education; living in a family that received food stamps or cash welfare payments; living in a single-parent household) were twice as likely as children with no risk factors to have reading scores that fell in the lowest 25% of the overall skill distribution. Similar differences were found for children's ability to identify letters of the alphabet, recognize two-digit numerals, identify ordinal positions of an object, and so on.

Data from the end of first grade in the ECLS showed the gap widening in some areas of achievement (West & Denton, 2002). Although children with at least one risk factor closed the gap in a few basic skills (e.g., recognizing letters and counting beyond 10), at the end of first grade they were further behind their more advantaged peers on tests of more sophisticated reading and mathematics knowledge than they had been at the end of kindergarten.

Even among economically disadvantaged children, small differences in family income are significantly associated with children's cognitive skills when they enter school. Stipek and colleagues studied the transition into school of nearly 400 children from ethnically diverse, low-income families.[1] More than three fourths of the families had incomes below $20,000, and one third had incomes below $12,000. Within this restricted range, children's Peabody Picture Vocabulary Test (PPVT) scores at 60 months and reading skills assessed at the end of kindergarten were significantly correlated with family income.

Many children entering the nation's elementary schools have the challenges of being an English language learner (ELL) added to risks associated with poverty. The English language learner student population has now reached a substantial proportion of the total population, especially in the early grades. One recent study (Kindler, 2002) estimates that in the year 2000–2001, about 10% of the total U.S. enrollment in pre-K to 12th grade were ELLs. In some states, such as California, enrollment is as high as 25%, and the numbers are increasing in many states that are not traditionally associated with large immigrant populations, such as Georgia, North Carolina, and Montana. The predominant language group remains Spanish, at 79% of the total ELL population.

Although the educational challenges facing this population are enormous, the particular circumstances of young ELLs have not been well documented. A

---

[1]The children are participants in a longitudinal study in which approximately 400 low-income children and their families are being followed from kindergarten or first grade through the fifth grade. Principal investigators include Deborah Stipek, Penny Hauser-Cram, Walter Secada, Heather Weiss, and Jennifer Greene. The study was funded by grants from the MacArthur Foundation, the W. T. Grant Foundation, and the U.S. Department of Education.

1995 national report on kindergarten readiness that examined the link between preschoolers' race and ethnicity found that Hispanic preschoolers had lower rates of kindergarten readiness (defined as emerging literacy and numeracy, small motor skills, physical activity, attention skills, speech development, and health) than non-Hispanic preschoolers (NCES, 1995). This report illustrates the challenges Hispanic children face when they enter school as well as the deficiencies in the knowledge base. Like most similar studies, the data are not disaggregated by home language use or English language proficiency, and it is not possible to determine what percentage of the Hispanic children had limited English proficiency. Furthermore, the conclusions are based entirely on parent reports; program or school information on the children's skills and dispositions were not collected. Moreover, only households with telephones were surveyed, using a survey conducted in English. The survey thus excluded households that could not afford telephone service and where all members were minority language speakers.

Although the special circumstances and needs of particular groups of children are not well-known, there is clear and consistent evidence that children from economically disadvantaged families start the race to success from far behind. And children who are not proficient in English, usually also from low-income homes, have additional challenges to succeed in a system that gives few points for proficiency in languages other than English.

The Starting Point Matters

There is reason to be concerned about the relatively poor cognitive skills of low-income children at school entry. Longitudinal studies suggest that students who enter school with poor skills rarely catch up; performance in the early years of school is highly predictive of achievement much later (see Stipek, 2001, for a review). In one study, the Hess School Readiness Scale, given just before or in kindergarten, correctly identified more than 70% of children who had academic difficulties (e.g., retention, 1 year behind grade level) 5 years later (Hess & Hahn, 1974). Stevenson and Newman (1986) found correlations ranging from .60 to .68 between scores on four assessments of cognitive competencies that were given before children entered kindergarten and children's 10th-grade reading achievement. Luster and McAdoo (1996) found a correlation of .71 between achievement test scores in first grade and achievement in eighth grade for the children in the High Scope study. Using eight national surveys to test students at different ages in a meta-analysis, Phillips, Crouse, and Ralph (1998) estimated that "about half of the total black–white math and reading gap at the end of high school can be attributed to the fact that blacks start school with fewer skills than whites" (p. 232).

Children's relative skills when they enter school may predict their academic success many years later in part because the quality of the schools children attend is associated with their family circumstances. If children who are the most disadvantaged and the least skilled when they enter school attend the lowest quality schools, then they will have a great deal of difficulty catching up with their more advantaged peers. We turn now to evidence related to this explanation.

Do Schools Compound Inequities?

Children who enter school with relatively low cognitive skills or English proficiency need special assistance and support to catch up with their peers. Extra attention in the early elementary grades may alter some children's long-term trajectories, and it is likely to be more cost-effective than intervention later on. The evidence reviewed in the following sections, however, suggests that children most in need of effective educational programs are least likely to get them.

Resources

Even with a disproportionate amount of federal categorical funding going to districts that serve a high proportion of low-income children, in most states these districts have less revenue than districts that serve more affluent children (Augenblick, Myers, & Anderson, 1997; Parrish, Hikido, & Fowler, 1998). Intradistrict differences in per-pupil expenditure also favor schools that serve middle-class children (Roza & Miles, 2002).

Whether looking across districts or within districts, low-income children also typically attend schools with less educated and less experienced teachers (Lankford, Loeb, & Wyckoff, 2002). A report by the National Center for Education Statistics (NCES, 1999) indicates, for example, that 37% of the teachers in schools with more than 60% of the students eligible for free or reduced-price lunch had masters degrees, compared with 57% in schools with less than 15% low-income students. Schools serving a relatively large proportion of low-income children also have less experienced teachers and lower teacher salaries (NCES, 1996).

Sobering and detailed information about inequities in schools serving high percentages of at-risk students was recently released in California in a survey by Louis Harris (2002). The study sampled 1,071 teachers representative of a cross-section of California schools. Data were reported that separated out teachers in schools serving students as "high-risk" and teachers in schools below the median in student risk factors. Harris highlighted the following:

> The high-risk students are 12 times more likely to have teachers lacking full credentials; 3.9 times more likely to be in schools with serious teacher turnover problems; 1.6 times more likely to be in schools where cockroaches, rats, and mice are commonly sighted; and 1.9 times more likely to have bathrooms that are not working or are closed. (Harris, 2002)

The data were equally striking when comparing schools serving 31% or more English language learners with those serving less than 31%. In their analysis of the Harris data, Gándara and Rumberger (2002) found that the high-ELL schools were 1.8 times more likely to have only fair or poor working conditions for teachers, 1.9 times more likely to have serious turnover rate problems with teachers, 1.6 times more likely to have difficulty filling teaching positions, 1.5 times more likely to have only fair or poor textbooks and instructional materials, and 1.8 times more likely to have had evidence of cockroaches, rats, or mice in the previous year.

Well-intentioned policy initiatives such as class size reduction appear to have exacerbated the situation for English learners who are predominantly in poor schools. Following California's class size reduction initiative, the percentage of uncredentialed teachers in schools with high proportions of ELLs jumped to as high as 23.9%, compared with fewer than 5% for those in schools with low proportions of ELLs. This was mostly attributable to the migration of credentialed teachers away from schools with a high level of ELLs to those with better working conditions (Stecher & Bohrnstedt, 2002).

Quality of Instruction

Inequities in resources and teacher credentials and experience have been well documented. Few studies, however, have examined instruction directly. We describe in some detail a study by one of the authors (Stipek, 2004) that reveals substantial evidence for differences in the quality of classroom instruction during the first 2 potentially crucial years of school. The study also provides information on the nature of instruction that economically disadvantaged children, children of color, and English language learners received.

The data come from the School Transition Study, mentioned previously. These analyses included 127 kindergarten and first-grade classrooms from 99 mostly public schools in 48 school districts in three states, two in the Northeast and one on the West coast. The schools varied considerably in the concentration of poverty, from 0% to 100% of their students being eligible for free or reduced-price lunch, with a mean of 49%. The proportion of non-White children varied from 0% to 100%, with a mean of 50%.

Although there is not complete agreement on effective educational practices in the early elementary grades, there is a developing consensus on effective learning environments for young children and on appropriate mathematics and literacy instruction. The measure of instructional quality used in this study was developed over many years of research and was based on an analysis of the early childhood education and the subject-matter literatures. The Early Childhood Classroom Observation Measure, developed by Stipek and her colleagues, assesses a wide range of observable classroom components (Stipek & Byler, 2004). The measure of "best practices" consists of 17 items rated on a scale ranging from 1 (*practices are rarely seen*) to 5 (*practices predominate*). The 17 ratings yield five dimensions of best practice: (a) the degree to which the social climate promotes respect for individuals and individual differences; (b) whether the classroom is managed with clear, well-understood routines and smooth, efficient transitions, with children having activity choices and other responsibilities that they can handle; (c) whether learning activities have clear standards and lessons are coherent and understandable; (d) the degree to which math instruction focuses on the development of understanding, using manipulatives, and guided practice; and (e) the degree to which literacy instruction involves diverse approaches to teaching reading and writing and a balance between phonics and comprehension. A parallel set of 17 items assesses the degree to which practices along these same five dimensions are highly teacher directed and didactic. Highly didactic, teacher-directed instructional strategies are not as well supported as the student-centered, problem-solving approaches described earlier in subject-matter research on reading and mathematics learning or in research found in the early childhood education literature. The classroom observation measure also assesses resources, including computers and equipment for gross motor activities and materials for literacy, math, science, dramatic play, and art.

Correlation coefficients were computed to assess associations between the school population and the various characteristics of the schools and teachers in the target classrooms. The higher the proportion of low-income children a school served, the larger the school ($r = .43$), the less spent per pupil ($r = -.24$), and the less educated the teachers of children enrolled in the study ($r = -.23$). Schools serving a relatively high proportion of children of color were also significantly larger ($r = .60$), spent less per pupil ($r = -.36$), and had relatively less educated teachers ($r = -.30$).

Analyses were also conducted to examine associations between the school population and teachers' practices and resources in the target classrooms. Four of the five best-practice scales mentioned previously were significantly and negatively correlated with the proportion of low-income children (rs ranging from $-.29$ to $-.41$) and the proportion of students of color (rs ranging from $-.25$ to $-.42$). All five of the scales assessing the degree to which highly teacher-directed practices were observed were positively correlated with both the proportion of low-income children (rs ranging from $.27-.46$) and the proportion of students of color (rs ranging from $.33-.48$). Resources, including the number of computers, were also observed less in the classrooms of schools serving a relatively high proportion of children of color. Regressions revealed further that the proportion of children of color had more predictive power than did the proportion of low-income children with regard to the nature and quality of instruction.

Our findings are consistent with Lee and Loeb's (1995) study, which was designed to investigate the possibility that low-quality schooling explains why the positive effects of preschool intervention programs often fade. The authors point out that the average family income of children who attend Head Start is lower than the average family income of all children who meet the Head Start low-income eligibility requirements. They proposed that Head Start effects fade because participants attend schools that are particularly low in quality. Using eighth-grade data from the National Education Longitudinal Study, they found, consistent with their hypothesis, that compared with middle-class children and low-income children who did not attend Head Start, Head Start children attended schools that had a higher concentration of low-income children and lower average student achievement; their schools were also rated less physically safe and students claimed to have relatively poor relationships with their teachers.

Taken together, these findings are cause for concern for low-income children, especially low-income children of color. Although the study conducted by Stipek (2004) was restricted to a set of districts in three states, the findings are strong and consistent in showing that during the first, critical years of school, children who entered with the greatest disadvantages received the poorest quality instruction. This finding is especially remarkable given that the variance in school population among the schools studied was somewhat restricted by the selection criterion of having a low-income study child enrolled. The two studies just described suggest that instead of serving a leveling function, schools reinforce the relatively low cognitive skills economically disadvantaged children often have when they enter kindergarten.

Policy Options

It is through no fault of their own that children born into poverty begin school with relatively low skills, on average, and typically do not catch up with their middle-class peers. Indeed, children from low-income families arrive at school just as eager to learn as children from more affluent families (Stipek & Ryan, 1997). Instead, many of the difficulties they encounter are a consequence of policy decisions that could be changed. In the next section, we discuss a few policy options that could prevent or reduce the achievement gap for young children, paying special attention to the needs of English language learners, who are often overlooked in both research and policy decision making.

Improving Elementary Education

It is clear that educators need to redouble their efforts to ensure that children who are in the greatest need of effective instruction in the early grades of school have access to experienced, well-trained teachers. Space constraints preclude a discussion of what is required to improve elementary education. We simply note that there is substantial knowledge about effective school and instructional practices that could be used to guide efforts to improve educational programs for low-income children and English language learners.

Increasing Access to Quality Day Care and Early Childhood Education

The gap in children's skill levels at school entry could be reduced by providing children from economically disadvantaged families more access to high-quality preschool programs. There has been a substantial increase in preschool programs available to low-income children. For example, a recent survey found that 42 states currently fund some kind of prekindergarten program through the public schools (Clifford, Saluja, & Crawford, 2001). Nevertheless, the need is not even close to being met. Head Start is able to serve only about 60% of the 3- and 4-year-old children who qualify, and children from low-income families are less likely to have any preschool experience at all (NCES, 1996) and much less likely to attend licensed day-care programs than middle-class children (Smith, 2002).

More, however, is not necessarily better. The evidence is very clear that quality counts. Simply creating additional slots in low-quality preschool programs is not likely to bring children from low-income families up to speed for the beginning of school. Quality has to be a central consideration in any effort to expand child-care and preschool opportunities for children.

We also recommend that more attention be paid to the needs of children from immigrant families. Few preschools are designed to meet the needs of low-income bilingual children. There is a severe shortage of bilingual preschool teachers, and teachers serving bilingual preschoolers are rarely trained in bilingual or second language acquisition methodology. For example, 14,000 language-minority Head Start youngsters are served in programs where there are no staff members who speak their first, and often only, language. Almost 10,000 native Spanish-speaking children attend Head Start centers without one Spanish-speaking staff member (Joseph & Chazan-Cohen, 2000).

Because the special needs of young English language learners are not discussed elsewhere in this volume, we consider issues related to preschool education for this group of children in more detail.

English Language Learners

Although there is consensus in the professional community that high-quality preschool experiences can have positive effects on children's skills, current understanding of effective practices for language-minority preschoolers is quite limited. Existing research is incomplete because studies either focus solely on English-speaking preschoolers or combine information on ELL preschoolers with native English-speaking preschoolers. Furthermore, most studies use standardized test scores as the primary indicator of preschool effectiveness. Because the tests are not usually offered in languages other than English, their validity is in question when applied to children who are not proficient in English. Research on the few preschools that are specially designed for the needs of language-minority children is also scarce. The majority of studies are descriptive and do not use an experimental design.

What is well-known is that low-income, language-minority children are underenrolled in formal care centers relative to socioeconomically comparable language-majority children. In one study (West, Hausken, & Chandler, 1993) of the Latino families with children between 3 and 5 years old that used some form of child care, only 39% used formal centers or preschools.

A central policy decision in designing preschool programs for language-minority children is whether they should be English-only or provide opportunities for children to develop language skills in their native language. The handful of studies that have compared outcomes of preschoolers in bilingual programs with outcomes of English-only programs suggests that children in bilingual preschools are better prepared for school than their peers in monolingual preschools. One such study was conducted by Campos (1995) on the Carpinteria Preschool, a program serving language-minority Latino youngsters, which offered instruction almost solely in Spanish. The report showed that even after a year in the program, Carpinteria preschoolers performed better on measures of English, Spanish, school readiness, and academic achievement than their peers in English-only day-care and Head Start centers. These advantages were found to extend well past children's participation in the preschool program. Indeed, middle school students who had participated in the Carpinteria program were found to be academically superior to students who had participated in English-only preschools. Advantages of bilingual preschools have been found in other studies as well (Bronson, 1994; Paul & Jarvis, 1992; Sandoval-Martinez, 1982).

Studies on the effects of bilingual preschool programs on children's native language proficiency yield conflicting conclusions. Wong Fillmore (1991) reported that English language preschool, even if offered through a bilingual program, causes students to reject, and ultimately lose proficiency in, their native language, and thus undermines their ability to communicate with their elders. Attrition of the native language through exposure to preschool has also been documented in a case study by Zentella (1997). In contrast, research by Winsler (1997) and Rodriguez, Diaz, and Duran (1995) found that exposure to English in a bilingual program did not cause preschoolers to lose proficiency in their native language within the 1-year time frame of the study. Different sampling as well as measurement strategies may account for the different findings.

A 1993 California Tomorrow report on home–school links suggests that English-only preschool instruction may also limit productive connections between Spanish-speaking parents and the school. The report claimed that when language-minority parents cannot participate in their child's preschool experience because of language barriers, a pattern of expectations of low involvement may be created that carries over into elementary school and beyond. Accordingly, the study's authors conclude from their survey of California preschools in five counties that language and cultural barriers between child-care providers and parents produce feelings of alienation for language- and cultural-minority parents. A case study of four Latina mothers, for example, suggested that language differences led to a feeling of alienation between the mothers and the monolingual English-speaking staff (Chang & Sakai, 1993).

Currently, the general understanding of bilingual preschools, language of instruction, and student outcomes is limited to evidence from only a few studies, and the studies that have been conducted are open to criticism for providing no information about the programs other than the language of instruction, for not specifying the proportion of English and native language used, and for lack of random assignment. Knowledge of the effect of English instruction in a bilingual program on students' native language use is also incomplete and vulnerable to criticism, for example, for relying on parent reports of children's language proficiency and failing to explore attitudes toward language or authentic language use, which might have implications for native language attrition or maintenance as children move through school.

It is clear that there is a need for more careful research on language-minority children in preschools that addresses issues of program characteristics and school readiness outcomes. Our best guess would suggest that high-quality preschool programs are just as beneficial for the ELL population as for native English speakers, and that a strong native-language development component would be highly desirable. A strong native-language component need not undermine English language development. To the contrary, the research on bilingualism and cognitive development suggests that under ideal conditions the two languages do not compete for mental capacity, and in fact reinforce and strengthen each other (Diaz, 1985).

We turn next to two additional policy options that should be considered as strategies for giving children in poverty a better start in elementary school: having children enter school at an earlier age and all-day kindergarten.

Earlier School Entry

An alternative to increasing access to early childhood education programs that are funded and managed outside of the public school system is to extend public school education programs to younger children. This could be achieved by changing the cutoff enrollment age, allowing children to begin kindergarten earlier than current policy, or by creating a new "grade" for 4-year-old children. Many public school systems have preschool programs linked to them, but they are often managed and funded independently of the regular school system, creating complicated bureaucracies and sometimes contradicting regulations. Extending school to younger children might be more cost-effective than separate programs and could promote greater continuity. Continuity, of course, should not be achieved by bringing developmentally inappropriate elementary school practices to 4-year-olds.

The cutoff birth date for kindergarten entry is typically set by the state, although a few states give school districts discretion. Currently, most states require children to turn 5 by the end of September, about the time school begins. The trend has been to move the cutoff date up, so that children enter kindergarten older on average. Between 1975 and 2000, 22 states moved the birth date required for school entry to an earlier point in the year. Nine of those changes were made since 1990. One state (Indiana) changed its law from allowing districts to set their own age cutoff to a state requirement of June 1. Only one state (Idaho) changed in the opposite direction (from August 16 to September 1). Legislation that moves the birth date cutoff to earlier in the school year is based in part on the assumption that later entry into school will result in higher academic achievement. This notion is articulated in the 1999 California bill (AB 25: Article 1.5, 48005.10).

> Comparisons between California pupils and pupils in other states on national achievement tests in the later grades are likely to be more equitable if the entry age of California pupils is more closely aligned to that of most other states.

Implicit in the theory underlying policies and practices that delay school entry is the debatable idea that for a child deemed unready for kindergarten the "gift of time" outweighs the benefits of experience in a school setting. Fortunately there are data that provide evidence on whether low-income children who are at risk for school failure are better served by having more time out-of-school or by having more time in an instructional environment.

One strategy that has been used to assess the effects of school entry age on children's academic achievement is to compare children who are in the same grade but have different birth dates. In any one grade there is at least a 12-month spread in ages. Assuming that children's birth dates are randomly distributed, associations between the natural variation in age of entry and child outcomes would suggest an entry-age effect. Few of the studies using this methodology assess change in achievement over the school year; they therefore cannot be used to determine whether older children benefit relatively more from schooling (make greater gains) than do younger children. They do, however, provide information on whether older children perform better on average than do younger children.

The findings from these studies vary somewhat, but a fairly clear picture emerges. Most studies report differences in the beginning grades of school that favor older children, and some studies report differences in the later elementary grades. A few studies find no difference in some or all achievement tests, even in kindergarten. In most of the studies that found significant age differences in the early grades, the differences were weaker or disappeared altogether by the upper elementary grades. (See Stipek, 2002, for a review of this research.)

In brief, extant research suggests some small advantage in being relatively older than classmates, but the advantage diminishes or disappears with age. The findings do not suggest that being older is better in some absolute sense because all of the studies use relative age as the independent variable. Depending on the birth-date cutoff, a relatively old child in one study could have been an average-aged child in another study. The findings also do not suggest that older children learn more in school than younger children. The age differences, when found, are usually stronger at the beginning of school than in the later grades, indicating that the younger children actually tended to learn more, often catching up with their older peers after a few years in school. Even in the early elementary grades, the magnitude of the effect of age appears to be small. Most studies do not compare age with other factors influencing student achievement, but in one that did, the proportion of the variance in achievement attributed to race and socioeconomic factors was 13 times larger than that contributed by age (Jones & Mandeville, 1990).

The most powerful strategy for assessing the effect of age of entry on children's learning compares children who are the same age but in different grades as well as children who are a year apart in age but in the same grade. The first comparison provides information on the effect of a year of schooling, holding age constant. The second comparison provides information on the effect of chronological age, holding the number of years of schooling constant. This strategy therefore provides information on the relative effects of an additional year of time (maturation and general out-of-school experience) versus an additional year of schooling.

Findings from studies using these methods suggest that schooling is the more potent contributor to most of the cognitive skills measured. In math and most aspects of reading and literacy, children who were in school gained more in a year than children the same age who were not in school. The evidence suggests also that age in the ranges studied was not a factor in how much children benefited from a year of schooling. (See Stipek, 2002, for a review.)

The studies comparing age and school effects suggest that school-based educational intervention contributes more to children's cognitive competencies overall than does maturation, and that relatively young children benefit from school as much as relatively older children. The school effect is strong in an absolute as well as a relative sense. In a study by Crone and Whitehurst (1999), for example, a year in school explained 62% of the literacy skill improvements at the kindergarten level and 81% in second grade. Cahan and Cohen (1989) reported that the effect of a year in school was twice the effect of a year of age.

In summary, the evidence suggests that within the 5- to 6-year-old range in which most children begin school in the United States (where most of the studies were conducted), age of school entry is not a significant predictor of ultimate academic success. Extant research does not support recent trends in the United States to raise the age at which children are eligible to begin school (e.g., from turning 5 by December of the year a child enters kindergarten to turning 5 in September or earlier). And it does not suggest that later school entry would enhance economically disadvantaged children's chances of academic success. To the contrary, time in school appears to contribute more to young children's cognitive skills than time outside of school. The results of these studies, if anything, suggest that low-income children should have access to instructional environments earlier, not later.

There is no evidence, to our knowledge, on the relative value of a preschool instructional program to early entry into elementary school. We suspect that the quality of the educational experience children have is more important than where it occurs or what it is called. Taken together, the research on the positive effects of quality center care and educational preschool programs and the research indicating that young children make more gains in than out of school, as previously discussed, suggest strongly that early education experiences— whether in or out of a regular school program—can help reduce the achievement gap in young children.

All-Day Kindergarten

Another possible strategy for getting all children off to a good start in school is to expand the amount of time they spend in kindergarten. An increasing number of children attend full-day kindergartens, rising from 13% in 1970, to 54% in 1995 (Elicker & Mathur, 1997), to 59.1% in 2000 (NCES, 2001a). Research suggests that there may be good reasons for this expansion of full-day programs.

The evidence on the effect of the longer kindergarten day is generally positive, although few studies meet the most rigorous research standards. Only one study we found involved random assignment, and only a few made efforts to match students or schools on demographics. Many studies did not collect or analyze data from the time students entered kindergarten, and bias that might have been introduced by parent choice is not known. Despite these shortcomings, the consistency of the findings, although not perfect, is impressive.

Fusaro (1997) conducted a meta-analysis of 21 studies that used achievement test results as the outcome measure. The results showed that students who attended full-day kindergartens had substantially and significantly higher achievement than students who attended half-day kindergartens. A few studies not included or completed after this meta-analysis provide further support for the benefits of full-day kindergarten. In a study by Elicker and Mathur (1997), children were randomly assigned to 4 full-day and 8 half-day programs. Analyses of developmental report card grades indicated that teachers rated the children who had attended full-day programs higher on literacy, math, general learning, social skills, and first-grade readiness, with prekindergarten developmental screening scores and parent income held constant. Hildebrand (2000), likewise, found that children who attended full-day kindergarten made significantly greater gains in reading than did children who attended half-day kindergarten, controlling for beginning reading ability. No differences were found between the groups in writing or math.

In one of the few studies that followed children beyond kindergarten, Gullo (2000) compared 947 second graders who had full-day or half-day kindergarten. Children who had full-day kindergarten scored significantly higher on both math and reading on the Iowa Test of Basic Skills and were less likely to be retained in either kindergarten or first grade. The study did not assess the possibility of preexisting differences in the two groups of children.

An atypically large study was conducted by Cryan, Sheehan, Wiechel, and Bandy-Hedden (1992). One of their samples included children from 27 school districts and the other sample included children from 32 districts in Ohio. An effort was made to match full- and half-day kindergartens on student demographics. In first grade the children who had been in full-time kindergarten scored 5 to 10 percentage points higher on Metropolitan Achievement Tests and were substantially less likely to be retained (17%–55% fewer retentions). A recent comparison of 17,600 Philadelphia children who attended half-day versus full-day kindergartens also found much lower retention rates among full-day students. Children who experienced full-day kindergarten were more than twice as likely as children without any kindergarten experience to reach third or fourth grade without being retained, and 26% more likely than children who had attended a half-day kindergarten (Del Gaudio Weiss & Offenberg, 2002).

In summary, although the research is both far from flawless and not perfectly consistent, the preponderance of the evidence suggests that children who begin school at a disadvantage would have a better chance of catching up if they attended a whole-day kindergarten program. In Philadelphia the savings from reducing retention rates was calculated to be 19% of the additional costs of a full-day program, indicating that some of the costs of expansion to full-day programs can be offset.

Universal or Targeted Policies

An important policy question for some of the options discussed in this chapter is whether expanded offerings should be made universal—available to all children—or targeted to children who are at risk of starting from behind. Arguments for universal services are usually based on the view that they enjoy a stronger, more powerful political base, and are thus less vulnerable to being red-lined in periods of tight budgets.

We acknowledge the wisdom of this perspective, but in light of current budget constraints we propose a more targeted approach. It is clear that it would not make sense to vary the date of school entry for children from different backgrounds or with different skill levels. But certainly Head Start as well as state and local preschool options for children who are at risk of school failure could be expanded and the quality of many existing programs could be improved. Schools that serve a substantial population of economically disadvantaged students might create prekindergarten programs to give these children an opportunity to develop cognitive and social skills that they may not develop out of school. Districts and schools that offer half-day kindergarten could provide an extended day for children whose skills lag behind their peers or who are English language learners.

At the very least, the inequities in resources and the quality of the public education offered to children from different ethnic and economic backgrounds should no longer be tolerated. Children who have not attended preschool, who have experienced low-quality day care, or who do not speak English need better, not worse, instruction in school. Schools that serve children who begin with these disadvantages need more, not fewer, resources. Until the current inequities are eliminated, the children who start from behind are sure to be left behind.

Choosing Among the Options

Our goals in this chapter were to make a case for attending more to the educational needs of young economically disadvantaged children and to suggest some policy options that are likely to improve these children's chances of success in school. We turn now to the task of choosing from among these and other options that might be considered to ensure that all children have a fair chance of succeeding in school. How might policymakers decide whether preschool programs should be expanded and improved, children should be allowed to enter school at a younger age, or kindergarten should be expanded to a full-day program?

This decision needs to be based on local resources and opportunities. For example, if the schools in a community are overcrowded, expanding freestanding preschool programs might be a better option than admitting children to kindergarten at an earlier age or creating school-based prekindergarten programs. The best option or combination of options in one context may not work in another. Whatever approach is chosen, it should be based on sound educational theory and it should be reevaluated and fine-tuned using data that reflect the goals of the program.

Strategies developed to address the needs of young children also need to be coordinated. Whether children's early educational experiences are in preschools independent of elementary schools or down the hall from the elementary grade classrooms, there needs to be continuity in children's experiences. For many years, people have believed the notion that children somehow become ready to succeed in school at some particular point in their development. All children at all ages are ready to learn. The meaningful question is not whether a child is ready to learn, but rather what a child is ready to learn at a particular point in time. The learning process is continuous, and so should be children's educational programs.

In summary, we are not prescribing a particular course of action, but we do recommend that decision making take into consideration what is known about the developmental needs of young children, and that they be adjusted on the basis of sound empirical evidence[2] and data that is collected after a policy is implemented. Continual systematic observations of the effect of policies and programs on children need to be collected locally as well, because the lessons learned from other sites need to be adapted to the specific circumstances and needs of the children in any particular context.

We are recognizably students of Zigler. He taught us the importance of scientifically based policy decision making early in our careers; that value has been reinforced by our own experience. There is much to be learned about how to ensure the academic success of all children, including children growing up in poverty and children who are not proficient in English. But extant research provides very good direction. Although we continue to fine-tune our knowledge base, we need to heed our mentor's advice, and use what we know.

References

Assembly Bill No. 25 (AB 25), Pupils: age of admission, Section 1.5, 48005.10 (1999).

Augenblick, J., Myers, J., & Anderson, A. (1997). Equity and adequacy in school funding. *The Future of Children, 7*, 63–78.

Bronson, M. (1994). The usefulness of an observation measure of children's social and mastery behaviors in early childhood classrooms. *Early Childhood Research Quarterly, 9*, 19–43.

Cahan, S., & Cohen, N. (1989). Age versus schooling effects on intelligence development. *Child Development, 60*, 1239–1249.

Campos, S. (1995). The Carpinteria Preschool Program: A long-term effects study. In E. Garcia & B. McLaughlin (Eds.), *Meeting the challenge of linguistic and cultural diversity in early childhood education* (pp. 34–48). New York: Teachers' College Press.

Chang, H., & Sakai, L. (1993). *Affirming children's roots: Cultural and linguistic diversity in early care and education*. San Francisco: California Tomorrow.

Clifford, R., Saluja, G., & Crawford, G. (2001). *Public school involvement in prekindergarten services*. Manuscript submitted for publication.

Crone, D., & Whitehurst, G. (1999). Age and schooling effects on emergent literacy and early reading skills. *Journal of Educational Psychology, 91*, 604–614.

Cryan, J., Sheehan, R., Wiechel, J., & Bandy-Hedden, I. (1992). Success outcomes of full-day kindergarten: More positive behavior and increased achievement in the years after. *Early Childhood Research Quarterly, 7*, 187–203.

Del Gaudio Weiss, A., & Offenberg, R. (2002). *Enhancing urban children's early success in school: The power of full-day kindergarten*. Unpublished manuscript.

Diaz, R. (1985). Bilingual cognitive development: Addressing three gaps in current research. *Child Development, 56*, 1376–1388.

Elicker, J., & Mathur, S. (1997). What do they do all day? Comprehensive evaluation of a full-day kindergarten. *Early Childhood Research Quarterly, 12*, 459–480.

Fusaro, J. (1997). The effect of full-day kindergarten on student achievement: A meta-analysis. *Child Study Journal, 27*, 269–277.

Gándara, P., & Rumberger, R. (2002, May). *The inequitable treatment of English learners in California's public schools*. Paper presented at the annual conference of the University of California Linguistic Minority Research Institute, Berkeley.

---

[2]Given the current enamored state of educational policymakers with "scientifically based research," mentioned more than 100 times in the No Child Left Behind Act of 2001 and in the authorization of the Institute of Education Sciences, it is worth mentioning that we reject the narrow equating of "scientific evidence" with "randomized field trials," and rather take the traditional scientific criteria of a dynamic interplay of theory and evidence that is mediated by the transparency of ideas and data and by a vigorous peer review process (see Shavelson & Towne, 2002).

Gullo, D. (2000). The long-term educational effects of half-day vs. full-day kindergarten. *Early Child Development and Care, 160*, 17–24.

Harris, L. (2002). *A survey of the status of equality in public education in California: A survey of a cross-section of public school teachers*. Retrieved January 1, 2004, from http://www.publicadvocates.org/equality_article-latest4.pdf

Hess, R., & Hahn, R. (1974). Prediction of school failure and the Hess School Readiness Scale. *Psychology in the Schools, 11*, 134–136.

Hildebrand, C. (2000). Effects of all-day and half-day kindergarten programming on reading, writing, math, and classroom social behaviors [Electronic version]. *National Forum of Applied Educational Research Journal, 13E*(3).

Jones, M., & Mandeville, K. (1990). The effect of age at school entry on reading achievement scores among South Carolina students. *Remedial and Special Education, 11*, 56–62.

Joseph, G. E., & Chazan-Cohen, R. C. (2000). *Celebrating cultural and linguistic diversity in Head Start*. Washington, DC: Administration on Children, Youth and Families.

Kindler, A. (2002). *Survey of the states' limited english proficient students and available educational programs and services: 2000–2001 summary report*. Washington, DC: National Clearinghouse for English Language Acquisition & Language Instruction Educational Programs.

Lankford, H., Loeb, S., & Wyckoff, J. (2002). Teacher sorting and the plight of urban schools: A descriptive analysis. *Education Evaluation and Policy Analysis, 24*, 37–62.

Lee, V., & Loeb, S. (1995). Where do Head Start attendees end up? One reason for why preschool effects fade out. *Educational Evaluation and Policy Analysis, 17*, 62–82.

Luster, T., & McAdoo, H. (1996). Family and child influences on educational attainment: A secondary analysis of the High/Scope Perry Preschool data. *Developmental Psychology, 32*, 26–39.

National Center for Education Statistics. (1995). *Approaching kindergarten: A look at preschoolers in the United States* (NCES No. 95-280). Washington, DC: Office of Education Research and Improvement, U.S. Department of Education.

National Center for Education Statistics. (1996). *Urban schools: The challenge of location and poverty* (NCES No. 96-184). Washington, DC: Office of Education Research and Improvement, U.S. Department of Education.

National Center for Education Statistics. (1999). *Digest of Educational Statistics* (NCES No. 99-036). Washington, DC: U.S. Department of Education.

National Center for Education Statistics. (2001a). *Digest of Educational Statistics*. Washington, DC: U.S. Department of Education.

National Center for Education Statistics (with N. Zill & J. West). (2001b). *Entering kindergarten: A portrait of American children when they begin school: Findings from the Condition of Education 2000* (NCES No. 2001-035). Washington, DC: U.S. Government Printing Office.

No Child Left Behind Act of 2001. Pub. L. No. 107-110 (2002).

Parrish, R., Hikido, C., & Fowler, W. (1998). *Inequalities in public school district revenues* (NCES Rep. No. 98-210). Washington, DC: U.S. Department of Education, National Center for Education Statistics.

Paul, B., & Jarvis, C. (1992, April). *The effects of native language use in New York City pre-kindergarten classes*. Paper presented at the annual conference of the American Educational Research Association, San Francisco, CA.

Phillips, M., Crouse, J., & Ralph, J. (1998). Does the black–white test score gap widen after children enter school? In C. Jencks & M. Phillips (Eds.), *The black–white test score gap* (pp. 229–272). Washington, DC: Brookings Institution Press.

Rodriguez, J., Diaz, R., & Duran, D. (1995). The impact of bilingual preschool education on the language development of Spanish-speaking children. *Early Childhood Research Quarterly, 10*, 475–490.

Roza, M., & Miles, K. (2002). *Moving toward equity in school funding within districts*. New York: Annenberg Institute for School Reform at Brown University.

Sandoval-Martinez, S. (1982). Findings from the Head Start bilingual curriculum development and evaluation effort. *The Journal for the National Association for Bilingual Education, 7*(1), 1–12.

Shavelson, R. J. & Towne, L. (Eds.). (2002). *Scientific research in Education*. Washington, DC: National Academy Press.

Smith, K. (2002). *Who's minding the kids? Child care arrangements: Spring 1997.* U.S. Census Bureau, Current Population Reports. Retrieved January 1, 2004, from http://www.census.gov/population/www/socdemo/childcare.html

Stecher, B., & Bohrnstedt, G. (2002). *Class size reduction in California: Findings from 1999–2000 and 2000–2001.* Sacramento: California Department of Education.

Stevenson, H., & Newman, R. (1986). Long-term prediction of achievement and attitudes in mathematics and reading. *Child Development, 57,* 646–659.

Stipek, D. (2001). Pathways to constructive lives: The importance of early school success. In C. Bohart & D. Stipek (Eds.), *Constructive & destructive behavior: Implications for family, school, & society* (pp. 291–315). Washington, DC: American Psychological Association.

Stipek, D. (2002). At what age should children enter kindergarten? A question for policy makers and parents. *SRCD Social Policy Report, 16*(2), 3–17.

Stipek, D. (2004). Teaching practices in kindergarten and first grade: Different strokes for different folks. *Early Childhood Research Quarterly, 19,* 548–568.

Stipek, D., & Byler, D. (2004). The Early Childhood Classroom Observation Measure. *Early Childhood Research Quarterly, 19,* 375–397.

Stipek, D., & Ryan, R. (1997). Economically disadvantaged preschoolers: Ready to learn but further to go. *Developmental Psychology, 33,* 711–723.

West, J., & Denton, K. (2002). *The kindergarten year: Findings from the Early Childhood Longitudinal Study, kindergarten class of 1998–99.* Washington, DC: National Center for Education Statistics.

West, J., Hausken, E., & Chandler, K. (1993). *Experiences in child care and early childhood programs of first and second graders prior to entering first grade: Findings from the 1991 National Household Education Survey.* Washington, DC: U.S. Department of Education, National Center for Educational Statistics.

Winsler, A. (1997, April). *Learning a second language does not mean losing the first: A replication and follow up of bilingual language development in Spanish-speaking children attending bilingual preschool.* Paper presented at the annual meeting of the American Educational Research Association, Chicago.

Wong Fillmore, L. (1991). When learning a second language means losing the first. *Early Childhood Research Quarterly, 6,* 323–346.

Zentella, A. (1997). *Growing up bilingual.* Oxford, England: Blackwell Publishers.

Part III ―――――――――――――――――――

Addressing the Needs of the Most Vulnerable Children and Families

9

Poverty and Child Development: New Perspectives on a Defining Issue

J. Lawrence Aber, Stephanie M. Jones, and C. Cybele Raver

In the emerging field of child development and social policy, two of the oldest concerns involved (a) how poverty and social deprivation influences children's development and (b) how programs and policies can ameliorate the effects of poverty on children's development. Indeed, it could be argued that these twin concerns were defining features of the birth of the field. Edward F. Zigler has labored mightily to address these concerns, from his early efforts to understand the role of poverty in the development of what was then called *cultural–familial retardation*; to his efforts to design, implement, protect, and reform Head Start; to more recent efforts to improve early care and education and elementary schooling for children from low-income families and communities. In this chapter, as former students of Ed's who were mentored by him at three different periods over nearly a 30-year span, we describe some of the changes in the scientific and theoretical understanding of the effects of poverty on child development over the last 4 decades. In addition, we describe the evolution of program and policy efforts to protect children from the negative effects of poverty, paying particular attention to whether and how evolution in practice and policy was influenced by developments in theory and research.

Where possible, we draw on Zigler's own work to support this examination. But we also extend the examination beyond his work to include critical developments in the field as a whole. Finally, we discuss the implications of these major developments over the last 40 years for future research, practice, and policy concerning poverty and child development.

We begin with a brief overview of the changing definitions and understanding of poverty and social deprivation over the last several decades. We then turn to a complementary overview of changing conceptions and basic theories of the influence of poverty on child development. We conclude by discussing the implications of these changes in theories and research for the evolution of programs and policies on behalf of low-income children and their families.

Changing Definitions of Poverty and Social Deprivation: 1960 to 2000

Despite current knowledge of the pernicious and multiple negative impacts of poverty on the development of children and youth (e.g., Aber, Jones, & Cohen, 2000; Gershoff, Aber, & Raver, 2002; McLoyd, 1998), poverty as a construct remains difficult to define. This is a problem because, as Zigler taught each of us, it is very difficult to rigorously study what you cannot clearly define. Indeed, various definitions of poverty have been used in both research studies and public policy analyses over the last several decades. In this section we aim to clarify distinctions among these multiple definitions.

The measurement of income poverty in the United States is based on an absolute measure, the *federal poverty threshold* (FPT), developed in 1963 by the Department of Agriculture. The FPT roughly determines poverty to represent any level of sustenance below the cost of the Department of Agriculture's economy food plan times a factor of three. The economy food plan equals the least expensive budget a household could devote to food and still receive adequate nutrition (Orshansky, 1963). The value of the economy food plan was multiplied by three because studies showed that food represented about one third of an average family's household expense at the time. Thresholds are adjusted annually in concurrence with the Consumer Price Index (Fisher, 1992). For the year 2004, the federal poverty guidelines (a simplification of the FPT used for administrative purposes, such as determining assistance eligibility) define the poverty line for a family of four at the income level of $19,157 (U.S. Census Bureau, 2004).

Although this definition of poverty is used in scores of programs and research studies, its limitations have been well documented. For example, since its development, it has not been adjusted for the decline in the proportion of families' total income devoted to food expenditures. Moreover, adjustments are not made for real differences in the cost of living in different geographic areas, and the standard definition ignores the increasing tax burden experienced by many lower income families (Citro & Michael, 1995; Edin & Lein, 1997). Using such a fixed-ratio definition does not allow other material costs to rise more rapidly than food (e.g., housing costs), nor does it account for other basic necessities such as transportation and child care. In addition, the FPT operates at an individual or family level and therefore cannot address larger contributing factors such as regional unemployment, job loss, or broader economic downturn (Aber et al., 2000; Gershoff et al., 2002).

Another limitation is that many programs and studies tend to use the FPT as a simple cutoff to identify the poor and nonpoor, despite the fact that it is broadly understood that the negative impact of poverty is not limited to those children living below 100% of the federal poverty threshold. Empirical studies document that living near the poverty threshold (variously defined as income between 100% and 185% or income below 200% of the federal poverty line) has also been linked to poor outcomes for children (e.g., Bolger, Patterson, Thompson, & Kupersmidt, 1995). Thus, any estimates of poverty's impact that fail to include children living near the poverty threshold are likely to grossly underestimate the scope of the problem. Indeed, recent estimates indicate that 45% of kindergarten-age children live in or near poverty (Gershoff, 2003).

Two alternative concepts and measures of income poverty are those of relative poverty and subjective poverty. *Relative poverty* is defined as a gross family income that falls below a certain percentage of a jurisdiction's median income (usually 40%–50% of the national median income). As is clear, in contrast to absolute definitions of poverty, relative poverty is determined contextually, and is contingent on the assessment of the income of a particular individual relative to the income of the population. The rationale behind the use of a relative poverty threshold is that what is considered an acceptable standard of living changes with time and that families whose resources are significantly below other members of their society will be unable to participate fully in that society. *Subjective poverty* is defined as the average answer to the following question, "What is the minimum income required for a family [of four] to just barely get by in your community?" Subjective definitions of poverty allows estimates of the degree to which families perceive and are adversely affected by financial hardship, such as the degree to which families are able to purchase sufficient food, clothing, or shelter. In addition, the manner in which poverty is measured, by whatever definition, is critical to understanding its effects on children and families.

Persistence of Poverty and Income Dynamics

Differential outcomes for children living in persistent poverty in contrast to transitory poverty are well established (Duncan & Brooks-Gunn, 2000). Families living in persistent poverty have limited access to viable social and economic opportunities. In contrast, transitory poverty is primarily marked by fluctuations in income, which may result in breaks in access to social services. Overall, families living in persistent poverty are more susceptible to negative psychological, emotional, and physical outcomes. However, considerable controversy still exists over whether it is persistent poverty per se or other factors associated with persistent poverty that are the causal factors leading to negative outcomes (Mayer, 1997).

Socioeconomic Status and Poverty

There has been considerable debate regarding the use of socioeconomic status (SES) as a proxy for family income level. Different means of calculating SES as well as the use of different variables to represent SES produce different findings. Thus, the distinction between SES and poverty is critical. As noted by Bradley and Whiteside-Mansell (1997), "the co-occurrence of an undereducated mother or a father employed in an occupation of low status adds to, but does not replace the impact of inadequate economic resources" (p. 17). Hauser (1994) proposed a set of guidelines when measuring SES in studies of child development. He suggested that the measurement of SES can be improved by ascertaining the occupation (and industry) held by one or both parents, levels of parental education, and residential mobility.

Poverty and Co-Occurring Demographic Risks

A considerable amount of research has described the co-occurrence of poverty and multiple familial and ecological risk factors, such as teen and single parenthood, negative life events, violence exposure, marital distress, and parent psychopathology (e.g., Aber et al., 2000). Some have argued that poverty's deleterious impact on child development may be due in part to exposure to these family and ecological risks, which, both individually and in combination, have been associated with negative outcomes for children and youth (e.g., Sameroff, Bartko, Baldwin, Baldwin, & Seifer, 1998).

More recently, psychological research has begun to identify measures of socioeconomic status that assess psychological aspects of poverty, rather than relying solely on external or distal conceptualizations of poverty. In particular, the notion of social exclusion has received increased attention of late. *Social exclusion* refers to the notion that children who face economic insecurity at varying degrees of severity are not only "poor" but also are excluded from situations and activities that are considered to be a normal or desirable part of life (Aber, Gershoff, & Brooks-Gunn, 2002).

When poverty is operationalized in multiple ways, at both proximal and distal contextual levels, and within and across time, it allows for the consideration of poverty as a pervasive life experience that exists and influences children and families in multiple ways and at multiple levels of their own ecologies. As such, *developmental contextual models* (e.g., Bronfenbrenner, 1979), which recognize and incorporate the importance of contextual effects for both healthy and psychopathological development, are particularly useful for poverty researchers. Such an ecological approach allows for the identification of multiple contexts important to development, and can encompass both objective and subjective dimensions (Bronfenbrenner & Morris, 1998). Directing attention to the immediate as well as larger social context allows researchers to consider the variety of factors that compose socioeconomic status as well as to understand how one's position in a socially stratified system affects the everyday life of children and families. This, in turn, facilitates investigations into the mechanisms through which poverty in its multiple contexts impacts developmental outcomes.

The last several decades have witnessed an increase in the sophistication and complexity with which researchers are defining *poverty* for use in studies of child development. What is particularly important about these changes is that the definitions and operationalizations of poverty are beginning to synchronize with the complexity and depth of current theoretical understandings of child development in context. We now turn to a complementary overview of changing conceptions and basic theories of the influence of poverty on child development.

The Evolution of Science and Theory in the Development of Poor Children

Each of us has had the privilege of knowing Ed as an advisor, inspiring us with his patience, compassion, and commitment to improving developmental outcomes for poor children across a span of more than 40 years. But what inspires Ed? In 1958, Zigler completed his dissertation research on the social potential of "feebleminded" children who had been institutionalized. Specifically, Ed examined the impact of providing positive feedback in the forms of verbal and nonverbal support to 60 children as they completed a simple, monotonous marble game. In his published dissertation research (Zigler, 1961) he reported in scholarly fashion that these children, because of their institutionalization and extensive social deprivation of supportive and loving contact with adults, played for longer periods of time than did children with less deprived histories. That is, his research participants could not have cared less about getting an experimenter's task "right;" for these children, Ed's marble task was an opportunity to engage, even if repetitively, with a new person who would share time and attention with them. But look more closely, through the scientific and technical language that can distance us so well from the lived experience of real children. What do we see? The heartbreaking image of Ed as a young graduate student, testing each of those 60 children in what was probably a quite desolate institutional context, with children willing to persevere on a completely boring task just to spend time sitting with him, receiving his encouragement and interest. Knowing Ed, what choice could he have had, as he turned and walked away from those institutions at the end of the day, but to commit with unending perseverance to the challenge of improving children's lives?

1960s

Zigler's work on removing obstacles to children's social and cognitive potential in the context of "social deprivation" was exactly the kind of work that policymakers needed as they launched the national Head Start program in 1965 with 500,000 children and families as part of the War on Poverty. A number of historians have argued that the history of federal assistance to poor Americans "left behind" in the wake of post–World War II prosperity has fundamentally been a struggle between those who see poverty as a consequence of individual flaws and deficits and those who see poverty as resulting from the state's inadequacies in protecting its citizens from market exploitation (Katz, 1996; O'Connor, 2002). Strands of that debate recurred throughout the last 4 decades of research on children and poverty.

What led to the policy choice in the War on Poverty to invest in a package of human capital investments in poor children's and adults' skills rather than in a plan of income redistribution or private market reforms that might have been equally plausible solutions to the problem of postwar poverty and income inequality? O'Connor (2002) and others argued that central to this choice during the 1960s was the increased visibility of social and behavioral sciences in the government's and public's eyes, and the inclination of the science of the time to focus on individual and cultural, noneconomic factors related to families' material hardship. Specifically, work by anthropologists such as Lewis (1966) and social psychologists such as McClelland (e.g., McClelland, Atkinson, Clark, & Lowell, 1953) emphasized that the skills, beliefs, and motivations of poor adults and their children were intertwined with, if not responsible for, the perpetuation of poverty. Although this obscured social structural class stratification explanations for poverty, it was also reflective of a remarkable sense of optimism: that children born into families in the lowest socioeconomic stratum were not barred by constitutional or social barriers from moving up.

What were the intellectual anchors in research on poor children's development that would have led the architects of Head Start to take such a stance? Within the field of child development generally, the first intellectual anchor was that children's futures (such as their likelihood of above-poverty earnings as adults) relied on some set of skills or abilities that were internal to the child and that demonstrated some degree of continuity over time (Jones & Zigler, 2002). Research by Hunt (1961) and B. S. Bloom (1964) suggested that cognitive skills were plastic and amenable to intervention early in life but became increasingly resistant to change over time. Thus, early childhood represented a critical period in which to intervene.

And what were our views of the development of poor children at that time? Head Start teachers were to serve as providers of cognitive stimulation and motivational support, in addition to ensuring children's health, social, emotional, and nutritional needs were being met (Zigler & Muenchow, 1992). Lewis (1966) set the stage for a focus on motivation by discussing the intense level of apathy and demoralization that poor adults felt in conditions of chronic material hardship. This depiction was consistently translated into a sense of hopelessness and despair on the part of children as well. Work by Harlow and Harlow (1965), Spitz (1945), and Bowlby (1969) underscored the costs of the absence of a nurturing and supportive adult caregiver in infants' lives. These investigators also offered the promise that dysfunction resulting from deprivation could be reversed, providing policymakers and the public with the kinds of metaphors that undergirded support for the role that Head Start teachers might be able to play in offering opportunities for "culturally deprived" children to build a sense of "effectance motivation" and mastery in formal learning environments (White, 1959). In light of nativist views of poor children's intellectual inferiority and a strong social psychological emphasis on motivation as a chief behavioral drive that leads to individual success, it is easy to see ways that well-intentioned policymakers might reach for a solution that included stimulating young children's curiosity as well as teaching them the basics of early schooling.

Zigler was among the first to suggest that public and policymaker expectations for Head Start were falsely inflated and that cognitive skills should not represent the only targeted outcome for poor children (Zigler, 1970). When reading today his works from the first 20 years of Head Start's implementation, it is clear that the field simply had not caught up with the depth or comprehensiveness of his insight into children's well-being and potential. In an *American Psychologist* article published in 1978 (Zigler & Trickett, 1978), for example, Zigler lays out clear, compelling quantitative evidence for ways that children's performance on standardized IQ tests is not wholly reliant on nor reflective of their potential. Zigler changed the policy environment and the field of scholarship by refuting the notion of "cognitive defect" as the key difficulty faced by a "culturally deprived" child, demanding that more complex models of childhood and poverty be considered (Zigler & Butterfield, 1968). Zigler gives the case example of a child who replies "I don't know" to a teacher's question of "What is your name?":

Something is wrong with this child, but it is not a cognitive defect. He is defective in the sense that he is interacting with the teacher in a way that is self-defeating to the child. His psychological stance, his orientation, is overly cautious to the extent that it takes him out of the mainstream of an educational system as it is typically structured. If the teacher wishes to help, the answer is not careful teaching of the child's own name, but giving him those experiences that will lead to his interacting with a strange adult in a trusting way. (Zigler, 1970, p. 408)

Zigler's early concerns both anticipated and were informed by early evaluation results. Generally dismal findings on the fade-out effects of Head Start on IQ gains were bad news to a model in which children were to be able to escape poverty simply by improving their human capital and cognitive potential in preschool (e.g., McKey et al., 1985).

1970s

When the simpler models of the influence of poverty and deprivation on children's development dominant in the 1960s failed to explain the emerging data, developmental psychologists began to offer a more complex portrait of poverty and child development in the early 1970s by considering children's experiences along a continuum of risk and resilience. For example, Elder (1974) studied child well-being in the context of large and unexpected income loss during the Great Depression. This work pushed psychologists and policymakers to recognize both the considerable variability in poor children's outcomes and the extent to which poverty was itself likely to be a result of exogenous economic forces as much as a result of personal failing on the part of the poor. Work by Bronfenbrenner in 1979 was central in locating children's experiences within the multiple ecologies of family, neighborhood, and formal institutions such as school. This ecological framework drew explicit attention to structural forces that might cause changes in interpersonal relations, family relationships, and dyadic interactions.

Although some developmentalists considered poor children's well-being in the context of exo- and macrosystems, other developmentalists considered the extensive biologic and neurologic risks that low-income infants were likely to face and also argued for complex, transactional models to predict prospects for positive versus negative developmental outcomes. Sameroff and Chandler's (1975) work was critical in convincing both social scientists and policymakers of the importance of considering biologic and environmental risks along a continuum, where neither anoxia nor low birth weight were guaranteed predictors of children's lower cognitive skill, nor was competent caregiving always a protective factor. The work of Belsky (1984) and Cicchetti and colleagues (e.g., Cicchetti & Rizley, 1981), focusing both on genetic and environmental sources of vulnerability, generated significant theoretical contributions in making clear that developmental processes were ongoing, complex, and transactional. Attachment research, research on parent–infant interaction, and research on cognitive stimulation continued to stress the primacy of parenting as the mediating nexus through which intervention and prevention efforts would likely offer the greatest prospects for success (e.g., Sroufe & Fleeson, 1986).

1980s

One important implication of this new decade of research was that policymakers increasingly recognized the need for much more intensive prevention efforts initiated earlier in children's lives, including efforts to support parents as the most proximal influences on children's development. Home visiting programs received more attention and funding at both the federal and state levels (Behrman, 1999). A number of intensive parenting and infancy-focused interventions (e.g., the Abecedarian Project and the Infant Health and Development Project) were implemented in multiple contexts such as child-care centers and homes to increase children's chances of success both in the context of biologic risk posed by low birth weight and environmental risk posed by cumulative disadvantage (Bennett, 1987; Ramey et al., 1990).

In the 1980s, developmental psychologists focused more clearly on parenting as a dynamic process, with wide variance among low-income families and more critically, with the possibility that parenting styles could change (for better and for worse) over time with rising and falling family fortunes. Perhaps most important to theory, conceptual lenses shifted to integrate both individual and structural factors that might seriously impede children's development in studies of multiple, cumulative disadvantage or risk (Rutter, 1987; Sameroff, Seifer, Barocas, Zax, & Greenspan, 1987). These studies offered evidence suggesting that it was no single characteristic (e.g., parental psychopathology, family structure, low income) but rather the accumulation of multiple stressors that place children's optimal development in jeopardy.

Again, rereading this literature today reveals the ways that our earliest theoretical models were pejorative in focusing only on negative outcomes among poor families. The field experienced an increasing emphasis on the construct of resilience in long-term, longitudinal studies that followed research participants from infancy to adulthood, such as Werner and Smith's (1982) study of infants followed into adulthood in Hawaii and Rutter's (1987) research on the children of women who had severe psychiatric histories.

Perhaps most important to policy was the new emphasis in the latter half of the 1980s on the role of earned income and the impact of income loss in families' lives. This model was proposed with newly introduced path analytic methods, clearer conceptualization of multivariate models in terms of mediation and moderation (Baron & Kenny, 1986), and new correlational data suggesting that sudden drops in income were associated with significant decrements in parenting skills and child functioning (e.g., Conger, Ge, Elder, Lorenz, & Simmons, 1994). McLoyd's critical (1990) paper marked a turning point in our discussion of the negative sequelae of child poverty as a function of parental unemployment or underemployment rather than as a function of cultural or familial dysfunction. This research focus on income loss paralleled a policy focus in welfare reform on increasing family income through low-income women's attachment to the labor force and through earnings. In addition, some psychologists recognized that the "other America" was being driven farther and farther into material hardship in the Reagan era, as the disparity between affluent Americans and poor Americans grew; as financing for public goods available to low-income families, children, and communities were cut; and as means-tested transfers were reduced (Strawn, 1992).

Investigators also began to measure the costs of poverty in material as well as psychological terms by assessing the children's home environments and child-care environments in careful detail. Designed and implemented in 1984, Bradley and Caldwell's HOME observer assessment was integrated into large scale survey research such as the National Longitudinal Study of Youth and the Panel Study of Income Dynamics, offering a common metric with which to identify the costs of economic hardship in terms of poor children's constrained educational opportunities. Some investigators were concerned that the HOME measure promoted a deficit-oriented perspective toward poor families and failed to assess other forms of human and cultural capital that might be more frequently provided in ethnic minority, low-income households. Despite these limitations, the Bradley and Caldwell (1984) measure provided a key means of measuring environments as well as children, offering a way for the field to distance itself empirically from nativist views of the intractability of poor children's average lower performance on standardized tests (e.g., Scarr, 1981).

Similarly, large-scale survey research of child-care quality began to document the serious inadequacy of out-of-home care received by low-income children in terms of safety, staffing, and cognitive stimulation. Early findings from the first wave of randomized early childhood interventions such as the Perry Preschool Project (Berrueta-Clement, Schweinhart, Barnett, Epstein, & Weikart, 1984), the Abecedarian Project (Ramey & Campbell, 1984), and demonstration home visiting programs such as Olds' Elmira nurse visiting program (Olds et al., 1998) made clear that with sufficient economic investment in poor children's early care and education, children's health, cognitive performance, and social outcomes improved.

Whereas some investigators focused on economic context, others placed the lens of scholarly critique and innovation squarely on cultural context, emphasizing the extent to which ethnic minority family practices, values, and beliefs represented sources of strength as well as potential conduits for alienation, with strong critique of the long tradition of focusing on ethnic and cultural difference as a source of deficit (e.g., Ogbu, 1985). Psychologists called themselves and the field to task for the implicit racism of past models and instituted stronger editorial and funding requirements to guard against the exclusion of ethnic and racial minority families from basic research, and to avoid the inclusion of racial stereotypes from published research (National Institutes of Health, 1994).

1990s

The pathbreaking April 1994 *Child Development* issue on children and poverty, now over 10 years old, highlighted many of these transitions in the field. Many of the studies published in that volume underscored the value of examining within-group differences among samples of poor, African American, inner-city youth, adults, and children as "necessary to understand why some youth fail, some survive, and some even thrive in high-risk environments" (Connell, Spencer, & Aber, 1994, p. 493). Closer empirical attention to within-group differences was complemented by a number of studies' application of greater statistical sophistication and model complexity in comparing young children's cognitive functioning and behavioral problems across poor and nonpoor as well as White and non-White groups of children in large-scale survey research (e.g., Duncan, Brooks-Gunn, & Klebanov, 1994). These studies demonstrated that much of the gap in test scores between young White children and young children of color could be accounted for by large disparities in family income, with much larger proportions of families of color experiencing much material hardship for much longer periods of time (Duncan et al., 1994). At the same time, the field offered clearer, more detailed economically grounded conceptualizations of child poverty at individual, family, neighborhood, and state levels (e.g., Aber, 1994). Increasingly, investigators have moved away from the use of the Hollingshead multifactor assessment of socioeconomic status to the use of income-to-needs ratios and to subjective measures of families' experiences of material strain, as well as to more structurally focused conceptualizations of neighborhood poverty (e.g., Brooks-Gunn, Duncan, & Aber, 1997; Wilson, 1987).

The 1990s also saw renewed debate regarding the direction of causal influence when considering models of poverty, income, family functioning, and child well-being. In some ways, it is tempting to view this debate as a resurrection of the old one raised when the War on Poverty was started: Some recent models of family poverty emphasize personal flaws, with income modeled as endogenous to parents' problems and poor choices (Mayer, 1997), whereas other models emphasize ways in which low-income families struggle to remain competent and psychologically healthy despite their exposure to such exogenous shocks as neighborhood violence or income loss (e.g., Morris, Huston, Duncan, Crosby, & Bos, 2001). Indeed, several new studies are striving to test which of these models fit the data emerging from new studies better (e.g., Gershoff, Aber, & Raver, 2002). Some of Zigler's former students are in the thick of these new projects. So there is much to suggest that the debate has shifted and become more complex, largely because of Zigler's intellectual legacy.

Are today's debates similar to or different from those of 40 years ago? First, the debate has shifted to consider income inequality, material hardship, and social exclusion as we search for better means of modeling structural as well as individual socioeconomic factors that may have an adverse impact on child development (e.g., Aber et al., 2002). As a vocal participant in debates regarding poor families' access to institutional supports such as paid family leave upon the birth of a child and high-quality child care, Zigler has consistently highlighted the gaps between services offered for affluent families versus those services available to poor families. In short, by emphasizing developmental processes and child-focused policy from both universal and targeted perspectives, Zigler has consistently asked us to examine the ways in which institutional supports for families can and should be more equitably distributed.

Second, Ed has impressed each of us repeatedly with the need to maximize our understanding of individual differences within groups. His commitment to understanding the developmental trajectories that support positive outcomes among families and children facing the highest levels of psychosocial, behavioral, or neurological risk has remained constant and sterling throughout his and our careers. Ed has counseled us to be patient, careful, and thorough when analyzing the problems of poor families. There is no one community of poor, no one community of advantaged, and Ed has supported each of us in examining rather than turning away from that diverse, complicated story.

Third, Ed's legacy is clear in that, in the face of conflicting findings suggesting that individual characteristics versus societal inequities are responsible for low family income, he expects us to forge ahead rather than to falter. If evidence were to mount on both sides of the poverty debate, Ed would (and does) expect us to come up with policy solutions for both individual obstacles and for societal disadvantages that young children face. Given such findings, how will we transcend ideological fights and press on with the work that needs to be done? What policy would represent an effective solution and an effective test? In short, Ed would not be satisfied with the simpler solution of antipoverty critique, but he has consistently demanded that we move antipoverty action forward with good antipoverty science.

The Evolution and Evaluation of Program and Policy Initiatives

As definitions, theories, and research unfolded over the last 40 years, antipoverty programs and policies also underwent change. The modern history of efforts in the United States to address the problems faced by poor families is rooted in a much larger history, is enormously complex, and is fraught with wide ideological differences in the perspectives that various scholars have brought to their analyses. For example, contrast the perspectives of Murray, Mead, and Himmelfarb on the right (who believe that the basic causes of poverty reside in the character of individuals or the cultures of families and communities), with Katz, Skocpol, and O'Connor on the left (who attribute the basic causes to the structure of modern societies and economies, or to some combination of all of the above).

This chapter is not the place (nor are we the right authors) to offer a careful historical analysis of the multiple and competing foci affecting the evolution of antipoverty programs and policies over the last half of the 20th century. But it is the right place to sketch for the reader something of the content and nature of changes in antipoverty programs and policies over the period of time Zigler has been working on behalf of poor children and their families.

Table 9.1 summarizes some of the more significant antipoverty program and policy initiatives of the last 5 decades at the federal government level. We have organized the entries both by time (from the 1960s to the first decade of the 21st century) and by focus (i.e., Does the program or policy focus primarily on poor children, their poor parents, or their poor schools or communities?). It is interesting to note that well in advance of having a formal ecological theory of human development (Bronfenbrenner, 1979), the pragmatism of program and policy appears to have driven the field to adopt an implicit ecological perspective, generating strategies that addressed all four foci.

In the 1960s, as part of Lyndon Johnson's War on Poverty, Head Start was created to close the huge gap between poor and middle-income families in their young children's readiness for school. The Elementary and Secondary Education Act (1965) was enacted to provide additional resources to serve poor chil-

Table 9.1. Prototypical Program and Policy Initiatives on Behalf of Low-Income Children, Families, and Communities: 1960–2000

Decade	Child focused	Adult focused	School focused	Community focused
1960s	Head Start	Office of Economic Opportunity	Elementary Secondary Education Act (1965)	Model Cities
1970s	Follow Through	Comprehensive Employment and Training Act (1973)	Community schools movement	Community development corporations
1980s	Comprehensive Child Development Program	Family Support Act (1988)	Education for All Handicapped Children Act (1975)	Comprehensive Community Initiatives for Children, Youth, and Families
1990s	Early Head Start	Personal Responsibility and Work Opportunity Reconciliation Act (1996)	Whole-school and standards-based reforms	Empowerment zones and enterprise communities

dren (in poor schools), the Model Cities initiative was launched to combat the housing problems of the poor, and the Office of Economic Opportunity was charged with orchestrating much of the War. Although the content of these issues look quite moderate by today's standards, the 1960s is remembered as the decade of the birth of liberal domestic social policy toward the poor, perhaps because the programs and policies contrasted so much with those of the immediate postwar period and earlier.

From the 1960s to the 1970s and 1980s, programs and policies shifted from more of a focus on single services and individuals to comprehensive services and communities. Just as researchers realized that no single factor explained the nonoptimal development of low-income children in the science of the times, advocates found that no single factor was an adequate target for programs and policies. Comprehensive programs and community initiatives for children became promising approaches. But as providing more services through comprehensive initiatives appeared not to make the positive difference many had hoped for, a new desire for bottom-line responsibility grew among policymakers in the 1990s. This impetus to hold service providers accountable for outcomes ushered in an era of promoting individual responsibility and system accountability. This approach both supported and was supported by a growing popular attraction to more conservative approaches to domestic policy in general and to child and family policy in particular.

Even this cursory sketch of the evolution of domestic programs and policies toward poor children, families, and communities allows us to draw a few general conclusions. Our first conclusion is obvious but merits consideration anyway: The evolution in programs and policies was influenced much more by ideological debate, political negotiations, fiscal realities, public and policymaker perceptions of need, and the history of program and policy successes and failures than they were influenced by theory and research. This does not mean that research has had no impact (more on this point later), but it does mean that power, money, and values usually trump knowledge as bases for program and policy formulation.

Second, theory and research can be valuable even if not frequently determinative. As we already noted, research can indirectly and positively influence the general zeitgeist surrounding decision making, as it did in the 1980s when basic research on the multivariate influences on the development of poor children helped shift program and policy away from magic bullet and single-factor models of intervention toward comprehensive, multitarget models.

Another important way that research can influence program and policy is through the design and conduct of rigorous evaluations. Negative findings from some evaluations of early initiatives for low-income children and families both decreased support for existing programs and simultaneously stimulated the development of new approaches. For example, the Westinghouse evaluation of Head Start perhaps slowed the growth of the program (due to finding the fadeout effect) and so provided the impetus for Follow Through. Similarly, the evaluation of the Comprehensive Child Development Program may have dampened state government's interests in truly comprehensive early childhood initiatives but may have fostered the more focused but multitarget approach of Early Head Start. Finally, evaluations and meta-analyses of several different types of welfare reform strategies have led policymakers to favor rapid workforce attachment models over human capital investment models (Gueron & Pauly, 1991) for reducing welfare caseloads and suggest that strategies that reduce welfare dependency have positive effects on poor children's learning and development only if they lead to increased family income as well (Morris, Gennetian, & Duncan, 2005). Rigorous evaluations are increasingly able to identify what antipoverty programs and policies work, for whom, and under what conditions. But identifying what works is not sufficient to convince policymakers, or the public for that matter, that they should spend the money and the political capital to adopt what works. To address these challenges of advocacy and social marketing requires a different set of skills, abilities, and sentiments, as laid out by Gruendel and Aber (see chap. 3, this volume).

It is interesting to note that the examples of rigorous evaluations noted previously were experiments in which individuals were randomly assigned to experimental (e.g., Comprehensive Child Development Program or Early Head Start) or control conditions. But the program and policy initiatives listed in the two right-hand columns of Table 9.1 include initiatives aimed at schools and communities as well. Over the last decade, there has been growing interest in and commitment to "place-randomized trials" (Boruch, 2005). When program or policy interventions are delivered at the group level (e.g., classrooms, schools, organizations, or neighborhoods), it is usually most appropriate to randomize at the group level to most rigorously assess the impact of the intervention. Recent examples of group-randomized evaluations of place-based program or policy interventions on behalf of low-income children and families include the recent experiment that randomized poor schools to Success-for-All or business as usual (Borman, Slavin, & Cheung, 2005) and the Progresa experiment in Mexico that randomized villages to a set of fiscal incentives to promote health care and education for young children or business as usual (Gertler & Boyce, 2001). The scientific methodology to conduct place-randomized trials is advancing at a rapid pace (see H. Bloom, 2005). But the theory and measurement strategies to assess variation in places (contexts) and over time lag behind. Fortunately, federal (e.g., National Institutes of Health) and private (e.g., W. T. Grant Foundation) sponsors of research have recognized the scientific value of place-randomized trials in the evaluation of antipoverty programs and policies. Funders have also recognized that until theory on and measurement of key features of places progress, we will still not be in a position to learn what we need to about what works, for whom, and under what conditions when targeting schools and communities as the loci of change. Thus, the emergent field of child development and social policy has recognized for nearly a half century (a) the vital role that schools and communities play in the development of low-income children and (b) the valuable role that rigorous evaluation research can play in improving programs and policies, but it is only now beginning to generate rigorous evaluations of (school and community) place-based strategies.

Implications for the Future

In this chapter, we have described two of the oldest concerns of the emerging field of child development and social policy: how poverty and social deprivation influences children's development and how programs and policies can ameliorate the effects of poverty on children's development. Further, we have tried to capture some of the most important changes in theory, research, programs, and policies over the 4 decades of Zigler's work in this emerging field. What lessons can we take away from the last 40 years that will serve us well as we and our students (and our students' students), Ed's intellectual and professional grandchildren (and great-grandchildren), prepare to face the challenges of the next 40 years? Like our mentor, we'll try to keep those lessons brief and to the point.

1. Our theoretical and scientific understanding of poverty, deprivation, impacts on development, and program and policy strategies to enhance development will continue to undergo rapid transformation. New generations of scientists willing and able to mount creative studies and rigorous evaluations will play an invaluable role in helping to develop the knowledge base needed to help guide effective action.
2. The knowledge base will never be wholly adequate to guide action. In the end, there will be a sizable gap between what researchers know with confidence and what policymakers need to know to act with confidence. Consequently, the field will usually be in the position that it needs to move beyond the information given. This will be a great challenge. It will be important to honestly and dis-

passionately pursue and represent the truth about how poverty affects children and about whether and how well antipoverty programs and policies improve the life chances of low-income children, families, and communities. But researchers and policymakers will also need to make decisions that extend beyond what is known with certainty. Said a different way, Head Start and welfare reform would never have been started if anyone waited for the knowledge base needed to fully inform their design. At the same time, both were influenced by the knowledge base that prevailed at the time and were probably better for it. Theory and research will necessarily and could productively compete with power, values, and money to guide intervention efforts. Thus, we must develop our capacity in the field of child development and social policy for discriminating judgment to find our way among these competing influences on program and policy decisions.

3. Mistakes are most likely to be made in child development and social policy if (a) sound research never effectively engages or informs practical program and policy decisions or (b) program and policy decisions are made solely on the basis of ideology and political power without being queried by the knowledge base emerging from sound research.

Zigler's work on poverty and child development—together with the work of many of his students and colleagues—have generated these lessons that we expect to be very important to us as we move into an uncertain future.

References

Aber, J. L. (1994). Poverty, violence, and child development: Untangling family and community level effects. In C. Nelson (Ed.), *Threats to optimal development: Integrating biological, psychological, and social risk factors* (pp. 229–272). Hillsdale, NJ: Erlbaum.

Aber, J. L., Gershoff, E. T., & Brooks-Gunn, J. (2002). Social exclusion of children in the United States: Identifying potential indicators. In A. J. Kahn & S. B. Kamerman (Eds.), *Beyond child poverty: The social exclusion of children* (pp. 245–286). New York: The Institute for Child and Family Policy, Columbia University.

Aber, J. L., Jones, S. M., & Cohen, J. (2000). The impact of poverty on the mental health and development of very young children. In C. H. Zeanah (Ed.), *Handbook of infant mental health* (2nd ed., pp. 113–128). New York: Guilford Press.

Baron, R. M., & Kenny, D. (1986). The moderator–mediator variable distinction in social psychological research: Conceptual, strategic, and statistical considerations. *Journal of Personality and Social Psychology, 51*, 1173–1182.

Behrman, R. E. (1999). Statement of purpose. Home visiting: Recent program evaluations. *Future of Children, 9*(1), 1.

Belsky, J. (1984). The determinants of parenting: A process model. *Child Development, 55*, 83–96.

Bennett, F. C. (1987). The effectiveness of early intervention for infants at increased biological risk. In M. J. Guralnick & F. C. Bennett (Eds.), *The effectiveness of early intervention for at-risk and handicapped children* (pp. 79–112). New York: Academic Press.

Berrueta-Clement, J., Schweinhart, L. J., Barnett, W. S., Epstein, A. S., & Weikart, D. P. (1984). *Changed lives: The effects of the Perry Preschool Program on youths through age 19.* Ypsilanti, MI: The High/Scope Press.

Bloom, B. S. (1964). *Stability and change in human characteristics*. New York: Wiley.

Bloom, H. (2005). *Learning more from social experiments: Evolving analytic approaches*. New York: Russell Sage Foundation.

Bolger, K. E., Patterson, C. J., Thompson, W. W., & Kupersmidt, J. B. (1995). Psychosocial adjustment among children experiencing persistent and intermittent family economic hardship. *Child Development, 66*, 1107–1129.

Borman, G. D., Slavin, R., & Cheung, A. (2005). Success for All: First-year results from the national randomized field trial. *Educational Evaluation & Policy Analysis, 27*(1), 1–22.

Boruch, R. (2005). Better evaluation for evidence-based policy: Place randomized trials in education, criminology, welfare, and health. *Annals of the American Academy of Political & Social Science, 599*, 6–18.

Bowlby, J. (1969). *Attachment and loss: Vol. 1. Attachment*. New York: Basic Books.

Bradley, R. H., & Caldwell, B. M. (1984). The relation of infants' home environments to achievement test performance in first grade: A follow-up study. *Child Development, 55*, 803–809.

Bradley, R. H., & Whiteside-Mansell, L. (1997). Children in poverty. In R. T. Ammerman & M. Hersen (Eds.), *Handbook of prevention and treatment with children and adolescents: Intervention in real world context* (pp. 13–58). New York: Wiley.

Bronfenbrenner, U. (1979). *The ecology of human development: Experiments by nature and design*. Cambridge, MA: Harvard University Press.

Bronfenbrenner, U., & Morris, P. (1998). The ecology of developmental processes. In R. M. Lerner (Ed.), *Handbook of child psychology: Vol. 1. Theoretical models of human development* (5th ed., pp. 993–1028). New York: Wiley.

Brooks-Gunn, J., Duncan, G. J., & Aber, J. L. (1997). *Neighborhood poverty: Vol. 1. Context and consequences for children*. New York: Russell Sage Foundation.

Cicchetti, D., & Rizley, R. (1981). Developmental perspectives on the etiology, intergenerational transmission, and sequelae of child maltreatment. *New Directions for Child Development, 11*, 31–56.

Citro, C. F., & Michael, R. T. (Eds.). (1995). *Measuring poverty: A new approach*. Washington, DC: National Academy Press.

Comprehensive Employment and Training Act of 1973, Pub. L. No. 93-204 (1973).

Conger, R. D., Ge, X., Elder, G. H., Lorenz, F. O., & Simons, R. L. (1994). Economic stress, coercive family process, and developmental problems of adolescents. *Child Development, 65*, 541–561.

Connell, J. P., Spencer, M. B., & Aber, J. L. (1994). Educational risk and resilience in African-American youth: Context, self, action, and outcomes in school. *Child Development, 65*, 493–506.

Duncan, G. J., & Brooks-Gunn, J. (2000). Family poverty, welfare reform, and child development. *Child Development, 71*, 188–196.

Duncan, G. J., Brooks-Gunn, J., & Klebanov, P. (1994). Economic deprivation and early childhood development. *Child Development, 65*, 296–318.

Edin, K., & Lein, L. (1997). *Making ends meet: How single mothers survive welfare and low wage work*. New York: Russell Sage Foundation.

Education for All Handicapped Children Act, S. 6, 94th Cong. (1975).

Elder, G. H. (1974). *Children of the Great Depression: Social change and life experience*. Chicago: University of Chicago Press.

Elementary and Secondary Education Act, Pub. L. No. 89-10 (1965).

Family Support Act of 1988, Pub. L. No. 100-485 (1988).

Fisher, G. M. (1992). *The development and history of the U.S. poverty thresholds: A brief overview*, Retrieved January 15, 2004, from http://aspe.hhs.gov/poverty/papers/hptgssiv.htm

Gertler, P. J., & Boyce, S. (2001). *An experiment in incentive-based welfare: The impact of PROGRESA on health in Mexico*. Unpublished manuscript. Haas School of Business, University of California, Berkeley.

Gershoff, E. T. (2003). *Low income and hardship among America's kindergarteners*. New York: National Center for Children in Poverty, Columbia University Mailman School of Public Health.

Gershoff, E. T., Aber, J. L., & Raver, C. C. (2002). Child poverty in the U.S.: An evidence-based conceptual framework for programs and policies. In R. M. Lerner, F. Jacobs, & D. Wertlieb (Eds.), *Handbook of applied developmental science: Vol. 2. Promoting positive child, adolescent, and family development through research, policies, and programs* (pp. 81–136). Thousand Oaks, CA: Sage.

Gueron, J., & Pauly, E. (1991). *From welfare to work.* New York: Russell Sage Foundation.

Harlow, H. F., & Harlow, M. K. (1965). The affectional systems. In A. Schrier, H. F. Harlow, & F. Stollnitz (Eds.), *Behavior of nonhuman primates: Modern research trends* (pp. 287–384). New York: Academic Press.

Hauser, R. M. (1994). Measuring socioeconomic status in studies of child development. *Child Development, 65,* 1541–1545.

Hunt, J. M. (1961). *Intelligence and experience.* New York: Ronald Press.

Jones, S. M., & Zigler, E. (2002). The Mozart effect: Not learning from history. *Journal of Applied Developmental Psychology, 23,* 355–372.

Katz, M. B. (1996). *In the shadow of the poorhouse: A social history of welfare in America.* New York: Basic Books.

Lewis, O. (1966). The culture of poverty. *Scientific American, 215,* 19–25.

Mayer, S. E. (1997). *What money can't buy: Family income and children's life chances.* Cambridge, MA: Harvard University Press.

McClelland, D. C., Atkinson, J. W., Clark, R. A., & Lowell, E. I. (1953). *The achievement motive.* New York: Appleton-Century.

McKey, R. H., Condelli, L., Ganson, H., Barrett, B., McConkey, C., & Plantz, M. (1985). *The impact of head start on children, families and communities.* Washington, DC: CSR.

McLoyd, V. C. (1990). The impact of economic hardship on black families and children: Psychological distress, parenting, and socio-emotional development. *Child Development, 61,* 311–346.

McLoyd, V. C. (1998). Socioeconomic disadvantage and child development. *American Psychologist, 53,* 185–204.

Morris, P., Gennetian, L., & Duncan, G. (2005). *Effects of welfare and employment policies on young children: New findings on policy experiments conducted in the early 1990s.* (Social Policy Report No. 19). Ann Arbor, MI: Society for Research in Child Development.

Morris, P. A., Huston, A. C., Duncan, G. J., Crosby, D. A., & Bos, J. M. (2001). *How welfare and work policies affect children: A synthesis of research.* New York: MDRC.

National Institutes of Health. (1994). NIH guidelines on the inclusion of women and minorities as subjects in clinical research. *NIH Guide, 23*(10). Retrieved on January 15, 2004, from http://www4.od.nih.gov/ocm/contracts/rfps/womenmin.htm

O'Connor, A. (2002). *Poverty knowledge: Social science, social policy and the poor in 20th century U.S. history.* Princeton, NJ: Princeton University Press.

Ogbu, J. (1985). A cultural ecology of competence among inner-city blacks. In M. B. Spencer & G. K. Brookins (Eds.), *Beginnings: The social and affective development of black children* (pp. 45–66). Hillsdale, NJ: Erlbaum.

Olds, D., Henderson, C. R., Cole, R., Eckenrode, J., Kitzman, H., Luckey, D., et al. (1998). Long-term effects of nursing home visitation on children's criminal and antisocial behavior: 15-year follow-up of a randomized controlled trial. *Journal of the American Medical Association, 280,* 1238–1244.

Orshansky, M. (1963). Children of the poor. *Social Security Bulletin, 26*(7), 3–13.

Personal Responsibility and Work Opportunity Reconciliation Act of 1996, H.R. 3734, 104th Cong. (1996).

Ramey, C. T., Bryant, D. M., Wasik, B. H., Sparling, J. J., Fendt, K. H., & LaVange, L. M. (1990). The Infant Health and Development Program for low birthweight, premature infants: Program elements, family participation, and child intelligence. *Pediatrics, 3,* 454–465.

Ramey, C. T., & Campbell, F. A. (1984). Preventative education for high-risk children: Cognitive consequences of the Carolina Abecedarian Project. *American Journal of Mental Deficiency, 88,* 515–523.

Rutter, M. (1987). Psychosocial resilience and protective mechanisms. *American Journal of Orthopsychiatry, 57,* 316–331.

Sameroff, A. J., Bartko, W. T., Baldwin, A., Baldwin, C., & Seifer, R. (1998). Family and social influences on the development of child competence. In M. Lewis & C. Feiring (Eds.), *Families, risk, and competence* (pp. 161–186). Mahwah, NJ: Erlbaum.

Sameroff, A. J., & Chandler, M. (1975). Reproductive risk and the continuum of caretaking casualty. In F. D. Horowitz (Ed.), *Review of child development research* (Vol. 4, pp. 179–244). Chicago: University of Chicago Press.

Sameroff, A. J., Seifer, R., Barocas, R., Zax, M., & Greenspan, S. (1987). Intelligence quotient scores of 4-year-old children: Social and environmental risk factors. *Pediatrics, 79*, 343–350.

Scarr, S. (1981). Race, social class and IQ. In S. Scarr (Ed.), *Race, social class, and individual differences in IQ* (pp. 183–208). Hillsdale, NJ: Erlbaum.

Spitz, R. (1945). Hospitalism: An inquiry into the genesis of psychiatric conditions in early childhood. *Psychoanalytic Study of the Child, 1*, 53–74.

Sroufe, L. A., & Fleeson, J. (1986). Attachment and the construction of relationships. In W. Hartup & Z. Rubin (Eds.), *Relationships and development* (pp. 51–76). Hillsdale, NJ: Erlbaum.

Strawn, J. (1992). *The states and the poor: Child poverty rises as the safety net shrinks* (Social Policy Report No. 6). Ann Arbor, MI: Society for Research in Child Development.

U.S. Census Bureau. (2004). *Poverty thresholds 2004.* Washington, DC: U.S. Census Bureau, Housing and Household Economic Statistics Division; also available at http://www.census.gov/hhes/www/poverty/threshld/thresh04.html

Werner, E. E., & Smith, R. S. (1982). *Vulnerable but invincible: A longitudinal study of resilient children and youth.* New York: Adams.

White, R. W. (1959). Motivation reconsidered: The concept of competence. *Psychological Review, 66*, 297–333.

Wilson, W. J. (1987). *The truly disadvantaged: The inner city, the underclass, and public policy.* Chicago: University of Chicago Press.

Zigler, E. (1958). *Preinstitutional social deprivation and rigidity in the performance of feebleminded children.* Unpublished doctoral dissertation, University of Texas, Austin.

Zigler, E. (1961). Social deprivation and rigidity in the performance of feebleminded children. *Journal of Abnormal and Social Psychology, 62*, 413–421.

Zigler, E. (1970). The environmental mystique: Training the intellect versus development of the child. *Childhood Education, 46*, 402–412.

Zigler, E., & Butterfield, E. C. (1968). Motivational aspects of changes in IQ test performance of culturally deprived nursery school children. *Child Development, 39*, 1–14.

Zigler, E., & Muenchow, S. (1992). *Head Start: The inside story of America's most successful educational experiment.* New York: Basic Books.

Zigler, E., & Trickett, P. K. (1978). IQ, social competence, and evaluation of early childhood intervention programs. *American Psychologist, 33*, 789–798.

10

Intervention and Policy Implications of Research on Neurobiological Functioning in Maltreated Children

Dante Cicchetti

In 1999, more than 2.9 million children were reported as abused or neglected in the United States and an estimated 826,000 children were confirmed as victims of maltreatment (U.S. Department of Health and Human Services, 2001). Child maltreatment is an enormous problem that exerts a toll, not only on its victims but also on society. In a National Institute of Justice report (Miller, Cohen, & Wierseman, 1996), the direct costs (e.g., medical expenses, lost earnings, public programs for victims) as well as indirect costs (e.g., pain, diminished quality of life) of child abuse and neglect were estimated at $56 billion annually. A 2001 study conducted by Prevent Child Abuse America estimated that the total cost of child abuse and neglect in the United States is more than $94 billion per year (Fromm, 2001). Annual direct costs, estimated at $24 billion, include hospitalization, chronic physical health problems, mental health care, welfare costs, law enforcement, and court action. Yearly indirect costs, estimated at $70 billion, include special education, mental and physical health care, delinquency, criminality, and lost productivity to society.

Thus, conducting research that elucidates the developmental processes by which maltreatment exerts its deleterious impact on children, as well as developing theoretically and empirically informed interventions for maltreated children and their families, should be a national priority (Cicchetti & Toth, 1993; National Research Council, 1993). Studies of the sequelae of maltreatment are critical for enhancing the quality of clinical, legal, and policy-making decisions for maltreated children. Decisions concerning such issues as whether to report a child as maltreated, whether to remove a child from the home, how to develop prevention and intervention programs to meet the specific biological and psychological needs of maltreated children, and how to evaluate these programs would all benefit greatly from a more thorough and sophisticated knowledge base on the processes through which child abuse and neglect affect developmental outcomes (Aber & Zigler, 1981; Cicchetti & Toth, 2000).

The writing of this chapter was supported, in part, by grants received from the Administration on Children, Youth and Families; the National Institute of Mental Health; the Office of Child Abuse and Neglect; and the Spunk Fund, Inc. This chapter is dedicated to Edward F. Zigler, developmentalist and child advocate extraordinaire.

Child maltreatment may represent one of the greatest failures of the environment to offer opportunities to foster normal developmental processes (Cicchetti & Lynch, 1995). In contrast to what occurs in response to an average expectable environment, the ecological, social, biological, and psychological conditions that are associated with maltreatment set in motion a probabilistic path of epigenesis for maltreated children characterized by an increased likelihood of failure and disruption in the successful resolution of the major stage-salient issues of development, resulting in grave implications for functioning across the life span (Cicchetti & Toth, 1995; Trickett & McBride-Chang, 1995). These repeated developmental disruptions in the formation of secure attachment relationships; an autonomous, integrated, and coherent self-system; effective peer relations; and successful adaptation to school create a profile of relatively enduring vulnerability factors that increase the probability of the emergence of maladaptation and psychopathology as negative transactions between the child and the environment continue (Cicchetti & Lynch, 1995).

Although more distal early developmental factors and current influences are both viewed as important to the process of development, individual action is seen as a central impetus for development. Individuals gain knowledge through an active process in which they continually structure and restructure their experiences and create and interpret meaning for comprehending the world through self-regulated mental activity (Cicchetti & Tucker, 1994). Early experience and prior levels of adaptation neither destine the individual to continued maladaptive functioning nor inoculate the individual from future problems in functioning.

In this chapter, after presenting a conceptualization that depicts the brain as a self-organizing, dynamic system that both affects, and is affected by, experience, I discuss the impact that child maltreatment exerts on neurobiological function. Drawing predominantly from investigations conducted within my laboratory, I address what is known about how child maltreatment affects brain function. In the concluding section, I proffer several prescriptions, emanating from extant research, that have implications for intervention and social policy.

The Developing Brain as a Self-Organizing Dynamic System

Until the past decade, scientific investigations on child maltreatment focused almost exclusively on psychological processes and outcomes. As research on the neurobiological functioning of maltreated children has begun to burgeon, it is conceivable that the examination of the multifaceted neurobiological systems affected by child maltreatment will provide insight into some of the mediators linking maltreatment and negative socioemotional and cognitive outcomes.

Not only do biological factors influence psychological processes but also social experiences, such as child maltreatment, exert actions on the brain by feeding back upon it to modify gene expression and brain structure and function (Cicchetti & Tucker, 1994; Kandel, 1998). For example, empirical evidence from research conducted with rodents and nonhuman primates has demonstrated that the experience of traumatic events early in life can alter behavioral and neuroendocrine responsiveness, the morphological characteristics of the brain, and the activation of genes associated with negative neurobiological and behavioral outcomes (Sanchez, Ladd, & Plotsky, 2001). Moreover, findings from animal studies reveal that early traumatic experiences may exert harmful effects on the normative developmental processes that have been implicated in the etiology of mental disorders (Sanchez et al., 2001). Specifically, studies reveal that early experiences of trauma are associated with long-term alterations in coping, emotional and behavioral regulation, the responsiveness of the neuroendocrine system to stress experience, brain structure, neurochemistry, and gene expression (Cicchetti & Walker, 2001; Meaney, 2001). Furthermore, both experimental and naturally occurring investigations of variations in maternal care have been found to alter the expression of genes whose function is to regulate behavioral and endocrine responses to stress and to modify synaptogenesis in the hippocampus, as well as to influence the responsivity of the hypothalamic–pituitary–adrenal (HPA) axis to later life stressors (Levine, 1994; Meaney et al., 1996).

It also has been discovered that alterations in gene expression induced by learning and through social and psychological experiences produce changes in patterns of neuronal and synaptic connections, and thereby in the functioning of nerve cells (Kandel, 1998). Such neuronal and synaptic modifications not only exert a prominent role in initiating and maintaining the behavioral anomalies that are provoked by social and psychological experiences but also contribute to the biological bases of individuality, as well as to individuals' being differentially affected by similar experiences, regardless of their positive or negative–adverse valence (Kandel, 1998).

In addition, although brain development is guided and controlled to some degree by genetic information (Rakic, 1988a, 1988b), a not insignificant portion of postnatal brain structuration, neural patterning, and organization are thought to occur through interactions and transactions of the individual with the environment (Black, Jones, Nelson, & Greenough, 1998; Cicchetti & Cannon, 1999). Consequently, each individual may traverse a potentially unique and partly self-determined developmental pathway of brain building that researchers believe may have important consequences for the development of normal, abnormal, and resilient adaptation (Black et al., 1998; Cicchetti & Tucker, 1994; Curtis & Cicchetti, 2003).

In self-organizing brain development, some regions of the brain serve to stabilize and organize information for other areas, whereas other regions use experience to fine-tune their anatomy for optimal function. In this manner, individuals can use the interaction of genetic constraints and environmental information to self-organize their highly complex neural systems. Synaptogenesis appears to be generated in response to events that provide information to be encoded in the nervous system. This experience-dependent synapse formation involves the brain's adaptation to information that is unique to the individual (Greenough, Black, & Wallace, 1987). Because all individuals encounter distinctive environments, each brain is modified in a singular fashion. Experience-dependent synaptogenesis is localized to the brain regions involved in processing information arising from the event experienced by the individual. Unlike the case with experience-expectant processes, experience-dependent processes do not take place within a stringent temporal interval because the timing or nature of experience that the individual engages or chooses cannot be entirely and dependently envisioned (Bruer, 1999). An important central mechanism for experience-dependent development is the formation of new neural connections in contrast to the overproduction and pruning back of synapses often associated with experience-expectant processes (Greenough et al., 1987).

For example, children who develop in a resilient fashion even though they have experienced significant adversity play an active role in seeking and receiving the experiences that are developmentally appropriate for them (Black et al., 1998; Cicchetti & Tucker, 1994). Through the use of experience-dependent processes, children who function resiliently likely modify and protect their brain anatomy to ensure an adaptive developmental outcome. At one level, different parts of the brain may attempt to compensate, and at another level, the organism may seek out new experience in areas where it has strength (Black et al., 1998). Because experience-dependent plasticity is a central feature of the mammalian brain (M. Johnson, 1999), neither early brain anomalies nor aberrant experiences should be considered as determining the ultimate fate of the organism (Cicchetti & Tucker, 1994).

Moreover, given that the mechanisms of neural plasticity cause the brain's anatomical differentiation to be dependent on stimulation from the environment, it is now clear that the cytoarchitecture of the cerebral cortex is shaped by input from the social environment. Cortical development and organization should not be viewed as passive processes that depend exclusively on genetics and environmental input. Development, both psychological and biological, is more than nature–nurture interaction. Thus, corticogenesis should be conceived as processes of self-organization guided by self-regulatory mechanisms (Cicchetti & Tucker, 1994).

Children endowed with normal brains may encounter a number of experiences, including child maltreatment, extreme poverty, and community and domestic violence, that can exert a negative impact on brain structure, function, and organization and contribute to distorting these children's experiences of the world (Pollak, Cicchetti, & Klorman, 1998). Perturbations that occur during brain development can potentiate a cascade of maturational and structural changes that eventuate in the neural system proceeding along a trajectory that deviates from that generally taken in normal neurobiological development (Courchesne, Chisum, & Townsend, 1994; Nowakowski & Hayes, 1999). Early stresses, either physiological or emotional, may condition young neural networks to produce cascading effects through later development, possibly constraining the child's flexibility to adapt to new challenging situations with new strategies rather than with old conceptual and behavioral prototypes. Thus, early psychological trauma such as that incurred by maltreated children may eventuate not only in emotional sensitization (Maughan & Cicchetti, 2002) but also in pathological sensitization of neurophysiological reactivity (Cicchetti & Tucker, 1994; Pollak et al., 1998). Such early developmental abnormalities may lead to the development of aberrant neural circuitry and often compound themselves into relatively enduring forms of psychopathology (Cicchetti & Cannon, 1999; Nowakowski & Hayes, 1999).

Children may be especially vulnerable to the effects of pathological experiences during periods of rapid creation or modification of neuronal connections

(Black et al., 1998). Pathological experience may become part of a vicious cycle, as the pathology induced in brain structure may distort the child's experience, with subsequent alterations in cognition or social interactions causing additional pathological experience and added brain pathology (Cicchetti & Tucker, 1994; Pollak et al., 1998). Children who incorporate pathological experience during ongoing experience-expectant and experience-dependent processes may add neuropathological connections into their developing brains instead of functional neuronal connections (Black et al., 1998).

The Impact of Child Maltreatment
on Neurobiological Processes

Because maltreated children experience the extremes of caregiving casualty, they provide one of the clearest opportunities for scientists to discover the multiple ways in which social and psychological stressors can affect biological systems. Numerous interconnected neurobiological systems are affected by the various stressors associated with child maltreatment. Moreover, each of these neurobiological systems influences and is influenced by multiple domains of psychological and biological development.

In the next section, I review the extant literature on the effects that child abuse and neglect have on neurobiological function. Research in our laboratory examining different components of brain functioning, each representing fairly distinct neural systems, converges in the finding that all of the neurobiological systems investigated exhibited dysregulation. Moreover, because not every maltreated child exhibited anomalous brain functioning, it is conceivable that the effects of social experiences, such as child abuse and neglect, on brain microstructure and biochemistry may be either pathological or adaptive.

Acoustic Startle in Maltreated Children

The acoustic startle reflex is an obligatory response to a sudden and unexpected stimulus that is marked by the cessation of ongoing behaviors and by a particular series of protective behaviors (Davis, 1984). The complete startle response in humans consists of a patterned sequence of rostral to caudal flexor movements in which the first feature is a brief closing of the eyes (i.e., an eyeblink) and a facial grimace, followed by neck flexion, and then shoulder and back contraction and flexion of the legs as the body assumes a defensive shrunken posture. Of this group of movements, the eyeblink is the most sensitive and consistent across individuals, and this is the response that is most often measured in studies of this reflex. The startle eyeblink in humans is measured from electromyographic activity detected by electrodes overlying the *obicularis oculi* muscle, located below each eye.

Startle expression in humans and in laboratory animals is affected by emotional factors, a connection that may be grounded in the evolutionary value of startle for immediate protection and its enablement of a basic posture from which other defensive or aggressive responses might quickly emerge. The effects of unpleasant stimulation or content are presumed to enhance startle through evocation of learned or innate responses in the amygdala, which then potentiate the startle reflex (Davis, 1990; Koch, 1999).

The disturbances of anxiety and traumatization that have been found in childhood maltreatment and the sensitivity of the startle reflex to these conditions suggested the utility of examining startle patterns in maltreated children for developing objective physiological markers of the severity of traumatization. Accordingly, my colleagues and I (Klorman, Cicchetti, Thatcher, & Ison, 2003) investigated acoustic startle in maltreated and nonmaltreated comparison children to a range of auditory intensities to describe any abnormalties in response magnitude, onset latency, and habituation. In addition, we examined startle differences among subtypes of maltreated children.

To the best of our knowledge, this study was the first prospective investigation of startle abnormalities in maltreated children. In addition to the lack of previous research on child maltreatment, inconsistencies in the literature on startle in traumatized children and adults made it difficult to propose specific confirmatory hypotheses. Specifically, the only study involving pediatric anxiety in children, conducted by Ornitz and Pynoos (1989), detected smaller than normal amplitude of startle eyeblinks in boys and girls with posttraumatic stress disorder (PTSD). In contrast, studies on startle in adults with PTSD have found exaggerated startle eyeblinks in men and have reported inconsistent findings in women.

We examined acoustic startle to 24 randomly ordered 50-millisecond binaural white noise burst probes of 70, 85, 100, and 115 dB while children were watching silent cartoons. The participants were 109 maltreated children and 103 nonmaltreated children matched for age, sex, and socioeconomic status (see Klorman et al., 2003).

Maltreated boys' startle blinks had smaller amplitude and slower onset latency and were less affected by increasing probe loudness than were those of comparison boys. Among maltreatment subtypes, this pattern was most salient for physically abused boys. Unfortunately, there were not enough physically abused girls in our sample to detect any potential differences from comparison children. Our results for maltreated boys also are consistent with those of Ornitz and Pynoos (1989) for diminished startle responses among children with PTSD. These investigators suggested that startle diminution in traumatized children may reflect cortically mediated attentional dysfunction that affected brainstem mechanisms for startle responses.

The findings obtained with the physically abused boys are consistent with those of Cicchetti and Rogosch (2001a), who found that physically abused children displayed a suppression of cortisol and significantly less diurnal variation in HPA functioning than did other subtypes of maltreated children. Although startle responsiveness and cortisol regulation are linked to separate, but interconnected, neurobiological systems, in both investigations physically abused children exhibited diminished responsiveness. Physically abused children are often exposed to threat and danger, and their smaller responses to startle and their suppression of cortisol may reflect allostatic load, the cumulative long-term effect of physiologic responses to stress (McEwen & Stellar, 1993). Repetitive social challenges in a child's environment, such as that engendered by child abuse and neglect, can cause disruptions in basic homeostatic and regulatory processes that are essential to the maintenance of optimal physical and mental health (Repetti, Taylor, & Seeman, 2002).

It is interesting to note that the findings in both the Klorman et al. (2003) and the Ornitz and Pynoos (1989) investigations diverge from reports that adult men with PTSD exhibit larger amplitude acoustic startle responses. The discrepancy might be clarified by longitudinal investigations. This strategy could help in establishing whether the timing of traumatization or age at testing determines an outcome of under- or overresponding to startle probes. Because 80% of the maltreated children in the Klorman et al. (2003) study experienced their onset of maltreatment within the first 2 years of life and also had current active monitoring by the Department of Social Services, it is impossible to disentangle whether age of onset versus chronicity of the trauma drove our findings on startle responsiveness.

Neuroendocrine Functioning

The study of child maltreatment also can be used to illustrate how traumatic social experiences can alter the activity of the HPA axis. Child abuse and neglect are stressful and threatening experiences that pose adaptational challenges, and the HPA axis is one of the physiological systems that has evolved in mammals to help focus and sustain cognitive, emotional, behavioral, and metabolic activity in response to conditions of threat (Lopez, Akil, & Watson, 1999; Vazquez, 1998). Basal activity of this neuroendocrine system follows a circadian rhythm such that the highest levels appear around the time of awakening and then decline to low levels near the onset of sleep (Kirschbaum & Hellhammer, 1989). Basal levels of cortisol are essential to ensure normal brain growth and to support the metabolic activity necessary to sustain general functioning (McEwen, 1998).

The capacity to elevate cortisol in response to acute trauma is necessary for survival. Although brief elevations in cortisol subsequent to acute stressors appear to improve the individual's ability to manage stressful experiences successfully, chronic hyperactivity of the HPA axis may eventuate in hippocampal neuronal loss, inhibit the process of neurogensis, decrease the rate at which myelination develops, contribute to abnormalities in synaptic pruning, and increase the probability of impairments in cognitive, memory, and affective functioning (Gould, Tanapat, McEwen, Flugge, & Fuchs, 1998; Sapolsky, 1992). Moreover, the elimination of glucocorticoids, or what is known as *hypocortisolism*, also can cause damage to neurons (Gunnar & Vazquez, 2001). Thus, some individuals who experience ongoing chronic stressors, such as children who are repeatedly physically abused by their parents, may manifest reduced adrenocortical secretion, decreased adrenocortical reactivity, or enhanced negative feedback of the HPA axis (DeBellis, Keshavan, et al., 1999). Accordingly, it is in the best interest of all individuals to avoid both chronic glucocorticoid hyper- and hyposecretion (Sapolsky, 1996).

Instances of child physical and sexual abuse, as well as child neglect, can be viewed as potentially massive stressors. Research with animals has revealed that threats of physical injury and pain produce intense activation of physiological systems associated with fear and stress (Kalin & Takahashi, 1990). By definition, child neglect creates opportunities for unrelieved fearfulness and discomfort, resulting in increased risk for accident, injury, and abusive interactions that would also be expected to activate stress systems such as the HPA axis. The activity level of the HPA system also may be related to the psychological characteristics of maltreated children and may play a role in the emergence of psychopathology among individuals with a history of child maltreatment.

HPA dysregulation has been found in children who have been sexually abused. For example, DeBellis, Lefter, Trickett, and Putnam (1994) discovered that girls who had been sexually abused excreted significantly greater amounts of the dopamine (DA) metabolite homovanillic acid than did girls who had not experienced sexual abuse. Augmented mean morning serial plasma cortisol levels also have been found in sexually abused girls, implicating altered glucocorticoid functioning in the HPA axis (Putnam, Trickett, Helmers, Dorn, & Everett, 1991). In addition, the attenuated plasma adrenocorticotropin hormone (ACTH) response to the ovine corticotropin releasing hormone (CRH) stimulation test in sexually abused girls further suggests a dysregulatory disorder of the HPA axis, associated with hyperresponsiveness of the pituitary gland to exogenous CRH and normal overall cortisol secretion to CRH challenge (DeBellis et al., 1993). Moreover, it has been demonstrated that sexually abused children with PTSD excrete significantly greater concentrations of baseline norepinephrine and DA in comparison with nonabused anxious and normal healthy comparison children (DeBellis, Baum, et al. 1999). Thus, it seems that the combination of sexual abuse experiences and PTSD is associated with relatively enduring alterations of biological stress systems.

Two investigations conducted in separate laboratories converge on the finding that maltreated children with major depressive disorder (MDD) fail to display the expected diurnal decrease in cortisol secretion from morning to afternoon (Hart, Gunnar, & Cicchetti, 1996; Kaufman, 1991). Furthermore, when compared with depressed nonabused and normal comparison children, maltreated prepubertal depressed abused children who were continuing to live under conditions of chronic ongoing adversity exhibited an increased human CRH-induced ACTH response, but normal cortisol secretion. In contrast, depressed children with prior histories of abuse but currently residing in stable environments did not differ in their HPA functioning from the depressed abused or the normal comparison children (Kaufman et al., 1997).

In our laboratory, two investigations of cortisol regulation have been conducted with school-age maltreated and nonmaltreated children (Cicchetti & Rogosch, 2001a, 2001b). These studies were implemented within the context of a research summer day camp program. Because attendance at this summer camp was a novel experience, these youngsters did not know what to expect from the adult camp counselors (who were unfamiliar to the children). Moreover, children in the camp were unfamiliar with each other. Thus, the camp context constituted a social challenge for the children in attendance.

Saliva samples were collected twice daily through the week as children participated in camp. One advantage of the naturalistic camp setting was that it permitted saliva to be collected from the children during uniform time periods (i.e., at 9 a.m. and at 4 p.m.; for details see Cicchetti & Rogosch, 2001a, 2001b). Cortisol assays were conducted without awareness of the maltreatment status of participating children.

In the first investigation, Cicchetti and Rogosch (2001a) found substantial elevations in the morning cortisol levels of maltreated children who had been both sexually abused and physically abused, as well as neglected or emotionally maltreated. In addition, many of the children in this multiple abuse group also exhibited elevated cortisol concentrations in both the morning and afternoon assayed saliva collections. Children in the multiple abuse group thus displayed patterns akin to hypercortisolism and may be at extremely high risk of developing compromised neurobiological structure and function. These children have experienced chronic maltreatment across a range of developmental periods. This multifaceted assault on cognitive, social, emotional, and biological systems most likely contributes to these children's expectations of continued adversity. The pervasive negative experiences that these multiply abused children have encountered contribute significantly to these children's construction of their worlds as marked by fear and a hypersensitivity to future maltreatment.

Unlike what was obtained in the multiple abuse group of children, a subgroup of youngsters who had experienced physical abuse evidenced a trend toward lower morning cortisol concentrations relative to the nonmaltreated children. Moreover, this physically abused subgroup of children displayed a significantly smaller decrease in cortisol levels from morning sample concentrations to afternoon sample concentrations. This pattern of cortisol production suggests relatively less diurnal variation for the physically abused group of children. They manifested reduced adrenocortical reactivity, or enhanced negative feedback of the HPA axis, a pattern suggestive of hypocortisolism and that also may cause long-term neurobiological sequelae. Finally, no differences in patterns of cortisol regulation were obtained between the neglected and the emotionally maltreated groups of children and the comparison group of nonmaltreated children. The divergent patterns of cortisol regulation for the varying subgroups of maltreated children suggest that it is highly unlikely that the neurobiological development of all children is uniformly affected by the experience of maltreatment. Not all maltreated children exhibited HPA axis functioning dysregulation and the type of dysfuction varied by subgroup.

In the second investigation, Cicchetti and Rogosch (2001b) examined the relations between neuroendocrine functioning and psychopathology in maltreated school-age children. The study also was implemented in a summer research day camp context, with salivary samples collected at 9 a.m. and 4 p.m. All samples were subsequently assayed for cortisol without knowledge of the children's maltreatment status. At the conclusion of the week, camp counselors completed the Teacher Report Form (TRF; Achenbach & Rescorla, 2001) and children completed the Child Depression Inventory (CDI; Kovacs, 1985). Counselors were unaware of the children's maltreatment status. Children were identified as exhibiting clinical-level internalizing-only psychopathology if they had clinical-level scores on the TRF Internalizing scale or the CDI and did not exhibit clinical-level problems on the TRF Externalizing scale.

Cicchetti and Rogosch (2001b) discovered that maltreated children with clinical levels of internalizing problems exhibited increased morning and across the day average levels of cortisol, compared with the other groups of maltreated and nonmaltreated children. These results suggest that the presence of maltreatment moderated the impact of case-level internalizing problems. Furthermore, maltreated children with case-level internalizing problems displayed higher afternoon cortisol than did nonmaltreated children with clinical-level internalizing problems.

The increased levels of cortisol found in the maltreated children with clinical levels of internalizing problems differ from those typically obtained in samples of children and adolescents with MDD. The latter groups rarely exhibit the increase in cortisol that is characteristic of a regulatory dysfunction of the HPA axis (Dahl & Ryan, 1996). Consistent with this literature, the nonmaltreated children with case-level internalizing problems in our study did not display increased levels of cortisol and an HPA axis dysregulation. Thus, it appears that the experience of maltreatment intensifies the usual effects of childhood depressive disorder on neuroendocrine functioning. Accordingly, maltreated children with significant internalizing psychopathology may be at risk for developing the neurobiological anomalies associated with hypercortisolism. The HPA axis abnormalities of the maltreated children with clinical levels of internalizing problems bear interestingly striking similarity to those obtained with maltreated children with PTSD and MDD reported by DeBellis, Baum, et al. (1999) and with depressed adults who were sexually or physically abused during their childhoods (Heim, Newport, Bonsall, Miller, & Nemeroff, 2001; Lemieux & Coe, 1995).

It is important to note that not all maltreated children with clinical case levels of internalizing psychopathology displayed the same pattern of cortisol regulation. This finding provides further evidence that maltreatment experiences do not uniformly affect behavioral and neurobiological functioning. Future investigations must strive to uncover the mechanisms that enable maltreated children with case-level internalizing symptomatology to construct and interpret their experiences in such a way as to eventuate in nonpathological behavioral and biological functioning.

Cognitive Brain Event-Related Potentials and Emotion Processing

My colleagues and I have conducted two experiments that have examined maltreated children's psychophysiological processing of emotional information. The goal of this research was to elucidate possible mechanisms through which the chronic stress experienced by children who have been maltreated could bring about problems in their processing of emotion stimuli (Pollak et al., 1998). Attachment systems have been theorized to be constructed to permit flexible responses to environmental circumstances, influence emotion regulation, and function through internal working models (Bowlby, 1988) that children hold of themselves and of their relationships with others (Cassidy, 1994). The activation of these representations may be reflected through physiological activity as well as behavior. In our work, we have focused on one type of physiological reaction, the event-related potential (ERP). The ERP is an index of central ner-

vous system functioning thought to reflect the underlying neurological processing of discrete stimuli (Hillyard & Picton, 1987). ERPs represent scalp-derived
changes in brain electrical activity over time, obtained by averaging time-locked
segments of the electroencephalogram (EEG) that follow or precede the presentation of a stimulus. In this manner, ERPs allow for monitoring of neural
activity associated with cognitive processing in real time (Donchin, Karis,
Bashore, Coles, & Gratton, 1986).

One particular ERP component, the P300, is a positive wave that occurs
approximately 300 to 600 milliseconds after the presentation of a task-relevant
stimulus and is maximal at the central-parietal scalp. The amplitude of the
P300 varies as a function of task relevance and stimulus probability (R. Johnson,
1993), and it has been used in conjunction with behavioral measures to classify
specific cognitive operations such as the evaluation of stimulus significance.
The P300 also may reflect processes involved in the updating of mental representations in working memory (Donchin et al., 1986). In general, such psychological processes serve to maintain accurate representations of one's environment by highlighting events that are significant. Therefore, we reasoned that
the P300 component may be useful in illuminating the cognitive processes that
accompany the encoding of salient emotional stimuli and highlight differences
in such processes between maltreated and nonmaltreated children.

The requirements of the task for both experiments were to recognize and
respond to facial expressions of emotions. For all conditions, children were instructed to depress a hand-held button whenever they recognized the target
facial expression (e.g., happy, angry, fearful). This emotional expression, the
target, was only one of three emotions that were presented to the children.
Across a variety of experimental conditions, children were required to attend to
different facial expressions of emotion, and the probability of occurrence (rare
or frequent) and task relevance (target or nontarget) were manipulated.

In the first experiment, Pollak, Cicchetti, Klorman, and Brumaghin (1997)
compared the ERPs of school-age maltreated and nonmaltreated children of
comparable socioeconomic background and cognitive maturity. Children were
instructed to respond to either a happy or an angry face. Because the amplitude
of the ERP is influenced by the probability of occurrence of the stimuli, both
happy and angry faces appeared infrequently (i.e., on 25% of the trials), whereas
the nontarget neutral faces were displayed more frequently (i.e., on 50% of the
trials). For both groups of children, there were few performance errors; thus, no
distinctions could be made between emotion conditions (i.e., happy, angry, neutral) or between maltreated and nonmaltreated children with respect to accuracy or reaction time. The ERPs of the nonmaltreated children were equivalent
in both the happy and angry target conditions. The amplitude of the ERP was
largest to the target stimuli, intermediate to the rare nontarget, and smallest to
the frequent nontarget stimuli. In contrast, the ERPs of the maltreated children were larger in the angry than in the happy target conditions. The differential pattern of responding to emotion conditions suggests that, compared with
nonmaltreated children, maltreated children exhibited different patterns of information processing depending on the emotion to which they were attending
(Pollak et al., 1997).

Pollak and colleagues (1997) interpreted these results as suggesting that angry and happy targets activated affective representations differentially for maltreated versus nonmaltreated children, and they theorized that the ERP responses of the maltreated children reflected more efficient cognitive organization in the anger condition than in the happy condition. Such patterns of neurophysiological activation would be adaptive for coping with the stressful and threatening environments in which maltreated children reside (Cicchetti, 1991). However, biases toward negative affect or diminished responsiveness toward positive affect would place maltreated children at increased risk for encountering difficulties in their interactions with peers and adults (Cicchetti, Lynch, Shonk, & Manly, 1992; Howes, Cicchetti, Toth, & Rogosch, 2000).

Emotion systems have been postulated to function as associative networks wherein input that matches significant mental representations activates memory systems (Lang, 1994). Pollak and colleagues (1997) conjectured, in this regard, that P300 amplitude may mark the match of facial stimuli with more complex emotional memories. Information processing theorists have invoked constructs such as schemas and working models to describe the mechanisms by which children integrate biologically relevant information with existing knowledge structures (Bowlby, 1988; Bretherton, 1990). The findings reported by Pollak et al. (1997) provide empirical support for such developmental processes.

In the second experiment, Pollak, Klorman, Thatcher, and Cicchetti (2001) compared the ERP responses of maltreated and nonmaltreated children with happy, angry, and fearful facial expressions. This investigation was conducted to determine the specificity of the relation between the ERP responses of the maltreated children and the nature of the eliciting stimuli. Specifically, Pollak and colleagues (2001) were interested in whether the ERPs of maltreated children generalized to positive versus negative emotional valence, or were restricted to emotional displays of happiness versus anger. Negative emotions in addition to anger are frequently associated with maltreatment experiences (e.g., fear; see Hennessy, Rabideau, Cicchetti, & Cummings, 1994). Consequently, it is important to ascertain whether each discrete emotion may convey its own unique information and be processed in a distinct fashion.

Pollak et al. (2001) discovered that, as was the case in their earlier study, nonmaltreated children exhibited equivalent ERP amplitude responses to all of the target facial expressions of affect. However, the ERP amplitude responses of the maltreated children exceeded those of the nonmaltreated comparison children only in response to the angry target, but not to the fear or happy targets. These results suggest that there was specificity in maltreated children's differential processing of the emotional information: when their attention is deployed to angry facial expressions, these youngsters are uniquely sensitive in detecting this emotion expression over others. In further tests of this hypothesis, Pollak and Sinha (2002) demonstrated that physically abused children required less sensory input than nonmaltreated comparison children to accurately identify faces of anger. These investigators used a gradual evolution of images depicting facial expressions of various emotions. Physically abused children detected angry emotions at lower steps of the sequence but did not exhibit increased sensitivity for the other facial displays. Pollak and Sinha (2002) concluded that physically abused children have facilitated access to representations of anger. Similarly, in a task in which pairs of photographs of emotional expressions were morphed into each other, Pollak and Kistler (2002) found that physically abused children detected anger with lower signal strength than did nonmaltreated comparison children. Taken in tandem, these studies suggest that physically abused children can detect facial expressions of anger more accurately and at lower levels of perceptual intensity in comparison to other emotions.

Findings from these two investigations, in combination with the literature on the effects of maltreatment on psychological development, demonstrate that the socioemotional and behavioral difficulties observed in maltreated children affect multiple neurobiological systems. In particular, the ERP data suggest that the experiences that maltreated children encountered during their development caused particular stimuli to become personally meaningful on the basis, in part, of the stored mental representations that have been associated with that stimulus over time (Pollak et al., 1998). Prior experiences of maltreated children are reflected in these children's psychophysiological responses.

It is highly plausible that the stresses associated with child abuse and neglect may enhance the memory of salient stimuli in the environment (Pollak et al., 1998; Toth & Cicchetti, 1998). In a related manner, maltreatment also appears to affect children's interpretation and comprehension of particular emotional displays (Pollak, Cicchetti, Hornung, & Reed, 2000). Specifically, neglected children, who often suffer from an extremely limited emotional environment, have more difficulty discriminating among emotional expressions than do physically abused or nonmaltreated comparison children. Moreover, physically abused children, who are often exposed to impending threat, display a response bias for angry facial expressions.

Implications for Social Policy

I next offer several social policy prescriptions that hold promise for promoting competent biological and psychological functioning in maltreated children, as well as for ensuring that necessary and effective interventions are available for these children and their families.

1.   *The primary prevention of child maltreatment must become a national priority.* Given the adverse neurobiological, psychophysiological, and psychological consequences of child maltreatment (Cicchetti & Valentino, 2006), we, as a nation, must be committed not only to treating this societal ill and the victims but also to preventing the occurrence of maltreatment. In a time of increased fiscal austerity, prevention as a priority is becoming secondary to the belief that only the most seriously ill must be treated. It behooves us to continue to conduct investigations of the effects of maltreatment on brain structure and functioning, and to link these aberrations to cognitive and socioemotional functioning so as to make a stronger case for the criticality of prevention.

2. *Assessments of maltreated children should include biological as well as psychological measures to ensure that each maltreated child receives the best intervention possible.* The incorporation of biological measures into clinical as-

sessments of maltreated children will provide a more comprehensive portrayal of functioning, as well as provide valuable input into the provision of efficacious interventions.

3. *Interventions must be directed toward the prevention of the biological and psychological sequelae associated with child maltreatment.* In addition to preventing the occurrence of child maltreatment, we also must strive to prevent the emergence of its negative sequelae. Thus, every effort should be made to implement interventions as soon after the detection of child maltreatment as possible. Again related to funding limitations, there is a press to provide treatment only to children who are evidencing a diagnosable mental disorder. This is a disservice to children and also costlier to our nation in the long run.

4. *In providing both preventive and psychotherapeutic interventions, various levels of the child's social ecology, including the community, school, and family, must be considered and addressed* (Cicchetti & Toth, 2000). Given our knowledge of the importance of intervening at multiple levels of the ecology to bring about the most salubrious effects on psychological functioning, it is similarly likely that such multicontextual interventions will be necessary to address the neurobiological and psychophysiological sequelae of maltreatment.

5. *Mechanisms must be developed that allow for the early provision and subsequent continuity of services for maltreated children.* Because the effects of maltreatment cut across multiple developmental systems, it is likely that developmental reorganizations could result in vulnerabilities not previously evident. As such, accessibility to "booster" interventions across time must be made available to maltreated children and to their families.

6. *Policymakers, clinicians, and educators all need to appreciate that the consequences of maltreatment extend to the biological level and that these neurobiological aberrations may mediate problems in academic functioning, interpersonal relations, regulation of anger and violence, and work performance, as well as the intergenerational transmission of child maltreatment.* In this regard, the criticality of assessing biological functioning, both in research investigations and in randomized preventive interventions, is underscored.

7. *As researchers, we must become increasingly sophisticated at providing legislators and policy advocates with information gained from basic research investigations, as well as from randomized preventive interventions and psychotherapeutic treatment trials* (see, e.g., Cicchetti, Rogosch, & Toth, in press; Zigler & Hall, 2000). Documenting the presence of biological aberrations in maltreated children might serve to underscore the importance of prevention and intervention and, ultimately, facilitate the availability of services to this vulnerable population.

It is crucial that researchers design and conduct the scientific investigations that are necessary to provide definitive answers to the questions concerning the effects of child maltreatment on brain functioning and psychological development. The knowledge gleaned from these studies will enable maltreated children to receive interventions that are based on sound scientific research. It is critical that theoretically and empirically informed interventions be conducted in a scientifically rigorous fashion that enables researchers to document their efficacy. Moreover, it is imperative that information derived from investigations of neurobiological and psychological functioning in maltreated children be incorporated into the intervention and social policy arenas.

References

Aber, J. L., & Zigler, E. (1981). Developmental considerations in the definition of child maltreatment. *New Directions for Child Development, 11*, 1–29.

Achenbach, T. M., & Rescorla, L. A. (2001). *Manual for the ASEBA School-Age Forms & Profiles.* Burlington: University of Vermont, Research Center for Children, Youth, and Families.

Black, J., Jones, T. A., Nelson, C. A., & Greenough, W. T. (1998). Neuronal plasticity and the developing brain. In N. E. Alessi, J. T. Coyle, S. I. Harrison, & S. Eth (Eds.), *Handbook of child and adolescent psychiatry* (pp. 31–53). New York: Wiley.

Bowlby, J. (1988). Developmental psychiatry comes to age. *American Journal of Psychiatry, 145,* 1–10.

Bretherton, I. (1990). Open communication and internal working models: Their role in the development of attachment relationships. In R. Thompson (Ed.), *Nebraska Symposium on Motivation: Vol. 36. Socioemotional development* (pp. 57–113). Lincoln: University of Nebraska Press.

Bruer, J. (1999). *The myth of the first three years: A new understanding of early brain development and life-long learning.* New York: Free Press.

Cassidy, J. (1994). Emotion regulation: Influences of attachment relationships. *Monographs of the Society for Research in Child Development, 59*(2–3), 228–283.

Cicchetti, D. (1991). Fractures in the crystal: Developmental psychopathology and the emergence of the self. *Developmental Review, 11*, 271–287.

Cicchetti, D., & Cannon, T. D. (1999). Neurodevelopmental processes in the ontogenesis and epigenesis of psychopathology. *Development and Psychopathology, 11*, 375–393.

Cicchetti, D., & Lynch, M. (1995). Failures in the expectable environment and their impact on individual development: The case of child maltreatment. In D. Cicchetti & D. Cohen (Eds.), *Developmental psychopathology: Vol. 2. Risk, disorder and adaptation* (pp. 32–71). New York: Wiley.

Cicchetti, D., Lynch, M., Shonk, S., & Manly, J. (1992). An organizational perspective on peer relations in maltreated children. In R. D. Parke & G. W. Ladd (Eds.), *Family-peer relationships: Modes of linkage* (pp. 345–383). Hillsdale, NJ: Erlbaum.

Cicchetti, D., & Rogosch, F. A. (2001a). Diverse patterns of neuroendocrine activity in maltreated children. *Development and Psychopathology, 13*, 677–694.

Cicchetti, D., & Rogosch, F. A. (2001b). The impact of child maltreatment and psychopathology upon neuroendocrine functioning. *Development and Psychopathology, 13*, 783–804.

Cicchetti, D., Rogosch, F. A., & Toth, S. L. (in press). The reorganization of attachment insecurity in maltreated infants through preventive interventions. *Development and Psychopathology.*

Cicchetti, D., & Toth, S. L., (Eds.). (1993). *Child abuse, child development and social policy.* Norwood, NJ: Ablex Publishing.

Cicchetti, D., & Toth, S. L. (1995). A developmental psychopathology perspective on child abuse and neglect. *Journal of the American Academy of Child and Adolescent Psychiatry, 34*, 541–565.

Cicchetti, D., & Toth, S. L. (2000). Developmental processes in maltreated children. In D. Hansen (Ed.), *Nebraska Symposium on Motivation: Vol. 46. Child maltreatment* (pp. 85–160). Lincoln: University of Nebraska Press.

Cicchetti, D., & Tucker, D. (1994). Development and self-regulatory structures of the mind. *Development and Psychopathology, 6*, 533–549.

Cicchetti, D., & Valentino, K. (2006). An ecological transactional perspective on child maltreatment: Failure of the average expectable environment and its influence upon child development. In D. Cicchetti & D. J. Cohen (Eds.), *Developmental psychopathology: Vol. 3. Risk, disorder, and adaptation* (2nd ed., pp. 129–201). New York: Wiley.

Cicchetti, D., & Walker, E. F. (2001). Stress and development: Biological and psychological consequences. *Development and Psychopathology, 13*, 413–418.

Courchesne, E., Chisum, H., & Townsend, J. (1994). Neural activity-dependent brain changes in development: Implications for psychopathology. *Development and Psychopathology, 6*, 697–722.

Curtis, W. J., & Cicchetti, D. (2003). Moving research on resilience into the 21st century: Theoretical and methodological considerations in examining the biological contributors to resilience. *Development and Psychopathology, 15*, 773–810.

Dahl, R., & Ryan, N. (1996). The psychobiology of adolescent depression. In D. Cicchetti & S. L. Toth (Eds.), *Rochester Symposium on Developmental Psychopathology: Vol. 7. Adolescence: Opportunities and challenges* (pp. 197–232). Rochester, NY: University of Rochester Press.

Davis, M. (1984). The mammalian startle response. In R.C. Eaton (Ed.), *Neural mechanisms of startle behavior* (pp. 287–351). New York: Plenum Press.

Davis, M. (1990). Animal models of anxiety based on classical conditioning: The conditioned emotional response (CER) and the fear-potentiated startle effect. *Pharmacological Therapeutics, 47*, 147–165.

DeBellis, M. D., Baum, A. S., Birmaher, B., Keshavan, M. S., Eccard, C. H., Boring, A. M., et al. (1999). Developmental traumatology: Part I. Biological stress systems. *Biological Psychiatry, 45*, 1259–1270.

DeBellis, M. D., Chrousos, G., Dorn, L., Burke, L., Helmers, K., Kling, M., et al. (1993). Hypothalamic–pituitary–adrenal axis dysregulation in sexually abused girls. *Journal of Clinical Endocrinology & Metabolism, 77*, 1–7.

DeBellis, M. D., Keshavan, M. S., Casey, B. J., Clark, D. B., Giedd, J., Boring, A. M. et al. (1999). Developmental traumatology: Biological stress systems and brain development in maltreated children with PTSD: Part II. The relationship between characteristics of trauma and psychiatric symptoms and adverse brain development in maltreated children and adolescents with PTSD. *Biological Psychiatry, 45*, 1271–1284.

DeBellis, M. D., Lefter, L., Trickett, P. K., & Putnam, F. W. (1994). Urinary catecholamine excretion in sexually abused girls. *Journal of the American Academy of Child and Adolescent Psychiatry, 33*, 320–327.

Donchin, E., Karis, D., Bashore, T. R., Coles, M. G. H., & Gratton, G. (1986). Cognitive psychophysiology and human information processing. In M. G. H. Coles, E. Donchin, & S. W. Porges (Eds.), *Psychophysiology* (pp. 244–267). New York: Guilford Press.

Fromm, S. (2001). *Total estimated cost of child abuse in the United States: Statistical evidence.* Retrieved January 1, 2004, from http://member.preventchildabuse.org/site/DocServer/cost_analysis.pdf?docID=144

Gould, E., Tanapat, P., McEwen, B.S., Flugge, G., & Fuchs, E. (1998). Proliferation of granule cell precursors in the dentale gyrus of adult monkeys is diminished by stress. *Proceedings of the National Academy of Sciences, 95*, 3168–3171.

Greenough, W., Black, J., & Wallace, C. (1987). Experience and brain development. *Child Development, 58*, 539–559.

Gunnar, M. R., & Vazquez, D. M. (2001). Low cortisol and a flattening of expected daytime rhythm: Potential indices of risk in human development. *Development and Psychopathology, 13*, 515–538.

Hart, J., Gunnar, M., & Cicchetti, D. (1996). Altered neuroendocrine activity in maltreated children related to depression. *Development and Psychopathology, 8*, 201–214.

Heim, C., Newport, D. J., Bonsall, R., Miller, A.. H., & Nemeroff, C. B. (2001). Altered pituitary–adrenal axis responses to provocative challenge tests in adult survivors of childhood abuse. *American Journal of Psychiatry, 158*, 575–581.

Hennessy, K., Rabideau, G., Cicchetti, D., & Cummings, E. M. (1994). Responses of physically abused children to different forms of interadult anger. *Child Development, 65*, 815–828.

Hillyard, S. A., & Picton, T. W. (1987). Electrophysiology of cognition. In V. Mountcastle (Ed.), *Handbook of physiology: Vol. 5. Higher functions of the brain* (pp. 519–583). Bethesda: MD: American Physiological Society.

Howes, P., Cicchetti, D., Toth, S. L., & Rogosch, F. (2000). Affective, organizational, and relational characteristics of maltreating families: A systems perspective. *Journal of Family Psychology, 14*, 95–110.

Johnson, M. H. (1999). Cortical plasticity in normal and abnormal cognitive development: Evidence and working hypotheses. *Development and Psychopathology, 11*, 419–438.

Johnson, R. (1993). On the neural generators of the P300 component of the event-related potential. *Psychophysiology, 30,* 90–97.

Kalin, N. H., & Takahashi, L. K. (1990). Fear-motivated behavior induced by prior shock experience is mediated by corticotropin-releasing hormone system. *Brain Research, 509,* 80–84.

Kandel, E. R. (1998). A new intellectual framework for psychiatry. *American Journal of Psychiatry, 155,* 457–459.

Kaufman, J. (1991). Depressive disorders in maltreated children. *Journal of the American Academy of Child and Adolescent Psychiatry, 30,* 257–265.

Kaufman, J., Birmaher, B., Perel, J., Dahl, R. E., Moreci, P., Nelson, B., et al. (1997). The corticotropin-releasing hormone challenge in depressed abused, depressed nonbused, and normal control children. *Biological Psychiatry, 42,* 669–679.

Kirschbaum, C., & Hellhammer, D. H. (1989). Salivary cortisol in psychobiology research: An overview. *Neuropsychobiology, 22,* 150–169.

Klorman, R., Cicchetti, D., Thatcher, J. E., & Ison, J. R. (2003). Acoustic startle in maltreated children. *Journal of Abnormal Child Psychology, 31,* 359–370.

Koch, M. (1999). The neurobiology of startle. *Progress in Neurobiology, 59,* 107–128.

Kovacs, M. (1985). The Children's Depression Inventory. *Psychopharmacology Bulletin, 21,* 995–998.

Lang, P. J. (1994). The varieties of emotional experience: A meditation on James–Lange theory. *Psychological Review, 101,* 211–221.

Lemieux, A. M., & Coe, C. L. (1995). Abuse-related posttraumatic stress disorder: Evidence for chronic neuroendocrine activation in women. *Psychosomatic Medicine, 57,* 110–115.

Levine, S. (1994). The ontogeny of the hypothalamic-pituitary-adrenal axis: The influence of maternal factors. *Annuals of the New York Academy of Sciences, 746,* 275–288.

Lopez, J. F., Akil, H., & Watson, S. J. (1999). Neural circuits mediating stress. *Biological Psychology, 46,* 1461–1471.

Maughan, A., & Cicchetti, D. (2002). The impact of child maltreatment and interadult violence on children's emotion regulation abilities. *Child Development, 73,* 1525–1542.

McEwen, B. S. (1998). Protective and damaging effects of stress mediators. *Seminars in Medicine of the Beth Israel Deaconess Medical Center, 338,* 171–179.

McEwen, B. S., & Stellar, E. (1993) Stress and the individual mechanisms leading to disease. *Archives of Internal Medicine, 153,* 2093–2101.

Meaney, M. J. (2001). Maternal care, gene expression, and the transmission of individual differences in stress reactivity across generations. *Annual Review of Neuroscience, 24,* 1161–1192.

Meaney, M. J., Di Orio, J., Fancis, D., Widdowson, J., LaBlante, P., Caldji, C., et al. (1996). Early environmental regulation of forebrain glucocorticoid receptor gene expression: Implications for adrenocortical response to stress. *Developmental Neuroscience, 18,* 49–72.

Miller, T. R., Cohen, M. A., & Wierseman, B. (1996). *Victim costs and consequences: A new look.* Washington, DC: National Institute of Justice.

National Research Council. (1993). *Understanding child abuse and neglect.* Washington, DC: National Academy Press.

Nowakowski, R. S., & Hayes, N. L. (1999). CNS development: An overview. *Development and Psychopathology, 11,* 395–418.

Ornitz, E. M., & Pynoos, R. (1989). Startle modulation in children with posttraumatic stress disorder. *American Journal of Psychiatry, 146,* 866–870.

Pollak, S. D., Cicchetti, D., Hornung, K., & Reed, A. (2000). Recognizing emotion in faces: Developmental effects of child abuse and neglect. *Developmental Psychology, 36,* 679–688.

Pollak, S. D., Cicchetti, D., & Klorman, R. (1998). Stress, memory, and emotion: Developmental considerations from the study of child maltreatment. *Development and Psychopathology, 10,* 739–759.

Pollak, S. D., Cicchetti, D., Klorman, R., & Brumaghim, J. T. (1997). Cognitive brain event-related potentials and emotion processing in maltreated children. *Child Development, 68,* 773–787.

Pollak, S. D., & Kistler, D. J. (2002). Early experience is associated with the development of categorical representations for facial expressions of emotion. *Proceedings of the National Academy of Sciences, 99,* 9072–9076.

Pollak, S. D., Klorman, R., Thatcher, J. E., & Cicchetti, D. (2001). P3b reflects maltreated children's reactions to facial displays of emotion. *Psychophysiology, 38,* 267–274.

Pollak, S. D., & Sinha, P. (2002). Effects of early experience on children's recognition of facial displays of emotion. *Developmental Psychology, 38*, 784–791.

Putnam, F. W., Trickett, P. K., Helmers, K., Dorn, L., & Everett, B. (1991). Cortisol abnormalities in sexually abused girls. *Proceedings of the 144th Annual Meeting of the American Psychiatric Association*, 107, 107–128.

Rakic, P. (1988a). Intrinsic and extrinsic determinants of neocortal parcellation: A radial unit model. In P. Rakic & W. Singer (Eds.), *Neurobiology of neocortex* (pp. 5–27). New York: Wiley.

Rakic, P. (1988b, July 8). Specification of cerebral cortex areas. *Science, 241*, 170–176.

Repetti, R., Taylor, S., & Seeman, T. (2002). Risky families: Family social environments and the mental and physical health of offspring. *Psychological Bulletin, 128*, 330–366.

Sanchez, M. M., Ladd, C. O., & Plotsky, P. M. (2001). Early adverse experience as a developmental risk factor for later psychopathology: Evidence from rodent and primate models. *Development and Psychopathology, 13*, 419–450.

Sapolsky, R. M. (1992). *Stress, the aging brain and the mechanisms of neuron death*. Cambridge, MA: MIT Press.

Sapolsky, R. M. (1996). Stress, glucocorticoids, and damage to the NS: The current state of confusion. *Stress, 1*, 1–19.

Toth, S. L., & Cicchetti, D. (1998). Remembering, forgetting, and the effects of trauma on memory: A developmental psychopathology perspective. *Development and Psychopathology, 10*, 589–605.

Trickett, P., & McBride-Chang, C. (1995). The developmental impact of different types of child abuse and neglect. *Developmental Review, 15*, 311–337.

U.S. Department of Health and Human Services, National Center on Child Abuse and Neglect (2001). *Child maltreatment 1999: Reports from the states to the National Child Abuse and Neglect Data System*. Washington, DC: U.S. Government Printing Office.

Vazquez, D. M. (1998). Stress and the developing limbic–hypothalamic–pituitary–adrenal axis. *Psychoneuroendocrinology, 23*, 663–700.

Zigler, E., & Hall, N. (2000). *Child development and social policy*. New York: McGraw-Hill.

11

The Sexually Mature Teen as a Whole Person: New Directions in Prevention and Intervention for Teen Pregnancy and Parenthood

Joseph P. Allen, Victoria Seitz, and Nancy H. Apfel

More than 3 decades ago, Edward F. Zigler, to whom this chapter is dedicated, noted the dangers of getting so swept up by a single behavior or phenomenon that individuals begin to consider that behavior or phenomenon as existing outside the context of the "whole person." In an article on mental retardation entitled, "The Retarded Child as a Whole Person," Zigler (1971) argued persuasively that both theory and intervention that treat fundamental social behaviors as existing in a social and developmental vacuum are bound to be intrinsically flawed. Although Ed's argument was made at another time and in another context, we believe that this chapter will demonstrate that it is highly applicable even to fields in which Ed has never worked, including adolescent pregnancy prevention.

Overview

Adolescent sexuality and its consequences have been a concern of numerous societies across many generations—and for good reason. Teenage pregnancy, teenage childbearing, and teenage acquisition of sexually transmitted diseases bring a unique set of costs both to the adolescents involved and to society as a whole. In the United States each year, more than 450,000 adolescents age 19 or younger become pregnant (Martin, Park, & Sutton, 2002). Rates have declined somewhat from their recent peak around 1990, with declines attributed primarily to increased adolescent contraceptive use (accounting for 75% of the decline) and secondarily to decreased adolescent sexual activity (accounting for 25% of the decline; Darroch, 2001; National Center for Health Statistics, 2002). Nevertheless, pregnancy rates still range from 50% to 550% higher than rates in other Western societies (Darroch, Singh, & Frost, 2001). Each year, 3 million teens in the United States (1 in 4 sexually experienced teens) contract a sexually transmitted disease (Alan Guttmacher Institute, 1994), and teen pregnancies result in more than 200,000 abortions each year (Jones, Darroch, & Henshaw,

2002; National Center for Health Statistics, 2002). For teens who continue their pregnancies to term, 83% of the resulting births now occur out of wedlock (Bachu & O'Connell, 2001), and even in carefully controlled studies teen mothers have been found to have significantly lower lifetime levels of educational attainment (Hotz, Mullin, & Sanders, 1997).

Most disturbing, however, is evidence that the costs of teen childbearing may actually accrue with greatest severity to members of the next generation. Pregnant adolescents are at well-documented risk of delivering a low-birth-weight baby (Institute of Medicine Committee to Study the Prevention of Low Birthweight, 1985), and such children often have later health problems and difficulties in school. Even if they are born healthy, children of teenage mothers are likely to show poorer cognitive functioning and school adjustment than are children born to older mothers (Brooks-Gunn & Furstenberg, 1986; Osofsky, Eberhart-Wright, Ware, & Hann, 1992). In adolescence, researchers have found massive school failure, delinquency, and risk for early parenthood among the offspring of teenage mothers (Furstenberg, Brooks-Gunn, & Morgan, 1987; Horwitz, Klerman, Kuo, & Jekel, 1991a, 1991b).

Teen Pregnancy Prevention With Adolescents

A Historical Perspective

The history of efforts to prevent adolescent pregnancy and sexually transmitted diseases has been in many ways filled with more conflict, contention, and sheer irrationality than many adolescent romances. If sexuality is a lightning-rod issue in our society, adolescent sexuality represents the point where the charges are greatest and most unstable. Given the fundamental tension in our society around the meaning of adolescent sexual activity—as either a marker of moral debasement or a normal, healthy, and adaptively unfolding developmental process—it is perhaps not surprising that the debates about approaches to preventing adolescent pregnancy have produced more thunderclaps of angry vitriol than they have produced usable energy. One purpose of this chapter is to suggest, regardless of which side one takes in these debates, that much of the text of this debate may be fundamentally misguided with respect to preventing adolescent pregnancy.

The culture wars surrounding adolescent pregnancy have focused heavily on the role of sex education as preventive intervention. Two opposing lines of theory have long existed. One perspective suggests that because a very significant percentage of adolescents become sexually active prior to age 18, educating them about the nature and consequences of this behavior—and teaching them how to prevent pregnancies while becoming sexually active—should be one of the most effective means of preventing teenage pregnancies. From this perspective, pregnancy is best prevented by acknowledging a role for adolescent sexual activity as normative, perhaps even as healthy, but certainly as warranting open and direct discussion unencumbered by moral prescriptions.

The alternative view posits that any assumption that adolescents might become sexually active cannot help but implicitly condone such activity. Although explicit sex education programs might not overtly condone sexual activity, they are seen as suggesting to naïve adolescents who might not have otherwise considered it that sexual activity is a normative behavior. At a minimum, such programs have been viewed as reducing teens' sense that sexual activity is universally viewed by adults as inappropriate prior to adulthood and marriage. Such programs are thus believed to be likely to increase rates of adolescent sexual activity, with a good chance that these increases will lead to higher rates of pregnancies and sexually transmitted infections as well.

The debate between these two camps has been long-standing and carried on with both intensity and acrimony. Yet, in reviewing the empirical evidence regarding this debate, what is most striking is that the two apparently diametrically opposed viewpoints could be argued so strenuously for so long and yet both turn out to be fundamentally wrong in their assumptions and predictions. Reviews of myriad programs that provide solely fact-based sex education to adolescents yield a point estimate of the effects of such programs on behavior that is remarkably close to 0.00 (Philliber & Namerow, 1995). Simple fact-based education programs appear to do nothing to prevent adolescent pregnancies or sexually transmitted diseases (Kirby et al., 1994). However, neither do they lead to increases in teens' likelihood of engaging in sexual activity.

In our discussions with adolescents who have experienced such programs, the reasons for their ineffectiveness, and the hubris of adults who have spent so much effort fighting about them, rapidly become apparent. Some perspective on what is actually occurring emerges quickly if one imagines a hypothetical female adolescent who is also an academically marginal student. Imagine that in September of her sophomore year, our student's world history class studies details of the reign of Charlemagne in medieval Europe. She takes a test on this, is fortunate to get 80% of the questions correct, and moves on to other concerns. Consider what would happen if we retested our adolescent about Charlemagne 6 months later, on a Friday night, after she had had several beers and while she was "making out" with her boyfriend in the back seat of a car. I think most high school teachers would be amazed if our hypothetical teen could recall even half of what she had learned under such conditions. Although this scenario may be moderately troubling for world history teachers, when we apply this rationale to material taught in sex education courses, it becomes clear that the odds of remembering a high-enough percentage of material taught in a regular high school course to adequately protect against a pregnancy are slim. The problem is that material taught in high school courses generally has little impact on adolescents' immediate lives, and little staying power as a result. Explicit sex education programs by themselves do not produce sexual behavior nor do they prevent pregnancies for the simple reason that they do not have much more impact on the behavior, thinking, emotions, and motivation of the adolescents in them than does the material taught in most of their other courses.

There is an alternative. The remainder of this chapter is devoted to outlining the ways in which Zigler's (1971) whole-person perspective might explain current findings regarding adolescent sexuality and transform the general approach to it. We begin by considering interventions that do have a positive impact on adolescents' sexual behavior, focusing on programs with solid research designs (e.g., those using experimental or quasi-experimental designs, adequate sample sizes, and pre- and postassessments of actual behavioral indicators). Next, we examine what happens when we try to help those for whom pregnancy prevention has failed. We will show that this high-risk group can help provide a clear perspective on the directions we need to follow to reduce teen pregnancy rates—along with a basis for hope that even when primary prevention has failed, positive outcomes can emerge with well-timed and thoughtful intervention. Finally, we will suggest directions for future research and intervention.

Prevention Programs That Work—Common Elements

One approach to sex education programs has been effective. This approach combines educational material with substantial amounts of in vivo skills training surrounding assertive and sexual behaviors. Main et al. (1994) reported, for example, that skill-based HIV preventive interventions implemented widely within Colorado schools have led to increases in condom use and declines in numbers of sexual partners. On a similar note, Sikkema, Winett, and Lombard (1995) described a successful AIDS prevention study in which educational material combined with social skills training was compared with an education-only approach and found clearly superior. Other researchers have similarly found that combinations of information-based programs with other developmentally oriented components, such as teaching self-efficacy skills, fare better than information alone in leading to reductions in risky behavior or pregnancy rates (Walter & Vaughan, 1993). Programs that teach safe sex but that place a heavy emphasis on pride and responsibility in decision making also appear to fare better than programs that simply teach safer sex practices (Jemmott, Jemmott, & Fong, 1998). Finally, although narrowly focused abstinence-only education programs have yet to yield well-documented findings of efficacy (Kirby, 2002), there is evidence that abstinence programs may lead to reductions in sexual activity when tied to skill-training programs (Frost & Forrest, 1995).

One interpretation of these findings is that the social and emotional development components of these prevention programs serve as the catalyst that helps leverage the power of educational or abstinence-based approaches. We think, however, that a careful consideration of these findings suggests a more radical interpretation: What if the developmentally oriented components of these pregnancy prevention programs are the primary active ingredient, and the sexuality focus is of only peripheral relevance?

This idea is further bolstered by findings from several programs that were not directly oriented toward altering adolescensts' sexual behavior but focused instead on enhancing overall psychosocial development. One such approach focuses on helping youth to become involved in volunteer service activities within their communities. Perhaps the best documented of these programs is the Teen Outreach Program, which works primarily with high school age youth and links regular community volunteer work to classroom-based discussions of life skills and life options. Notably, the program addresses adolescent sexuality only in a relatively small (less than 10%) and optional part of the curriculum. In short, this is a program that would not be recognized by either program staff or the youth they serve as primarily targeting teenage pregnancy prevention. Instead, the community service component of Teen Outreach is undoubtedly its most unique feature. For Teen Outreach students, volunteer service in the community provides them with the chance to expand their education beyond the walls of the classroom (Sarason, 1982). Yet, unlike paid employment, volunteer activities that are performed as part of a carefully designed curriculum do not compete with schoolwork, nor do they undermine parental influence by providing teens with early financial independence (Steinberg, Fegley, & Dornbusch, 1993).

Experimental data in which youth were randomly assigned to a treatment or control condition indicated that over the course of an academic year, the program yielded approximately 50% reductions in youth pregnancy rates (Allen, Philliber, Herrling, & Kuperminc, 1997). The program also led to reductions in academic course failure rates and rates of academic suspensions. In short, this volunteer service program appeared to reduce teen pregnancy rates by enhancing the adolescent's overall level of psychosocial adaptation. Further research suggested that these impacts have been greatest among those youth who were most at risk at the outset of the program (as evidenced either by demographic risk factors or by prior histories of pregnancy or course failure; Allen & Philliber, 2001). These findings are echoed in at least one other independent study of volunteerism and community service (O'Donnell et al., 1999), in which participation was found linked to lower levels of sexual activity among eighth-grade students.

One possible mechanism for these effects is that when teens succeed as volunteers, they come to believe that they can succeed in other attempts at competent behavior. Their self-efficacy is enhanced, and higher levels of self-efficacy have been found linked to lower levels of a variety of problem behaviors (Allen, Leadbeater, & Aber, 1990, 1994). In addition, the opportunity as an adolescent to perform work that is of real value to others may also help cement the relationship of the teen to important adults in their lives in ways that reduce the likelihood of problem behaviors (Gottfredson & Hirschi, 1994). Research has also found that implementation of volunteer service activity was a core component related to successful program outcomes at the site level (Allen, Philliber, & Hoggson, 1990). In addition, surveys of youth within the program reveal that the sites in which youth feel the greatest sense of autonomy and sense of connection to other adults and students—two critical aspects of psychosocial development in adolescence—achieve the best outcomes, thus furthering the sense that the program works by enhancing basic social developmental processes in adolescence (Allen, Kuperminc, Philliber, & Herre, 1994).

Other program evaluations further the idea that some of the most effective approaches to preventing teenage pregnancies may seemingly have little directly to do with adolescent sexuality. Rotheram-Borus, Koopman, Haignere, and Davies (1991) reported, for example, that simply providing needed services to a high-risk runaway population significantly reduced the incidence of risky sexual behavior. Perhaps the most striking data come from programs that took place long before adolescence. David Olds created a program in which nurses made home visits and provided services to young mothers during their pregnancy with a firstborn child and for 2 years afterwards. Follow-up data indicated that nurse home visitation to young mothers significantly reduced the risky sexual behavior of their children 15 years later when these children had become adolescents (Olds et al., 1998). This finding raises the obvious question of how services directed toward mothers can lead to such long-term benefits for their children. A recurrent theme in research with teen parents is that improving the lives of mothers often improves their children's lives as well. Nurse home visitation helped young mothers return to school more quickly, delay subsequent childbearing, and obtain better employment (Olds, Henderson, Tatelbaum, & Chamberlin, 1988). Improving mothers' lives evidently changed the childrearing environment in ways that produced enduring benefits for their children, a topic to which we now turn in detail.

Teen Pregnancy Prevention With Teen Parents and Their Children

Research with adolescent mothers both helps explain the long-range findings of the nurse home visitation project and provides suggestions for effective teen pregnancy prevention for the next generation of children. Although most children of teen mothers do not become teen parents themselves, they are significantly more likely to do so than are children born to older mothers (Furstenberg, Levine, & Brooks-Gunn, 1990), a finding that remains even when a number of prebirth differences between teen mothers and older mothers are statistically controlled (Haveman, Wolfe, & Peterson, 1997).

The life trajectories of adolescent mothers and their children are closely interwoven. Frank Furstenberg and his colleagues (Furstenberg et al., 1987; Furstenberg et al., 1990) studied pregnant teenagers in Baltimore who delivered their babies during the mid-1960s. When the children of these young mothers were 15 and 16 years old, the researchers found a very high incidence of early sexual activity among them and reported that prolonged maternal welfare dependency was a significant predictor of this early sexual intercourse. Conditions in the mothers' lives thus strongly affected their children's life outcomes.

At about the same time as the Furstenberg study, two epidemiologists at Yale, Lorraine Klerman and James Jekel, studied pregnant teenagers in New Haven, Connecticut. These researchers and their colleagues (Horwitz et al., 1991a, 1991b) reported that depression in teen mothers predicted early parenthood for their children. They also found that when teen mothers moved away from their parents' homes soon after their children were born, the children were three times more likely to become teenage parents than were children who continued to co-reside with their grandparents. The authors argued that the loss of mature, grandparental care for the children was very important, and suggested that "emotional deprivation, particularly at an early age, may predispose adolescents to seek emotional closeness through sexual activity and early parenthood" (Horwitz et al., 1991a, p. 168).

Our own research in New Haven sheds further light on the predictors of early parenthood in this high-risk group and the kinds of interventions that can reduce its likelihood. The participants were firstborn children of 115 young mothers who gave birth in 1979 and 1980. The mothers were all the African American residents of New Haven, Connecticut, who had delivered a firstborn child over a 1-year time span and who were younger than 18 years old when their baby was born. When the children were 17 to 18 years old, we obtained information about parenthood from the teenagers and their mothers, and from medical record review. We obtained information about parenthood for 94% of the sample.

Almost one third of the daughters of the former teen mothers became school-age mothers themselves, and approximately one fifth of the sons became school-age fathers. An important predictor of early parenthood for children of both sexes was the length of time that they remained an only child. The magnitude of the effect was substantial: Almost half the girls who had a younger sibling by the time they were 30 months old later became a school-aged mother, compared with only 19% of the girls who had remained an only child for at least 30 months. None of the boys who remained an only child at least 5 years became a school-age father, whereas almost one third of the remaining boys did so (Seitz & Apfel, 1999).

In a sample that had not received intervention, maternal intelligence would likely be confounded with rapid repeated childbearing. More intelligent mothers might be expected to delay subsequent childbearing and also to rear children who have higher IQs, perform better in school, and have better life outcomes. However, many of the present sample received an early intervention program and subsequently showed a lower likelihood of rapid repeated childbearing in a manner that was unrelated to their cognitive ability (Seitz & Apfel, 1993). The kind of support the young mother received from her family also affected how long she waited before having a second child, and family support was also unrelated to maternal cognitive ability (Apfel & Seitz, 1999).

As noted earlier, Horwitz and her colleagues found that early loss of co-residence with grandparents predisposed children eventually to become teen parents. Although these researchers did not relate this finding to childbirth spacing, the two are likely related, and we believe that the spacing of children is the more fundamental causal factor. A child's removal from the grandmother's home often occurred after a mother's second pregnancy or the birth of a new sibling, and was only one of many negative events likely to occur when a teen mother had a second child soon after her first.

Mothers who spaced their children at least 30 months apart subsequently had significantly smaller families, completed more education, and remained welfare dependent for fewer years. In contrast, rapidly having a second child set the young mothers on a life path that became progressively more difficult to alter. An additional small child makes continuing in school or entering the labor force much more difficult, and mothers with two very young children were likely to have still more children, eventually having large welfare-dependent families, an observation also noted by Furstenberg and his colleagues in Baltimore (1987).

In addition to childbirth spacing, the young mother's educational success was an important predictor of early parenthood for the boys. As was true for childbirth spacing, timing was important. Early educational success (within the first 2 years after delivery) was more critical than success occurring later. Mothers who had graduated from high school by the time their sons were 2 years old, or who were still enrolled in school and making normal progress toward graduation, had sons who were considerably less likely to become school-age fathers (only 5% did so) than did mothers who were not educationally successful (32% of whose sons became young fathers). As was true for fertility control, educational success was not confounded with maternal intelligence in this highly intervened-with sample.

It is not surprising that fertility control and educational success were related. Nevertheless, early maternal educational success significantly predicted early parenthood over and above the childbirth spacing factor. The benefits of early educational success for the mothers largely were found in their later economic success. By the time their boys were entering adolescence, mothers who had been educationally successful at 2 years postpartum were more than four times more likely to be raising their child in a self-supporting family. Our finding that prolonged welfare dependency is related to early parenthood is thus consistent with findings by Furstenberg et al. (1987), and further shows the importance of changing the parents' lives to change the children's.

Factors Leading to Maternal Educational Success and Fertility Control

As noted earlier, nurse home visitation is one form of community intervention that is known to help young mothers space their children more widely and attain educational success. Our study shows that communities can also use a school-based program to achieve the same outcomes, and thereby help prevent early parenthood among their children. We have evaluated the effects of the Polly T. McCabe Center, a school for pregnant students. In an analysis of programs for pregnant and parenting adolescents, Lorraine Klerman and her colleagues have emphasized the need for programs to be "comprehensive," providing educational, social, and medical services to address the many problems such teenagers experience (Klerman & Horwitz, 1992). The McCabe Program provides services in all three domains.

More extensively than in the average urban school, the McCabe school's social worker helps, if needed, to address problems such as dealing with a substance-abusing parent or trying to find affordable housing. Medical services at McCabe are provided by nurses, who monitor students for any signs of pregnancy-related problems and who teach courses that supplement and reinforce information that the teenagers are receiving in their regular prenatal care. Such services closely resemble what David Olds has called "enhanced prenatal care" (Olds, Henderson, Tatelbaum, & Chamberlin, 1986) as provided by the nurses in his program who make home visits. In sum, the Polly T. McCabe Center is an excellent example of a comprehensive program.

We have found this program effective in helping young mothers improve their educational success and control their fertility. In the best research design, persons are assigned randomly either to receive a program or to be part of a comparison group. This is rarely feasible in evaluating a public school. However, program rules sometimes mimic random assignment when they do not allow attendees choice about how long to attend. We found that if we limited our analyses to students who attended the McCabe Center as long as the rules permitted, then we were able to create good comparison groups (Seitz & Apfel, 1993, 1994; Seitz, Apfel, & Rosenbaum, 1991).

Educationally, the McCabe program offered better students a safe environment in which to continue their schooling without disruption. For poorer students, however, it actually turned their academic careers around, raising them to the same level of educational success as students who had previously been academically competent. In a specialized program such as McCabe, individual attention is possible because of small class sizes. Also, support is available to help a student overcome personal problems that could interfere with academic success. The marginal student who is able to attend for a longer time thus may be able to establish an increasingly strong sense that she is capable of being an adequate student. This positive response of poorer students to a smaller, personalized setting agrees with evidence from many studies of scholastically at-risk students.

To determine whether attending McCabe helped students postpone additional childbearing, we divided the group at the median length of time students were allowed to remain after their baby was born. Students who were allowed to attend the McCabe Center for more than 7 weeks after their baby was born were much less likely to have a second baby within the next 5 years than were students who were required to leave before their baby was 7 weeks old. (In fact, more than half of the young mothers who had stayed more than 7 weeks postnatally still had not had a second child when their first child was 5 years old.) The two groups of students were similar in age, the amount of family support they received, the kind of students they were, their cognitive ability, and in every other way we examined, but they had very different patterns of later childbearing (Seitz & Apfel, 1993). The services that made the program effective went far beyond help with birth control. Reasons for program success were probably similar for both educational and fertility outcomes: small class sizes, nurturance, and personalized guidance. Students appeared to identify with the staff and to consider new life options based on an assumption that they should finish high school. These results with pregnant students thus are similar to those reported earlier for primary prevention programs that increase self-efficacy.

Support provided by the teenager's family also affected her educational success and fertility control. In interviews with the young mothers and with the babies' grandmothers, when the babies were 18 months old, we discerned four models of support (Apfel & Seitz, 1991). When we categorized these models as extreme or nonextreme, they predicted the teen mothers' speed of subsequent childbearing (Apfel & Seitz, 1999). Extreme models were those providing too much support (replacing the young mother entirely) or too little (leaving her with almost total caregiving responsibility). Nonextreme models included a *supplemental* style, in which the teen mother and her family shared child care, and an *apprentice* style, in which the teen's mother coached her daughter in parenting and helped her as she learned but did not supplant her. Teen mothers who received nonextreme forms of family support were only about half as likely to have a second baby quickly as were those whose families provided extreme support. Good family support also helped promote educational success

(43% of teens with nonextreme family support versus 27% with extreme family support were educationally successful at 2 years postpartum).

Community Support Can Compensate for Inadequate Family Support

We then considered whether community support can compensate for poor family support and discovered the answer was affirmative. Among teens who had extreme forms of family support, 50% of those who also did not receive enough time at McCabe postnatally had a second baby within 30 months; the incidence dropped to 18% for those who attended McCabe for enough time postnatally. For students who had had poor academic records before becoming pregnant and who had poor family support and inadequate time at the McCabe program, only 7% had a good educational outcome at 2 years postpartum. If they did receive an adequate time, 57% had a good educational outcome at 2 years postpartum, despite poor family support.

Our findings show that it is possible to reduce significantly the likelihood that high-risk children will eventually become teen parents, and that teen parents will have further children as teenagers, by directing intervention toward those parents when their children are very young. Our study thus extends Olds et al.'s finding that communities can accomplish this goal through nurse home visitation by showing that community support can also take the form of a special school program. We have also discovered that community intervention can effectively compensate for cases in which the young mother's own family does not provide good early support for her.

Toward a Model of the Sexual Adolescent as a Whole Person

As just shown, although the idea of preventing teenage pregnancies, repeat pregnancies, or parenting failures by focusing on something other than sexual behaviors might at first glance appear hopelessly indirect, this approach actually appears far more effective than are programs that focus solely and primarily on sexual behaviors. Adolescent problem behavior theory (Donovan & Jessor, 1985; Jessor, Donovan, & Costa, 1991) has long recognized that precocious sexual activity in adolescence tends to co-occur with higher levels of delinquency and substance use and abuse. Thus, it may make less sense to view problem behaviors in isolation than to see them as part of a unified syndrome in which an underlying risk basis may be manifest in many different forms (Bell, 1986). This theory is now thought to apply to patterns of problematic behavior well into adulthood (Jessor et al., 1991) and begins to shed some light on the findings presented earlier. Effects of programmatic interventions on behaviors far removed from the immediate targets of the interventions begin to make more sense if researchers and others understand adolescents' risky sexual behavior not so much as reflecting specific attitudes toward sexuality, but rather as reflecting underlying difficulties that might give rise to a host of problematic outcomes. In brief, thinking about the adolescent as a whole person is not simply a nice catch phrase—it may be fundamental to understanding the phenomenon.

Putting these findings together, the appropriate model for risk prevention appears not to be a pathogen model in which adolescents are viewed as susceptible to becoming pregnant in the same way in which some individuals are susceptible to nearsightedness or to illnesses such as West Nile virus. Rather, a nutritional metaphor provides a more adequate explanation. Some adolescents appear psychosocially poorly nourished in a way that leaves them susceptible to a wide array of pathological outcomes. Lack of a sense of how one might fit into the larger adult world appears as one of the key nutrients lacking in the lives of many at-risk adolescents.

Discussions with never-pregnant adolescents engaged in volunteer activities reveal that volunteering provides them with precisely this type of vision about how they might fit into the larger adult world. For some this vision involves possible career options; for others, it simply involves a way in which they can engage in activities that are meaningful to other people. This contrasts starkly with the life experiences of many adolescents, which were aptly described by a late adolescent in one of our college courses as being "a bubble, which consists of the walls of my room, the shopping mall, the TV, Internet, and my classroom at school." It is important to note that almost nothing that happened within this "bubble" had any significant impact on other people, let alone on the larger society of individuals outside the adolescent's age-segregated social world.

Programs that engage youth in volunteer service pop the bubble in which teens live. They not only expose teens to a larger adult community, but also they give them a productive and valued role within it. This exposure may be most important for teenagers who are unhappy within their social worlds. We know that teenagers who are having difficulties at home and at school, and who are somewhat marginal in their interactions with peers, are at higher risk for teenage pregnancies (Zabin & Cardona, 2002). These teens are not only isolated in the bubble of adolescent life, they are struggling within it. For them, volunteer work may offer the best avenue to do something that they and others can view as impressive and worthwhile. In a similar manner, programs that provide youths with needed social skills—be they assertion skills or a sense of self-efficacy—may also enhance the youths' sense of their ability to succeed as adolescents. From this perspective, then, it is not at all surprising that the impact of these programs is greatest for those youths who enter the programs at greatest risk (i.e., with the least nurturance in their existing environments). These are the youths who are most likely to lack ways of connecting and feeling capable of being productive and valued members of a larger community.

Teenage parents face a challenge that on the surface may seem far different from that of their never-pregnant counterparts. The limits they face are less aptly compared to a bubble than to a box or prison. For these adolescents, the constraints on their future lives may include lack of education, lack of educational opportunity, poor child care, poor health care for themselves and their children, lack of social supports, and lack of job opportunities. Yet, although the effort to intervene with these adolescents may require a different model— tailored along the lines of the Polly McCabe Center—than the efforts required to mount volunteer service-oriented programs, the fundamental goals of both approaches may be the same: to prevent future pregnancies by giving youth a clear vision and better prospects of a successful future role in society.

Risky behavior of all sorts, sexual and otherwise, is likely to appeal to adolescents who see little value in their present or future lives. Long-term interventions may work in part by helping youths increase their sense of connection to the larger community, by increasing their assertiveness, their sense of self-efficacy, their impulse control, and their optimism about the future. Without such interventions, teens who are hungry for intimacy and a sense of connection in their lives are more likely to turn to sexual behavior for which they are not well-prepared (Allen, 2002). The nutritional model may be particularly apt here, as these adolescents may be literally starving for the sense of connection and place within a broader social world—a connection that broader, developmentally focused programs may help provide. In short, focusing on the development of the adolescent as a whole person may target precisely those behaviors and developmental factors that are most directly linked to preventing risky sexual behavior and its negative outcomes. These programs are likely to build competencies in youth that can dramatically increase both their motivation and their skill at avoiding early childbearing (Kirby & Coyle, 1997), even though they may not directly address sexual behavior.

Implications

Several lessons can be drawn from this perspective on adolescent sexual behavior. One is that teen pregnancy prevention can be achieved by what might seem to be indirect routes. By helping adolescents achieve educational success and control their fertility—even if they have already become parents—evidence shows we are preventing teen pregnancy in the next generation. We now have several tools available for reducing the frequency of negative outcomes tied to adolescents' sexual behavior—and none of them require fighting or winning the culture wars regarding how sexuality should be viewed within our society.

These findings also suggest a critical distinction between approaches that narrowly target adolescent sexual behavior versus those that target risk-taking behavior more broadly. Although most adolescent sexual behavior carries some element of risk, the critical question appears to be not adolescents' attitudes toward sex but rather their attitudes toward protecting themselves from risk. A motivated adolescent with an optimistic view of the future may choose to remain abstinent, or may choose to become sexually active, but only in a very careful and relatively protected manner. Although abstinence-only advocates would rightly point out that the abstinent adolescent faces the fewest risks, it is unarguable that both abstinent and highly responsible sexually active adolescents face dramatically lower levels of risk than do unmotivated risk-taking adolescents. This latter group is unlikely to take pleas for abstinence or for sexual responsibility seriously unless they are presented in a way that provides a vision of a future role for them that they will want to safeguard. In short, neither side in the culture wars surrounding adolescent sexuality is likely to prevent the most feared outcomes unless they address the basic socioemotional needs of the adolescent—unless they treat the adolescent as a whole person, and not as a bundle of sexual urges to be controlled.

Said a different way, our problem is not so much that adolescents are preoccupied with sex—although all evidence suggests they are and always have been—but that adults are preoccupied with adolescents' sexuality to the exclusion of a thoughtful focus on the developing adolescent as a whole person. Focusing exclusively on adolescent sexual behavior to reduce its negative outcomes seems as likely to be successful as telling a starving person to carefully control their intake of junk food. Proper nourishment (whether physical or psychosocial) requires a far broader focus.

The good news is that a clear path exists both for programmatic intervention and research that involves fleshing out our picture of risky adolescent sexual behavior as it relates to broader aspects of social development. Understanding the link between risky sexual behavior and difficulties in the normative development of adolescent autonomy, competence in social interactions with peers, and risk-taking propensities appears as a highly promising route to pursue in this regard. Even if as a society we cannot reach easy agreement about what are acceptable levels of adolescent sexual activity, we already have widespread agreement on the need to promote adaptive social development in adolescence. The successful programs described in this chapter suggest that we already have the tools to begin this work. What we now need is to turn our attention from a narrow and unhealthy focus on how to respond to the presence of adolescent sexual behavior in our society to a consideration of the sexually active adolescent as a whole person. This is an idea that has deep roots in the wisdom and theories Zigler (1971) propounded decades ago. It is an idea that has been strangely ignored in spite of its potential in this area. And it is an idea whose time has clearly come.

References

Alan Guttmacher Institute. (1994). *Sex and America's teenagers.* New York: Author.

Allen, J. P. (2002, April). *Observed autonomy and connection with parents and peers as predictors of early adolescent sexual adaptation.* Paper presented at the biennial meeting of the Society for Research in Adolescence, New Orleans, LA.

Allen, J. P., Kuperminc, G., Philliber, S., & Herre, K. (1994). Programmatic prevention of adolescent problem behaviors: The role of autonomy, relatedness, and volunteer service in the Teen Outreach Program. *American Journal of Community Psychology, 22,* 617–638.

Allen, J. P., Leadbeater, B. J., & Aber, J. L. (1990). The relationship of adolescents' expectations and values to delinquency, hard drug use, and unprotected sexual intercourse. *Development and Psychopathology, 2,* 85–98.

Allen, J. P., Leadbeater, B. J., & Aber, J. L. (1994). The development of problem behavior syndromes in at-risk adolescents. *Development and Psychopathology, 6,* 323–342.

Allen, J. P., & Philliber, S. P. (2001). Who benefits most from a broadly targeted prevention program? Differential efficacy across populations in the Teen Outreach Program. *Journal of Community Psychology, 29,* 637–655.

Allen, J. P., Philliber, S. P., Herrling, S., & Kuperminc, G. P. (1997). Preventing teen pregnancy and academic failure: Experimental evaluation of a developmentally based approach. *Child Development, 68,* 729–742.

Allen, J. P., Philliber, S. P., & Hoggson, N. (1990). School-based prevention of teen-age pregnancy and school dropout: Process evaluation of the national replication of the Teen Outreach Program. *American Journal of Community Psychology, 18*, 505–524.

Apfel, N. H., & Seitz, V. (1991). Four models of adolescent mother–grandmother relationships in Black inner-city families. *Family Relations: Journal of Applied Family & Child Studies, 40*, 421–429.

Apfel, N. H., & Seitz, V. (1999, April). *Sibship spacing affects life outcomes of children of adolescent mothers.* Paper presented at the biennial meeting of the Society for Research in Child Development, Albuquerque, NM.

Bachu, A., & O'Connell, M. (2001). *Fertility of American women: June 2000.* Washington, DC: U.S. Census Bureau.

Bell, R. Q. (1986). Age specific manifestations in changing psychosocial risk. In D. C. Farran & J. D. McKinney (Eds.), *The concept of risk in intellectual and psychosocial development.* (pp. 169–183). New York: Academic Press.

Brooks-Gunn, J., & Furstenberg, F. F. (1986). The children of adolescent mothers: Physical, academic, and psychological outcomes. *Developmental Review, 6*(3), 224–251.

Darroch, J. E. (2001). Adolescent pregnancy trends and demographics. *Current Women's Health Reports, 1*(2), 102–110.

Darroch, J. E., Singh, S., & Frost, J. J. (2001). Differences in teenage pregnancy rates among five developed countries: The roles of sexual activity and contraceptive use. *Family Planning Perspectives, 33*, 244–250.

Donovan, J. E., & Jessor, R. (1985). Structure of problem behavior in adolescence and young adulthood. *Journal of Consulting and Clinical Psychology, 53*, 890–904.

Frost, J. J., & Forrest, J. D. (1995). Understanding the impact of effective teenage pregnancy prevention programs. *Family Planning Perspectives, 27*, 188–195.

Furstenberg, F. F., Brooks-Gunn, J., & Morgan, S. P. (1987). *Adolescent mothers later in life.* New York: Cambridge University Press.

Furstenberg, F. F., Jr., Levine, J. A., & Brooks-Gunn, J. (1990). The children of teenage mothers: Patterns of early childbearing in two generations. *Family Planning Perspectives, 22*, 54–61.

Gottfredson, M. R., & Hirschi, T. (1994). A general theory of adolescent problem behavior: Problems and prospects. In R. D. Ketterlinus & M. E. Lamb (Eds.), *Adolescent problem behaviors: Issues and research* (pp. 41–56). Hillsdale, NJ: Erlbaum.

Haveman, R., Wolfe, B., & Peterson, E. (1997). Children of early childbearers as young adults. In R. A. Maynard (Ed.), *Kids having kids* (pp. 257–284). Washington, DC: Urban Institute Press.

Horwitz, S. M., Klerman, L. V., Kuo, H. S., & Jekel, J. F. (1991a). Ingenerational transmission of school-aged parenthood. *Family Planning Perspectives, 23*, 168–172.

Horwitz, S. M., Klerman, L. V., Kuo, H. S., & Jekel, J. F. (1991b). Predictors of long-term educational and economic outcomes. *Pediatrics, 87*, 862–868.

Hotz, V. J., Mullin, C. H., & Sanders, S. G. (1997). Bounding causal effects using data from a contaminated natural experiment: Analysing the effects of teenage childbearing. *Review of Economic Studies, 64*, 575–603.

Institute of Medicine Committee to Study the Prevention of Low Birthweight. (1985). *Preventing low birthweight.* Washington, DC: National Academy Press.

Jemmott, J. B., III, Jemmott, L. S., & Fong, G. T. (1998). Abstinence and safer sex HIV risk-reduction interventions for African American adolescents. *Journal of the American Medical Association, 279*, 1529–1536.

Jessor, R., Donovan, J. E., & Costa, F. M. (1991). *Beyond adolescence: Problem behavior and young adult development* (15th ed.). New York: Cambridge University Press.

Jones, R. K., Darroch, J. E., & Henshaw, S. K. (2002). Patterns in the socioeconomic characteristics of women obtaining abortions in 2000–2001. *Perspectives on Sexual and Reproductive Health, 34*, 226–235.

Kirby, D. (2002). *Do abstinence-only programs delay the initiation of sex among young people and reduce teen pregnancy?* Washington, DC: National Campaign to Prevent Teen Pregnancy.

Kirby, D., & Coyle, K. (1997). School-based programs to reduce sexual risk-taking behavior. *Children & Youth Services Review, 19*, 415–436.

Kirby, D., Short, L., Collins, J., Rugg, D., Kolbe, L., Howard, M., et al. (1994). School-based programs to reduce sexual risk behaviors: A review of effectiveness. *Public Health Reports, 109*, 339–360.

Klerman, L. V., & Horwitz, S. M. (1992). Reducing the adverse consequences of adolescent pregnancy and parenting: The role of service programs. *Adolescent Medicine: State of the Art Reviews, 3,* 299–316.

Main, D. S., Iverson, D. C., McGloin, J., Banspach, S. W., Collins, J. L., Rugg, D. L., & Kolbe, L. J. (1994). Preventing HIV infection among adolescents: Evaluation of a school-based education program. *Preventive Medicine: An International Journal Devoted to Practice and Theory, 23,* 409–417.

Martin, J. A., Park, M. M., & Sutton, P. D. (2002). Births: Preliminary data for 2001. *National Vital Statistics Reports, 50*(10).

National Center for Health Statistics. (2002). *Health, United States, 2002: With chartbook on trends in the health of Americans.* Washington, DC: Author.

O'Donnell, L., Stueve, A., Doval, A. S., Duran, R., Haber, D., Atnafou, R., et al. (1999). The effectiveness of the reach for health community youth service learning program in reducing early and unprotected sex among urban middle school students. *American Journal of Public Health, 89,* 176–181.

Olds, D. L., Henderson, C. R., Cole, R., Eckenrode, J., Kitzman, H., Luckey, D., et al. (1998). Long-term effects of nurse home visitation on children's criminal and antisocial behavior: 15-year follow-up of a randomized controlled trial. *Journal of the American Medical Association, 280,* 1238–1244.

Olds, D. L., Henderson, C. R., Tatelbaum, R., & Chamberlin, R. (1986). Improving the delivery of prenatal care and outcomes of pregnancy: A randomized trial of nurse home visitation. *Pedatrics, 77,* 16–28.

Olds, D. L., Henderson, C. R., Tatelbaum, R., & Chamberlin, R. (1988). Improving the life-course development of socially disadvantaged mothers: A randomized trial of nurse home visitation. *American Journal of Public Health, 78,* 1436–1445.

Osofsky, J. D., Eberhart-Wright, A., Ware, L., & Hann, D. (1992). Children of adolescent mothers: A group at risk for psychopathology. *Infant Mental Health Journal, 13,* 49–56.

Philliber, S. P., & Namerow, P. (1995, March). *Trying to maximize the odds: Using what we know to prevent teen pregnancy.* Paper presented to The Pregnancy Prevention Program, Division of Reproductive Health, National Center for Chronic Disease Prevention and Health Promotion, Centers for Disease Control and Prevention, Atlanta, GA.

Rotheram-Borus, M. J., Koopman, C., Haignere, C., & Davies, M. (1991). Reducing HIV sexual risk behaviors among runaway adolescents. *Journal of the American Medical Association 266,* 1237–1241.

Sarason, S. B. (1982). *The culture of the school and the problem of change* (2nd ed.). Boston: Allyn and Bacon.

Seitz, V., & Apfel, N. H. (1993). Adolescent mothers and repeated childbearing: Effects of a school-based intervention program. *American Journal of Orthopsychiatry, 63,* 572–581.

Seitz, V., & Apfel, N. H. (1994). Effects of a school for pregnant students on the incidence of low-birthweight deliveries. *Child Development, 65,* 666–676.

Seitz, V., & Apfel, N. H. (1999, April). *Style of family support predicts the subsequent childbearing and parenting success of teen mothers.* Paper presented at the biennial meeting of the Society for Research in Child Development, Albuquerque, NM.

Seitz, V., Apfel, N. H., & Rosenbaum, L. K. (1991). Effects of an intervention program for pregnant adolescents: Educational outcomes at 2 years postpartum. *American Journal of Community Psychology, 19,* 911–930.

Sikkema, K. J., Winett, R. A., & Lombard, D. N. (1995). Development and evaluation of an HIV-risk reduction program for female college students. *AIDS Education & Prevention, 7*(2), 145–159.

Steinberg, L., Fegley, S., & Dornbusch, S. M. (1993). Negative impact of part-time work on adolescent adjustment: Evidence from a longitudinal study. *Developmental Psychology, 29,* 171–180.

Walter, H. J., & Vaughan, R. D. (1993). AIDS risk reduction among a multiethnic sample of urban high school students. *Journal of the American Medical Association, 270,* 725–730.

Zabin, L. S., & Cardona, K. M. (2002). Adolescent pregnancy. In G. M. Wingood & R. J. DiClemente (Eds.), *Handbook of women's sexual and reproductive health. Issues in women's health* (17th ed., pp. 231–253). New York: Kluwer Academic/Plenum Publishers.

Zigler, E. (1971). The retarded child as a whole person. In H. E. Adams & W. K. Boardman (Eds.), *Advances in experimental clinical psychology* (pp. 47–121). New York: Pergamon Press.

12

Children in Foster Care

Ellen E. Pinderhughes, Brenda Jones Harden,
and Amanda E. Guyer

One of Edward F. Zigler's many contributions to the field of developmental psychology was to broaden its focus to include the unique trajectories of children at environmental risk. His efforts have resulted in a large corpus of evidence concerning the development of children reared in poverty, children experiencing familial and community violence, and children exposed to prenatal and postnatal environmental toxins. In addition, he has made important contributions to our understanding of child maltreatment and its sequelae (e.g., Aber & Zigler, 1981; Zigler, 1979; Zigler & Styfco, 2000). Perhaps no other group of children experiences the magnitude of individual and ecological risks to optimal development than do children whose maltreatment results in their removal from home and placement in foster care. However, empirical attention to these vulnerable children's development has been lacking. In keeping with his dedication to the development of children at environmental risk, Ed nourished several of his students' interest in foster children, which has generated greatly needed empirical data on this important population.

In the United States, children enter foster care through the child welfare system, which aims to ensure the safety, permanence, and well-being of the children relegated to this service system (Adoption and Safe Families Act, 1997). Foster children enter care because they cannot be adequately or appropriately cared for by their birth parents. Typically, states assume legal guardianship for these children and place them in alternative caregiving arrangements. In this chapter, we present the extant knowledge about children in the U.S. foster care system. We start with an epidemiological profile of these children, including their foster care trajectories, followed by a theoretical framework for understanding developmental issues for foster children, and a summary of the effects of foster care on children's development. We then describe research challenges, propose new research directions, and end with a consideration of policies that determine the child welfare system's response to the needs of foster children and the intersection of research and policy.

An Epidemiological Profile of Children in Foster Care

Despite the trend toward decreasing rates of children entering foster care in the United States, the most recent national statistics indicate that 523,000 children were in foster care in 2003 (U.S. Department of Health and Human Services [USDHHS], 2005). Of these children, 53% were boys and 55% were children of color (USDHHS, 2005). Children enter the system for a variety of reasons, most typically maltreatment. Approximately 15% of maltreated children are subsequently placed in foster care (USDHHS, 2005). The majority of children who are placed in foster care have experienced substance abuse (alcohol or illicit drugs) within their families of origin (Wulczyn, 1991). Increases in family stressors such as interspousal violence and poverty also are linked to child placement, especially for children who are victims of neglect (Edleson, 2001).

The placement options for children in foster care include traditional (i.e., unrelated) foster family homes, kinship family homes, group homes, or institutions. Across the nation, 46% of foster children reside in the homes of unrelated caregivers who are licensed by the local jurisdiction to care for children in state custody. Currently, almost one quarter (23%) of foster children are formally placed with kinship caregivers (USDHHS, 2005); this number does not include the many children who are informally placed with relatives or placed in guardianship status. Kinship homes are increasingly seen as viable placements, given the decline of nonrelative foster homes and the increased demand for alternative placements for maltreated children. Aside from children in kinship and nonrelative foster care, another 9% of foster children live in group homes and 10% are placed in institutions. The remaining 12% are scattered in various settings (e.g., independent living, preadoptive home; USDHHS, 2005).

Certain characteristics of children make them more vulnerable to foster care entry. For example, children of particular ages are more likely to enter foster care. Almost one third of children under 5 years are placed into care following a maltreatment report. At a national rate of 14% (USDHHS, 2005), infants under 1 year are even more likely to enter care (Wulczyn, Hislop, & Harden, 2002). With a national entry rate of 40% (USDHHS, 2005), adolescents are more likely to be placed in foster care than are preschool and school-age children (Wulczyn & Hislop, 2002).

Race also is implicated in children's rates of foster care entry (USDHHS, 2005). For example, despite comparable maltreatment rates, African American children are overrepresented in the foster care system when compared with European American children. There is considerable controversy regarding whether this disparity among races reflects the needs of the specific populations or discriminatory practices in the child welfare system (see Barth, Goodhand, & Dickinson, 2000).

Children's Trajectories Through the Foster Care System

Foster children traverse through the child welfare system through multiple pathways. Most foster children are in stable living situations, having only one or two placements while in foster care. However, a significant minority experiences multiple placements while in care. Children with multiple placements tend to be older, have special needs, and be African American. Placement disruptions arise because of child behavior problems, foster parent decisions to leave the child welfare system, child abuse by foster parents, and conflicts with the birth family (Wulczyn et al., 2002).

Fortunately, few children child spend their entire youth in foster care. Children still linger in the system for prolonged periods, however, depending on their age of entry and their post-foster-care situation. Younger children are adopted quickly but are returned to birth families more slowly, whereas older children are returned home more quickly and adopted more slowly (Wulczyn et al., 2002). This trend holds regardless of child ethnicity. Children who are adopted were in foster care 4 times as long as children who were reunited with their birth parents, most likely because of delays in court proceedings. Studies of foster care document that African American children leave foster care at a slower rate than do other children, regardless of their destination after discharge (Wulczyn et al., 2002).

The majority (nearly 60%) of children leaving foster care are reunited with their birth parents (Wulczyn et al., 2002). Approximately 10% are formally placed with relatives, and another 10% are adopted. The remaining children exit the system by entering a guardian's care (relative or nonrelative), running away, emancipating, or transferring to another service system (e.g., juvenile justice; Courtney & Barth, 1996). Foster care reentry rates peak for children with the shortest stays in care, and are lowest for children placed with relatives. Rates of return to care from adoption range from 10% to 14%, and from guardianship rates of return range from 8% to 15%. Other factors associated with high reentry rates are race, age, and maltreatment type, with African American, older, and neglected children having the highest reentry rates (Barth et al., 2000).

The Development of Children in Foster Care

An understanding of the developmental sequelae of foster care requires a useful conceptual framework. Of the relevant theories, we find the bioecological model most useful in that it integrates several theoretical perspectives. The bioecological model emphasizes that children's developmental trajectories are differentially shaped by dynamic interactions and reciprocal transactions occurring over time that operate at the biological and environmental levels within multiple nested contexts (Bronfenbrenner & Ceci, 1994). Because foster care experiences affect children differently, it is important to consider genetic and environmental influences as probabilistic in how they shape developmental pathways. As such, children in foster care are at risk for problematic functioning in adolescence and adulthood largely because of their pre-foster-care experiences, experiences in foster care, and transactions between the child's history, the child's and foster family's functioning, and aspects of the foster care placement. These critical influences include inherent biological vulnerabilities, attachment-related disturbances, and more distal ecological risks.

Individual vulnerabilities such as demographic characteristics and health and developmental needs affect the likelihood and trajectory of foster care placement. For example, children now entering foster care have more severe behavioral, emotional, and medical problems than previously documented (Haugaard & Hazan, 2002), and children with special needs are more likely to enter foster care, remain in care for prolonged periods, experience multiple placements, and live in restrictive settings (e.g., group homes; Wulczyn, 1991). Foster children are at particularly high risk for having parents with psychiatric disorders, and thus, for an increased genetic loading of similar psychiatric disorders. Prenatal exposure to substances can lead to a host of medical and developmental problems, such as prematurity, fetal alcohol syndrome, HIV infection, and social–emotional and behavioral problems (see review by Harden, 1998). Both parental mental illness and prenatal drug exposure may negatively alter characteristics such as temperament and self-regulatory competencies, which in turn may make it more difficult to care for the child (Schutter & Brinker, 1992). Finally, the stress and trauma associated with maltreatment negatively influence brain development and the functioning of neurotransmitter and neuroendocrine systems (see chap. 10, this volume).

Caregiving processes represent proximal factors that shape foster children's development. Prior to foster care, a child most likely has experienced maltreatment (e.g., neglect, physical abuse, sexual abuse, emotional abuse), which typically prompts the removal of a child from home (Curtis, 1999). As suggested by attachment theory, the context and quality of children's caregiving histories shape their perceptions and interactions with the social environment. Unpredictable, unresponsive, and threatening caregiving experiences may lead to insecure representational models of attachment figures, of oneself, and relations with significant others (Crittenden & Ainsworth, 1989). In the only known published empirical study of attachment to one's foster caregivers, a higher proportion of foster children had insecure attachments than the general population of young children (Stovall & Dozier, 2000).

The impact of individual child characteristics and relationship disturbance on children's development is further compounded by larger contextual and ecological influences. For example, family functioning (e.g., parents' mental health, family interactions) and structural characteristics of the family (e.g., socioeconomic status (SES), marital–partnership status) individually and collectively operate to increase children's risk for problematic outcomes (see, e.g., McLoyd, 1998). In addition to increasing risk for problematic outcomes, poverty is a strong predictor of a child's removal from home, suggesting that the prevalence (but not necessarily the occurrence) of maltreatment is enmeshed with SES (Lindsey, 1991). Evidence shows that nearly half of all foster children come from families eligible for public assistance (Curtis, 1999). Parental substance abuse is a risk for foster care entry: 50% to 80% of children entering foster care have birth parents who abused substances (Besinger, Garland, Litrownik, & Landsverk, 1999).

Family influences do not operate in a vacuum. Distal influences such as the child's community and neighborhood can heighten children's risk for problematic outcomes. Neighborhood danger and poverty, and few public services can undermine parenting, particularly parental warmth and harsh punishment (e.g., Pinderhughes, Nix, Foster, Jones, & Conduct Problems Prevention Research Group, 2001). It has been suggested anecdotally and empirically that neighborhood quality has an impact on foster care placement, exit timing and type, as well as experiences during foster care.

Minority status further adds to family and contextual risks that surround foster care placement. For example, among low SES adults, African Americans are more likely to suffer psychological distress than are European Americans, thus placing them at greater risk for harsh parenting (Pinderhughes, Dodge, Bates, Pettit, & Zelli, 2000), and perhaps abuse. Three times as many African American children as European American live in poverty; and African American children are 20 times as likely as European American children to live in communities where at least 40% of the residents are poor (Duncan & Aber, 1997). Thus, family poverty, stress, and neighborhood conditions place African American children and other children of color at greater risk for entering foster care. This has been borne out by the overrepresentation of minority children in the foster care system and the differential experiences they have while in care.

Finally, more distal, systemic, and cultural influences affect foster children's development (e.g., local stipulations for removing a child from her home, cultural beliefs in corporal punishment, national child welfare policies). Although designed to protect vulnerable children, the child welfare system may pose further risk for foster children. Some children in foster care are at risk for further maltreatment (Zuravin, Benedict, & Somerfield, 1993). Furthermore, today's child welfare system is beset with overwhelming caseloads for professionals, unpredictable and high foster caregiver turnover, and repeated moves between foster families, which can undermine children's relationship formation with families and professionals (Newton, Litrownik, & Landsverk, 2000). Because of poor access to mental health, health, and other critical services (e.g., Leslie, Landsverk, Horton, Ganger, & Newton, 2000), foster children may lack the intended compensatory experiences from the child welfare system. Despite these challenges, it appears that, overall, foster children benefit from child welfare services (see Taussig, 2002).

In sum, the conceptual framework underlying the discussion in this chapter posits that children are at risk for entering and remaining in foster care because of multiple factors and that these factors negatively influence development. These factors include (a) biologically based individual child characteristics; (b) relationship disturbances that undermine children's ability to form, maintain, and benefit from healthy relationships; (c) transactionally based family problems; (d) family level influences such as parental psychopathology, parental substance abuse, family interactions, poverty, and social support; and (e) neighborhood level effects such as danger and lack of resources. Once in care, children's risk status can be exacerbated by systemic problems that undermine the delivery of compensatory experiences.

Developmental Sequelae Among Foster Children

The American Academy of Pediatrics (2000) suggested that maltreated children in foster care demonstrate (a) the same developmental needs of all children, (b) unique needs as foster or adopted children, and (c) needs that stem from a history of maltreatment. Despite the multiple risk factors present in foster children's lives and the influence of foster care on development, the well-being and mental health of foster children has received little attention until recently (see reviews by Dore, 2000; Landsverk & Garland, 1999). This is particularly glaring, given the amount of research focused on maltreatment sequelae (Schweder, 2002). Research on maltreatment sequelae, however, has not typically examined the impact of children's foster care experiences on development. The study of foster children's mental health and psychological development grew primarily out of initial concern for their poor physical health status and lack of health care. Several studies using data from foster children's medical records documented high rates of both poor physical health and current or past psychological impairment or behavioral problems (e.g., Halfon, Mendonca, & Berkowitz, 1995). Current research indicates that mental health issues, particularly behavior problems, are among the most frequently cited problems for foster children (Dore, 2000; Leslie et al., 2000).

PREVALENCE STUDIES. Research on the prevalence of developmental, behavioral, and emotional problems among foster children indicates that twice as many foster children are developmentally delayed when compared with children in the larger population (e.g., Leslie, Gordon, Ganger, & Gist, 2002). Many prevalence studies of developmental delay have suggested that upward of one third of foster children had behavioral problems in the clinical range (e.g., Clausen, Landsverk, Ganger, Chadwick, & Litrownik, 1998).

LONGITUDINAL STUDIES OF FOSTER CHILDREN'S ADJUSTMENT. Although earlier longitudinal studies were methodologically flawed, they are reported briefly here because of their uniqueness in foster care research. In one study, nearly 25% of children were deemed psychologically "abnormal" or "suspect for abnormality" at any assessment period (Fanshel & Shinn, 1978). However, many children improved on a number of outcomes within the first 6 months of care, some of which held over time. Wald, Carlsmith, and Leiderman (1988) found that maltreated children placed in care tended to experience less abuse, have better physical care, attend school more often, and have higher school achievement than did maltreated, home-reared children. In both studies, researchers concluded that foster care positively affected maltreated children's development, and children's histories negatively affected outcomes more than foster care did. A recent study of young adult outcomes following emancipation from Casey Family Services suggests that youth who had longer stays in privately run foster care were functioning better than those who left foster care at or before age 18 (Kerman, Wildfire, & Barth, 2002).

A recent project, the National Survey of Child and Adolescent Well-Being (NSCAW), is the first nationally representative, longitudinal study of the functioning, service needs, and service utilization of children (from infancy to adolescence) and families involved with the child welfare system (NSCAW Research Group, 2002). NSCAW follows two groups of children: those in foster care for 1 year and those entering care for the first time. Preliminary findings from both groups indicate that foster children have more impaired functioning in achievement, adaptive skills, behavior, cognition, language, and social skills relative to normative samples of children (Barth, Green, Wall, & NSCAW Research Team, 2001). A larger proportion of foster children also have scores in the clinical range in terms of cognitive–language and social–emotional measures. However, the majority of foster children are functioning in the normal range and their rates of negative outcomes are similar to those of children in poverty. Children entering foster care at later ages demonstrate substantial developmental risk that is not linked to growing up in foster care.

STABILITY, PERMANENCY, AND DEVELOPMENT. Foster children who endure long spells in foster care may experience multiple placements that compromise the stability and continuity of their caregiving environment (Goldstein, Solnit, Goldstein, & Freud, 1996). Most data on outcomes and placement stability are descriptive and correlational, making it difficult to determine the directionality of effects. Many children enter care with preexisting behavior problems that can lead to repeat placements and a lasting and pervasive cycle of problems. For some children, behaviors seen as problematic in a new context may have been adaptive in a prior context. Nonetheless, having multiple placements can be significantly associated with the severity of externalizing behaviors (Marcus, 1991), high aggression, poor home adjustment, and low self-concept (Kurtz, Gaudin, Howing, & Wodarski, 1993). Children with these problems in functioning experience more placements than do children without such problems (Halfon et al., 1995). Widom (1991) found that foster children with juvenile records of behavior problems had been placed more readily and had made more frequent moves than did children without behavior problems. In a recent prospective study, behavioral problems were positively linked to numerous placement problems, which, in turn, predicted behavior problems 17 months after placement entry (Newton et al., 2000). Finally, the degree to which a placement is viewed as permanent also is associated with children's behavioral adjustment. For example, Dubowitz, Zuravin, Starr, Feigelman, and Harrington (1993) found that children whose permanency plans were unclear were at greater risk for externalizing behaviors than were children with clear plans.

Foster Caregivers and Children's Functioning

Whether nonrelative or kin, the caregiver's primary tasks with children are to help restore them to a positive trajectory toward adulthood; help them maintain connection with their birth family where appropriate and planned; and prepare them for reunification or adoption.

NONRELATIVE FOSTER CARE. As the number of children entering and remaining in foster care has increased, the number of available foster families has declined. This decline likely is due to the increasing severity of foster children's problems, the state of systemic supports for foster parents, and an increasing demand for two incomes in families (Haugaard & Hazan, 2002). With few new and younger caregivers, the foster parent population also has aged.

Foster parents face helping children enter a new family and develop new relationships that will serve as compensatory experiences, maintaining or realigning the child's developmental trajectory. Like families adopting older children (e.g., Pinderhughes, 1996), foster families may function with different boundaries, rules, and interactions than those with which foster children have experience. Thus, knowledge of foster family functioning would facilitate an understanding of its impact on foster children's development. Far too little research has focused on foster family processes and functioning and their impact on children's functioning (Orme & Buehler, 2001). Replete with methodological limitations (e.g., inadequate or poorly described sample sizes, lack of comparison groups, few parenting or family variables, minimal use of psychometrically sound measures, an emphasis on cross-sectional inquiry), the literature indicates that in general 15% to 20% of foster families experienced problems in family functioning and parenting. Rare longitudinal studies show the benefit of foster parents' previous experience, knowledge about the child, and positive home settings on children's functioning (Cautley, 1980; Fanshel & Shinn, 1978). Cross-sectional studies have also yielded negative links between family functioning and children's problems (Orme & Buehler, 2001). These associations suggest evolving transactional processes in foster families, with mutual child and parent influences.

Children's functioning and previous relationship organization also affect parent–child interactions and family functioning. Foster parents of infants have been drawn into a pattern of interactions and emotions that paralleled the attachment cycle between the infant and his or her birth parent (Stovall & Dozier, 2000). Among older children entering care, internal representations of their foster parents mirrored their previous representations of birth parents and were linked to their current attachment-related behaviors (Milan & Pinderhughes, 2000). Although intended to break a dysfunctional pattern of relating with compensatory caregiving, the transaction between foster parent and foster child actually may maintain this pattern of relating. When parent–child interactions fail to alter children's problem behaviors, placement outcomes may be affected (Landsverk, Davis, Ganger, Newton, & Johnson, 1996).

KINSHIP CARE. Two types of kinship care exist: *public kinship care*, involving state placement of the child with relatives, and *private kinship care*, involving informal placement from birth caregivers to kin caregivers. An estimated 200,000 children reside in public kinship care, whereas about 2.1 million children live in private kinship care (USDHHS, 2000). Children in public kinship care tend to be younger than those in private kinship care, who also are older than children in nonrelative foster care (USDHHS, 2000). Children in public kinship care tend to live with aunts or uncles, whereas children in private care tend to live with grandmothers (Ehrle & Geen, 2002b). Much less is known about children in private kinship care, so this discussion will center on children in public kinship care (hereinafter referred to as *kinship care*).

Children in kinship care have different experiences from children in nonrelative care. First, the pathways differ: Children in kinship care tend to have experienced neglect (e.g., Ehrle & Geen, 2002a; Landsverk et al., 1996) from single birth parents who abused drugs (e.g., Benedict, Zuravin, & Stallings, 1996; USDHHS, 2000), whereas children in nonrelative care tend to have experienced abuse. Once in care, children's experiences differ, as well. Kinship caregivers are older, disproportionately African American, single, and reside in urban communities with few resources (Ehrle & Geen, 2002b; USDHHS, 2000). Kinship caregivers face more challenges with their physical health, with daily stressors and hassles, and with caring for more children. Unfortunately, kinship caregivers also receive a relative lack of systemic resources, such as foster parent training, preparation for a placement, ongoing supervision, health and mental health services for the family, and comparable levels of financial support (USDHHS, 2000). Children in kinship care also remain in foster care longer and are less likely to leave foster care (USDHHS, 2000).

The outcomes for children who are placed in kinship care are equivocal. Despite a kinship family context of greater risk, children in kinship care do not fare more poorly than do children in nonrelative care (USDHHS, 2000). In fact, several small studies consistently indicate that children in kinship care have more competencies, fewer behavioral problems, and better physical and mental health (e.g., Benedict, Zuravin, & Stallings, 1996; Leslie et al., 2000; USDHHS, 2000). These patterns are most aptly illustrated in a longitudinal study of children's functioning and reunification decisions: Problematic functioning was negatively associated with reunification only among children living in nonrelative foster care (Landsverk et al., 1996). However, other studies suggest that rates of behavior problems in children in kinship care exceed those expected for the general population (Dubowitz et al., 1993).

Because almost all of these studies are cross-sectional, it is impossible to determine whether children with less severe problems disproportionately enter kinship care or the stability of a kinship placement facilitates more resilient functioning. Children in kinship placements also have more stable placements, more contact with birth families, and on leaving foster care, they have greater chances at reunification (e.g., Benedict et al., 1996; Leslie et al., 2000). When youth face emancipation from foster care, those leaving kinship care are more likely to expect to have contact with their birth families than are those leaving nonrelative care (Iglehart, 1995). However, kinship placements may provide few other long-term advantages over nonrelative placements for adult functioning (Benedict et al., 1996).

GROUP-BASED (CONGREGATE) FOSTER CARE. Approximately 19% of children in foster care live in a group home or residential institution. Very young children have been placed in group home settings at much higher rates than previously because of drug epidemics. Infants and preschoolers raised in congregate care settings can exhibit a multitude of problems, such as attention-seeking behaviors; disciplinary problems; disorganization; hyperactivity and restlessness; low school achievement; motor, cognitive, and language delays; and adaptive behavior and relationship difficulties, some of which persist into adolescence (see Harden, 2002). Additional documentation of the negative consequences of congregate care on young children comes from the data on children reared in institutions, such as Romanian orphans (e.g., O'Connor, Bredenkamp, Rutter & the English Romanian Adoptees Study Team, 1998). Increased use of congregate care also evolved from a recognition that family-based care does not meet the needs of all children, such as older youth and children with emotional problems (Courtney, 1994). However, group settings offer fewer opportunities that simulate parent–child interactions and also expose youth to others who have problems. Research on interventions with youth who are at risk for delinquency suggests that group-based interventions heighten the risk for offending in adulthood (Dishion, McCord, & Poulin, 1999).

Research Challenges

The previous sections highlighted the extant research on foster children, which has seen dramatic growth in the past decade. However, with few exceptions (e.g., Billing, Ehrle, & Kortenkamp, 2002; Dubowitz et al., 1993), foster children's development and well-being have been ignored. Moreover, until the NSCAW project began (NSCAW Research Group, 2002), research on foster children's functioning over time has been virtually nonexistent (Waldfogel, 2000).

This gap may derive from two barriers. First, psychologists apparently viewed child-welfare-related phenomena as the purview of social service researchers. Fortunately, research in developmental psychopathology (e.g., Cicchetti & Lynch, 1995) and areas such as adoption (e.g., Brodzinsky, 1990) have highlighted how the study of deviations in development can enhance understanding normative development. Foster care is one major experience linked to deviations in development that cries out for more developmentally based investigation. Second, researchers in child welfare have faced significant conceptual, methodological, and logistical challenges. Conceptual challenges include identifying the appropriate developmental constructs to measure and identify the unique contributions from foster children, birth parents, foster parents, and system-related experiences to children's development and outcomes. Methodological challenges include selection of appropriate comparison samples and informants, frequency of assessment, and disentangling the effects of multiple influences. Logistical challenges include tracking and retaining research participants through various placements, gaining access to children in their current placements, and obtaining consent from the appropriate guardian. Because local and state jurisdictions have different criteria for foster care entry and different standards for decision making about placements and service delivery, the use of administrative records as data sources and the generalizability of findings of any study design are affected. Ethical and legal issues include selection of study design, the appropriate source of informed consent (parent or child welfare representative), obtaining assent from children, and relying on children as informants as they experience multiple failed placements.

Developmental Processes: The Next Frontier of Research on Children in Foster Care

Empirical attention should be given to key normative developmental processes among foster children. Children entering care are at risk for dysfunctional outcomes because of their experiences with and separation from their birth parents. Later experiences in care with foster families and birth parents also influence well-being, developmental trajectories, and outcomes. Thus, research should address how foster family life, contact with birth family, and foster care experiences interact with children's functioning across the developmental spectrum to reduce risk and enhance outcomes or to exacerbate risk and undermine outcomes.

SHORT-TERM TRANSACTIONS AND EFFECTS. One critical question centers on the additional risks children of different ages face on entry into foster care and new families. For example, disruption of the parent–child relationship may have a differential impact depending on the child's level of development. Another critical area is the evolving processes of readjustment that foster families and children undergo as the child enters the new family. Because the foster family is the mechanism for compensatory experiences, how the family readjusts may facilitate or impede the delivery of such experiences. Another relevant question centers on the contexts in which the family must help the foster child adjust. These contextual influences include the foster family's functioning, new neighborhoods and schools, visitation with birth parents, and the new permanency planning emphasis of concurrent focus on reunification and adoption. In sum, this area is ripe for the application of a transactional perspective in studying foster family–foster child readjustment. Research should include careful process-oriented approaches to understand evolving patterns of interactions and behaviors over time.

LONG-TERM TRANSACTIONS AND EFFECTS. With almost one third of all children in foster care stranded there for 3 years or more (USDHHS, 2005), research must examine the long-term impact of foster family life, contact with birth parents, and foster care experiences (e.g., number of placements and service utilization) on children's trajectories. During a 3-year period, many foster children must negotiate normative transitions such as school entry or graduation to middle or high school. Research should examine how foster care experiences affect these normative developmental processes over time. Unpacking the associations between children's functioning and their foster care experiences (e.g., number of placements and service utilization) will require a longitudinal approach that allows researchers to examine causal pathways between foster care experiences and child outcomes. The empirical focus should include consideration of the meaning of each experience for the child, family, and caseworker.

Research on postexit outcomes would yield critical information about children's well-being and functioning. For example, there is a paucity of research on the effect of reunification on children's developmental outcomes. Knowledge also is needed about adolescents' transition to independence from different foster care settings. In sum, longitudinal studies that include follow-ups after youth are emancipated, reunified, or adopted will enable tracking of children's developmental trajectories and a more valid assessment of the impact of foster care experiences.

Finally, the evidence base must be broadened to include the effectiveness of extant child welfare policies and programs. Scholars have criticized the implementation of practices that have no research support. Thus, research must evaluate the effect of specific policies such as expedited permanency decisions and kinship care, and their associated practices such as concurrent planning and subsidized guardianship on children's development. More empirical validation of demonstration programs (e.g., shared family care, independent living) and their impact on child well-being would benefit child welfare practice.

The Policy Framework

American child and family policy stems from a complex array of laws, regulations, and procedures lacking a cohesive philosophy and an interconnected funding stream (Kamerman & Kahn, 2001; Jacobs & Davies, 1994). Many federal policies affect foster children, including policies on child maltreatment and income supports for low-income families (see Allen & Bissell, 2004), which are beyond the scope of this chapter.

We conclude this chapter with brief descriptions of policies specific to children in foster care and a developmental analysis of those policies. One of the oldest pieces of child welfare legislation, Title IV-E of the Social Security Act (1935), created the largest funding source for services to children in the foster care system. Included in this law are provisions for the board and maintenance payments to foster parents, as well as funds to be used for training of foster care providers and child welfare staff.

Extending the provisions of Title IV-B of the Social Security Act (1935), the Promoting Safe and Stable Families Act (1997) authorized funding for services to reunify foster children with their birth parents, to promote and support adoption of foster children, and to improve court systems responsible for monitoring permanency for foster children.

The Adoption and Safe Families Act (ASFA, 1997) addressed several issues of concern to advocates for foster children. It shortened the time frame for permanency decisions from 18 to 12 months after foster care entry, mandated initiation of termination of parental rights for children in care for 15 of the last 22 months, emphasized the safety of children in foster care, excluded long-term foster care as a permanency option, identified unreasonable situations for reunification, provided monetary incentives to states for adoption, and promoted concurrent planning (i.e., permanency through reunification and adoption are addressed simultaneously).

Finally, the Foster Care Independence Act (1999) focused on the needs of adolescents transitioning out of foster care by providing funds to pay for the board and maintenance of 18- to 21-year-old foster youth and preparation for foster parents to provide care for them. This legislation also authorized funds for programs to facilitate these youths' independence, as well as for a variety of support services (e.g., housing, education, and health care).

The many complexities in child welfare policy are amplified when viewed through a child development lens. For example, despite links between the placement and developmental trajectories of foster children, foster care policy has treated placement outcome and child well-being separately. Although ASFA (1997) requires that states measure child well-being as a performance outcome, there is ambiguity regarding how this goal should be accomplished and who is administratively and fiscally responsible for services to promote child well-being. Developmentally, the involvement of a child in the child welfare system is an important opportunity to alter the child's trajectory. However, if child well-being is an explicit child welfare goal, then legislation and funding to facilitate relevant outcomes must exist. For example, given the high rates of developmental and mental health problems found among foster children, scholars and policymakers have called for mandatory universal developmental and mental health screening, followed by appropriate services (e.g., Landsverk & Garland, 1999).

Further, child welfare policies have not typically capitalized on extant data on developmental processes in high-risk children, particularly children in foster care. For example, despite clinical and research attention to children's attachment to their birth and foster families, policymakers have to a great extent ignored this critical issue for young children. Proponents of ASFA (1997) considered this issue when creating expedited permanency time limits for children. However, for infants, the 12-month time limit can fall within a developmental window when loss of a caregiver can be particularly devastating (i.e., 12–24 months of age).

Policy has been somewhat responsive to the unique issues posed by foster children of certain ages. The Foster Care Independence Act (1999) meets the overarching needs of older adolescents in care, even beyond independent living goals. Special provisions for abandoned infants also reflect policymakers' vision to avoid prolonged foster care stays for the most vulnerable children. Yet, the more global needs of infants, who today represent the largest proportion of children in the foster care system, remain poorly met, as are the needs of preschool and school-age children.

To meet the broad and complex needs of families, the child welfare system historically has had to collaborate with other systems of care. However, still missing is a federal and local policy agenda that integrates service sectors at the uppermost level and provides incentives for joint planning and servicing for this vulnerable population. Scholars and practitioners suggest that integration of services would yield substantial cost savings by emphasizing prevention, reducing service duplication, and coordinating services for families who require services from multiple service sectors. Finally, the extant spending formula that many contend fiscally rewards child welfare systems to place and maintain children in foster care must be scrutinized. Various child welfare advocates have argued for more flexible federal funding for children and families in this system. Such flexibility would allow for state experiments with prevention and reunifications efforts, and more germane to this chapter, would allow greater creativity in how child welfare systems meet the developmental and mental health needs of foster children.

References

Aber, J. L., & Zigler, E. (1981). Developmental considerations in the definition of child maltreatment. *New Directions for Child Development, 11*, 1–29.

Adoption and Safe Families Act, 42 U.S.C. § 671 et seq. (1997).

Allen, M. L., & Bissell, M. (2004) Safety and stability for foster children: The policy context. *Future of Children, 14*(1), 49–73.

American Academy of Pediatrics. Committee on Early Childhood and Adoption and Dependent Care. (2000). Developmental issues for young children in foster care. *Pediatrics, 106*, 1145–1150.

Barth, R. P., Goodhand, J., & Dickinson, N. S. (2000). Reconciling competing values in the delivery of child welfare services under ASFA, MEPA, and community-based child protection. In J. Zlotnick (Ed.), *Changing paradigms of child welfare practices: Responding to opportunities and challenges* (pp. 7–33).Washington, DC: U.S. Department of Health and Human Services, Administration on Children, Youth, and Families, Children's Bureau.

Barth, R. P., Green, R. L., Wall, A., & the NSCAW Research Team. (2001, March). Environmental, behavioral, and developmental status of foster children one year after placement. In R. Clyman (Chair), *Policy implications of a national study of the mental health and developmental status of abused children and services they received.* Symposium conducted at the biennial meeting of the Society for Research on Child Development, Minneapolis, MN.

Benedict, M. I., Zuravin, S., & Stallings, R. Y. (1996). Adult functioning of children who lived in kin versus nonrelative family foster homes. *Child Welfare, 75*, 529–549.

Besinger, B. A., Garland, A. F., Litrownik, A. J., & Landsverk, J. A. (1999). Caregiver substance abuse among maltreated children placed in out-come-home care. *Child Welfare, 78*, 221–239.

Billing, A., Ehrle, J., & Kortenkamp, K. (2002). *Children cared for by relatives: What do we know about their well-being?* Washington, DC: The Urban Institute.

Brodzinsky, D. M. (1990). A stress and coping model of adoption adjustment. In D. M. Brodzinsky & M. D. Schechter (Eds.), *The psychology of adoption* (pp. 3–24). Oxford, England: Oxford University Press.

Bronfenbrenner, U., & Ceci, S. J. (1994). Nature-nurture reconceptualized in developmental perspective: A bioecological model. *Psychological Review, 101*, 568–586.

Cautley, P. (1980). *New foster parents*. New York: Human Sciences Press.

Cicchetti, D., & Lynch, M. (1995). Failures in the expectable environment and their impact on individual development: The case of child maltreatment. In D. Cicchetti & D. J. Cohen (Eds.), *Developmental psychopathology* (Vol. 2, pp. 32–71). New York: Wiley.

Clausen, J. M., Landsverk, J., Ganger, W., Chadwick, D., & Litrownik, A.. (1998). Mental health problems of children in foster care. *Journal of Child and Family Studies, 7*, 283–296.

Courtney, M. E. (1994). Factors associated with entrance into group care. In R. P. Barth, J. D. Berrick, & N. Gilbert (Eds.), *Child welfare research review* (Vol. 1., pp. 185–204). New York: Columbia University Press.

Courtney, M. E., & Barth, R. P. (1996). Race and child welfare services: Past research and future directions. *Child Welfare, 75*, 99–136.

Crittenden, P. M., & Ainsworth, M. D. (1989). Child maltreatment and attachment theory. In D. Cicchetti & V. Carlson (Eds.), *Child maltreatment: Theory and research on the causes and consequences of child abuse and neglect* (pp. 432–463). New York: Cambridge University Press.

Curtis, P. A. (1999). Introduction: The chronic nature of the foster care crisis. In P. A. Curtis, G. Dale Jr., & J. C. Kendall (Eds.), *The foster care crisis: Translating research into policy and practice* (pp. 1–14). Lincoln: University of Nebraska Press in association with the Child Welfare League of America.

Dishion, T. J., McCord, J., & Poulin, F. (1999). When interventions harm: Peer groups and problem behavior. *American Psychologist, 54*, 755–764.

Dore, M. M. (2000). Emotionally and behaviorally disturbed children in the child welfare system: Points of preventive intervention. *Children and Youth Services Review, 21*, 7–29.

Dubowitz, H., Zuravin, S., Starr, H., Feigelman, S., & Harrington, D. (1993). Behavior problems of children in kinship care. *Developmental and Behavioral Pediatrics, 14*, 386–393.

Duncan, G. J., & Aber, J. L. (1997). Neighborhood models and measures. In G. J. Duncan, J. Brooks-Gunn, & P. K. Klebanov (Eds.), *Neighborhood poverty: Vol. 1. Context and consequences for children* (pp. 62–78). New York: Russell Sage Foundation.

Edleson, J. (2001). Studying the co-occurrence of child maltreatment and domestic violence in families. In S. Graham-Bermann & J. Edleson (Eds.), *Domestic violence in the lives of children* (pp. 91–110). Washington, DC: American Psychological Association.

Ehrle, J., & Geen, R. (2002a). Children cared for by relatives: What services do they need? *New federalism: National survey of America's families* (Rep. No. B-47). Washington, DC: The Urban Institute.

Ehrle, J., & Geen, R (2002b). Kin and non-kin foster care: Findings from a national survey. *Children and Youth Services Review, 24*, 15–35.

Fanshel, D., & Shinn, E. B. (1978). *Children in foster care: A longitudinal investigation*. New York: Columbia University Press.

Foster Care Independence Act, 42 U.S.C. § 677 (1999).

Goldstein, J., Solnit, A. J., Goldstein, S., & Freud, A. (1996). *The best interests of the child: The least detrimental alternative*. New York: The Free Press.

Halfon, N., Mendonca, A., & Berkowitz, G. (1995). Health status of children in foster care. *Archives of Pediatric and Adolescent Medicine, 149*, 386–392.

Harden, B. J. (1998). Building bridges for children: Children exposed to drugs and the child welfare system. In R. Hampton (Ed.), *Substance abuse, family violence, and child welfare*. Thousand Oaks, CA: Sage.

Harden, B. J. (2002). Congregate care for infants and toddlers: Shedding new light on an old question. *Infant Mental Health Journal, 23*, 476–495.

Haugaard, J., & Hazan, C. (2002). Foster parenting. In M. H. Bornstein (Ed.), *Handbook of parenting: Vol. 1. Children and parenting* (2nd ed., pp. 313–327). Mahwah, NJ: Erlbaum.

Iglehart, A. P. (1995). Readiness for independence: Comparison of foster care, kinship care, and non-foster care adolescents. *Children and Youth Services Review, 17*, 417–432.

Jacobs, F., & Davies, M. (Eds.). (1994). *More than kissing babies? Current child and family policy in the United States.* Westport, CT: Greenwood Press.

Kamerman, S., & Kahn, A. (2001). Child and family policies in the U.S. at the opening of the 21st century. *Social Policy and Administration, 35*(1), 69–84.

Kerman, M., Wildfire, J., & Barth, R. P. (2002). Outcomes for young adults who experienced foster care. *Children and Youth Services Review, 24*, 319–344.

Kurtz, P. D., Gaudin, J. M., Howing, P. T., & Wodarski, J. S. (1993). The consequences of physical abuse and neglect on the school age child: Mediating factors. *Children and Youth Services, 15*, 85–104.

Landsverk, J., Davis, I., Ganger, W., Newton, R., & Johnson, I. (1996). Impact of child psychosocial functioning on reunification from out-of-home placement. *Children and Youth Services Review, 18*, 447–462.

Landsverk, J., & Garland, A. F. (1999). Foster care and pathways to mental health services. In P. A. Curtis, G. Dale Jr., & J. C. Kendall (Eds.), *The foster care crisis: Translating research into policy and practice* (pp. 193–210). Lincoln: University of Nebraska Press in association with the Child Welfare League of America.

Leslie, L. K., Gordon, J. N., Ganger, W., & Gist, K. (2002). Developmental delay in young children in child welfare by initial placement type. *Infant Mental Health Journal, 23*, 496–516.

Leslie, L. K., Landsverk, J., Horton, M. B., Ganger, W., & Newton, R. R. (2000). The heterogeneity of children and their experiences in kinship care. *Child Welfare, 79*, 315–334.

Lindsey, D. (1991). Factors affecting the foster care placement decision: An analysis of national survey data. *American Journal of Orthopsychiatry, 61*, 272–281.

Marcus, R. F. (1991). The attachments of children in foster care. *Genetic, Social, and General Psychology Monographs, 117*, 265–394.

McLoyd, V. C. (1998). Socioeconomic disadvantage and child development. *American Psychologist, 53*, 185–204.

Milan, S. E., & Pinderhughes, E. E. (2000). Factors influencing maltreated children's early adjustment in foster care. *Development and Psychopathology, 12*, 63–81.

Newton, R. R., Litrownik, A. J., & Landsverk, J. A. (2000). Children and youth in foster care: Disentangling the relationship between problem behaviors and number of placements. *Child Abuse and Neglect, 24*, 1363–1374.

NSCAW Research Group. (2002). Methodological lessons from the National Survey of Child and Adolescent Well-Being: The first three years of the USA's first national probability study of children and families investigated for abuse and neglect. *Children and Youth Services Review, 24*, 513–541.

O'Connor, T. G., Bredenkamp, D., Rutter, M., & the English and Romanian Adoptees Study Team. (1998). Attachment disturbances and disorders in children exposed to early severe deprivation. *Infant Mental Health Journal, 20*, 10–29.

Orme, J. G., & Buehler, C. (2001). Foster family characteristics and behavioral and emotional problems of foster children: A narrative review. *Family Relations: Journal of Applied Family & Child Studies, 50*, 3–15.

Pinderhughes, E. E. (1996). Toward understanding family readjustment following older child adoptions: The interplay between theory generation and empirical research. *Children and Youth Services Review, 18*, 115–138.

Pinderhughes, E. E., Dodge, K. A., Bates, J. E., Pettit, G. S., & Zelli, A. (2000). Discipline responses: Influences of parents' socioeconomic status, ethnicity, beliefs about parenting, stress, and cognitive–emotional process. *Journal of Family Psychology, 14*, 380–400.

Pinderhughes, E. E., Nix, R. L., Foster, E. M., Jones, D., & the Conduct Problems Prevention Research Group. (2001). Parenting in context: Impact of neighborhood poverty, residential stability, public services, social networks and danger on parental behaviors. *Journal of Marriage and Family, 63*, 941–953.

Promoting Safe and Stable Families Act of 1997, 42 U.S.C. § 629 (1997).

Schutter, L. S., & Brinker, R. P. (1992). Conjuring a new category of disability from prenatal cocaine exposure: Are the infants unique biological or caretaking casualties? *Topics in Early Childhood Special Education, 11*, 84–111.

Schweder, A. E. (2002). *Out-of-home care and externalizing behavior problems in maltreated children*. Unpublished manuscript. New Haven, CT: Yale University.

Social Security Act of 1935, 42 U.S.C. § 301–1397jj (1935).

Stovall, K. C., & Dozier, M. (2000). The development of attachment in new relationships: Single subject analyses for 10 foster infants. *Development and Psychopathology, 12*, 133–156.

Taussig, H. (2002). Risk behavior in maltreated youth placed in foster care: A longitudinal study of protective and vulnerability factors. *Child Abuse and Neglect, 26*, 1179–1199.

U.S. Department of Health and Human Services, Administration on Children, Youth, and Families, Children's Bureau. (2000). *Report to the Congress on kinship foster care*. Washington, DC: U.S. Government Printing Office.

U.S. Department of Health and Human Services, Administration for Children and Families, Administration on Children, Youth and Families, Children's Bureau. (2005). *The Adoption and Foster Care Analysis and Reporting System (AFCARS) report: Preliminary FY 2003 estimates as of April, 2005*. Retrieved April 20, 2005, from http://www.acf.hhs.gov/programs/cb

Wald, M. S., Carlsmith, J. M., & Leiderman, P. H. (1988). *Protecting abused and neglected children*. Stanford, CA: Stanford University Press.

Waldfogel, J. (2000). Child welfare research: How adequate are the data? *Children and Youth Services Review, 22*, 705–741.

Widom, C. S. (1991). The role of placement experiences in mediating the criminal consequences of early childhood victimization. *American Journal of Orthopsychiatry, 6*, 195–209.

Wulczyn, F. (1991). Caseload dynamics and foster care reentry. *Social Service Review, 65*, 133–156.

Wulczyn, F., & Hislop, K. B. (2002). *Foster care dynamics in urban and non-urban counties. Report to the Office of the Assistant Secretary of Planning and Evaluation*. Washington, DC: U.S. Department of Health and Human Services.

Wulczyn, F., Hislop, K. B., & Harden, B. J. (2002). The placement of infants in foster care. *Infant Mental Health Journal, 23*, 454–475.

Zigler, E. (1979). Controlling child abuse in America: An effort doomed to failure? In D. G. Gil (Ed.), *Child abuse and violence* (pp. 37–48). New York: AMS Press.

Zigler, E., & Styfco, S. J. (2000). Preventing child abuse through quality early care and education: A plea for policy makers to act. *UMKC Law Review, 69*, 15–24.

Zuravin, S. J., Benedict, M., & Somerfield, M. (1993). Child maltreatment in family foster care. *American Journal Orthopsychiatry, 63*, 589–596.

Part IV

Strengthening Children, Families, and Communities

13

Parent Education:
Lessons Inspired by Head Start

LaRue Allen, Anita Sethi, Sheila Smith,
and Jennifer Astuto

In 1965, the original goals of Head Start were outlined in the "Cooke memo," a summary of recommendations for the program as envisioned by a "Panel of Experts Chaired by Dr. Robert Cooke." This document, elegant in its brevity, described many of the aspects of Head Start that are still in place today, including specific requirements with regard to the role of parents in Head Start. The decision to include and educate parents reflects the political and academic research climate of the time in which Head Start was born, but the effects of that decision are still seen today in Head Start policy as well as in recommended standards for early childhood program quality (e.g., Harms, Clifford, & Cryer, 1998, see also Congress's Goals 2000: Educate America Act, 1994; National Association for the Education of Young Children, 1998). In this chapter we briefly discuss the decision to include parents in Head Start and the implications of that decision. We then focus on enduring challenges in the design and delivery of parent education programs and recommend an agenda for future research that can further develop the knowledge we need to create effective programs for different kinds of families.

We define parent education as a means for teaching parents about their children in an effort to maximize their children's competence, using a formal curriculum or set of activities, and involving face-to-face contact between educator and parent. This encompasses the definition provided by Smith, Perou, and Lesesne (2002, p. 389): "Educational efforts that attempt to enhance or facilitate parent behaviors that will influence positive developmental outcomes in their children," but excludes programs that are solely based on manuals, the Internet, or television programs.

The Arrival of Head Start

Although parent education had clear historical precedents (see Schlossman, 1983, for a review), the policy of mandating it as a prominent component of a new national program represented a bold advance. To be exact, the Cooke memo required parent involvement, not education, but implicit in this requirement was the notion that parents would be educated as a consequence of their involvement.

The decision to include parents as agents of change in Head Start was influenced by Urie Bronfenbrenner's (1977) theory about the importance of multiple contexts for children's development. Bronfenbrenner, a member of the Head Start Planning Committee, believed that real effects on children's lives could only be gained by changing multiple, nested environments that shaped their development, including the home and the larger neighborhood, and not by simply removing children from their families for certain hours of the week.

There were other reasons to support parent involvement as well. Technically, parent participation was mandated as a result of the funding source, because Head Start was considered a Community Action Program (CAP) and the legislation that funded CAPs required "maximum feasible participation." But the idea for maximum feasible participation itself came out of the growing belief that schools in poor and minority areas had no cultural links to, and no awareness of, the communities in which they existed. Involving parents at the management level would, theoretically, provide them with greater ownership of the Head Start program and help them forge links with other community agencies and, as a result, create a better fit between their needs and the services provided in that community. In addition, the sense of self-determination and belonging that should come from having such effects on one's community was expected to enhance parental mental health and, by extension, parenting and child outcomes (Bromley, Valdez, & Bowles, 1972). As Zigler and Freedman (1987) pointed out, the hope was that the sense of community gained by participating in Head Start would ameliorate some of the isolation felt by modern parents.

The goal, then, of improving children's prospects was being pursued at two levels within the parent domain—through the parents as direct agents of their children's socialization and through the parents as activists who could change the quality and tenor of services in their own neighborhoods. These sets of goals came into conflict with one another almost from the start. According to some researchers (e.g., Hess, Block, Costello, Knowles, & Largay, 1971), the problem was that there was an inherent contradiction in encouraging parents to take pride in their skills and ownership of a program, on the one hand, and telling them to follow the guidelines of parenting "experts" on the other. The implication of the former approach is that the parents have skills and capacities with regard to child rearing that have not been recognized or tapped, whereas the implication of the latter approach is that parents have deficits that need to be remedied.

Head Start identified and confronted these challenges (see Kagan, 2002, for a description of how Head Start and Edward F. Zigler in particular addressed issues related to parent inclusion). The experiences of programs as they navigated new territory and the ongoing responsiveness of Head Start leaders to problems as they arose provided an impetus to the further expansion and evolution of parenting programs. One outgrowth of the mandate to include parents in Head Start was the development of programs with a singular focus, both through Head Start and independent of it. The idea of these programs was to identify a particular set of needs and target it by articulating a theory, a specific intervention plan, and a desired outcome. Such programs included the Teenage Pregnancy Intervention Project and Education for Parenthood (aimed at teen parents) and Parent Training and Information Centers (aimed at parents of children with disabilities).

Other programs addressed multiple needs and defined their target populations and outcomes in broad terms, while sometimes adapting features of the program for different types of families. Meld, for example, targets multiple needs, and offers different "curricula" based on the family's characteristics (e.g., one for a family with a child with disabilities vs. another for a teen parent; see http://www.meld.org/main.cfm?PageID=1004). There has also been a continued evolution of programs, such as the Prenatal/Early Infancy Project, that provide a wide array of services with parent education as one component. Such programs may be more accurately termed *family support* programs rather than strictly parent education programs (see Kagan & Weissbourd, chap. 15, this volume). Nevertheless, the family support movement finds its origins in the parent education and support philosophy articulated by Head Start (Weissbourd, 1987) and can be considered a product of the same early efforts as the other programs listed here.

Evaluations of Parent Education Programs

Many single and multicomponent parent education programs have been evaluated, with studies varying in quality and scope. Synthesizing results across these studies is a challenge, not only because the studies used different methodologies but also because the programs achieved variable levels of fidelity to their goals and service models. Keeping these issues in mind, however, we briefly summarize recent evaluations of parent education programs (for a more complete review, please contact the first author).

Overall, these evaluations present a mixed picture. Although it is difficult to identify success across the board, there are programs that have had sizable impacts on parents and children. An ongoing challenge is to identify what it is that successful programs are able to provide that differentiates them from their less successful counterparts. In general, the results suggest that parent education programs are most successful in terms of children's outcomes when they are combined with center-based services for the target child. This may, in part, be a function of the fact that far more evaluations have been conducted of multimodal interventions than of stand-alone parent education programs, which, in turn, may be due to the greater number of the former type of program compared with the latter. It may also be a result of the fact that children benefit from the direct exposure to learning and stimulation in the center-based setting, benefits that are not accessible at home.

Evaluations of Head Start and Early Head Start programs provide a window into the effects of parent education in combination with a center-based program. A recent evaluation (Administration for Children and Families [ACF], 2002) revealed important differences in social–emotional competence among children who attended center-based programs and whose parents participated in an array of parent education programs. Positive parental behaviors, including reading books to and greater positive social interactions with the target children, were observed in this group as well. Behavioral benefits of parent education programs have also been observed in the evaluation of a specific social-competence parenting curriculum linked to a Head Start program (Webster-Stratton, 1994). Parents were randomly assigned to participate in small groups that revolved around discussion of video segments of parenting behaviors. Those who participated in the intervention, which was designed to decrease harsh, inconsistent, critical parenting, demonstrated an increase in positive affect, praise, and consistency and a decrease in harsh behavior toward their children. These changes were maintained at 1-year follow-up. Children's social competence in the classroom was also higher for those in the intervention group.

Parent education focused on children's emergent literacy also shows promise as a component of center-based programs and as a stand-alone intervention. For example, a highly focused parent training intervention that involves shared book reading has been successfully implemented in Head Start and child-care programs. This intervention, called *dialogic reading*, trains parents and teachers to ask children different kinds of questions to elicit conversation about a book during shared reading. Dialogic reading has been shown to have a significant positive impact on children's language skills when combined with a classroom-based literacy intervention and also when implemented only by parents (Lonigan & Whitehurst, 1998; Whitehurst et al., 1994). It is interesting to note that this intervention improves children's language only when parents participate—a classroom-based program alone is not as effective in enhancing children's language—and in one study, selected child outcomes in the parent-only dialogic reading condition were superior to the classroom-based and combined classroom-home intervention (Lonigan & Whithurst, 1998). Whitehurst et al. (1994) observed that parents play a critical role in the development of preschoolers' language skills and can deliver a language-promoting intervention such as dialogic reading with greater intensity and specificity than center-based programs. Whereas a teacher conducts shared reading with conversation in small groups, parents can enjoy one-on-one shared reading and discussion, possibly more frequently and more targeted to the child.

In contrast to the mixed (center- and home-based) programs just described, a prevalent model of a stand-alone parent education intervention can be found in home-visiting programs. (It should be kept in mind, however, that many home-visiting programs encompass more than just parent education, as seen, for example, by the Nurse Home Visiting Program, which includes guidance on maternal health and contraception as well as on career development.) A recent review of six early childhood home-visiting programs found no consistent positive effects on parents or children across programs (Gomby, Culroos, & Behrman, 1999), but examination of individual studies indicates that some programs do have a positive impact on parents (most often mothers) and children. For example, home-visiting programs designed for parents of young children have been found to increase rates of sensitive, responsive parenting (e.g., Olds, Henderson, & Kitzman, 1994) and quality of the home environment (Erickson, Korfmacher, & Egeland, 1992). Differences in maternal attitudes about physical abuse (Duggan et al., 1999) and fewer hospital visits in the first 4 years of life have also been associated with families receiving home-visiting services

(Olds & Kitzman, 1993). Other effects on children include better performance on tests of cognitive and social development among Latino children whose mothers participated in Parents as Teachers (PAT; Wagner & Clayton, 1999). At a 13-year follow up, children whose mothers had participated in the Nurse Home Visiting Program exhibited less running away, less promiscuity, and less alcohol use than control group teenagers, whose mothers had not received these services when their children were toddlers (Olds & Kitzman, 1993).

Webster-Stratton (1994) has tested a parent-training program that involves visits with a therapist as well as supplementary clinic-based videotape viewing. In this training, which is a good example of stand-alone parent training outside the home, positive effects were observed for both parent–child communication and parents' reports of their children's behavior.

The challenge for these programs, again, is to identify what characteristics of family or program are associated with success. On the program side alone, differences in levels of staff training and supervision, curriculum content, staff fidelity to the program model, and staff turnover contribute to the varied levels of success of these programs. Obtaining reliable measures of these highly changeable variables presents another obstacle to identifying links with outcomes. In the next sections, we discuss enduring issues such as these that will need to be addressed in practice and program design, and we outline a research agenda for the future.

Challenges for Practice

A review of literature on practical issues confronting parent educators suggests that challenges fall into three general categories: (a) creating a match between program and staff qualities and parents' characteristics, (b) identifying parents' capacity to benefit from the program, and (c) addressing the inherent conflict between the "expert" role of parent educators and the goal of programs to respect and use parents' expertise. The ways in which programs resolve these challenges have implications for program design and practice, and they effect outcomes including levels of participation and achievement of program goals. Additional practice challenges include recruitment and retention of families, training of staff (particularly with a focus toward maintaining fidelity of the program), and finding ways to build the social capital of families and neighborhoods (because programs face an uphill battle with families in highly distressed neighborhoods), but for present purposes we focus on these core issues.

Creating a match between program and parent does not necessarily mean that parent educators need to have the same socioeconomic status or child-rearing values as the parents they are serving, but that awareness exists of the impact of variables such as parental characteristics and family circumstances upon parents' ability to connect with program staff and learn from them. The PAT study noted earlier, for example, found better effects for Latino families (Wagner & Clayton, 1999). A recent evaluation of Early Head Start, which included home-based and mixed interventions, found that African American and Latino families demonstrated more benefits from participation than did White families (ACF, 2002). On a similar note, in a family support study, McCurdy,

Gannon, and Daro (2003) found lower levels of attrition in African American and Latino families than in White families. The question that remains for practitioners in these settings is, what contributes to the differential results by, in this case, race/ethnicity, and how can one broaden those effects to participants of a different race/ethnicity?

Another major challenge has to do with the capacity of parents to benefit from a particular program. Familial risk factors can influence the effectiveness of an intervention, although not always in predictable ways. For example, Barnard (1998) demonstrated that the most effective intervention for a particular mother varied by the quantity of risk factors she was experiencing: Higher risk mothers benefited from one type of intervention (mental health support), whereas lower risk mothers benefited from another type (education). The recent evaluation of Early Head Start (ACF, 2002) found that families with moderate levels of demographic risk benefited most from the program. Families with fewer risks exhibited little gain from the program, and families with many risks actually demonstrated negative effects as a consequence of program participation. The researchers hypothesize that families with particularly high levels of risk might find the demands of program participation so overwhelming that their level of functioning actually drops. Yet a Nurse Home Visiting Program study (Olds et al., 1999) found the strongest effects in terms of levels of child abuse for those families who felt most overwhelmed before intervention. The implication of this for parent education programs is twofold. First, it is possible that certain sets of risk factors (e.g., maternal depression) are incompatible with the ability to benefit from educational programs at a given time. The roles of these risk factors need to be evaluated and addressed at the program level, however, because the inconsistent relationship between risk level and program success suggests that a high number of risk factors might not always mean that the family is a poor fit for a given program, and because certain risk factors might only have an impact in certain programs. Second, programs must consider whether it is feasible and imperative—in light of program capacity, goals, and philosophy—to try to help parents attain a level of well-being and resources such as adequate food and housing that will permit them to participate and benefit from parent education programs.

A third challenge for practice has to do with maintaining a balance between a didactic relationship and partnership. This hearkens back to the initial conflicts in parents' roles in Head Start, but it remains an issue even when focusing on parent education. Zigler explicitly addressed this concern more than 30 years ago, in the memorandum he wrote regarding parent involvement. Referring to the relationships between professionals and parents on Policy Councils, he stated, "[Professionals] must learn to ask parents for their ideas, and listen with attention, patience and understanding" (Department of Health, Education, and Welfare, Office of Child Development, 1970, p. 7).

The balance between didactic and partnership relationships remains an issue because many programs hire former parents or community members as educators on the basis of the idea that parents can better identify with them and they, in turn, can better appreciate the challenges and beliefs of the parents they are working with. But hiring less trained members of the community may have an impact on program fidelity. Other issues may arise as well. For example, Korfmacher, O'Brien, Hiat, & Olds (1999) found that paraprofessionals had higher turnover than trained nurses, despite the extensive supervision provided to the less trained group.

The challenge of this balance has, itself, generated its own area of controversy in that some researchers and practitioners disagree with the entire concept of parent education. According to some researchers (e.g., Dockecki & Moroney, 1983; Howrigan, 1988), the academic shortcomings of particular subgroups of children are incorrectly attributed to poor upbringing or values, and should be seen as "differences," not deficits. Schlossman (1978), an early and vocal opponent of parent education, stated that it essentially blames the victim and assigns to poor parents jobs that should be done by the government or other social supports. According to Schlossman, encouragement of parent education programs lets the larger powers in society off the hook, because when children do not succeed, the parent can be blamed.

This view of parent education provides a lesson for practitioners in that it encourages them to consider the broader range of influences in a child's life, even if they cannot address all of them. As stated by Howrigan (1988), "Trying to change mothers' interactional style and children's cognitive functioning without considering whether other aspects of families' settings can support the changes is unproductive" (p. 97). This insight is important to keep in mind when considering the reasons why some families might not achieve all the goals a program has set out for them.

Just as some practice issues will continue to challenge professionals who design and implement parent education programs, there are challenges to evaluating these programs that will persist in the next generation of studies. In the following section we review these challenges and discuss potentially fruitful directions for future research.

A Parent Education Research Agenda for the Future

More than 4 decades of research on parent education programs has yielded valuable lessons about how research in this field should be conducted. This same literature, along with our expanding knowledge from other areas of child development research, suggests important new questions that should be investigated in the next generation of parent education research. In this section, we discuss general methodological approaches that will be essential to ongoing studies of parent education programs and highlight new areas of investigation that should be part of a research agenda that can help extend the general knowledge about the kinds of programs that can benefit children and their families.

A major challenge in the study of parent education programs is understanding child and parent outcomes in relation to the actual program that was delivered to participants. In large-scale interventions, programs have often varied from their prototype because sponsors and implementers have confronted the need to make services responsive to particular communities. For example, Zigler and Freedman (1987) noted that the Parent Child Center (PCC) in Vermont provided center- and home-based services, whereas the PCCs in many southern states had to find alternatives to center-based care because out-of-home care was illegal for infants in these states at the time. Programs also deviate from a model as a result of the many variables that affect program implementation, including the nature of preexisting services, staff training, organizational capacities, and unanticipated events such as a change in agency leadership. A marked lack of program fidelity was found, for example, in the evaluation of the federal Comprehensive Child Development Program (CCDP) initiative. CCDP sites varied in their capacity to help families gain access to comprehensive services, in part due to the availability of services in the different sponsoring agencies and their community settings (Goodson, Layzer, St. Pierre, Bernstein, & Lopez, 2000). Evaluators hypothesized that one possible reason for CCDP's failure to produce desired program impacts was that the amount and quality of services received by some families was lower than what was prescribed by the program model. More recently, the evaluation of Early Head Start found that programs that fell short of performance standards set by research staff and the Head Start Bureau were less successful in achieving benefits for families than programs that met the standards (ACF, 2002).

Whatever the source of programs' deviation from a model, sound interpretations of outcome findings will depend on good information about programs as they were actually implemented. In addition to tracking the types and amounts of delivered services (e.g., the number of parent training sessions provided), strong attention should be paid in future research to the content and quality of these services. Just as some previous home-visiting studies have documented the content of home-based sessions (Powell, 1994), future studies of parent education programs need to assess exactly what is being taught as well as the quality of the sessions (e.g., facilitators' use effective adult learning methods).

Related to issues of fidelity, it is also important for parent education programs to articulate a coherent (i.e., programwide) theory of change. This has been pointed out by Weiss and Greene (1992) as well as by Brooks-Gunn, Berlin, and Fuligni (2000), and refers to the understanding that program staff have about how the intervention will lead to intended outcomes. Brooks-Gunn et al. (2000) suggested that the coherence of staff's theory of change may be related to program success. They suggested that if program staff members have differing theories about what is contributing to change, then these theories and their related practices might work against one another. Future research is needed to test the idea that a coherent theory of change affects practice and program outcomes.

A dimension of quality that may prove especially important for understanding outcomes is participants' perceptions of their relationship with the parent educator. Wasik (1993) observed that positive, growth-promoting relationships in parenting education programs are likely to occur when parents experience parent educators as empathic, respectful, and genuine, qualities found in effective clinician–client relationships in more traditional therapeutic settings. In contrast, parent educators who assume an overly authoritative or judgmental stance are unlikely to be effective. Supporting this observation, Boger, Kuipers, and Berry (1969) observed, anecdotally, that in the parent groups they held, parental attrition seemed to be influenced by the teachers' personalities. The inclusion of more fine-grained, theory-based measures of service quality in future studies of parent education should contribute to the general understanding of provider and program characteristics that affect parenting and child outcomes.

Even when a program achieves a high degree of fidelity to a model, differential levels of parent participation sometimes influence outcomes, suggesting the need for careful subgroup analyses of families' involvement in the intervention. In the Infant Health and Development Program, for example, families' involvement in home visits and center-based services predicted children's outcomes after controlling for demographic characteristics (Liaw, Meisels, & Brooks-Gunn, 1995). On a similar note, Osofsky, Culp, and Ware (1988) found that teenage mothers who had higher levels of participation in a parenting skills program were more likely to achieve program goals of sensitivity and responsiveness toward their infants. Given the relevance of participation as a variable affecting outcomes, it will be important to continue assessing both families' engagement and the factors that may influence engagement. These factors are likely to include both features of the program (e.g., incentives, quality of services) and characteristics of families (e.g., risk status). In larger scale studies, the use of planned variations in program design and enrollment could allow the testing of specific strategies for enhancing participation of different groups of families.

The investigation of parent and family characteristics that either affect program participation or independently influence program outcomes is another important avenue for subgroup analyses. Beyond demographic variables, it will be important to investigate the extent to which a variety of mental health and social risk factors, such as parental depression, perception of self-efficacy, style of coping with stress, capacity for self-awareness, and ability to use social support affect parents' involvement in and response to parent education programs. As mentioned earlier, the recent evaluation of Early Head Start (ACF, 2002) found differences in the extent to which families at different levels of risk benefited from the program. Recent research suggests that, under certain conditions, low-income parents with mental health risk factors can become as engaged in parenting training as parents lacking these factors, and they can also enjoy similar benefits from the intervention (Baydar, Reid, & Webster-Stratton, 2003). Such research can help program developers to avoid faulty assumptions about the role these factors play in parents' response to programs.

The next generation of parent education programs should continue efforts to identify predictors of parent engagement and experiment with new strategies to enhance parents' capacities to fully use parent education. Generic program strategies that have been found to foster engagement should be tested with different populations and parenting interventions. These include the provision of child care and meals for program participants; the use of varied session times and make-up classes to accommodate parents' schedules; and formats, such as problem solving and discussion that encourage parents' active participation in sessions (Baydar et al., 2003). It will also be informative to probe more deeply into the reasons that parents drop out of programs or participate at less than optimal levels. In-depth interviews with hard-to-engage parents may reveal aspects of the program and participants' lives that limit parents' participation and conditions that would encourage their engagement.

The current knowledge about experiences that contribute to the development of social and cognitive competencies in the preschool years and beyond will help future studies of parent education programs specify pathways by which interventions are likely to affect child outcomes. In this regard, Brooks-Gunn et al. (2000) have observed that specific mediators of child outcomes have rarely been analyzed in previous studies of parent education programs. As programs become more theory and research based, it will be important to analyze whether and how specific intervention-targeted parenting behaviors have mediated children's outcomes. In a related vein, Howrigan (1988) has noted that parent education evaluations presume unidirectionality of effects from parent to child, disregarding the possibility that children's behavior is influencing the parent. Therefore, children's characteristics (e.g., temperament, cognitive functioning) should be entered into analyses as potential mediators of parent behavior and of the success of parent education programs. Just as parent characteristics may enhance or minimize programs' impacts on parenting behavior, parenting programs may have differential effects on children by virtue of their characteristics.

With regard to content of parenting programs, recent research highlights the critical importance of children's social–emotional competence (e.g., Raver & Zigler, 1997) and early literacy skills and interests (e.g., Whitehurst & Lonigan, 2000) for school readiness and success. Much of this research points to specific experiences in the family setting that contribute to the social, self-regulatory, and emergent literacy skills that help children learn effectively in school. This body of knowledge argues for the design and evaluation of new interventions that attempt to increase parent–child experiences that are likely to contribute to competencies in the social–emotional and literacy domains. In the domain of social–emotional development, Webster-Stratton's (1994) work with parents of children at risk for conduct disorders is a good example of this sort of evaluation. In the area of emergent literacy, an example of this approach is research on training parents in dialogic reading, as previously discussed (Whitehurst & Lonigan, 1998).

Because there are many parent–child experiences that can simultaneously support development in the social–emotional and early literacy domains (e.g., shared book reading and conversation with children that expands children's understanding of positive relationships, prewriting activities and pretend play that help children build communication and self-regulatory skills; Thompson, 2002), new parent education interventions that have a dual focus on the development of children's social–emotional competence and early literacy skills should be designed and investigated. Although past studies have sometimes included a broad array of fairly global cognitive and social–emotional outcome measures, the current state of knowledge should permit increasingly refined designs of both programs and evaluations. For example, drawing on recent theoretical and research literature regarding preschoolers' social competence, parent education programs that include a focus on children's social and emotional development might attempt to foster and assess parents' modeling of prosocial behavior, use of effective conflict resolution strategies, and explicit support for children's ability to interpret social situations.

Even as the field tests new program models, there is an ongoing need to investigate the state-of-the-field of practice in parent education across different settings, especially those serving large numbers of preschool-age children. Extensive surveys are needed to investigate current practices in parent education programs that are attached to center-based settings. In particular, it would be useful to know the scope and content of parent education components and levels of parent participation. More information is also needed about circumstantial obstacles to participation, such as parents' mandatory involvement in work or training programs. Information from current programs can be used in several ways. First, it is helpful to know the extent to which current parent education practices are incorporating new research-based information about early experiences that promote children's school readiness. A failure to use this information suggests the need for technical assistance and other dissemination methods to bring programs in closer alignment with our knowledge base. Second, the continuing refinement of welfare, health, and related policies depends on researchers' and scholars' understanding of their impact on families and children. Third, the field has much to teach about innovation. Novel and promising practices that merit careful evaluation are likely to be found in a wide-scale investigation of how early childhood programs and other sponsors are conducting parent education.

In summary, though questions remain to be answered, the field of parent education has demonstrated its capacity to evolve with new information and with time. The continuing innovation in parent education programs since the inception of Head Start and the growing body of knowledge about influences on children's development that can be applied to further refinements of program models suggest a promising future for the field of parent education. Ongoing collaboration between families, communities, policymakers, and researchers will ensure that the field continues to grow and provide services to children and families.

References

Administration for Children and Families. (2002). *Making a difference in the lives of infants and toddlers and their families: The impacts of Early Head Start.* Washington, DC: U.S. Department of Health and Human Services.

Barnard, K. (1998). Developing, implementing, and documenting interventions with parents and young children. *Zero to Three, 18,* 23–99.

Baydar, N., Reid, M. J., & Webster-Stratton, C. W. (2003). The role of mental health factors and program engagement in the effectiveness of a preventive parenting program for Head Start mothers. *Child Development, 74,* 1433–1453.

Boger, R., Kuipers, J., & Berry, M. (1969). *Parents as primary change agents in an experimental Head Start program of language intervention. Experimental program report.* Washington, DC: Office of Economic Opportunity.

Bromley, K., Valdez, D., & Bowles, W. (1972). *Investigation of the effects of parent participation in Head Start* (Tech. Rep. No. 251). Washington, DC: Department of Health, Education, and Welfare.

Bronfenbrenner, U. (1977). Toward an experimental ecology of human development. *American Psychologist, 32,* 513–531.

Brooks-Gunn, J., Berlin, L., & Fuligni, A. (2000). Early childhood intervention programs: What about the family? In J. Shonkoff & S. Meisels, (Eds.), *Handbook of early childhood intervention* (2nd ed., pp. 549–587). New York: Cambridge University Press.

Department of Health, Education, and Welfare, Office of Child Development. (1970). *Head Start policy manual 70.2: The parents.* Washington, DC: Author.

Dokecki, P., & Moroney, R. (1983). To strengthen all families: A human development and community value framework. In R. Haskins & D. Adams (Eds.), *Parent education and public policy* (pp. 40–64). Norwood, NJ: Ablex Publishing.

Duggan, A., McFarlane, E. C., Windham, A. M., Rohde, C. A., Salkever, D. S., Fuddy, L., et al. (1999). Evaluation of Hawaii's Healthy Start program. *The Future of Children, 9,* 66–90.

Erickson, M., Korfmacher, J., & Egeland, B. (1992). Attachments past and present: Implications for therapeutic intervention with mother–infant dyads. *Development and Psychopathology, 4,* 495–507.

Goals 2000: Educate America Act, H.R. 1804, 103d Cong (1994); also available at http://www.ed.gov/legislation/GOALS2000/TheAct/index.html

Gomby, D., Culross, P., & Behrman, R. (1999). Home visiting: Recent program evaluations. Analysis and recommendations. *The Future of Children, 9,* 4–27.

Goodson, B. D., Layzer, J. I., St. Pierre, R. G., Bernstein, L. S., & Lopez, M. (2000). Effectiveness of a comprehensive five-year family support program for low-income families: Findings from the comprehensive child development program. *Early Childhood Research Quarterly, 15,* 5–39.

Harms, T., Clifford, R. M., & Cryer, D. (1998). *Early Childhood Environment Rating Scale* (Rev. ed.). New York: Teachers College Press.

Hess, R., Block, M., Costello, J., Knowles, R., & Largay, D. (1971). Parent involvement in early education. In E. Grotberg (Ed.), *Day care: Resources for decision* (pp. 265–298). Washington, DC: Office of Economic Opportunity.

Howrigan, G. (1988). Evaluating parent–child interaction outcomes of family support and education programs. In H. Weiss & F. Jacobs (Eds.), *Evaluating family programs* (pp. 95–130). New York: Aldine de Gruyter.

Kagan, J. (2002). Empowerment and education: Civil rights, expert-advocates, and parent politics in Head Start, 1964–1980. *Teachers College Record, 104,* 516–562.

Korfmacher, J., O'Brien, R., Hiatt, S., & Olds, D. (1999). Differences in program implementation between nurses and paraprofessionals providing home visits during pregnancy and infancy: A randomized trial. *American Journal of Public Health, 89,* 1847–1851.

Liaw, F., Meisels, S., & Brooks-Gunn, J. (1995). The effects of experience of early intervention on low birthweight, premature children: The Infant Health and Development Program. *Early Childhood Research Quarterly, 10,* 405–431.

Lonigan, C., & Whitehurst, G. (1998). Relative efficacy of parent and teacher involvement in a shared-reading intervention for preschool children from low-income backgrounds. *Early Childhood Research Quarterly, 13,* 263–290.

McCurdy, K., Gannon, R., & Daro, D. (2003) Participation patterns in home-based family support programs: Ethnic variations. *Family Relations: Interdisciplinary Journal of Applied Family Studies, 52,* 3–11.

National Association for the Education of Young Children. (1998). *Accreditation criteria and procedures of the National Association for the Education of Young Children.* Washington, DC: Author.

Olds, D. L., Henderson, C. R., & Kitzman, H. (1994). Does prenatal and infancy nurse home visitation have enduring effects on qualities of parental caregiving and child health at 25 to 50 months of life? *Pediatrics, 98,* 89–98.

Olds, D. L., Henderson, C. R., Kitzman, H., Eckenrode, J., Cole, R., & Tatelbaum, R. (1999). Prenatal and infancy home visitation by nurses: Recent findings. *The Future of Children, 9,* 44–65.

Olds, D. L., & Kitzman, H. (1993). Review of research on home visiting for pregnant women and parents of young children. *The Future of Children, 3,* 53–92.

Osofsky, J. D., Culp, A. M., & Ware, L. M. (1988). Intervention challenges with adolescent mothers and their infants. *Psychiatry: Journal for the Study of Interpersonal Processes, 51,* 236–241.

Powell, D. R. (1994). Evaluating family support programs: Are we making progress? In S. L. Kagan & B. Weissbourd (Eds.), *Putting families first: America's family support movement and the challenge of change* (pp. 441–470). San Francisco: Jossey-Bass.

Raver, C. C., & Zigler, E. (1997). Social competence: An untapped dimension in evaluating Head Start's success. *Early Childhood Research Quarterly, 12,* 363–385.

Schlossman, S. (1978). The parent education game: The politics of child psychology in the 1970s. *Teachers College Record, 79,* 788–808.

Schlossman, S. (1983). The formative era in American parent education: Overview and interpretation. In R. Haskins & D. Adams (Eds.), *Parent education and public policy* (pp. 7–39). Norwood, NJ: Ablex Publishing.

Smith, C., Perou, R., & Lesesne, C. (2002). Parent education. In M. Bornstein (Ed.), *Handbook of parenting: Vol. 4. Social conditions and applied parenting* (pp. 389–410). Mahwah, NJ: Erlbaum.

Thompson, R. (2002). The roots of school readiness in social–emotional development. *The Kauffman Early Education Exchange, 1,* 8–29.

Wagner, M., & Clayton, S. (1999). The Parents as Teachers program: Results from two demonstrations. *The Future of Children, 9,* 91–115.

Wasik, B. H. (1993). Staffing issues for home visiting programs. *The Future of Children, 3,* 140–157.

Webster-Stratton, C. (1994). Advancing videotape parent training: A comparison study. *Journal of Consulting and Clinical Psychology, 62,* 583–593.

Weiss, H., & Greene, J. (1992) An empowerment partnership for family support and education programs and evaluations. *Family Science Review, 5,* 131–149.

Weissbourd, B. (1987). A brief history of family support programs. In S. Kagan, D. Powell, B. Weissbourd, & E. Zigler (Eds.), *America's family support programs* (pp. 38–56). New Haven, CT: Yale University Press.

Whitehurst, G. J., Epstein, J. N., Angell, A. L., Payne, A. C., Crone, D. A., & Fischel, J. E. (1994). Outcomes of an emergent literacy intervention in Head Start. *Journal of Educational Psychology, 86,* 542–555.

Whitehurst, G. J., & Lonigan, C. J. (1998). Child development and emergent literacy. *Child Development, 68,* 848–872.

Whitehurst, G. J., & Lonigan, C. J. (2000). Emergent literacy: Development from prereaders to readers. In S. B. Neuman & D. K. Dickinson (Eds.), *Handbook of early literacy research* (Vol. 1, pp. 11–29). New York: Guilford Press.

Zigler, E., & Freedman, J. (1987). Head Start: A pioneer of family support. In S. Kagan, D. Powell, B. Weissbourd, & E. Zigler (Eds.), *America's family support programs* (pp. 57–76). New Haven, CT: Yale University Press.

Zigler, E., & Meunchow, S. (1992) *Head Start: The inside story of America's most successful educational experiment.* New York: Basic Books.

14

Mental Health:
A Neglected Partner in the Healthy
Development of Young Children

Kathryn Taaffe McLearn, Jane Knitzer,
and Alice S. Carter

> The value of theories does not lie in the comfort they provide the user, but
> rather in the things that the user can do now which he would not be able to
> do in absence of a theory. . . . This is true whether our goals are navigating
> between celestial spheres or raising children.

—Edward F. Zigler (1963, p. 487)

Using theory and knowledge to inform action has been a hallmark of Edward F.
Zigler's philosophy and work in child development for more than 40 years. When
Head Start opened its doors in 1965, its founders, which included Zigler, viewed
the program as a "national proving ground for a new era of mental health theory
building" (Cohen, Solnit, & Wohlford, 1979, p. 262). They recognized the importance of establishing a comprehensive program, in which all aspects would promote a young child's mental health. Included in this agenda was the notion that
the provision of mental health services could not be isolated from other aspects
of service delivery or the broader life circumstances of families.

Consistent with the ecological model of development, Head Start's philosophy emphasized the whole child and the central roles of family and community
to facilitate the child's optimal development. The program included social and
emotional development in its performance standards; pioneered unproven concepts of prevention, outreach, early detection, and parent involvement; and de-
emphasized the traditional mental health paradigm of diagnosis and treatment
for psychopathology. Despite the promise, the Head Start community currently
acknowledges that its innovative approach to children's mental health has been
weakly implemented within its comprehensive services strategy (Piotrkowski,
Collins, Knitzer, & Robinson, 1994). The Head Start experience is not the ex-

---

We thank Elisabeth Marks for providing valuable assistance in the preparation of this chapter. The work reflected in this chapter was funded, in part, by the Commonwealth Fund, Annie E.
Casey Foundation, the Marguerite Casey Foundation, and federal Grant NIH-MH-55278.

ception. Far too often young children's mental health is neglected in discussions of what researchers and scholars know about the development of young children and of what needs to done to raise healthy young children.

We begin this chapter suggesting why children's mental health has been neglected and then proceed to describe fundamental principles for understanding the mental health of young children. We then selectively review the developmental theory and science that have contributed to the understanding of young children's mental health. Using this knowledge we then turn to action and discuss the challenges for future research, policy, and practice to better understand and address the mental health needs of young children and their families in this country.

Why Young Children's Mental Health Is Neglected

First, there has been skepticism about the importance of mental and social–emotional health for later adaptive functioning. The recent explosion of research in the neurological, behavioral, and social sciences provides robust evidence that adaptive social–emotional development underlies all growth and development in young children (Shonkoff & Phillips, 2000). Yet psychologists' and educators' emphasis on cognition and academic preparedness continues to overshadow attention to the importance of mental health and connections between young children's social and emotional development and success in school.

Second, the mental health of young children is neglected because there is a myth about "happy early childhood." Overall, parents and other adults do not believe that infants and very young children are suffering emotionally—that they are capable of being profoundly sad, disruptive, angry, or that social–emotional disorders can be apparent early in life. Despite reliable evidence that young children do have mental health disturbances at rates similar to older children (Briggs-Gowan, Carter, Skuban, & Horwitz, 2001; Lavigne et al., 1996), a report on mental health by the Surgeon General contends that most young children do not receive treatment early in life and there are vast inequities in health insurance coverage (U.S. Public Health Service, 2000). As a country, we ignore the fact that young children can suffer emotionally, providing early intervention services to children with developmental delays but fundamentally ignoring children with severe mental health disturbances (Horwitz, Gary, Briggs-Gowan, & Carter, 2003).

Third, the mental health of young children is neglected because of the societal stigma associated with mental health in general, and particularly young children's mental health. Recognizing that a very young child may have concerns in the area of mental health can be threatening to parents and other family members (U.S. Public Health Service, 2000). Culturally bound differences in belief systems, approaches toward parenting, and acceptance of mental health issues affect parents, teachers, and health care clinicians and their likelihood to address children's emotional and behavioral problems. It is a challenge to find a comfortable language to reduce stigma and explain the importance of mental health needs in young children to the public, policymakers, and service providers.

The final reason the mental health of young children has been neglected is because of the politicized environment in the health system about treatment for young children's mental health. The line between promoting mental health in young children and what to do to treat children with mental health problems is blurry. At present, the majority of mental health service systems require that a child receive an individual diagnosis in order for the child or family to receive mental health services. Yet, until preschool, there are few clear guidelines to distinguish the child with an extreme temperament in the typical range and the child with an affective, regulatory, or attentional disorder. In addition, extant psychiatric nosology, as presented in the *Diagnostic and Statistical Manual of Mental Disorders* (4th ed., text rev.; American Psychiatric Association, 2000), is not adequate to capture the symptomatology that infants and toddlers present, and even where the nosology may be appropriate, there is no reliability or validity data to support the use of these diagnoses. Furthermore, many young children may be in a setting with a single caregiver, making the determination of whether a mental health problem or impairment resides within the child or within the parent–child system very challenging.

Determining how to rectify the neglected issues of young children's mental health requires an understanding of the contexts and environments in which children grow and the multifaceted nature of young children's mental health and development. Before moving on to what we know about early social and emotional development, we must discuss the field's current understanding of the mental health of infants and young children.

Principles for Understanding the Mental Health of Infants and Young Children

Although a commonly accepted definition of early childhood mental health is still a work in progress (Zeanah, 2000), in this chapter we propose that young children who are mentally or emotionally healthy are—in an age-appropriate manner—self-confident; reasonably trusting of others; capable of relating well; empathetic toward others; able to constructively channel frustration and anger; able to inhibit or contain unwanted or inappropriate emotions, impulses, and desires; motivated to master cognitive, physical, and social tasks; and able to cope with adversity. On the basis of existing research, three principles provide a framework to understand the complexity of young children's emotional lives and to address the challenges for research, policy, and practice (Shonkoff & Phillips, 2000; Zeanah, 2000).

The first principle recognizes that the mental health of infants and young children is best understood in the context of their primary caregiving and nurturing relationships. From very early on, infants and young children rely on the social interactions with their caregivers to help them understand and manage their own feelings, strengthen their sense of competency and efficacy, and learn skills for later, more externally oriented social interactions. Children with insecure, coercive, or otherwise troubled attachments may be at significant risk for mental health problems.

The second principle recognizes the interdependence of parents and children and that infants and young children's mental health functioning is embedded within the broader relational contexts of family and family life circumstances. As such, it is important to adopt a whole-child and whole-family approach to early childhood mental health and development.

The third principle recognizes that because infants and young children are so dependent on their environments for the opportunity to develop competently, any discussion of early childhood mental health must include a careful consideration of the interdependent and active contexts of biology, relationships, and culture. Stated so aptly by Shonkoff and Phillips (2000), "a child's responses to the family, neighborhood, and the culture hinge significantly on genetically based ways of feeling, interpreting, and responding to environmental events" (p. 55).

Developmental Theory and Research: What Researchers Know About the Mental Health of Young Children

Although the mental health of young children has been a comparatively neglected field in both scientific inquiry and intervention research, in the past 2 decades researchers and scholars have gained knowledge to appreciate the intricacy and intensity of emotional development in children's early years and to identify the contexts that benefit or compromise children's trajectories for healthy emotional development. Developmental theory and research offer several frameworks that, together, provide the scientific basis for understanding children's early social and emotional development, their trajectories, and their impact on later mental health and socioemotional well-being.

Theoretical Perspectives

Ecological and transactional theories and the tenets of developmental psychopathology inform our conceptualization of infant mental health and guide the principles and recommendations set forth in this chapter. Bronfenbrenner's ecological theory (Bronfenbrenner, 1986, 1995) provides a framework for embedding young children's development within multiple interacting levels of the environment that affect development. Although expanded to include biological influences, the main emphasis remains on five environmental systems that range from unique, direct interactions between individuals within the family system to the global cultural and historical settings in which development takes place. Consistent with ecological theory, Sameroff's transactional model (e.g., Sameroff, 1995) highlights the active role of the child and the importance of viewing young children within the environmental contexts in which they reside, learn, and play. The transactional model traces the ways in which genetic and acquired characteristics of children interact, or transact, over time, with characteristics of their environment to influence later child outcomes.

The principles of developmental psychopathology that are most relevant for conceptualizing infants', toddlers', and preschoolers' mental health include the following: (a) the study of normative development informs psychologists' understanding of psychopathological development, and reciprocally, the study of psychopathology deepens this understanding of normative development; (b) individual differences in normative and atypical functioning must be examined in the context of stage salient tasks, normative transitions, and broader ecological risks; (c) normative and atypical development are best understood when multiple risk factors and multiple developmental domains are assessed; and (d) developmental psychopathology is concerned with longitudinal change with respect to both continuities and discontinuities in development (Cicchetti, 1990).

Research Perspectives

The study of threats to children's mental health has shifted dramatically from a focus on vulnerability and risk factors to an increasing emphasis on resilience and protective factors. Three types of protective factors emerge as recurrent themes in the diverse group of studies cited in the literature: (a) dispositional attributes of young children that elicit positive responses from their environments, (b) affectional ties and interactions within families, and (c) external support systems. Researchers have also found a shifting and intricate balance between resilience and vulnerability that depends on complex interactions among young children's constitutional characteristics, children's developmental stages, environmental circumstances, family relationships and processes, and the larger social context in which young children live (Masten & Garmezy, 1985; Werner, 1990). Research evidence suggests that the most significant threats to young children's mental health are poverty, parental depression and mental illness, and other parental psychosocial risks.

POVERTY. Poverty is a known risk factor for negative outcomes for children's mental health. Across all classifications, poverty has consistently shown strong associations with critical aspects of child development, including social and emotional development (Shonkoff & Phillips, 2000). One significant public health issue in the United States is the fact that more than 8 million children under age 5 live in families with incomes below 200% of the official poverty level and 19% of children under age 5 live in families with incomes below the poverty level (U.S. Census Bureau, 2003).

The effects of poverty on young children's social and emotional development can be seen in the higher levels of mental health problems that poor children exhibit (Brooks-Gunn & Duncan, 1997). Evidence has demonstrated that poverty affects young children's mental health through a large variety of mechanisms. Macrolevel effects have been thoroughly explored by research on poverty and young children's mental health. Poor families often do not have access to or the ability to afford resources that can contribute to healthy social and emotional development, such as high-quality child care and consultations with mental health professionals; environments in which poor children live are often harmful; and treatment costs can be prohibitive for low-income families (Aber, Jones, & Cohen, 2000). Research in this area has also examined the negative effects of poverty on family processes and parenting behaviors and their impact on young children's social and emotional development, such as increased rates of marital discord, parental irritability and hostility, and harsh discipline practices (Elder, Eccles, Ardelt, & Lord, 1995; Shonkoff & Phillips, 2000).

PARENTAL DEPRESSION AND MENTAL ILLNESS. Parental depression is a significant threat to young children's healthy social and emotional development because of the potential intensity of its effects on child development, particularly when present in the context of additional ecological risk factors, and because of the high prevalence of depression among mothers with young children (Lyons-Ruth, Wolfe, Lyubchik, Steingard, 2002; Young, Davis, Schoen, & Parker, 1998). The effects of maternal depression are evident very early in life and span a wide range of outcomes: infants of depressed mothers are less likely to engage in exploratory or active play and more likely to exhibit a generalized negative affect toward others, have a more muted interactive style, have lower scores on developmental assessments on the Bayley developmental tests, and be insecurely attached (Goodman & Gotlib, 1999).

Maternal depression affects later social and emotional outcomes for children as well. Children of depressed mothers are more likely to display poorer social competence, are more prone to helpless behaviors, and more often demonstrate impaired problem-solving abilities. Other studies have found that children of depressed mothers are at risk for poor emotional regulation strategies, lower self-esteem, more fear and anxiety, and more externalizing and aggressive behaviors than children of nondepressed mothers (Hammen, Gordon, Burge, Jaenicke, & Hiroto, 1987) and are at higher risk of developing serious psychopathology (Lyons-Ruth et al., 2002).

Although the deleterious impact of maternal depression on a wide range of children's outcomes has been documented, the mechanisms whereby maternal depression confers risk are not well understood. Possible mechanisms include the following: (a) genetic transmission of general temperamental attributes or genes for specific psychopathology, (b) prenatal exposure to heightened maternal stress, (c) suboptimal parenting practices, (d) risk factors in the broader interpersonal context (e.g., marital discord, limited social supports), and (e) concomitant psychopathology in the mother or the family (Carter, Garrity-Rokous, Chazan-Cohen, Little, & Briggs-Gowan, 2001).

OTHER PARENTAL PSYCHOSOCIAL RISKS. Many investigators have called attention to the life circumstances that often co-vary with a diagnosis of maternal depression. Factors such as low socioeconomic status, marital discord, poor parent–child interactions, parental substance abuse, family violence, and increased psychosocial stress are common in parents experiencing depression and put young children at risk for seriously compromised psychosocial development and increased risk for social and emotional developmental impairment and mental illness (Knitzer, 2000a; Shonkoff & Phillips, 2000). Even in the absence of parental mental health problems, young children in poverty are also more likely to be exposed to combinations of risk factors that are associated with higher rates of emotional and behavioral disorders such as disadvantageous parental marital or employment status, low educational attainment level of parents, environmental health risks, community effects, and lack of access to health and other services (Aber et al., 2000).

Prevention and Intervention Research

Early childhood preventive intervention research is broadly defined by three types of interventions: preventive interventions that are targeted to low-income children and families, early intervention programs targeted to children with documented disabilities, and prevention programs that are targeted to new parents. Typically, these interventions (a) are derived from normative theories, (b) recognize that relationships with primary caregivers have a primary impact on early development, and (c) seek to affect young children directly through structured experiences or the caregiving environment. Although there is a generally accepted conceptual foundation, the empirical knowledge base on the efficacy of early childhood intervention is mixed (Shonkoff & Phillips, 2000). Notwithstanding methodological and design issues, quality comprehensive early childhood interventions targeting poor children have shown short-term improved cognitive performance as well as longer term gains marked by increased work experience and decreased involvement with juvenile or adult criminal activity (Reynolds, Temple, Robertson, & Mann, 2001). Research on home-visiting programs for low-income families has shown a pattern of mixed effects (Gomby, Culross, & Behrman, 1999).

Preventive Interventions and Social and Emotional Issues

Perhaps most striking is that, typically, the body of research on preventive interventions includes neither outcome measurements related to social and emotional competencies or analyses of the impact of the intervention on subgroups of children who are at risk or who are already showing signs of social–emotional delay or behavioral disturbance. Fortunately, this is beginning to change. For example, the Early Head Start evaluation is documenting modest but important gains about the impact of this two-generation intervention on young children's social and emotional development and the prevention of problems (Love et al., 2002). With 17 programs (center, home, or a combination) and more than 3,000 families, the evaluation documented that the children showed improved language and cognitive outcomes and had lower ratings of aggressive behavior. By age 3, the children were also more able to engage their parents, were less negative with their parents, and were more attentive in play than the control children. Mothers of children enrolled in Early Head Start were less detached and showed fewer negative parenting behaviors compared with control parents; enrolled fathers engaged in fewer spankings and less intrusive interactions. These effects, however, varied depending on the nature of the program, with the mixed programs showing the best balance of positive cognitive and social–emotional outcomes

Early Head Start researchers have also conducted analyses of the impact of the intervention on subgroups of parents and children especially vulnerable to poor social and emotional outcomes. For example, research on teen parent families showed that the teens were more likely to increase school attendance, and there were positive developmental impacts on their young children, something not found in most other teen-focused interventions. Research on parents showing signs of depression also shows a positive impact from being involved in Early Head Start. Families facing more than three demographic risks, however, do not show the same pattern of gains, and on some outcome measures, worsen.

Although carried out on a far smaller scale, some of the patterns of findings in the Early Head Start data have also been replicated in research carried out on children and families participating in Starting Early Starting Smart (SESS). Carried out in 11 Head Start, child-care, and primary health care settings, the intervention at each site involved some mix of four core services: family–parenting services, child development services, mental health services, and substance abuse services. Preliminary data suggest not just reductions in aggressive behavior but also increased verbal and cognitive skills and improved parent–child relationships (Casey Family Programs & U.S. Department of Health and Human Services, 2001).

Reports accumulated from other interventions complement the lessons from Early Head Start and SESS and shed light on the effective delivery of relationship-based interventions to parents. For example, the Keys to Caregiving intervention tested the efficacy of two contrasting service approaches to families for whom traditional home-visiting nursing were ineffective. One focused on decreasing the mother's sense of isolation and increasing her sense of competence, the other focused on transmitting knowledge; the relationship-based approach yielded significantly more positive effects (Barnard, Morisset, & Spieker, 1993).

Another example of relationship-based intervention is Healthy Steps for Young Children (McLearn, Zuckerman, Parker, Yellowitz, & Kaplan-Sanoff, 1998). This national experiment incorporates child developmental specialists and enhanced developmental services into pediatric primary care. Evidence suggests that Healthy Steps parents improved their parenting behaviors around child safety and book-sharing activities, reduced their use of physical punishment practices, and began to interact more positively with their young children (Minkovitz et al., 2003).

For preschool-age children in Head Start, the Incredible Years: Parent, Teacher, and Child Training Series, in which parents and Head Start teachers work through a curriculum that has grown out of clinical work with aggressive children, has documented positive results for parenting practices with parents who themselves have experienced multiple risks (e.g., abuse or foster care; Baydar, Reid, & Webster-Stratton, 2003). Encouragingly, there is an increasing amount of research on explicit interventions designed for young children and parents already identified as having serious problems. These include preliminary research on manualized interventions, targeted to high-risk parents of infants and toddlers, that focus on parent–child relationships and assist parents in becoming more attuned and responsive to their young children (McDonough, 2000).

Toward the Future of Intervention Research on Social and Emotional Issues

Even though the research reported here is important and groundbreaking, it is still preliminary and continually points to challenges that desperately need to be overcome to help vulnerable young children and families more effectively. There are critical questions that need to guide the next generation of intervention research: (a) How can the trinity of parental risks (i.e., substance abuse, domestic violence, and maternal depression) be addressed in the context of early intervention; (b) how can intervention programs help adults and transform impaired parent–child relationships; (c) what kind of training and support to staff can assist the promotion of more positive trajectories in children whose early experiences have been compromised; (d) how can the impact of early interventions best document young children's early achievement when they enter school; and (e) what will be most effective in making the case for resource investments and funding? Developmental research suggests that social and emotional development is foundational for later development. But only intervention research can help the field develop the tools and strategies needed to repair the foundation when it is shaky.

Making Mental Health a Full Partner in Healthy Child Development: Research and Policy Priorities

Advances in developmental and intervention research have increased our understanding of the complexity of young children's mental health. As such, both provide promising directions and challenges for future research and have clear implications for policy and practice.

Research Challenges

Despite incorporation of a focus on social–emotional, behavioral, and mental health outcomes within the earliest phases of Head Start, it is only recently that researchers are addressing the mental health needs of very young children. Indeed, only in the last 10 years have assessment instruments become available that allow researchers to gather systematic data on the prevalence of young child behavior problems and social–emotional competencies. Parent and child-care report questionnaires (e.g., Child Behavior Checklist 1.5-5 [Achenbach & Rescorla, 2000], the Infant–Toddler Social and Emotional Assessment [Carter, Briggs-Gowan, Jones, & Little, 2003]) and a diagnostic interview, the Preschool Age Psychiatric Assessment (Egger & Angold, 2004), are available for dissemination. Among the many research challenges facing the field, we highlight the following four: (a) developing guidelines to synthesize information across informants and methods of data collection, (b) documenting the mental health needs of young children and their families, (c) using intervention science to move beyond correlational studies to experimental model testing, and (d) demonstrating the benefits of early detection and intervention.

INTEGRATING INFORMATION ACROSS ASSESSMENT METHODOLOGIES AND INFORMANTS. Despite significant gains in the assessment of early emerging social–emotional and behavior problems and disorders in early childhood (Del Carmen-Wiggins & Carter, 2004), there are few guidelines for integrating the multiple sources of information that are necessary to complete a thorough evaluation of a young child's mental health status. There is now consensus that evaluation of infant, toddler, and preschool children's mental health must attend to contextual factors such as parent–child relationships and culture, as well as to the temperamental, regulatory, and developmental characteristics of the child, and focus attention on both strengths and weaknesses within the child and caregiving systems (Del Carmen-Wiggins & Carter, 2004). Further, because young children cannot provide self-report data and parents may offer biased reports of their children's behaviors, observation is a critical facet of young child assessment. Developing systematic strategies for integrating multi-informant, multimethod assessments is critical for identifying children at risk for and exhibiting psychopathology.

DOCUMENTING THE MENTAL HEALTH NEEDS OF VERY YOUNG CHILDREN. Epidemiological studies are now needed to document young child mental health needs and current service utilization. Extant studies indicate that rates of a mental health disorder approach those of older children (Briggs-Gowan et al., 2001) and highlight the lack of mental health services in this age range (Horwitz et al., 2003). However, to date no epidemiological studies of very young children's mental health needs have been conducted. As the boundary between typical and atypical functioning may vary with developmental and contextual constraints, epidemiological studies of very young children need to attend to variations in normative and psychopathological functioning in the context of stage salient tasks and broader ecological risks (Sroufe, 1990) and include longitudinal components to examine the role of competencies and assets in parental and child mental health trajectories. There is consensus that the number of children entering kindergarten who are ill prepared to learn because of behavioral difficulties is a public health crisis (e.g., Huffman et al., 2000; U.S. Public Health Service, 2000). There is also consensus regarding the value of early intervention to minimize the consolidation of maladaptive behavior problems (cf. Fox, Dunlap, & Cushing, 2002). Only with the appropriate data can developmental psychologists advocate for and develop an adequate national policy response to this crisis.

USING EXPERIMENTAL MODEL TESTING. The vast majority of our knowledge regarding the impact of risk factors on young children's social–emotional and behavioral development is based on correlational studies of children living in a range of conditions of risk. Both cumulative risk and individual risk models have been studied, and all indicate strong associations between the number of sociodemographic and psychosocial risks that young children experience and the emergence and maintenance of behavior problems and delays in the acquisition of competence (cf. Sameroff, Seifer, & McDonough, 2004). What is needed is a much stronger emphasis on model testing through experimental assignment to combinations of community, family, and child interventions. By studying the impact of treatment response, it is possible to gain greater insights into the role of specific risk factors on specific child outcomes as well as the impact of children's increased social competence on maternal depressive symptoms. Moreover, there is a paucity of interventions that address the deleterious impact of community poverty and violence (Ceballo, 2000). Investment in creative ecologically based initiatives is needed. It is notable that Zigler has not only been an advocate for Head Start and other programs that enhance child development but also a consistent advocate for high-quality evaluation.

DEMONSTRATING THE BENEFITS OF EARLY DETECTION AND INTERVENTION ACROSS THE MULTIPLE CONTEXTS IN WHICH CHILDREN CAN BE SERVED. Studies are needed to document the benefits of implementing widespread early detection and intervention efforts. Consistent with the evidence currently available that demonstrates cost savings associated with prevention programs that target low-income families having their first child (Olds, Henderson, & Cole, 1998), it is likely that both benefits to children's development and cost savings in later special education and juvenile justice system spending will be documented by further studies. Studies documenting the advantages of early detection and intervention are needed to shape policies that support early detection efforts as well as to highlight the need for professional training about young child mental health among pediatric, psychology, and social work practitioners.

Challenges for Policy and Practice

Research suggests that promoting the social and emotional resilience of young children should be a high priority on the early childhood agenda. But to achieve this many policy and practice challenges must be overcome. Some of these are long-standing challenges; for example, maximizing the use of existing resources in ways that promote healthy social and emotional development and strategically allocating new resources. Some challenge professional mindsets that minimize the reality of social and emotional problems in young children. Other challenges are more recent ones; for example, the growing tendency to equate school readiness only with the cognitive aspects of early literacy, ignoring the powerful evidence that early literacy involves achieving age-appropriate developmental milestones across multiple domains. Despite the fact that many of these challenges are daunting, there is evidence that all across this country, states and communities are trying to respond. Although there is limited research on most of these system-building efforts (see Exhibit 14.1), researchers are generating

Exhibit 14.1. Principles to Guide Early Childhood Mental Health Practice and Policy

---

- Programs need to be individualized to meet varying child and family needs and cultural contexts; there can be no "one size fits all."
- Support systems and services must be based on developmental knowledge and utilize relationship-based approaches to foster healthy relationships.
- Community-based early childhood delivery systems must be infused with the capacities to address mental health needs of children and families.
- The development of an early childhood mental health infrastructure must be grounded in efforts to support and strengthen families and incorporate a two-generation approach.
- To develop a sustainable infrastructure, attention to fiscal strategies is as important as is attention to program and clinical strategies.
- Attention to outcomes, particularly those linked to school readiness, is critical to incorporate into any planning and implementation processes.
- Programs and policies must be sensitive to the stigma associated with mental health issues and attempt to build awareness about the social and emotional development of young children.

---

principles and yielding practical guidelines to guide early childhood mental health policy and practice (Knitzer, 2000b).

As one example, the state of Vermont, in response to the high percentage of third-grade children not reading at grade level, used a federal children's mental health program called the Children's UPstream Services Program to jumpstart early childhood mental health planning and service delivery statewide. Drawing on the powerful body of research and incorporating the guiding principles listed in Exhibit 14.1, the following are six steps for policymakers, service providers, and researchers to promote early social and emotional development in children.

1. Ensure family economic security. Research suggests that improving family economic security either through increased income, improved work supports (such as certain access to child care and health care benefits), or increased assets tends to improve child outcomes. The converse is also true, the first line of defense in promoting strong, healthy young children and families is the creation of policies to ensure that families have adequate resources to raise their children. Thus the first line of defense in promoting strong, healthy families is the creation of policies to ensure that families have adequate resources to raise their children.

2. Increase capacity of early childhood programs to address social and emotional development. Early childhood care is a critical entry point for systematic interventions. These systems must be infused with the capacity to promote emotional wellness, intervene quickly, and address the mental health needs of the most vulnerable. This requires that developmental psychologists expand and train the workers who have a direct relationship with families and young children. Those who work with young children need trained mentors and consultants available to help them navigate the muddy and turbulent waters of emotional development in young children.

3. Expand prevention-oriented and relationship-based mental health systems in the early childhood community. The message from the science of early childhood is that the nature of early relationships has lasting effects—for better or for worse. State and community infrastructure is needed for effective expansion of systems that foster healthy early relationships. Research from Early Head Start suggests that a sound investment would be to rapidly expand Early Head Start to all low-income young children.

4. Enhance capacity of the primary health care system. The child health care system is uniquely positioned to offer behavioral and developmental health care services because pediatric offices are visited often by families with infants and young children. Pediatric primary care participation in the social and emotional development of young children could provide possibilities for early prevention and intervention activities for both children and families, and allow continued collaboration to ensure that services are individualized, efficient, and effective.

5. Address fiscal and administrative barriers that prevent the development of more responsive strategies. Existing funding streams, especially Medicaid, need to be more responsive to the developmental realities of young children, especially incorporating more flexibility in terms of diagnosis requirements. Funding streams must be created for screening and interventions for children facing multiple risks. In addition, partnerships and funding mechanisms for collaboration between adult mental health and substance abuse systems and early childhood mental health are required.

6. Promote state and federal legislation for resilience-promoting services for young children at risk. Young children in families facing multiple risks are the least likely to meet the public policy goal of ensuring that every child enters school ready to succeed. However, to date, early childhood mental health challenges are largely hidden from the policy community. The current policy framework must be restructured to maximize the impact of current resources and to remove the barriers that require medical diagnosis as the point of entry for services.

In this chapter, we have described the necessity of understanding and addressing young children's mental health in the context of environments and relationships. These principles are also essential for the future of efforts that seek to promote social and emotional development and prevent mental health problems in young children. Change must happen in multiple contexts, but the challenge for all is to take children's social and emotional development and mental health as seriously as children's cognitive development and physical health. As long as research, programs, and policies neglect to make mental health a full partner in young children's healthy development, children and their families will continue to fall through the cracks. Ever the pragmatic optimist, Zigler wrote that attending to the mental health of young children "is far from a sentimental leaning; . . .[it] is good science, good business and good politics" (Zigler, Hopper, & Hall, 1993, p. 490). We are in complete agreement.

References

Aber, J. L., Jones, S., & Cohen J. (2000). The impact of poverty on the mental health and development of very young children. In C. H. Zeanah Jr. (Ed.), *Handbook of infant mental health* (2nd ed., pp. 113–128). New York: Guilford Press.

Achenbach, T. M., & Rescorla, L. A. (2000). *Manual for the ASEBA preschool forms and profiles.* Burlington: University of Vermont.

American Pyschiatric Association. (2000). *Diagnostic and statistical manual of mental disorders* (4th ed., text rev.). Washington, DC: Author.

Barnard, K. E., Morisset, C. E., & Spieker, S. J. (1993). Preventive interventions: Enhancing parent-infant relationships. In C. H. Zeanah (Ed.), *Handbook on infant mental health* (pp. 386–401). New York: Guilford Press.

Baydar, N., Reid, M. J., & Webster-Stratton, C. (2003). The role of mental health factors and program engagement in the effectiveness of a preventive program for Head Start mothers. *Child Development 74,* 1433–1453.

Briggs-Gowan, M. J., Carter, A. S., Skuban, E. M., & Horwitz, S. M. (2001). Prevalence of social–emotional and behavioral problems in a community sample of 1- and 2-year-olds. *Journal of the American Academy of Child and Adolescent Psychiatry, 40,* 811–819.

Bronfenbrenner, U. (1986). Ecology of the family as a context for human development: Research perspectives. *Developmental Psychology, 22,* 723–742.

Bronfenbrenner, U. (1995). The bioecological model from a life course perspective. In P. Moen, G. H. Elder, & K. Luscher (Eds.), *Examining lives in context* (pp. 599–618). Washington, DC: American Psychological Association.

Brooks-Gunn, J., & Duncan, G. J. (1997). The effects of poverty on children. *The Future of Children, 7*(2), 55–71.

Carter, A. S., Briggs-Gowan, M., Jones, S. M., & Little, T. (2003). The Infant-Toddler Social and Emotional Assessment (ITSEA): Factor structure, reliability, and validity. *Journal of Abnormal Child Psychology, 31,* 495–514.

Carter, A. S., Garrity-Rokous, F. E., Chazan-Cohen, R., Little, C., & Briggs-Gowan, M. J. (2001). Maternal depression and comorbidity: Predicting early parenting, attachment security, and toddler social-emotional problems and competencies. *Journal of the American Academy of Child and Adolescent Psychiatry, 40,* 18–26.

Casey Family Programs & U.S. Department of Health and Human Services. (2001). *Starting Early Starting Smart: Summary of early findings.* Washington, DC: Author.

Ceballo, R. (2000). The neighborhood club: A supportive intervention group for children exposed to urban violence. *American Journal of Orthopsychiatry, 70,* 401–407.

Cicchetti, D. (1990). An historical perspective on the discipline of developmental psychology. In J. Rold, A. Mastter, D. Cicchetti, K. Neuchterlein, & S. Weinthraub (Eds.), *Risk and protective factors in the development of psychopathology* (pp. 2–28). New York: Cambridge University Press.

Cohen, D., Solnit, A., & Wohlford, P. (1979). Mental health services in Head Start. In E. Zigler & J. Valentine (Eds.), *Project Head Start* (pp. 259–290). New York: Free Press.

Del Carmen-Wiggins, R., & Carter, A. S. (Eds.). (2004). *Handbook of infant, toddler, and preschool mental health assessment.* Oxford, England: Oxford University Press.

Egger, H. L., & Angold, A. (2004). The Preschool Age Psychiatric Assessment (PAPA): A structured parent interview for diagnosing psychiatric disorders in preschool children. In R. Del Carmen & A. S. Carter (Eds.), *Handbook of infant, toddler and preschool mental health assessment* (pp. 223–243). Oxford, England: Oxford University Press.

Elder, G. H., Eccles, J. S., Ardelt, M., & Lord, S. (1995). Inner-city parents under economic pressure: Perspective on the strategies of parenting. *Journal of Marriage and Family, 57,* 771–784.

Fox, L., Dunlap, G., & Cushing, L. (2002). Early intervention, positive behavior support, and transition to school. *Journal of Emotional and Behavioral Disorders, 10,* 149–157.

Gomby, D. S., Culross, P. L., & Behrman, R. E. (Eds.). (1999). Home visiting: Recent program evaluations. *The Future of Children, 9*(1), 4–26.

Goodman, S. H., & Gotlib, I. H. (1999). Risk for psychopathology in the children of depressed mothers: A developmental model for understanding mechanisms of transmission. *Psychological Review, 106,* 458–490.

Hammen, C., Gordon, G., Burge, D., Jaenicke, C., & Hiroto, D. (1987). Maternal affective disorders, illness, and stress: Risk of children's psychopathology. *American Journal of Psychiatry, 144,* 736–741.

Horwitz, S. M., Gary, L. M., Briggs-Gowan, M., & Carter, A. S. (2003). Do needs drive services or do services drive needs? *Pediatrics, 112*, 1373–1378.

Huffman, L. C., Mehlinger, S. L., Kerivan, A. S., Cavanaugh, D. A., Lippitt, J., & Moyo, O. (2000). *Off to a good start: Research on the risk factors for early school problems and selected federal policies affecting children's social and emotional development and their readiness for school.* Chapel Hill: University of North Carolina, FPG Child Development Center.

Knitzer, J. (2000a). *Promoting resilience: Helping young children and parents affected by substance abuse, domestic violence and depression in the context of welfare reform.* New York: The National Center for Children in Poverty, Mailman School of Public Health, Columbia University.

Knitzer, J. (2000b). Using early childhood mental health services through a policy and systems development perspective. In J. P. Shonkoff & S. J. Miesels (Eds.), *Handbook of early childhood intervention* (2nd ed., pp. 416–438). New York: Cambridge University Press.

Lavigne, J. V., Gibbons, R. D., Christoffel, K. K., Arend, R., Rosenbaum, D., Binns, H., et al. (1996). Prevalence rates and correlates of psychiatric disorders among preschool children. *Journal of the American Academy of Child and Adolescent Psychiatry, 35*, 204–214.

Love, J. M., Kisker, E. E., Ross, C. M., Schochet, P. Z., Brooks-Gunn, J., Paulsell, D., et al. (2002). *Making a difference in the lives of infants and toddlers and their families: The impacts of Early Head Start.* Washington, DC: U.S. Department of Health and Human Services.

Lyons-Ruth, K., Wolfe, R., Lyubchik, A., & Steingard, R. (2002). Depressive symptoms in parents of children under age 3: Sociodemographic predictors, current correlates, and associated parenting behaviors. In N. Halfon, K. T. McLearn, & M. A. Schuster (Eds.), *Child rearing in America* (pp. 217–259). New York: Cambridge University Press.

Masten, A. S., & Garmezy, N. (1985). Risk, vulnerability and protective factors in developmental psychology. In B. B. Lahey & A. E. Kazdin (Eds.), *Advances in child clinical psychology* (Vol. 8, pp. 1–52). New York: Plenum Press.

McDonough, S. C. (2000). Interaction guidance: An approach for difficult-to-engage families. In C. H. Zeanah (Ed.), *Handbook of infant mental health* (2nd ed., pp. 485–493). New York: Guilford Press.

McLearn, K. T., Zuckerman, B. S., Parker, S., Yellowitz, M., & Kaplan-Sanoff, M. (1998). Child development and pediatrics for the 21st century: The Healthy Steps approach. *Journal of Urban Health: Bulletin of the New York Academy of Medicine, 75*, 704–723.

Minkovitz, C. S., Hughart, N., Strobino, D., Scharfstein, D., Grason, H., Hou, W., et al. (2003). A practice-based intervention to enhance quality of care in the first three years of life: Results from the Healthy Steps for Young Children Program. *Journal of the American Medical Association, 290*, 3081–3091.

Olds, D., Henderson, C. R., & Cole, R. (1998). Long-term effects of nurse home visitation on children's criminal and antisocial behavior: 15-year follow-up of a randomized controlled trial. *Journal of the American Medical Association, 280*, 1238–1244.

Piotrkowski, C. S., Collins, R. C., Knitzer, J., & Robinson, R. (1994). Strengthening mental health services in Head Start: A challenge for the 1990s. *American Psychologist, 49*, 133–139.

Reynolds, A. J., Temple, J. A., Robertson, D. L., & Mann, E. A. (2001). Long-term effects of an early childhood intervention on educational achievement and juvenile arrest: A 15-year follow-up of low-income children in public schools. *Journal of the American Medical Association, 285*, 2330–2346.

Sameroff, A. J. (1995). General systems theories and developmental psychopathology. In D. Cicchetti & D. J. Cohen (Eds), *Developmental psychopathology: Vol. 1. Theory and methods* (pp. 659–695). New York: Wiley.

Sameroff, A., Seifer, R., & McDonough, S. C. (2004). Contextual contributors to the assessment of infant mental health. In R. Del Carmen-Wiggins & A. S. Carter (Eds.), *Handbook of infant and young child mental health assessment* (pp. 61–76). Oxford, England: Oxford University Press.

Shonkoff, J. P., & Phillips, D. A. (Eds.). (2000). *From neurons to neighborhoods: The science of early child development.* Washington, DC: National Academy Press.

Song, Y., & Lu, H. (2002). *Child poverty fact sheet.* New York: The National Center for Children in Poverty, Mailman School of Public Health, Columbia University.

Sroufe, L. A. (1990). Considering normal and abnormal together: The essence of developmental psychopathology. *Development and Psychopathology, 2,* 335–347.

U.S. Census Bureau. (2003). People in families by family structure, age, and sex, iterated by income-to-poverty ratio and race. *Current Population Survey, 2003 Annual Social and Economic Supplement.* Retrieved November 21, 2003, from http://ferret.bls.census.gov/macro/032003/pov/new02_000.htm

U.S. Public Health Service. (2000). *Report of the Surgeon General's Conference on Children's Mental Health: A national action agenda.* Washington, DC: U.S. Department of Health and Human Services.

Werner, E. E. (1990). Protective factors and individual resilience. In S. J. Meisels & J. P. Shonkoff (Eds.), *Handbook of early childhood intervention* (pp. 97–115). New York: Cambridge University Press.

Young, K. T., Davis, K., Schoen, C., & Parker, S. (1998). Listening to parents: A national survey of parents with young children. *Archives of Pediatric and Adolescent Medicine, 152,* 255–262.

Zeanah, C. H., Jr. (2000). *Handbook of infant mental health* (2nd ed.). New York: Guilford Press.

Zigler, E. (1963). Metatheoretical issues in developmental psychology. In M. Marx (Ed.), *Theories in contemporary psychology* (pp. 341–369). New York: Macmillan.

Zigler, E., Hopper, P., & Hall, N. W. (1993). Infant mental health and social policy. In C. H. Zeanah Jr. (Ed.), *Handbook of infant mental health* (pp. 480–492). New York: Guilford Press.

15

Family Support: A Force for Change

Sharon Lynn Kagan and Bernice Weissbourd

Early on in my family support efforts, I adopted the principle that we shouldn't force millions of families to fit themselves to our programs, but rather make our programs as comprehensive and as family-friendly as possible.

—Edward F. Zigler (2002, p. 20)

Family support began as a grassroots movement, created by and for practitioners who run programs. Although supported and advanced by academics, including Edward Zigler, its pulse is not academic or theoretical in orientation; rather, family support etched its way on to the practice landscape, emerging as a robust, vital social phenomenon. Following suit, scholarly efforts to define family support, to delimit its parameters, to clarify its intentions, and to evaluate its success have emerged. In this chapter we provide a synopsis of the field, focusing on the challenges it faces and the efforts needed to support its continuing advancement. We summarize the definitional challenges and history of family support, discuss the most trenchant issues, and provide perspectives on the next steps for family support theory and practice.

The Definition and History of Family Support

The term *family support* is widely used but with very different meanings (Kagan & Shelly, 1987; Singer, Powers, & Olson, 1996). At one point in our social history, family support was the shorthand name for welfare (Moroney, 1987). Indeed, one reauthorization of welfare legislation was called the Family Support Act. In this context, family support was considered to focus primarily on poverty populations. More generically, the term *family support* refers to a broad array of social services that enhance family well-being. Using this frame, family support embraces social services, health services, mental health services, and education—a cadre of services that is not limited to poverty populations. From another perspective, family support has been used in conjunction with

The authors gratefully acknowledge the wonderfully helpful research and editorial assistance provided by Amy Lowenstein of the National Center for Children and Families, Teachers College, Columbia University.

environmental, transportation, housing, and economic development policies because each of these has impact on, and provides supports to, the family. Finally, from an international perspective, the term *family support* is often used to encapsulate diverse policies proffered by a society, including family leave, income supports, social insurances, and child allowance policies that, depending on the nation, may or may not focus on targeted populations.

In the late 1970s and early 1980s, when grassroots providers of a new and renegade type of service came together, they dubbed their efforts "family support" (Weissbourd, 1987). In adopting this terminology, hindsight suggests they did their work a great service and disservice simultaneously. In service to their efforts, the literal nomenclature *family support* suggests exactly what the programs purported to do, support families—all types of families. And because the range of services being provided was very diverse, such a general term seemed like a wise choice to brand what was hoped would become a large-scale national effort. Conversely, the use of the broad term *family support* to explicate this more limited ideology and approach to service provision has proven—as just noted—confusing at best and illusive at worst.

For the purposes of this chapter, and to chronicle Zigler's work, we use the term *family support* to discuss a rather circumscribed philosophy that manifests itself in diverse programs and services. Designed for poor and nonpoor individuals, grassroots family support efforts share a common set of principles that find operational expression in five primary program types. Defining *family support* as we use it in this chapter, therefore, demands that we discuss, first, a set of principles that frame family support efforts and, second, describe five service-delivery types that are most often associated with these principles.

Principles

Unlike, and established in response to, conventional service-delivery characteristics that prevailed at the time, family support principles include the following:

- staff and families working together in relationships based on equality and respect;
- staff enhancing families' capacities to support the growth of all family members;
- families acting as resources to their own and other families as well as communities;
- programs strengthening families' cultural, racial, and linguistic identities;
- programs supporting the development of their communities;
- programs acting as advocates for fair, responsible, and accountable services;
- programs remaining flexible to accommodate changing family needs; and
- program staff acting as resources to families.

Service-Delivery Types

In reality, and complicating the definition, these principles are not limited to one type of service or even one discipline. Indeed, contemporary family support finds itself at home in multiple settings, using multiple mechanisms for translating the principles into action (Diehl, 2002; Mason, 2003), with five primary service-delivery types.

First, family support principles may be carried out in family support centers. These centers are physical entities that offer a cadre of outreach and support services. They also provide environments for families and for families and children together that may be located in a housing project, a school, a library, or a self-contained facility. Family support centers may function independently, or they may be lodged within larger institutions; in this case they form the second type of family support service—family support programs nested within larger organizations. In these cases, the host programs often have primary missions that are broader than and allied with, but somewhat distinct from, family support. Examples include Boys and Girls Clubs, schools, and libraries. In these cases, the organization's values are compatible with family support, and often they append family support efforts to support their own institutional mission.

The third type of service delivery is organizations that adopt and work from the principles of family support practice but do not have special family support programs. Despite the fact that these host organizations may not elect to offer direct family support programs (characteristic of the second type), they alter their existing policies to reflect the principles of family support. For example, a child-care program may formally adopt family support principles and incorporate a family support ethos into all it does.

Like the third type, the fourth service-delivery type, community-level systems of family support, may not result in a single family support center or program being developed, but it may use principles of family support to guide its efforts—in this case community planning and mobilization efforts. For example, a community governance board might adopt principles of family support to which each of its local programs would adhere. A school board might adopt the principles of family support, with each local school deciding individually how to implement them.

The final manifestation of family support is family support at the workplace. In this service-delivery type, family support principles are adopted by businesses and corporations to support workers in managing work and family life. Often these arrangements include flexible work schedules and workplaces, child-care assistance, paid days off for volunteerism, and diversity training and related opportunities.

So, what began as a set of independent maverick programs has found expression in mainstream business, industry, public agencies, and private for-profit organizations. Family support, more than a network of programs, is becoming a way of thinking about how services might be delivered for all families. Defining *family support* as a field, then, remains challenging because it is constantly growing and changing. What binds the field is its unswerving commitment to the family support principles and to a new way of delivering services that respects diverse families and that honors their inherent capacities to nurture their children.

Framing Traditions and Disciplines

Although framed by pioneers, family support was firmly rooted in the traditions of the past. There is no need to reiterate the detailed history of the family support movement in America (Weissbourd, 1987, 1994). But to fully understand these unique efforts, it is helpful to review the institutions and disciplines that shaped family support.

From social work, family support drew a commitment to an ecological orientation and to supporting children and families within the context of the community. It drew from the urban settlement house movement, with its commitment to service, social reform, and advocacy. Its roots can also be traced to the self-help movement, with its commitment to validating and honoring individual strengths and contributions. From parent education, family support drew its commitment to two-generation services, to full cultural inclusion, and to developing the skills parents need to be advocates for themselves and their children (Smith, 1995).

With lesser force, family support was fueled by education and the need to engage families in schools and by education's commitment to life-long development. From community mental health, family support drew its commitment to family systems theory and its emphasis on the critical role of the family in preventing mental health problems. Child welfare contributed ideas about creating healthier environments for children and the development of community-based child abuse prevention services. And finally, family support took lessons from community development, stressing the need for developing social capital as well as economic capital.

To be sure, this amalgam of disciplines, theoretical dispositions, and services formed the base of family support. But what brought it to life? What made it a force on the social landscape that propelled hundreds of individuals from all states in the union, all ethnic backgrounds and religious persuasions to band together in this loosely configured field called family support? Much of the literature has traced the impetus for family support's emergence to three major factors: (a) evolving demographics, (b) sociopolitical trends, and (c) research. Changing demographics, including increases in family mobility, family isolation, teen parenting, poverty, social disruption, and community fragmentation, are well documented in the literature of the 1980s and 1990s (Dryfoos, 1994; Moynihan, 1986; Schulz, 1982; Steiner, 1981). As a result, more families needed support and conventional institutions, which were flooded with demand and could not meet their needs. The consequence was that family support emerged as an alternative to conventional service delivery. Simultaneously, a sociopolitical emphasis on personal responsibility and the importance of the family was being heralded across political lines. Families were encouraged to be self-reliant and not to depend on government. Family support, with its emphasis on self-help and peer support, gained currency in this sociopolitical context.

Fresh research emerged as a powerful impetus to the emergence of family support. Data revealed the benefits of an ecological orientation, one that suggests that the child is dramatically influenced by an entire social ecology that includes the family and community (Dunst, 1995). In contrast to scholars and practitioners who saw the unit of analysis or intervention as the child alone, family support conceptualized the family and the child together as the focus for change. Concurrently, data emerged that supported the viability of early childhood programs, noting not only their positive contributions to later development but their cost-effectiveness, too. Finally, an entire body of literature that focused on prevention and preventive strategies emerged (Cowan, 1977). In part because of their ability of preventive intervention to save taxpayer dollars and in part because of their ability to derail debilitating consequences of poverty, depression, unemployment, and other social sequelae, diverse types of prevention efforts drew much attention (Unger & Powell, 1990). All of this contributed to the social zeitgeist from which family support emerged.

Phases of Development

It is not at all surprising that chroniclers of the history of family support have talked about it in phases, almost akin to the phases of human development. In part, this orientation may exist because both human development and the development of family support pass through quite predictable phases, but phases that are not immune to powerful influence by both exogenous and endogenous factors. The "phase" construct might also be used to explain the historical evolution of family support because many of its scholars, Zigler foremost among them, are developmentalists, either by training or by exposure, so they would be inclined to see evolution as developmental in orientation.

The contemporary family support movement began modestly and inconspicuously, with individuals acting as program entrepreneurs. Often alone in their communities, these vanguard individuals understood that extant approaches to supporting families in large, impersonal institutions was not working. They knew that serving children in isolation from their home cultures, their families, and their neighborhoods was not working. In city after city, with almost no contact, these individuals set up neighborhood family support programs, often then called *family resource programs*. They provided information, support, and sometimes tangible resources. Not until 1981, when the Administration on Children, Youth, and Families provided a small grant to Family Focus (a pioneer family support program in Evanston, Illinois) did 200 of these pioneers come together. These individuals decided to form an organization that would support them and their work. Now called Family Support America, the organization was born in 1981 as the Family Resource Coalition. Other individuals became interested in the idea, including Edward Zigler, who, along with the Family Resource Coalition, sponsored a landmark conference and began chronicling existing programs (Zigler, Weiss, & Kagan, 1985). Indeed, Zigler's early endorsement of family support was extremely helpful in garnering the financial and ideological support for these still-embryonic efforts.

As family support programs flourished, involved individuals—filled with almost revolutionary zeal—recognized that in addition to freestanding family support programs, there was a need to lodge these programs, if not the principles they embodied, in mainstream institutions, most notably schools, human services entities, libraries, and health departments. Gradually these heretofore-strange services took hold in mainstream institutions, sometimes being merely tolerated and other times being embraced. In instances where the ideas of family support were embraced, institutional policies and actions often changed, rendering family support an agent of institutional reform. In other words, family support broadened from being a genre of direct services to providing the fodder for the reform of mainstream institutions. On an interesting and somewhat paradoxical note, when family support is most successful, it is often least observable and a part of the fabric of organizational culture.

As family support took hold, its branches expanded. No longer characterized by a set of programs and services, family support was altering mindsets and modi operandi. In the late 1980s and the early 1990s, the federal government began a large-scale federal initiative to advance both family support and family preservation (Weissbourd, 1994). Called the Family Preservation and Support Act of 1993, this legislation supported the development of programs as well as their evaluation. No longer the purview of a small band of revolutionaries, family support moved into the mainstream, bringing with its growth serious issues that command attention. With this history in mind, we turn to a discussion of contemporary issues affecting family support, suggesting that this genre of services is at a critical juncture.

Issues in Family Support

Many issues face those concerned about advancing family support. Among these, we discuss the following in this section: the ideological disjunct and the lack of support for prevention, family support as a service or a normative system, family support as a coherent professional field, and the absence of a national policy agenda.

The Ideological Disjunct and the Lack of Support for Prevention

> We have remarkable capacities to mobilize our creative skills to meet a crisis, but we do not utilize those same talents to prevent it.
>
> —Margaret Mead

Inherent in its fiber, family support is about the prevention of poor developmental outcomes and family dysfunction (Cameron & Vanderwoerd, 1997). Family support does not stand alone with its emphasis on prevention, but joins an increasing number of efforts that aim to prevent the negative consequences of, if not optimize, the social conditions of children and families (Weissberg, Gullotta, Hampton, Ryan, & Adams, 1997). Other manifestations of preventive services emerged in hospitals, where new parents learned about the abilities of the "amazing newborn," and in training institutions, where understanding infancy became as essential a component as understanding how school-age children learn. Indeed, so profound was this zeitgeist that prevention through early intervention began to grow.

Prevention, however, has not become as motivating a force in children's policy as was hoped. A crisis orientation that has long characterized U.S. policy is deeply embedded in our culture. For example, when the Family Preservation and Support Act of 1993 was replaced with the Adoption and Safe Families Act (1997; which focuses on adoption and time-limited family reunification), it represented a complete turnaround from the prevention orientation that characterized its forerunner (Barth, 1999). The justification for the turnaround was that there was insufficient research to bolster investments in prevention. In part, policymakers found it difficult to put resources into prevention services when there were so many children and families in dire situations crying out for help. Assuring that the prevention goal is not lost under the weight of immediate needs requires adequate funding for prevention programs, as well as the reorientation of services and policies toward this way of thinking. Overcoming this Herculean ideological disjunct between crisis and prevention orientations is the first critical challenge that requires concerted attention.

Family Support as a Service or a Normative System?

The second issue, one that directly stems from the crisis-versus-prevention issue, focuses on whether family support is seen as a special service for some (those in need or in crises) or as a normative service for all. In some circles, this issue is expressed as a targeted-versus-universal approach to family support. In actuality, we see the issue as one that transcends the scope of service delivery (the some-versus-all question) and is fundamental to the identity of family support itself. It raises the question of whether family support is framed from a normative (universal) or deficit (targeted) perspective.

Indeed, both approaches are taking hold. In some cities and states, family support is incorporated into school systems, therefore making family support services universally available. In other situations, family support is focused in communities that have the fewest resources or in those with particular populations in need (e.g., teen parents, ex-offenders and their families, children of single parents, and children being raised by grandparents). Although varied, these directions compose the fabric of family support and the foundation on which a comprehensive system can be built. They suggest that both targeted and universal strategies are needed.

Family Support as a Coherent Professional Field

Given growth, any field must face the question of its identity, its coherence, and its professionalism. Nowhere could this be more true than of contemporary family support. Looking backward, there is little question that as family support has expanded, its coherence has lessened. Once a small band of stand-alone programs, family support no longer has an identity that is uniquely its own. Concepts of family support now characterize scores of programs, services, and agencies, many of which do not acknowledge that what they are doing is part of a broader social movement. They enact principles of family support as part of their ongoing work. So, the ideas of family support are being spread and incorporated into the modi operandi of countless services.

Such diffusion, however, brings with it undeniable challenges. For example, the breadth and depth of family support—an issue that makes *family support* so difficult to define—still plagues many who question whether family support is a unique field comparable to, but separate from, other professional fields. But, if family support is a field in and of itself, it has yet to be professionalized and to acquire the accoutrements associated with professionalization. Family support does not have a system of certification for its workers or an accreditation system for its programs. It has not developed an explicit set of standards, though it does have guidelines for good practice. It has not formalized a statement of ethics. There is no established career ladder as exists in other fields.

However, if family support is not a field but a mindset that emphasizes respectful relationships, strength-based orientation, and empowerment of participants, what, then, is the need for these efforts? If the emphasis were the latter, perhaps there would be less need to acquire the structures and specifications associated with professionalism; emphasis could then focus on expanding the knowledge base of family support into many arenas. Taking this less formal and structured path, future directions for family support might include making connections with other fields to incorporate family support concepts or initiating extensive public education efforts. Not unique, the dilemma—essentially to professionalize or not—has been addressed by other fields. Presently, the cues in family support suggest that it is leaning toward more structure and professionalization without sacrificing its basic beliefs.

The Issue of Quality

Whether family support is ultimately manifest as a codified field or as a part of many diverse fields and services, the issue of quality persists. Indeed, it may be said that quality is at the heart of any discussion of the future of family support. Its central place in the debate stems less from dissatisfaction with the current quality of family support programs or from a deep-seated concern that all is not well in family support programs. To the contrary, the importance of focusing on quality now relates to the fact that promising innovations are proliferating in programs throughout the nation. The next important step is to capture those practices, build on them, and specify and translate them so that family support can move beyond its present state.

Necessary as it is, specifying the parameters of quality in family support is a large task involving the following quality correlates: (a) mandated regulation; (b) voluntary accreditation, monetary and nonmonetary incentives; (c) a focus on delivery (or input) standards; (d) a focus on performance (or outcome) standards; and (e) professional development (Kagan, 1994). A few words regarding each are in order.

Regulation traditionally provides a socially sanctioned vehicle for preventing harm to citizens while protecting the rights of the individual. Yet, despite their importance, regulations have fallen out of favor in recent years, as a decidedly antiregulatory movement has swept the nation. Given this ethos and given the complexity of developing and implementing regulations from ideological and cost perspectives, it is the most difficult of the six quality strategies listed in this section. The family support field needs to consider the pros and cons of such safeguards, discerning if and where their use, in either guideline or regulatory form, could be most helpful.

Voluntary accreditation is another quality strategy that has been used successfully in many fields. On the basis of a three-step process (program self-study, on-site peer evaluation, and review and decision by an accreditation body), accreditation is used by hospitals, psychiatric and geriatric facilities, child-care and early education organizations, and private schools, to mention a few (Bredekamp & Willer, 1996; Carter-Blank, n.d.). In each of these cases, establishing reliable and valid accreditation systems has forced careful scrutiny and the popularization of each field's values and priorities. Moreover, such accreditation recognizes quality programs for their accomplishments and simultaneously identifies them to the public.

The third method of quality enhancement, the use of *incentives*, manifests itself quite differently in for-profit and nonprofit settings. In the for-profit world, incentives—performance-based pay, profit sharing, stock options, and merit bonuses—are linked to notions of enhancing worker productivity on the assumption that productivity will lead to greater organizational profit. More recently, the idea of small group incentives has gained currency and spurs cooperative action on behalf of a larger organization. The use of monetary incentives in human services has been far less frequent and often fraught with social stigma, as in the use of "combat" pay to entice teachers to work in inner-city schools. Nonmonetary incentives have been used in nursing and in education and may serve as better models for family support. Teachers, for example, may be accorded more curricular and pedagogical autonomy in lieu of less monitoring as an incentive for increased student outcomes.

Both the fourth and fifth quality enhancements are related to standards. The *development of delivery (or input) standards*, the fourth strategy, is considered an accelerator not only of quality but of equality. Because such standards discern the nature and level of services necessary to produce anticipated positive performance standards, they provide, once implemented, a gauge of resource and quality differentials among programs, hence exposing inequities. Compared with the other five strategies, the development of delivery standards is not difficult, though care must be taken to assure the involvement of knowledgeable field experts in the process and to avoid overly prescriptive standardization in the product.

Performance (or outcome) standards refer to the specification of what service beneficiaries should know or be able to do as a result of the service. This poses challenges for family support because on the one hand there are multiple individual beneficiaries of family support (e.g., children, parents), but on the other hand, family support efforts are directed to the entire family, thus making it difficult and unfair to tease out standards for individuals. Second, if standards are to have utility, it is necessary to determine performance cutoffs, below which changes in performance are deemed unacceptable. Given the multiple definitions and multiple contexts in any one domain such as community enhancement, defining one set of performance standards is precarious business. Defining multiple sets of standards, however, defeats the purpose. Despite these enormous challenges, the need to specify standards (delivery and performance) is requisite for the advancement of the field.

Finally, any field that desires to promote quality must have a codified system of *professional development*, including pre- and in-service development. Professional development in family support has been primarily in-service and, as such, is flourishing. Curricula developed by diverse local programs are serving as training tools for other programs. The Midwest Learning Center, under the auspices of Family Focus and in collaboration with Family Support America, is bringing trainers together to coordinate and enhance learning opportunities (Family Focus, 1994; Stringfellow, 2003; Weissbourd, 2003). It is intended to serve as a model for other regional centers. The ultimate goal is a National Learning Center, consisting of regional centers linked to each other and connected to Family Support America. These regional centers would serve both as training centers and think tanks on family support issues. Although in-service opportunities for professional development in family support are robust, there is a dearth of preservice training in the field. Family support, as a specific set of courses, exists in a few universities; however, even in these, as in the School of Social Service Administration at the University of Chicago, the ongoing question is whether family support premises and principles should be taught as separate courses or integrated into all social work instruction.

The Absence of a National Policy Agenda

If one traces the evolution of family support programs, it is clear that they are largely an outgrowth of, first, local efforts to promote family support services and, second, state and federal efforts to promote categorical antidotes to social problems (e.g., child abuse and violence) and to promote development (e.g., youth development and neighborhood development). Looking across the nation, we see a proliferation of categorical or domain-specific family support programs, but there is limited evidence of any national policy on family support or a national conceptualization of what it might take to advance such a policy.

Although family support is all but absent from the national policy agenda, this was not always the case. As noted earlier, in 1993, Congress passed a landmark piece of legislation, the Family Preservation and Support Act. This legislation was designed to promote the advancement of family support and family preservation programs, along with their evaluation. Even though it was federally sponsored, it provided for state- and community-level planning; as such it engaged numerous individuals. Despite these provisions, which should have assured more long-term viability, the legislation was reframed several years later to emerge as largely adoption-related legislation.

Several instructive explanations might be proffered for its quick ascent and equally quick demise. First, this family support legislation spanned the conventional legislative committee structure. Its content was not limited to one jurisdiction and hence, speaking positively, could find support across committees. Conversely, lacking a home domain meant that this legislation (and presumably future family support bills) might not commandeer the intense congressional support of members to ensure bill introduction, monitoring, and passage. Indeed, the multidimensional aspects of family support that are regarded as its practical strength may, in fact, be its policy weakness.

Second, it may be said that the advocacy community that came together for the initial passage of the legislation had spent so much of its energy to promote understanding of the constructs of family support that it lacked the necessary momentum to monitor and sustain the legislation. Such a fact points to the need to build a strong and durable advocacy community for family support.

Moreover, some may argue that the original act was an accommodation and that it was never intended to energize the family support movement durably. If it had been proffered as such, the actual legislation would have looked very different. In addition to supporting direct services and evaluation, which it did, the legislation would have attended to supporting the infrastructure more systematically. Many would argue that its modest resources were never adequate for the task at hand.

The legislation was a high point in the federal commitment to family support, but it takes more than public funding to sustain an effort of such magnitude. To accomplish this, the strategy must artfully blend resource acquisition from public and private sources; the mix of local, state, and federal commitments; attention to direct services and infrastructural elements; and mechanisms that support the development of family support in all its forms. To date, such a national vision and such a national policy are lacking.

Next Steps

Given this array of complex problems coupled with the momentum that currently characterizes the field, what options exist for the future? We suggest two major strategies. First, we see the need to recognize, understand, and act on family support as an emerging social movement. Second, we see the need for a long-term vision, including planning, financing, and developing the infrastructure for the field.

Family Support as an Emerging Social Movement

Within the field of family support, there is a growing realization that family support is far more than programs, principles, and patterns of being; it is evolving into a large social movement. The evolution of family support is not at all surprising, because at its very inception, family support regarded itself as a fluid, evolving construct. Yet, it is important to understand what constitutes a social movement before branding family support as such.

There is a vast body of literature on theories of social movements and their classifications. Some suggest that social movements are attitudinal reactions to social and cultural breakdowns in society (Parsons, 1969). Rejecting this perspective, others regard social movements as highly rational efforts that demand political mobilization, often through informal networks and formal organizations (Morris, 1984). The new social movement approach describes social movements as both symptoms of and solutions to the conflict arising from emphasis on individual autonomy in a highly bureaucratic society (Habermas, 1981; Offe, 1985).

Commensurate with these perspectives, family support is a social movement. It is about attitudinal change, notably the reorientation from treatment to prevention and the shift from a focus on the child to the child, family, and community as the unit of intervention. Moreover, family support has emerged in response to the breakdown of bureaucratic institutions and societal failures. Although rooted in ideological discontent, family support has been most strategic in engaging new partners, in proffering alternative structures, and in mobilizing support to influence society at large.

The issue at hand, then, is for family support to conceptualize itself as a social movement, acknowledging that this marks another stage in its evolution. Such a reconceptualization raises many questions: How can family support, which began as a bottom-up movement, garner the top-down support necessary to achieve its goals? Is a social movement of this nature likely to gain momentum in the political atmosphere today? What steps can be taken to stimulate support? Does family support have the resources to pursue the public education efforts that facilitate cultural change? How can a link between family support and public policy leaders be forged?

The fact that questions such as these are not only relevant, but seemingly urgent, is evidence of the growth of family support and its place in the social service arena today. The time has come to think about how family support can be available and accessible to all and understood as an integral part of our social structure.

Visioning Family Support for the Future

At present, there is little consolidated vision of what the "promise" of family support actually is. If family support were fully implemented, what would service provision look like? In which institutions would services be provided? What would the outcomes be for children, families, and communities? To address these issues, it would be helpful to establish a national commission. Such a commission could discern a long-term, broad vision for family support; it could examine the ongoing realities of the domain-specific policy apparatus as well as the need to focus on the development of the practice and the policy infrastructure, as discussed next. In short, clarity on expectations for 20- and 10-year goals for family support is necessary.

UNDERSTANDING FAMILY SUPPORT IN THE 21ST-CENTURY CONTEXT. Although the social context in which family support was born continues to persist (e.g., childhood poverty, teen pregnancy), there are other elements of the social context that are quite different. The advent of near-universally available technology at just costs is upon us. Just how the use of technology can be infused so that the family support movement will become more efficacious must be considered. What do technological advances mean for service delivery? What do they mean for policy and advocacy capacity? And what do they mean for the preparation of those who elect to work in family support?

There is also a need to take into consideration the changing nature of the relationship between the for-profit and nonprofit sectors and between publicly and privately provided human services. There is little question that the distinction that once clearly demarked sectors is slipping away with increased public dollars being used to support private entities. How does this affect family support? What can and should the roles of business and the religious sector be in the future of family support?

It is important to better understand the changing nature of families and the nature of the current work–family relationship. With more flexibility in schedules for some segments of society, the new structure of work time and workplace will alter the conceptions of what family support might be. Changing immigration patterns, changing conceptions of the schools, and changing conceptions of public responsibility for its citizenry are critical to the next stage of family support's evolution. What is clear: Family support emerged as a responsive force to family need that was not being met by mainstream institutions. As family needs continue to change, it is imperative that family support not be calcified into its 1980s format. Its strength has been, and will continue to be, its ability to adapt to the changes in family, community, and society.

SPECIFYING PROGRAM AND PARTICIPANT OUTCOMES. There is a pressing need to develop clear specifications of family support program–service-delivery outcomes and participant performance outcomes. Difficult as these tasks appear, Family Support America (1996) has already delineated factors associated with quality programs. Using these as a base, work can be advanced on more specific program parameters, including the establishment of performance benchmarks. Such program–service delivery outcomes could become the basis for curriculum, training, and accreditation efforts. As such, they represent a prerequisite effort for the field. The development of participant performance outcomes is also necessary as they give program staff and families a clear picture of the intentions of family support. They also provide a means for holding frontline workers accountable for productive activities and provide policymakers with data essential for policy decisions.

DEVELOPING A PRACTICE INFRASTRUCTURE THAT ADVANCES *QUALITY*. To foster the quality of direct services, attention must be accorded to the infrastructure. By infrastructure, we mean the training and credentialing of individuals who work in family support as well as the development of a system of accreditation that signifies quality programs. Family support standards and the requirements that yield effective performance need to be specified. Once the requirements are determined, a plan must be developed to instantiate these requirements in law and regulation within the states. Simultaneously, work must ensue to alter the nature and content of offerings within institutions of higher education. Curriculum will need to be developed and made suitable for both in-service and preservice training. Systems of state credentialing and the apparatus to carry out such credentialing must be established. Finally, mechanisms to enhance program quality must be launched.

DEVELOPING A POLICY INFRASTRUCTURE AND CAPACITY. To advance family support policy, we recommend the establishment of a National Policy Institute (NPI). The NPI should consider the most potent ways to advance a family support agenda and should identify the research to do so. Structurally, the NPI should mature to have counterpart organizations in each state; together, the NPI and its state partners would coconstruct a policy strategy that would lead to the implementation of legislation to advance family support services. In addition, these state entities would mount the systematic development of an advocacy base for the field that would include advocacy training and mentoring.

DEVELOPING A RESEARCH CAPACITY FOR THE FIELD. The field of family support has no codified research apparatus. To expand the empirical knowledge base on family support, it is imperative that a multifaceted research agenda be crafted, one that includes cost–benefit analyses and program–service impact evaluations. Building on past research, researchers' efforts must address diverse delivery approaches and populations to better understand what approaches work best, for whom, and under what conditions (Powell, 1994). Case studies should be developed to explicate different forms of family support. Considerable funds from state governments, the federal government, and foundations should be earmarked for these purposes.

THE ED ZIGLER QUALITY. Most important, it will take leaders like Ed Zigler who possess the guts, vision, and fortitude to devote their lives to making a better America for children and families. Who can deny that the field has been made better by his dedication and commitment and that if only there were a new generation of Zigler protégés, family support would be in far better stead? Ed's enduring commitment helped bring family support to life: For that reason, and so many others, this chapter is dedicated to him.

References

Adoption and Safe Families Act of 1997, Pub. L. No. 105-89 (1997).

Barth, R. P. (1999). After safety, what is the goal of child welfare services: Permanency, family continuity, or social benefit? *International Journal of Social Welfare, 8*, 244–252.

Bredekamp, S., & Willer, B. (1996). *NAEYC Accreditation: A decade of learning and the years ahead.* Washington, DC: National Association for the Education of Young Children.

Cameron, G., & Vanderwoerd, J. (1997). *Protecting children and supporting families.* New York: Aldine De Gruyter.

Carter-Blank, D. (n.d.). *Cross-sector analysis of accreditation systems* (White paper prepared for the NAEYC Governing Board). Washington, DC: National Association for the Education of Young Children.

Cowan, E. L. (1977). Baby-steps toward primary prevention. *American Journal of Community Psychology, 5*, 1–22.

Diehl, D. (2002). *Issues in family support evaluation: Report from a meeting of national thought leaders.* Chicago: Family Support America.

Dryfoos, J. G. (1994). *Full-service schools: A revolution in health and social services for children, youth, and families.* San Francisco: Jossey-Bass.

Dunst, C. (1995). *Key characteristics and features of community-based family support programs.* Chicago: Family Resource Coalition.

Family Focus. (1994). *Annual report.* Chicago: Author.

Family Preservation and Support Act of 1993, Pub. L. No. 103-66 (1993).

Family Support Act of 1988, Pub. L. No. 100-485 (1988).

Family Support America. (1996). *Guidelines for family support practice.* Chicago: Author.

Habermas, J. (1981). New social movements. *Telos, 49*, 33–37.

Kagan, S. L. (1994). Defining and achieving quality in family support. In S. L. Kagan & B. Weissbourd (Eds.), *Putting families first: America's family support movement and the challenge of change* (pp. 375–400). San Francisco: Jossey-Bass.

Kagan, S. L., & Shelly, A. (1987). The promise and problems of family support programs. In S. L. Kagan, D. Powell, B. Weissbourd, & E. Zigler (Eds.), *America's family support programs: Perspectives and prospects* (pp. 38–56). New Haven, CT: Yale University Press.

Mason, V. L. (2003). Shared leadership with families: Social inclusion as a core strategy of family support. In F. Jacobs, D. Wertlieb, & R. M. Lerner (Eds.), *Handbook of applied developmental science: Vol. 2. Enhancing the life chances of youth and families: Contributions of programs, policies, and service systems* (pp. 507–533). Thousand Oaks, CA: Sage.

Moroney, R. (1987). Social support systems: Families and social policy. In S. L. Kagan, D. Powell, B. Weissbourd, & E. Zigler (Eds.), *America's family support programs: Perspectives and prospects* (pp. 38–56). New Haven, CT: Yale University Press.

Morris, A. (1984). *The origins of the civil rights movement: Black communities organizing for change.* New York: The Free Press.

Moynihan, D. P. (1986). *Family and nation.* San Diego: Harcourt Brace Jovanovich.

Offe, C. (1985). New social movements: Challenging the boundaries of institutional politics. *Social Research, 54*, 817–867.

Parsons, T. (1969). *Politics and social structure.* New York: The Free Press.

Powell, D. R. (1994). Evaluating family support programs: Are we making progress? In S. L. Kagan & B. Weissbourd (Eds.), *Putting families first: America's family support movement and the challenge of change* (pp. 441–470). San Francisco: Jossey-Bass.

Schulz, D. A. (1982). *The changing family: Its function and future.* Englewood Cliffs, NJ: Prentice Hall.

Singer, G. H. S., Powers, L., & Olson, A. L. (1996). *Redefining family support: Innovations in public-private partnerships.* Baltimore: Paul Brookes.

Smith, S. (Ed.). (1995). *Two generation programs for families in poverty: A new intervention strategy.* Norwood, NJ: Ablex Publishing.

Steiner, G. (1981). *The futility of family policy.* Washington, DC: Brookings Institution Press.

Stringfellow, C. (2003). Investing in our future: The Midwest Learning Center for Family Support. *America's Family Support Magazine, 22*, 39–41.

Unger, D. G., & Powell, D. R. (1990). *Families as nurturing systems: Support across the lifespan.* New York: Haworth Press.

Weissberg, R. P., Gullotta, T. P., Hampton, R. L., Ryan, B. A., & Adams, G. R. (Eds.). (1997). *Establishing preventive services.* London: Sage.

Weissbourd, B. (1987). A brief history of family support programs. In S. L. Kagan, D. Powell, B. Weissbourd, & E. Zigler (Eds.), *America's family support programs: Perspectives and prospects* (pp. 38–56). New Haven, CT: Yale University Press.

Weissbourd, B. (1994). The evolution of the family resource movement. In S. L. Kagan & B. Weissbourd (Eds.), *Putting families first: America's family support movement and the challenge of change* (pp. 28–47). San Francisco: Jossey-Bass.

Weissbourd, B. (2003, Spring/Summer). The time is right for a family support learning center. *America's Family Support Magazine, 22*, 28–29.

264 KAGAN AND WEISSBOURD

Zigler, E. (2002, Summer). A lifetime in the family support movement. *America's Family Support Magazine, 21*, 20–22.

Zigler, E., Weiss, H., & Kagan, S. L. (1985). *Programs to strengthen families*. New Haven, CT: Yale University Bush Center in Child Development; and Chicago: Social Policy and the Family Resource Coalition.

16

Using the Web to Disseminate Research and Affect Public Policy

Fred Rothbaum, Nancy F. Martland, and Sandra J. Bishop-Josef

The World Wide Web has generated considerable excitement about the potential to inform and connect various groups and thereby influence public policy about children. Although this potential has not yet been realized, we believe that the excitement is well founded. We envision a future in which parents can easily obtain online information about public policy issues relevant to their interests, and the means to connect with policymakers around these issues. Because child development researchers are among the best sources of information about children, they are essential to this process.

The Web offers a medium ideally suited to wide dissemination of information, and parents have displayed a willingness to make use of it. A recent study by the Pew Internet and American Life Project (Allen & Rainie, 2002) indicated that "70% of U.S. parents with a child under 18 use the Internet . . . there are almost 45 million online parents in the United States today, and they make up 43% of all U.S. Internet users" (p. 2). Even though the numbers are impressive, it is not clear what kind of information these parents were seeking. In a study by Zero to Three (2000) that focused on finding information about children, 38% of parents of children age 0 to 6 years indicated that they used the Web for this purpose on a regular (4 or more hours monthly) basis.

There are reasons to believe that the online informational needs and preferences of parents and policymakers have important similarities that can be addressed simultaneously. Both groups want brief, easy to digest information relevant to their current interests and problems. The interactive possibilities of the Web make it an excellent means of closing the loop between parents and policymakers because communication is easy and instantaneous.

Throughout his distinguished career, Edward F. Zigler has played a leadership role in bridging the gap between basic science, policy, and practice. Few have shown a keener interest in, and facility at, applying research findings to the design and implementation of policies, practices, and programs for children. Ed views dissemination as an essential tool in the effort to apply basic research findings. This is evident in the mission statement of the Yale Bush Center in Child Development and Social Policy, which he founded. The Center's mission is to "bring research-based knowledge of child development to the federal and state policy arenas in an effort to improve the lives of children and families in the United States" (Bush Center in Child Development, 2005, ¶ 1). Informing the public and thereby influencing their beliefs and understandings is a critical component of this effort; public opinion affects policy if for no other reason than that policymakers are so responsive to it.

Our goal in this chapter is to describe ways in which child development scholars can participate in the dissemination of research-based information to the public, especially to parents and policymakers. Such dissemination is a key element in developing more responsive public policy. Although we are concerned with the various ways in which the Web can affect dissemination efforts, we focus on a particular Web-based initiative, the Child & Family WebGuide, as an example of how to make the Web more accessible to parents and to foster parents' ability to contact and influence policymakers.

We divide the chapter into three sections corresponding to the following timeline: (a) a brief description of dissemination prior to widespread use of Web browsers in the mid-1990s, (b) ways in which the Web has transformed consumption and dissemination of research-based information during the past several years, and (c) the future potential of the Web. Our emphasis throughout is on the role of researchers in the translation of scientific, technical information about child development for parents and policymakers.

Researchers' Dissemination Activities Before the Web

For most researchers, public dissemination has been a secondary or nonexistent goal. This neglect persists despite the fact that both the Society for Research in Child Development (SRCD) and the American Psychological Association (APA) have a long-standing commitment to the dissemination of research findings. According to John Hagen (2003), the SRCD constitution, written in 1933, states that the Society's goals are "to stimulate and support research . . . and to encourage applications of research findings." Since as early as 1949, there has been a commitment to "bring research out of the laboratory . . . to reach not only scientists but also the larger public" (p. 1). Similarly, APA has a 100-year history of commitment to dissemination, perhaps best expressed by George Miller in his 1969 Presidential address, in which he encouraged members to "give psychology away" by sharing findings with the public (Fowler, 1999, p. 2).

Until about 1995, researchers who were interested in disseminating findings to the public and to policymakers often involved journalists as intermediaries. There were numerous problems in this relationship (McCall, 1988). Whereas researchers want "truth" with all its complexities and nuances, journalists have space limitations and an impatient public who want simple sound bites. Researchers are accustomed to, and have difficulty moving beyond, technical terms and abstruse language. Journalists know that their audience has little patience for either, and are often placed in the role of translating concepts and findings about which they have very limited understanding. When journalists' translations include errors of commission or omission, which is often the case, scholars bristle at the misrepresentations and actively avoid journalists.

The result is that journalists rely on a small group of scholars who are themselves savvy about translating difficult concepts, but journalists and thus the public are seldom privy to the most relevant or recent research. This is a matter of concern because parents frequently rely on journalists for information about child development (Kakinuma, 1993; Koepke & Williams, 1989; Zero to Three, 1997).

There are also difficulties in the relationship between researchers and policymakers—difficulties that have been noted by Zigler and others who straddle the two worlds (e.g., Bevan, 1980; Hayes, 1982; Maccoby, Kahn, & Everett, 1983; Phillips, 2002; Zigler & Hall, 2000). As noted earlier, researchers tend to speak and write in jargon, and they publish their findings in esoteric academic journals. Policymakers' informational needs are more similar to those of the public: They prefer "plain English" and tend to refer to popular outlets such as *Time*, *Newsweek*, TV news, and newspapers. In the past, researchers have made little attempt to draw connections between their findings and the practical implications or applications of those findings. Policy experts may not be well versed enough in science to make their own inferences about the applications and implications of academic findings.

Jack Shonkoff (2000, p. 182) maintained that the tensions between researchers and policymakers are "inevitable" for various reasons: (a) science focuses on what we do not know and on questions, whereas policymakers focus on what we should do and on answers; (b) researchers have a high tolerance for ambiguity and complexity, yet policymakers want clear, simple solutions to pressing social problems; (c) researchers have been trained to think and to generate knowledge, whereas policymakers have been trained to act; (d) researchers are influenced by data garnered from empirical study, yet policymakers are often influenced by anecdotes, values, and political factors, and consider them as important, or even more important, than scientific evidence.

Dissemination in the Web Era

The Web presents new opportunities and new liabilities regarding the dissemination of research-based information to the public and policymakers. The Web allows for instantaneous access to a great deal of information, but the information is not necessarily trustworthy and is rarely based on research. Web technology allows for user-friendliness (e.g., links, layering, and graphics), but many organizations lack the knowledge or the wherewithal to capitalize on these possibilities and instead post full-text academic articles without adapting them. These opportunities and liabilities are explored next in greater detail.

Web Effects on the Consumption of Information

As a result of the World Wide Web, the public can easily obtain a remarkable range of child and family information, from highly technical reports on U.S. government Web sites to "Joe's" personal page on attachment therapy. Researchers now have direct access to the public, obviating the need to work through journalists to reach the public, and parents increasingly avail themselves of this information (Zero to Three, 2000).

A serious problem posed by the Web's openness is that in addition to the "good stuff," viewers are exposed to a large amount of questionable or unverified material, and most consumers do not know how to sort the wheat from the chaff. Although newspapers and magazines are governed by journalistic codes of accuracy and honesty, anything can be posted on the Web. This is a particular problem for parents because they are " . . . less vigilant than non-parents in checking the source and sponsorship of the information (that they find on Web sites)" (Allen & Rainie, 2002, p. 3).

Policymakers have access to the same plethora of information. Similar to parents, they too lack sufficient expertise to evaluate the quality of the information on the Web. Federal policymakers (i.e., senators and representatives) rely heavily on their staffs to quickly find background information on policy issues relevant to pending legislation. Although time urgency encourages use of the Web, it discourages careful evaluation of the information found there.

The Child & Family WebGuide: A Directory of the Best Sites

The Child & Family WebGuide is an effort to address the issues and opportunities presented by online information. Founded in 2001 by faculty members of the Eliot-Pearson Department of Child Development at Tufts University, the WebGuide is a tool for enhancing the Web's ability to heighten public knowledge and understanding. The WebGuide searches the Web for sites that present research-based or resource information, systematically evaluates the sites to ensure their trustworthiness, and presents them at its Web site (http:// www.cfw.tufts.edu) organized by topic. Sites selected for listing receive a WebGuide Award for posting on their sites as a means of alerting consumers to the trustworthiness of the material. The effect is to assist consumers in negotiating the maze of options available to them online.

Each site listed on the WebGuide has undergone a rigorous evaluation. The WebGuide Evaluation Instrument was developed from recommendations generated by a Delphi panel of 19 nationally recognized child development scholars and practitioners (Martland, 2001). Each site is evaluated on the basis of the authority of the site's sponsor and the individual authors (credentials such as educational status), whether the content is based on documented research (citation of sources), ease of use (working links, ease of navigation), and stability (presence of copyright date). The Evaluation Instrument sets high standards; very few of the sites considered score well enough to be listed. Those that are listed can be used by the consumer with great confidence.

Our research (Rothbaum & Martland, 2003) indicated the public's need for and positive response to assistance navigating the Web. As part of a larger, 3-year study, we conducted 10 parent focus groups ($n = 80$) in the fall of 2001. When we mention "our research" throughout this chapter, we are referring to data from these focus groups unless otherwise noted. Before viewing the Child & Family WebGuide, parents in the focus groups ranked the Web fifth in preference, behind family and friends, books, pediatricians, and magazines as a source of child-rearing information (it was ranked significantly lower than all of these sources except magazines). After viewing the WebGuide, in contrast, use of the Web was ranked significantly ahead of all other sources. These findings held for low, middle, and upper socioeconomic status participants. Parents also expressed a preference for content that is user friendly—practical and easy to understand (Rothbaum & Martland, 2003). Unfortunately, it is rare to find content that is both user friendly and research based. To take maximum advantage of the Web and the opportunity it offers, this combination is critical.

Web Effects on the Dissemination of Information

The Web has opened the information floodgates. Not only is there much more basic research and applied information available online, there is also much more policy information. To determine the policy issues that have a research base, we examined three academic journals that focus on policy-relevant developmental research: SRCD's *Social Policy Reports* (January 1998–December 2002); APA's *Children's Services: Social Policy, Research, and Practice* (January 1998–December 2002), and *Applied Developmental Science* (January 2000–December 2002; only these issues were available on the Web). On the basis of our examination of these journals, we have compiled a list of 18 social policy topics that have a research base (see Table 16.1). Two topics—mental health treatment and education—have received the most research attention (at least 13 articles). An additional 8 topics have received considerable research attention (at least 6 articles): crime, adolescent development, youth civic engagement, child care and early childhood education, child abuse, chronic health conditions, parenting, and substance abuse. Finally, there were 7 topics that have received attention in at least one study. Further research involving a greater number of publications is needed to indicate the full range and popularity of topics within the broader policy literature.

This preliminary analysis suggests that there is an array of policy topics that have relevant empirical data. The task is to make these data more accessible to the public and policymakers. The Web can play a major role in accomplishing this task. Already, the most recent (from 1994) SRCD *Social Policy Reports* are available on the Web. Articles in *Applied Developmental Science* and APA's *Children's Services* are also available on the Web, but only through universities or other entities that subscribe to the journals. In the near future, we hope all of these topics will be available in easily accessible forms.

Although the Web enables child development researchers to reach an almost unlimited audience, the material posted by researchers will not grab the public's attention unless researchers make a concerted effort to make the material user friendly. Nothing in researchers' education or training prepares them for this task. The removal of journalists as brokers exacerbates this problem. As a result, much of the Web material presented by universities, as well as leading nonprofit and government organizations, is highly technical and user unfriendly. The failure to translate science into language that is comprehensible means that much of the good stuff (as rated by the WebGuide) is not as user friendly as the public and policymakers would like.

Table 16.1. Survey of Topics Addressed in Journals on Social Policy Research

Topic	Number of articles	Number of journals
Mental health treatment	15	1/3
Education	13	3/3
Crime or violence	10	3/3
Adolescent development	10	3/3
Youth civic engagement	10	2/3
Child care or early childhood education	9	3/3
Child abuse	9	2/3
Chronic health conditions	9	1/3
Parenting	7	3/3
Disorders or problems		
Substance abuse	6	2/3
HIV	1	1/3
Policy research—how-to articles	5	3/3
Early intervention	4	2/3
Programs for youth	4	2/3
Adolescent pregnancy/parents	3	3/3
Specific policies		
Welfare reform	3	1/3
Poverty	1	1/3
Homelessness	1	1/3

To help meet the need for material that is easy to read and understand, SRCD recently required authors of *Child Development* articles to write public summaries—short, user-friendly abstracts—to be posted on the SRCD site. This SRCD initiative encourages scholars to develop skill in writing for the public, and it increases the quantity of user-friendly material available online. APA does something very similar with its series of press releases on topics of interest to the public. The Web's effectiveness as a communication medium is encouraging leading research organizations in child development to post material of interest to the public and to policymakers.

How Research-Based Sites Can Successfully Compete

Attracting visitors is the critical factor in generating the resources necessary to maintain and expand sites and to take advantage of rapidly improving Web technologies. Sites that are maintained by educational, governmental, and other nonprofit organizations, which present much of the research-based content, are at a disadvantage as compared with commercial sites that have no academic requirements and can employ writers who know how to appeal to the public.

To successfully compete for public interest, a number of nonprofit organizations provide information about resources and recreation (e.g., services for locating child care, private schools, and summer camps; referrals for professional services; after school activities). Our focus group data indicated that parents very much want this information. Although the resource and recreation information is often not based on research, it can be evaluated using many of the criteria that are used to evaluate research-based sites, such as the authority of the sponsoring organization. Our focus group data also indicated that parents are very interested in research news and opportunities to ask an expert. The Child & Family WebGuide lists sites providing all of these kinds of information.

The Future Potential of the Web

We began this chapter with the suggestion that the Web can be a powerful force in influencing public policy. We envisioned a future in which the public is more informed about research and more engaged in important policy debates. Only a minority of the public is likely to become actively engaged—most likely those who are personally involved in an issue (e.g., special needs, giftedness, athletic participation) because it pertains to their child. When these individuals find relevant information, they are primed for further action. Sites providing useful information can encourage action by providing specific ways to become engaged—from opportunities to contact other parents, to links to relevant advocacy agencies, to invitations to give their opinions about public policy matters to their legislators. Equally important are those individuals who are not motivated to further actions but who avail themselves of the information and, as a consequence, are more aware of child policy issues. Even if they take little initiative, these individuals will affect policymakers because policymakers are highly responsive to public opinion polls and voting patterns.

In the next four sections we describe ways the Web can be used to attract a larger segment of the public to the conversation about children's social policy:

- to find out what is of interest to the public and provide it;
- to present policy information in contexts that are meaningful;
- to increase user-friendly content; and
- to provide easy access to policy materials and policymakers.

We end this section with a discussion of ways in which child development researchers can play a role in fostering needed changes.

Find Out What They Want and Give It to Them

As a first step, we need to determine which topics are of interest to the public. Once we know which topics are popular and thus likely to attract public interest, we can determine whether Web coverage of those topics includes research and policy information. In the following sections we describe three studies that indicate topics of interest to parents.

THE KUNKEL STUDY. One way to assess public interest is to examine the topics addressed in daily newspapers and network TV news. Dale Kunkel tracked stories about five child-related topics in 12 newspapers and four national networks from April 2001 to July 2001 (Shepard, 2002). The topics studied were child abuse or neglect, child care, children's health insurance, teen childbearing, and youth crime and violence.

In Kunkel's study, almost all of the stories in newspapers and on TV were on either youth crime or violence (54% and 50%, for newspapers and TV, respectively) or child abuse or neglect (40% and 46%, respectively). Only a small percentage were about teen childbearing (2% and 3%), child care (3% and 1%), or child health insurance (1% and 0%). It is interesting to note that these least covered stories were the ones that most frequently provided important contextual information: The stories on teen childbearing (90%), child care (75%), and child health care (36%) were more likely to provide background information deemed important by experts than were the stories on child abuse or neglect (5%) and youth crime or violence (3%).

The Kunkel study further examined the percentage of stories on each topic that addressed public policy perspectives. Here again the least covered stories did the best job. Most health insurance stories (91%), many child-care stories (47%), and a smaller percentage of stories about childbearing (24%), child abuse or neglect (16%), and youth crime (14%) provided a public policy perspective.

It appears that journalists rarely avail themselves of basic or policy research on topics that are already popular with the public (i.e., abuse and violence). We need to understand why this occurs. Because popular stories are often of the late-breaking type, journalists may not have the time to incorporate context and policy issues. Alternatively, journalists may have little incentive to add context or policy issues to stories that they know are already popular with their audience (i.e., "if it bleeds it leads"). The reasons for omitting context and policies are important because they will provide clues as to how to remedy the omission. It is unlikely that the solution is as simple as posting more reports about research and social policies relevant to these topics. The topics for which context and policy are most neglected—abuse and violence—are ones for which Web-based materials are already available (see Table 16.1). Rather, we suspect that the solution involves making that material more accessible to reporters or writing it in forms that make it easier to use.

TIME AND *NEWSWEEK* STUDY. To build on Kunkel's data, we conducted a survey of child-related articles in leading feature stories (i.e., 2,000 or more words) from recent issues (i.e., January 2001–December 2002) of *Time* and *Newsweek* magazines (see Table 16.2). There were 20 feature stories related to children in the two publications over the 2-year period. Parenting topics were the ones most commonly covered (six articles, e.g., parenting stress, unmarried parenthood). Child abuse, childhood disorders, and education were also frequently covered (at least three articles each).

The *Time* and *Newsweek* survey indicated that the topics covered in leading magazines differ from those covered in newspapers and on TV. This may be due to the nature of the coverage—the magazine stories are features and are considerably longer than are breaking news stories. The feature and breaking news difference may also be responsible for the greater attention to research in

Table 16.2. *Newsweek* and *Time* Survey

Topic	Research content?	Policy content?
Parenting		
Unmarried parents	Yes	Yes
Parenting stress	Yes	No
Spoiling children	Yes	No
Keeping divorced families intact	Yes	No
Costs of starting a family	No	No
TV for preschoolers	Yes	Yes
Child abuse		
Child pornography on Web	Yes	Yes
Pedophilia or sexual abuse	Yes	Yes
Catholic church child abuse	Yes	No
Andrea Yates—child abuse	Yes	No
Child disorders and problems		
Depression	Yes	No
Autism	Yes	No
Teen drinking	Yes	No
Bipolar disorder	Yes	No
Education		
School lunches	Yes	Yes
Home schooling	Yes	Yes
Training babies' brains	Yes	No
Children and war		
Palestinian and Israeli teens	Yes	Yes
United Nations meeting on children	No	No
Miscellaneous (adolescence)		
Choosing virginity	Yes	Yes
Total (20 articles)	18/20	8/20

Note. The survey examined feature articles (2,000 or more words) from January 1, 2001, through December 31, 2002, on child-related topics (search terms: children, child, childhood, adolescent, adolescents, adolescence, teen, teenage, teenager, teenagers, youth, youths).

the magazine stories—the vast majority of them (90%) had research content (typically statistics from government agencies) or data from psychological or sociological studies. Public policy perspectives were addressed in 40% of the *Time* and *Newsweek* stories (on topics ranging from children's television, to legal definitions of adulthood, to school lunch programs). These findings not only indicate that it is possible to integrate research findings and policy issues with topics of interest to parents but also that successful integration along these lines is already common in certain media.

FOCUS GROUP STUDY. To obtain a more direct assessment of the topics of interest to parents, and to better understand parents' preferences for Web-based

Table 16.3. Feedback From Parents in Focus Groups

Category	Topic	% of parents selecting topic
Health	Behavioral problems	39
	Depression	39
	Drugs or alcohol	30
	Anxiety or fears	28
Education	Literacy or reading	42
	Curriculum	42
	Testing	31
	Learning disabilities	27
Family	Discipline	76
	TV or media	35
	Fathers	27
	Abuse	25
Typical development	Self-esteem	72
	Teen sex	45
	Friends or peers	42

Note. The baseline (by chance) probability of selecting a topic in each of the four categories is as follows: health (14%), education (13%), family (16%), and typical development (25%).

information, we obtained feedback from parents in our focus groups. Specifically, parents were shown lists of topics in each of several categories—health, education, family, and typical development—and were asked to select the topics they found of greatest interest. The topics selected significantly more than chance and the percentages of parents who selected them (in parentheses) are listed in Table 16.3.

Six of these 15 topics (depression, drugs or alcohol, discipline, TV, abuse, and teen sex) parallel the topics covered in the *Time* and *Newsweek* articles. We suspect that more research along these lines will make it possible to identify a relatively small list of topics of particular interest to parents. It is worth noting that other methods used in the focus groups to assess parents' interest in topics yielded somewhat different findings. For example, when parents were asked open-ended questions (before viewing lists of topics) about which topics they were most likely to seek information on, they emphasized topics pertaining to medical problems. These differences in findings underscore the need to use multiple methods when exploring parents' preferred topics.

IMPLICATIONS OF THESE STUDIES. The Kunkel, *Time* and *Newsweek*, and focus group findings indicate the topics of interest to parents and provide suggestions as to how to engage parents in research and policy information. It is not surprising that some formats (feature stories) lend themselves more to inclusion of research and policy information than do others (breaking news stories). Because there are not space restrictions on the Web, it is well suited to providing in-depth feature articles. The findings also suggest that developmental psychologists should pay more attention to the connection between the topics of interest to parents and the availability of relevant research and policy materials. For example, the *Time* and *Newsweek* articles suggest that parents are most interested (not surprisingly) in topics related to parenting (see Table 16.2). Yet, policy-relevant research on parenting topics was much less common (see Table 16.1). Moreover the parenting topics that were of interest to parents bear little relationship to the policy issues involving parenting addressed in the journals (i.e., family leave and child care). Where connections between parents' interests and extant policy research do exist, we need to do a better job of highlighting those connections. For example, parents' interest in mental health topics (see Table 16.2 and Table 16.3) may translate into an interest in mental health treatment issues examined by policy experts (see Table 16.1), but only if the policy experts can clarify how the two relate to one another.

The bottom line is that to better disseminate knowledge, researchers and policy experts must attend more to topics of interest to parents and clarify how the issues they study are relevant to what parents want. Researchers and scholars need further research on topics of interest to parents, they need to better understand the policy issues to which these topics relate, and they need to determine whether there is sufficient research on those policy issues. The ultimate goal is to help parents understand how research and policies relate to their questions and concerns.

Present Policy Information in Contexts That Are Meaningful

Besides focusing on topics of interest to the public (e.g., abuse, crime, parenting, childhood disorders, and education), it is important to bundle together different kinds of information on a given topic. For example, parents who are interested in children and diet should be able to find practical advice, resources, basic research, and social policy information relevant to that topic. This will encourage the kind of cross-fertilization between different types of information that has been all too infrequent in the past and that the Web is uniquely suited to provide.

The goal is to package information in a way that leads viewers from their initial interest (typically practical advice) to other interests that are likely to arise as their understanding of the topic deepens. When parents go online, they typically want to know something specific, such as whether their child has a health problem, how many hours a day their grade-school–age child should be spending on homework, or how to judge the quality of a child-care program. In the latter case, parents may initially want advice or tips about what to look for when visiting a specific program, as well as resources (e.g., lists of programs in their area) and basic research (e.g., the effects of child care). From this information, parents may become increasingly interested in policy issues, such as the merits of half- versus full-day kindergarten or the need for family day-care regulations.

We believe that if policy issues are relevant to the viewers' everyday life, and if there is a logically compelling path from parents' initial questions to the policy issues, then many viewers who are not initially invested in (or perhaps aware of) policy issues will follow the path. For the subset of viewers who have a deep interest in the topic, links to relevant sites (e.g., chat rooms, advocacy groups, or opportunities to participate in surveys or contact legislators) may lead to even greater civic engagement.

Increase User-Friendly Content

Child and family organizations must do a better job of providing user-friendly, easy-to-understand information on the Web. Our interviews with social policy experts (as part of our larger study described earlier) indicated that they would like more user-friendly articles and summaries; the latter would help the experts decide whether to wade through full-text articles. If the goal is to inform the wider public, who have even less tolerance for technical information than do policy experts, then sites posting social policy information must be substantially modified.

Our research also indicated that user-friendliness is a multifaceted concept. It involves language, overall clarity of the material, visual presentation, and ease of navigation within a site. The first and perhaps most important facet is the reading level of the material presented. If the material is written at a level more difficult than the average newspaper story, then the visitor is likely to leave the site. *Layering* is a highly successful technique that offers the viewer a very brief, simply written abstract that links to more detailed but still nontechnical summaries that in turn link to full length academic reports. Your Child, which is a University of Michigan Health System site (http://www.med.umich.edu/1libr/yourchild/), makes excellent use of layering. Overall clarity of the material involves streamlining dense academic and professional writing. Material should concentrate on a coherent presentation of the main points of a study or argument and avoid unnecessary details. Definitions of technical terms, avoidance of jargon, and headings that clearly describe each section are all good ways to improve clarity. However, dissemination efforts should not abandon academic rigor. Links to references, for example, can be retained in a user-friendly document to maintain academic integrity.

Visual presentation of content is another often overlooked aspect of user-friendliness. The common practice of pasting a text file of an article on a Web site, resulting in screen after screen of text, leaves viewers cold. Much more successful is the strategy of breaking up text into chunks separated by graphics of some form—photographs or graphical dividers, for example. PDF format allows for much more attractive presentations (e.g., in brochure or newsletter format). Another way to increase user satisfaction is to provide navigational aids that enable the viewer to return to the home page, the search page, an index, or other pages.

Provide the Public Easy Access to Policymakers

The Web is ideally suited to connect the public with policymakers. Interviews we conducted with practitioners and policymakers suggest that both groups are already making extensive use of the Web to keep in touch with peers about issues of interest. In addition, many practitioners reported that parents with whom they work used the Web to find laypersons and experts who share an interest in a specific issue faced by their family. Our goal is to tap into the enormous communication potential of the Web to help informed parents contact policymakers. We believe that the resulting pressure has the potential to influence public policy, making it more responsive to the needs of families.

The Web can inspire the belief, so often lacking, that individuals can do something about issues that are of concern to them. There are at least two ways to facilitate parents' contact with policymakers. First, the sites that provide policy information could also provide links for contacting policymakers. Alternatively, a Web hub, such as Connect for Kids (http://www.connectforkids.org) or the WebGuide (http://www.cfw.tufts.edu) might provide a search engine that enables parents to type in their address and get a list of their elected officials, with email links. All the parent or visitor needs to do is click the e-mail link and compose a message to a policymaker. The pressure from parents generated in this manner could be a significant new force in the public policy arena. This approach could result in a more involved public, as well as policymakers who are better informed about which issues the public cares about and their positions on those issues. A number of advocacy groups such as The Children's Defense Fund use this method to focus communication with policymakers on targeted issues.

Of course, individual action on a mass scale is not the only means of influencing policymakers. Perhaps a more attainable goal in the near term is to raise the level of public awareness of policy issues. Awareness of social issues prompts policymakers to include them in the legislative agenda and shapes the public opinion that legislators monitor to help them make policy decisions (Bogenschneider, 2002, p. 142).

Despite our optimism, there are important gaps in our understanding of how to best capitalize on Web technology. The possibilities for concerted action on the Web, via electronic mailing lists and other emerging technologies, are rapidly expanding. A future goal of the WebGuide is to conduct research on the most effective technologies for coordinating different perspectives around pending policies and to work with policy experts to help implement them.

The Role of Researchers in Fostering Needed Changes

Child development researchers are key players in the effort to disseminate quality child development information to the public. Two important questions are, What should researchers do? and What will motivate them to do it?

What Should Researchers Do?

As already discussed, researchers need to get involved in disseminating their findings to the public. This could occur if researchers were to work with the media or public affairs offices of their universities. Most major universities have such offices, which help researchers interact with the press and disseminate their findings. Researchers can also enlist the help of journals and professional societies. The SRCD policy office and the Casey Journalism Center for Children and Families offer training in dissemination of research findings. The Yale Bush Center has long offered such training to its students, and similar programs at other universities have begun to follow its lead.

Researchers can play a pivotal role in enabling the WebGuide, for example, to accomplish several goals addressed in this chapter. Researchers could submit reviews of research that spell out implications for practice and policy, and encourage their students to do so as well. These reviews could be published on several of the excellent sites now available for the public, including sections of university sites devoted to research. Once published online, they could be listed on the WebGuide, making it easier for the public to find them.

How Can We Get Them to Do It?

There is little motivation for researchers to disseminate information to the public because, traditionally, there have been few rewards for doing so (cf. McCall & Groark, 2000). Although APA publishes a small number of press releases and SRCD is beginning to publish public summaries of articles in its flagship publication, *Child Development*, outlets for public dissemination remain sparse.

What are needed are true online journals for the public—not just online versions of existing journals. These new journals would be designed as Web publications with a separate editorial board and review process. Unlike the current online journals, these would be free of charge, their articles would come up in searches, they would be presented in user-friendly formats, and they would be aimed at the public and policymakers as well as at researchers. All of these audiences would be served if the articles provide layered content (i.e., user-friendly, nontechnical summaries of the literature that link to more detailed and technical literature reviews).

The aforementioned editorial structure and layering of content may enable the articles to count as publications for purposes of merit and tenure reviews. If a leading professional organization were to host the online journal, then it could enjoy considerable status among scholars. If the articles posted in the proposed journal count as professional publications, then researchers would have the incentives needed to encourage them to devote more energy to dissemination.

Conclusion

The activities we have described in this chapter have been inspired by Edward Zigler's work. The mission of the Yale Bush Center explicitly calls for the dissemination of research-based information, with the goal of improving the lives of America's children and families through informed social policy. In addition, Ed has long argued that children need an effective lobby to ensure that their needs are addressed in social policy. The Web is a powerful medium, and the

WebGuide is a useful tool, for advancing this agenda by providing information that the public could then use to influence social policy.

Throughout this chapter we focused on how child development researchers can participate in Web dissemination of information. Researchers can play an equally powerful role in their capacity as designers of the research agenda. Two major avenues of further study are indicated: (a) studies that add to the understanding of the policy process and (b) studies that generate knowledge to inform the policy process.

Understanding the Web's relevance to the policy process involves questions about how the Web is used to obtain information, how this information is used, and what can be done to enhance this process. Research questions that address this issue include the following: How do policymakers, journalists, and parents use the Web to gather the information they need and what are they looking for? What Web technologies exist that can enhance dissemination and audience engagement? What engages parents in the policy process and what role can the Web play in this engagement? How are policy topics and parent topics related to one another, and what are ways to connect the two?

Child development researchers also have a key role to play in generating knowledge that can inform the policy making process. This can include research aimed directly at illuminating policy issues. Quite often, it seems, policymakers seek research information about policy topics that simply do not exist, because, as noted earlier, the match between pending policy issues and extant research is poor. A good example of this mismatch is the lack of outcome studies for the Head Start program—or rather the lack of Web-based summaries of that research. Informed policy decisions ideally take into account program and intervention outcomes, costs, and effective implementation structures, for example; more research in these areas would result in more informed decisions. Basic and applied research on topics of interest to parents that will raise awareness of policy issues should also be included in the research agenda.

References

Allen, K., & Rainie, L. (2002). *Parents online*. Retrieved October 22, 2003, from http://www.pewinternet.org/reports/pdfs/PIP_Parents_Report.pdf

Bevan, W. (1980). On getting in bed with a lion. *American Psychologist, 35*, 779–789.

Bogenschneider, K. (2002) *Family policy matters*. Mahwah, NJ: Erlbaum.

Bush Center in Child Development. (2005). *The Edward Zigler Center in Child Development and Social Policy Yale University*. Retrieved March 20, 2006, from http://www.yale.edu/bushcenter/

Fowler, R. (1999). Giving psychology away. *APA Monitor, 30*, 2–3.

Hagen, J. (2003). Social policy, research and SRCD. *Developments: Newsletter of the Society for Research in Child Development, 46*(2), 1–12.

Hayes, C. D. (Ed.). (1982). *Making policies for children: A study of the federal process*. Washington, DC: National Academy Press.

Kakinuma, M. (1993). A comparison of the child rearing attitudes of Japanese and American mothers. *Childhood, 1*, 235–242.

Koepke, J. E., & Williams, C. (1989). Child-rearing information: Resources parents use. *Family Relations, 38*, 462–465.

Maccoby, E. E., Kahn, A. J., & Everett, B. A. (1983). The role of psychological research in the formation of policies affecting children. *American Psychologist, 38*, 80–84.

Martland, N. (2001). *Expert criteria for evaluating the quality of Web information*. Unpublished doctoral dissertation, Tufts University, Medford, MA.

McCall, R. B. (1988). Science and the press: Like oil and water. *American Psychologist, 43*, 87–94.

McCall, R. B., & Groark, C. J. (2000). The future of applied child development research and public policy. *Child Development, 171*, 197–204.

Phillips, D. (2002). Collisions, logrolls, and psychological science. *American Psychologist, 57*, 219–221.

Rothbaum, F., & Martland, N. (2003). *Web-based information about children and families*. Unpublished report. Tufts University, Medford, MA.

Shepard, A. C. (2002, March). Young lives, big stories: Crime, abuse and little context dominate coverage of children's lives. *American Journalism Review, 24*, 4.

Shonkoff, J. P. (2000). Science, policy, and practice: Three cultures in search of a shared mission. *Child Development, 171*, 181–187.

Zero to Three. (1997). *Key findings from a nationwide survey among parents of zero-to-three-year-olds*. Retrieved March, 20, 2006, from http://www.zerotothree.org/parent_poll.html

Zero to Three. (2000).*What grown-ups understand about child development: A national benchmark survey*. Retrieved March, 20, 2006, from http://www.zerotothree.org/parent_poll.html

Zigler, E., & Hall, N. W. (2000). *Child development and social policy*. Boston: McGraw-Hill.

Epilogue: Combining Basic and Applied Science in Constructing Sound Social Policy

Edward F. Zigler

When my students and colleagues joined to create this book about my influence on the broadening field of developmental psychology, they could not have chosen a better title. The words *Child Development and Social Policy: Knowledge for Action* precisely trace my professional voyage. I began my academic career as an empirical scientist, working to understand targeted facets of child development. I forayed into the world of social policy when I helped plan the nation's Head Start program and then became the federal official responsible for the project as well as chief of the U.S. Children's Bureau. After my brief stint in Washington, DC, I devoted most of my time to attempting and advocating knowledge for action, words that neatly tie the two spheres of my career into a meaningful whole.

I am grateful to have contributed to the union of basic and applied science, but I admit my involvement still surprises me. As a graduate student some 50 years ago, I was socialized in pure, basic behavioral science—then the aristocracy of psychology. My training focused on theory building, hypothesis testing, rigorous methodology, and sophisticated statistical analysis. These were the tools scientists needed to pursue knowledge. So equipped, I began my profession searching for facts and principles that could add to psychology's understanding of human development. I conducted experiment after experiment, valuing the findings not so much for whether they confirmed a hypothesis or uncovered a truth, but by how clearly they indicated the direction of the next experiment needed to refine the insights gleaned from those completed. In fact, in 1963 I wrote a paper somewhat grandly titled, "Metatheoretical Issues in Developmental Psychology," in which I implored developmentalists to focus more on empirical work to build a more sophisticated theoretical base (Zigler, 1963).

In that paper, I did admit that the value of a good theory is to lead to appropriate action. And I did try to reconcile how the artificial, standardized protocols researchers deployed in unnatural laboratory settings could possibly relate to what children encounter and how they behave in the real world. When Urie Bronfenbrenner (1974, p. 3) later took experimental work to task by writing that developmental psychology had become "the science of the behavior of children in strange situations with strange adults," I was still young and arrogant enough to take him to task. I actually wrote a letter to this icon in the field, pointing out that there are many roads to truth and that our only hope of attaining it is to travel all of them.

I am not quite sure how he took my unsolicited advice. One of my biggest claims to fame at the time was a creation called *marble-in-the-hole*. It consisted of a box with two holes at the top. Subjects, which were what research participants were called in those days, were instructed to put red marbles into one hole and blue ones into the other. When they got tired of that game, they played a "new" round that was exactly the same except the designated holes for the colored marbles were reversed. Now this was admittedly the most artificial task imaginable, and no child would ever encounter anything like it in the real world. But let me remind you of what became of it outside the laboratory door.

I devised this pointless activity as a simple test of the Lewin-Kounin formulation of cognitive rigidity among individuals with mental retardation. I hypothesized that if their cognitive systems were inherently rigid, they would engage in the repetitive motion of dropping marbles into holes for long periods of time and would have difficulty switching when the designated hole for the colored marbles was reversed. Some experimental tweaking and dozens of experiments later, my colleagues and I refuted cognitive rigidity and developed a new explanatory edifice for the performance of children with nonorganic forms of mental retardation. Our developmental approach incorporated personality features such as motivation for social reinforcement, wariness of adults, fear of failure, outerdirectedness, and other traits that we showed to hinder the performance of children with and without mental retardation who experienced adverse socialization histories.

Beyond the theoretical, the knowledge built from my surreal marble-in-the-hole device had a tangible impact. First, my work revealed that the experience of living in an institution itself resulted in infantilizing the behavior of residents with mental retardation. This set of findings came to be noted in court cases and played a role in the deinstitutionalization movement. Second, responses to my simple task indicated that like individuals with mental retardation, children from impoverished homes suffered a variety of negative consequences as a result of their debilitating life experiences. In particular, my work on the negative behavioral consequences of an inordinate number of failure experiences led to Robert Cooke's inviting me to join the Head Start planning committee.

It also led to much, much more, if the contents of this book are a valid indication. My students have taken my devotion to rigorous empirical science, and my belief that the knowledge derived from research must be put to work in bettering lives, into fields far removed from their original training. The diversity of their areas of scientific inquiry, practical application, and policy involvement make me at once proud and humble in the face of their power to change the world.

I leave my students—and their students—a lot of unfinished work. I have been striving for 40 years to raise Head Start quality, end its practice of socioeconomic segregation, and enroll all eligible children and families. After 4 decades and countless promises from generations of policymakers, quality remains uneven and funding insufficient to serve the population below the poverty line much less those above it. A reasonable conclusion to draw from this lack of progress is that Head Start will never be available to all poor children. They will all have access to early education only when preschool becomes universal. I say this with optimism. We have come a long way since the founding of Head Start. Our nation is clearly on the cusp of a nationwide commitment to universal access to preschool education for all children. Indeed, some states have already legislated such programs.

While the states slowly move in the direction of universal prekindergarten, I am thankful I have students in early care and education around the country to nudge the movement along. They must deploy their knowledge gained through science to shape these programs into quality preschool experiences that enable all children to meet the goal of school readiness. They must also promote the availability of comprehensive services to families and their children who need this level of intervention to better their chances of succeeding in school. Finally, they must shape new roles for Head Start, which I envision to be expanded services to infants and toddlers, treatment centers for preschoolers of all economic levels with special educational needs, and an invigorated national laboratory where more effective methods of early care and education are designed, tested, and refined (see chap. 11, written with Styfco, in Zigler, Gilliam, & Jones, 2006).

A national policy for paid infant-care leave is another consuming project my students have assumed. The seed began to grow back in the 1980s, when I chaired a committee of renowned experts and scholars to study the emerging social trend of mothers returning to work when their children were very young and the concomitant need for high-quality infant caregiving. The panel concluded that paid family leaves were needed to promote healthy child development and family functioning (Zigler & Frank, 1988). Our policy proposal wound its way through Congress for years before emerging as the Family and Medical Leave Act of 1993. It was a shadow of our idea, only protecting jobs after brief unpaid absences for workers in certain sized firms in nonexempt occupations. But it was a good start and has served as a springboard for more generous leaves mainly in slivers of the public sector. I have every faith that my students will deftly steer a national paid infant-care leave policy toward reality.

The greatest failure of my professional career remains the sorry state of child-care services in this wise and wealthy nation. Perhaps I would not feel the disappointment so heavily if we had not come so very close to founding a high-quality, affordable system of child care available to every American family. Such a system was part of the Comprehensive Child Development Act of 1971, which passed both houses of Congress with bipartisan support. The Nixon administration, which at the time included me, had helped draft the bill, so the president's support seemed assured. Richard Nixon's veto of the Act was therefore much more than a surprise. It was a crushing defeat. The hope that all children would have the opportunity to flourish in nonparental care never again burned as brightly in the history of our nation's family policies.

Today, the quality and price of child care are just as variable as they were when I called these services a "cosmic crapshoot." Some care is so horrific that it is harmful to a child's physical and emotional well-being and future developmental course. I tried mightily to help craft a remedy, but I failed. On this issue, I hand the torch to my students and others who care deeply about children and families. In my heart I believe that someday the United States will join the rest of the modern world in enabling families to nurture and support their children's development with both in-home and out-of-home care.

Our nation's efforts to meet the needs of children and families have expanded over time, and they will continue to expand and improve. The key to how well and how quickly child-friendly policies evolve is leadership. We need leading researchers in the science of child development who can enhance understanding of the myriad ingredients and principles of human growth and their intricate interactions. We need leaders who can apply the evidence derived from science to develop programs that work in meeting children's needs. Finally, we need leadership in the policy arena, including those who create and pass laws that affect children and those who serve as interpreters of the knowledge needed for effective social policy. Judging by the impressive contributions detailed in this book, my students are such leaders. If they are a mirror to the future, I am confident that the future for children and families is brighter than it has been during my own lifetime.

References

Bronfenbrenner, U. (1974). Developmental research, public policy, and the ecology of childhood. *Child Development, 45*, 1–5.

Comprehensive Child Development Act of 1971, H.R. 6748, 92d Cong. (1971)

Family and Medical Leave Act of 1993, 29 U.S.C § 2601 (1993).

Zigler, E. (1963). Metatheoretical issues in developmental psychology. In M. Marx (Ed.), *Theories in contemporary psychology* (pp. 341–369). New York: MacMillan.

Zigler, E., & Frank, M. (Eds.). (1988). *The parental leave crisis: Toward a national policy.* New Haven, CT: Yale University Press.

Zigler, E., Gilliam, W., & Jones, S. M. (2006). *A vision of universal preschool education in America.* New York: Cambridge University Press.

Author Index

Numbers in italics refer to listings in reference sections.

Subject Index